# CCNA® Cisco® Certified Network Associate Voice Study Guide

## (Exams 640-460 & 642-436)

Tom Carpenter

New York  Chicago  San Francisco  Lisbon  London  Madrid
Mexico City  Milan  New Delhi  San Juan  Seoul  Singapore  Sydney  Toronto

Cataloging-in-Publication Data is on file with the Library of Congress

McGraw-Hill books are available at special quantity discounts to use as premiums and sales promotions, or for use in corporate training programs. To contact a representative, please e-mail us at bulksales@mcgraw-hill.com.

**CCNA® Cisco® Certified Network Associate Voice Study Guide (Exams 640-460 & 642-436)**

1234567890 DOC DOC 109876543210

ISBN: Book p/n 978-0-07-174437-9 and CD p/n 978-0-07-174438-6
of set 978-0-07-174440-9
MHID: Book p/n 0-07-174437-1 and CD p/n 0-07-174438-X
of set 0-07-174440-1

| | | |
|---|---|---|
| **Sponsoring Editor** | **Copy Editor** | **Illustration** |
| Tim Green | Jan Jue | Lyssa Wald |
| **Editorial Supervisor** | **Proofreader** | **Art Director, Cover** |
| Jody McKenzie | Paul Tyler | Jeff Weeks |
| **Project Editor** | **Indexer** | **Cover Designer** |
| Emilia Thiuri, Fortuitous Publishing Services | Jack Lewis | Peter Grame |
| **Acquisitions Coordinator** | **Production Supervisor** | |
| Stephanie Evans | James Kussow | |
| **Technical Editor** | **Composition** | |
| Jim Geier | Apollo Publishing Service | |

# ABOUT THE AUTHOR

**Tom Carpenter** is a technical expert's expert. He teaches in-depth courses on Microsoft technologies, wireless networking, voice and data communications, security, and professional development skills such as project management, team leadership, and communication skills for technology professionals. Tom holds the CCNA, CCNA Voice, CCNA Security, Convergence+, CWNA, CWSP, and CWTS certifications with the CWNP program and is also a Microsoft Certified Partner. The "Wireless Networking," "Windows Administration," and "IT Project Management" boot camps that Tom offers annually provide the in-depth knowledge IT professionals need to succeed. He is married to his lovely wife, Tracy, and lives with her and their four children, Faith, Rachel, Thomas, and Sarah in Ohio. His company, SYSEDCO, provides training and consulting services throughout the United States. For more information about Tom and the services offered by his company, visit www.SYSEDCO.com.

## About the Technical Editor

**Jim Geier** is the founder of Wireless-Nets, Ltd., and the company's principal consultant. His 25 years of experience include the analysis, design, software development, installation, and support of numerous wireless network–based systems for municipalities, enterprises, airports, retail stores, manufacturing facilities, warehouses, and hospitals worldwide. Jim is the author of over a dozen books, including *Designing and Deploying 802.11n Wireless Networks* (Cisco Press), *Implementing 802.1X Security Solutions* (Wiley), *Deploying Voice over Wireless LANs* (Cisco Press), *Wireless LANs* (SAMS), *Wireless Networks – First Step* (Cisco Press), *Wireless Networking Handbook* (Macmillan), and *Network Reengineering* (McGraw-Hill). He is the author of numerous tutorials for www.Wi-FiPlanet.com and other publications. Jim has been active within the Wi-Fi Alliance, responsible for certifying interoperability of 802.11 (Wi-Fi) wireless LANs. He has also been an active participant of the IEEE 802.11 Working Group, responsible for developing international standards for wireless LANs. He served as chairman of the IEEE Computer Society, Dayton Section, and chairman of the IEEE International Conference on Wireless LAN Implementation. He is an advisory board member of several leading wireless LAN companies. Jim's education includes a bachelor's and master's degree in electrical engineering and a master's degree in business administration.

Contact Jim Geier at jimgeier@wireless-nets.com

## About LearnKey

**LearnKey** provides self-paced learning content and multimedia delivery solutions to enhance personal skills and business productivity. LearnKey claims the largest library of rich streaming-media training content that engages learners in dynamic media-rich instruction complete with video clips, audio, full motion graphics, and animated illustrations. LearnKey can be found on the Web at www.LearnKey.com.

# CONTENTS AT A GLANCE

# CONTENTS

**vii**

I would like to dedicate this book to my wonderful family. Rachel, you are growing into a fine young woman, and I'm grateful that you are showing commitment to that which you've started. Thomas and Sarah— you did great at the 2010 Bible Quizzing National competition. Faith, you're turning 18 this year, and I'm very proud of you for the maturity you've shown. And of course, to my loving wife, Tracy, who makes everything in my life better.

## ACKNOWLEDGMENTS

A book is a large project, and I would like to acknowledge the helpful staff at McGraw-Hill who made this book happen. Timothy Green, Meghan Riley, and Stephanie Evans, thanks for your patience and work along the journey. It is all appreciated. Jim Geier, thanks for taking on this project so soon after completing the last one with me. You are an excellent technical editor. And, of course, I desire to acknowledge God who gives me the health and strength to accomplish all things through Him.

# PREFACE

The objective of this study guide is to prepare you for the 640-460 and 642-436 exams by familiarizing you with the technology or body of knowledge tested on the exam. Because the primary focus of the book is to help you pass the test, we don't always cover every aspect of the related technology. Some aspects of the technology are only covered to the extent necessary to help you understand what you need to know to pass the exam, but we hope this book will serve you as a valuable professional resource after your exam.

## In This Book

This book is organized to serve as an in-depth review for the 640-460 IIUC and 642-436 CVOICE Cisco exams for both experienced Cisco professionals and newcomers to Cisco technologies. Each chapter covers a major aspect of the exam, with an emphasis on the "why" as well as the "how to" of working with and supporting Cisco Voice over IP (VoIP) technologies.

## On the CD

For more information on the CD-ROM, please see the appendix "About the CD-ROM" at the back of the book.

## Exam Readiness Checklist

At the end of the Introduction you will find an Exam Readiness Checklist. This table has been constructed to allow you to cross-reference the official exam objectives with the objectives as they are presented and covered in this book. The checklist also allows you to gauge your level of expertise on each objective at the outset of your studies. This should allow you to check your progress and make sure you spend the time you need on more difficult or unfamiliar sections. References have been provided for the objective exactly as the vendor presents it, along with a chapter and page reference of where the objective is covered in the study guide.

# In Every Chapter

We've created a set of chapter components that call your attention to important items, reinforce important points, and provide helpful exam-taking hints. Take a look at what you'll find:

■ Every chapter begins with **Certification Objectives**—what you need to know in order to pass the section on the exam dealing with the chapter topic. The Objective headings identify the objectives within the chapter, so you'll always know an objective when you see it!

■ **Exam Watch** notes call attention to information about, and potential pitfalls in, the exam. These helpful hints are written by authors who have taken the exams and received their certification—who better to tell you what to worry about? They know what you're about to go through!

*PSTN network signaling can be broken into three categories. The first is address signaling for endpoint location. The second is supervisory signaling for access to and termination of the connection with the network. The final is informational signaling, which includes things like the dial tone, busy signal, and call-waiting notifications for information feedback.*

■ **Step-by-Step Exercises** are interspersed throughout the chapters. These are typically designed as hands-on exercises that allow you to get a feel for the real-world experience you need to pass the exams. They help you master skills that are likely to be an area of focus on the exam. Don't just read through the exercises; they are hands-on practice that you should be comfortable completing. Learning by doing is an effective way to increase your competency with a product.

**on the job**

■ **On the Job** notes describe the issues that come up most often in real-world settings. They provide a valuable perspective on certification- and product-related topics. They point out common mistakes and address questions that have arisen from on-the-job discussions and experience.

■ **Inside the Exam** sidebars highlight some of the most common and confusing problems that students encounter when taking a live exam. Designed to anticipate what the exam will emphasize, getting inside the exam will help ensure you know what you need to know to pass the exam. You can get a leg up on how to respond to those difficult-to-understand questions by focusing extra attention on these sidebars.

- ■ The **Certification Summary** is a succinct review of the chapter and a restatement of salient points regarding the exam.

✓

- ■ The **Two-Minute Drill** at the end of every chapter is a checklist of the main points of the chapter. It can be used for last-minute review.

Q&A

- ■ The **Self Test** offers questions similar to those found on the certification exams. The answers to these questions, as well as explanations of the answers, can be found at the end of each chapter. By taking the Self Test after completing each chapter, you'll reinforce what you've learned from that chapter while becoming familiar with the structure of the exam questions.

- ■ The **Lab Question** at the end of the Self Test section offers a unique and challenging question format that requires the reader to understand multiple chapter concepts to answer correctly. These questions are more complex and more comprehensive than the other questions because they test your ability to take all the knowledge you have gained from reading the chapter and apply it to complicated, real-world situations. These questions are aimed to be more difficult than what you will find on the exam. If you can answer these questions, you have proven that you know the subject!

## Some Pointers

Once you've finished reading this book, set aside some time to do a thorough review. You might want to return to the book several times, and make use of all the methods it offers for reviewing the material:

1. *Reread all the Two-Minute Drills*, or have someone quiz you. You also can use the drills as a way to do a quick cram before the exam. You might want to make some flashcards out of 3×5 index cards that have the Two-Minute Drill material on them.

2. *Reread all the Exam Watch notes and Inside the Exam elements*. Remember that these notes are written by authors who have taken the exam and passed. They know what you should expect—and what you should be on the lookout for.

3. *Retake the Self Tests*. Taking the tests right after you've read the chapter is a good idea because the questions help reinforce what you've just learned. However, it's an even better idea to go back later and do all the questions in

the book in one sitting. Pretend that you're taking the live exam. When you go through the questions the first time, you should mark your answers on a separate piece of paper. That way, you can run through the questions as many times as you need to until you feel comfortable with the material.

4. *Complete the Exercises.* Did you do the exercises when you read through each chapter? If not, do them! These exercises are designed to cover exam topics, and there's no better way to get to know this material than by practicing. Be sure you understand why you are performing each step in each exercise. If there is something you are not clear on, reread that section in the chapter.

# INTRODUCTION

Voice over IP (VoIP) technologies have taken the telephony world by storm. Certainly, the majority of new telephony network implementations are VoIP-based, and most analog PBX systems are being upgraded, or future plans are being made to upgrade them. The recent release of the 802.11n high speed wireless data standard will provide for even greater support of VoIP across wireless LANs. For these reasons, learning about VoIP technologies is a very important task for today's network administrator.

This book was written to help you prepare for the IIUC or the CVOICE exam so that you can earn your CCNA Voice certification and potentially move on to the more advanced CCVP certification. This book will provide an excellent supplement to your certification preparation processes. In many cases, the book goes into greater depth than the certifications require, and in all cases it points you in the right direction for your studies. While nothing can replace hands-on experience with the technologies, this book can act as your guide to the preparation process.

As you prepare for the IIUC or CVOICE exam, be sure to use the Exam Readiness Checklists available at the end of the Introduction. These checklists will allow you to quickly locate the sections within the book where the specific objectives are addressed.

One of the most important decisions you'll make is whether to take the IIUC or the CVOICE exam. The decision should be a simple one. If you plan to sell and support small VoIP networks or implement small VoIP networks in your company, the IIUC exam is the best choice, and you'll need to go no further. However, if you want to eventually achieve your CCVP certification status, you should go the CVOICE route. The CVOICE exam is required to become a CCVP, but the IIUC exam is not.

# Exam 640-460 (IIUC)

| Official Objective and Study Guide Coverage | Ch # | Pg # | Beginner | Intermediate | Expert |
|---|---|---|---|---|---|
| **Describe the components of the Cisco Unified Communications Architecture** | | | | | |
| Describe the function of the infrastructure in a UC environment | 2, 9 | 38, 249 | | | |
| Describe the function of endpoints in a UC environment | 9 | 252 | | | |
| Describe the function of the call processing agent in a UC environment | 9 | 253 | | | |
| Describe the function of messaging in a UC environment | 9 | 255 | | | |
| Describe the function of auto attendants and the IVRs in a UC environment | 9 | 257 | | | |
| Describe the function of contact center in a UC environment | 9 | 257 | | | |
| Describe the applications available in the UC environment, including Mobility, Presence, and Telepresence | 9 | 258 | | | |
| Describe how the Unified Communications components work together to create the Cisco Unified Communications Architecture | 9 | 260 | | | |
| **Describe PSTN components and technologies** | | | | | |
| Describe the services provided by the PSTN | 3 | 92 | | | |
| Describe time division and statistical multiplexing | 14 | 381 | | | |
| Describe supervisory, informational, and address signaling | 2, 14 | 107, 385 | | | |
| Describe numbering plans | 3 | 112 | | | |
| Describe analog circuits | 14 | 380 | | | |
| Describe digital voice circuits | 14 | 381 | | | |
| Describe PBX, trunk lines, key systems, and tie lines | 3 | 113 | | | |
| **Describe VoIP components and technologies** | | | | | |
| Describe the process of voice packetization | 4 | 131 | | | |
| Describe RTP and RTCP | 5 | 161 | | | |
| Describe the function of and differences between codecs | 4 | 145 | | | |
| Describe H.323, SIP, MGCP, and SCCP signaling protocols | 6, 7, 8 | 193, 216, 236 | | | |

## Exam 640-460 (IIUC) *(continued)*

| Official Objective and Study Guide Coverage | Ch # | Pg # | Beginner | Intermediate | Expert |
|---|---|---|---|---|---|
| **Describe and configure gateways, voice ports, and dial peers to connect to the PSTN and service provider networks** | | | | | |
| Describe the function and application of a dial plan | 13 | 362 | | | |
| Describe the function and application of voice gateways | 14 | 376 | | | |
| Describe the function and application of voice ports in a gateway | 14 | 378 | | | |
| Describe the function and operation of call-legs | 14 | 364 | | | |
| Describe and configure voice dial peers | 14 | 387 | | | |
| Describe the differences between PSTN and Internet Telephony Service Provider circuits | 14 | 386 | | | |
| **Describe and configure Cisco network to support VoIP** | | | | | |
| Describe the purpose of VLANs in a VoIP environment | 2 | 77 | | | |
| Describe the environmental considerations to support VoIP | 2 | 79 | | | |
| Configure switched infrastructure to support voice and data VLANs | 2 | 79 | | | |
| Describe the purpose and operation of PoE | 2 | 70 | | | |
| Identify the factors that impact voice quality | 1 | 21 | | | |
| Describe how QoS addresses voice quality issues | 17 | 477 | | | |
| Identify where QoS is deployed in the UC infrastructure | 17 | 479 | | | |
| **Implement UC500 using Cisco Configuration Assistant** | | | | | |
| Describe the function and operation of Cisco Configuration Assistant | 10 | 283 | | | |
| Configure UC500 device parameters | 10 | 284 | | | |
| Configure UC500 network parameters | 10 | 287 | | | |
| Configure UC500 dial plan and voicemail parameters | 10 | 290 | | | |
| Configure UC500 SIP trunk parameters | 10 | 288 | | | |
| Configure UC500 voice system features | 10 | 289 | | | |
| Configure UC500 user parameters | 10 | 290 | | | |

# Exam 640-460 (IIUC) *(continued)*

| Official Objective and Study Guide Coverage | Ch # | Pg # | Beginner | Intermediate | Expert |
|---|---|---|---|---|---|
| **Implement Cisco Unified Communications Manager Express to support endpoints using CLI** | | | | | |
| Describe the appropriate software components needed to support endpoints | 12 | 322 | | | |
| Describe the requirements and correct settings for DHCP, NTP, and TFTP | 12 | 332 | | | |
| Configure DHCP, NTP, and TFTP | 12 | 332 | | | |
| Describe the differences between key system and PBX mode | 12 | 334 | | | |
| Describe the differences between the different types of ephones and ephone-dns | 12 | 334 | | | |
| Configure Cisco Unified Communications Manager Express endpoints | 12 | 336 | | | |
| Configure call-transfer per design specifications | 12 | 336 | | | |
| Configure voice productivity features, including hunt groups, call park, call pickup, paging groups, and paging/intercom | 12 | 337 | | | |
| Configure Music on Hold | 12 | 342 | | | |
| **Implement voicemail features using Cisco Unity Express** | | | | | |
| Describe the Cisco Unity Express hardware platforms | 10 | 291 | | | |
| Configure the foundational elements required for Cisco Unified Communications Manager Express to support Cisco Unity Express | 10 | 291 | | | |
| Describe the features available in Cisco Unity Express | 10 | 292 | | | |
| Configure AutoAttendant services using Cisco Unity Express | 10 | 295 | | | |
| Configure basic voicemail features using Cisco Unity Express | 10 | 294 | | | |
| **Perform basic maintenance and operations tasks to support the VoIP solution** | | | | | |
| Describe basic troubleshooting methods for Cisco Unified Communications Manager Express | 17 | 473 | | | |
| Explain basic troubleshooting methods for Cisco Unity Express | 17 | 474 | | | |
| Explain basic maintenance and troubleshooting methods for UC500 | 17 | 476 | | | |

# Exam 642-436 (CVOICE)

| Official Objective and Study Guide Coverage | Ch | Pg # | Beginner | Intermediate | Expert |
|---|---|---|---|---|---|
| **Describe the components of a gateway** | | | | | |
| Describe the function of gateways | 14 | 377 | | | |
| Describe DSP functionality | 11 | 376 | | | |
| Describe the different types of voice ports and their usage | 14 | 378 | | | |
| Describe dial peer types | 14 | 378 | | | |
| Describe codecs and codec complexity | 4 | 142 | | | |
| **Describe a dial plan** | | | | | |
| Describe a numbering plan | 13 | 362 | | | |
| Describe digit manipulation | 13 | 365 | | | |
| Describe path selection | 13 | 364 | | | |
| Describe calling privileges | 13 | 365 | | | |
| Describe call coverage | 13 | 365 | | | |
| **Describe the basic operation and components involved in a VoIP call** | | | | | |
| Describe VoIP call flow | 13, 14 | 364, 377 | | | |
| Describe RTP, RTCP, cRTP, and sRTP | 5, 18 | 176, 535 | | | |
| Describe H.323 | 6 | 188 | | | |
| Describe MGCP | 8 | 233 | | | |
| Describe SCCP | 8 | 234 | | | |
| Describe SIP | 7 | 206 | | | |
| Identify the appropriate gateway signaling protocol for a given situation | 14 | 395 | | | |
| Describe voice quality considerations | 1 | 26 | | | |
| Choose the appropriate codec for a given situation | 4 | 148 | | | |
| **Implement a gateway** | | | | | |
| Describe the gateway call routing process | 14 | 380 | | | |

# Exam 642-436 (CVOICE)
## (continued)

| Official Objective and Study Guide Coverage | Ch | Pg # | Beginner | Intermediate | Expert |
|---|---|---|---|---|---|
| Configure digital voice ports | 14 | 383 | | | |
| Describe considerations for PBX integration | 14 | 383 | | | |
| Configure dial peers | 14 | 383 | | | |
| Configure hunt groups and trunk groups | 14 | 393 | | | |
| Configure digit manipulation | 14 | 393 | | | |
| Configure calling privileges | 14 | 393 | | | |
| Verify dial-plan implementation | 14 | 388 | | | |
| Implement fax and modem support on a gateway | 16 | 432 | | | |
| Configure a gateway to provide DTMF support | 15 | 411 | | | |
| **Describe the function and interoperation of gatekeepers within an IP Communications network** | | | | | |
| Describe the function and types of gatekeepers | 14 | 389 | | | |
| Describe the interoperation of devices with a gatekeeper | 14 | 389 | | | |
| Describe gatekeeper signaling | 14 | 390 | | | |
| Describe Dynamic Zone Prefix Registration with a gatekeeper | 14 | 393 | | | |
| Describe gatekeeper redundancy | 14 | 393 | | | |
| **Implement a gatekeeper** | | | | | |
| Configure devices to register with a gatekeeper | 14 | 393 | | | |
| Configure gatekeeper to provide dial-plan resolution | 14 | 395 | | | |
| Configure gatekeeper to provide call admission control | 14 | 395 | | | |
| Verify gatekeeper operation | 14 | 396 | | | |
| **Implement an IP-to-IP gateway** | | | | | |
| Describe the IP-to-IP gateway features and functionality | 15 | 408 | | | |
| Configure gatekeeper to support an IP-to-IP gateway | 15 | 414 | | | |
| Configure IP-to-IP gateway to provide address hiding | 15 | 416 | | | |
| Configure IP-to-IP gateway to provide protocol and media internetworking | 15 | 416 | | | |
| Configure IP-to-IP gateway to provide call admission control | 15 | 418 | | | |
| Verify IP-to-IP gateway implementations | 15 | 419 | | | |

# 1

# The VoIP Market

> *A person with a new idea is a crank until the idea succeeds.*
>
> —Mark Twain

Voice over Internet Protocol (VoIP) has taken the business world by storm. Few companies are still holding out against VoIP and continuing the use of traditional PBX systems. The vast majority have implemented it in at least small departments, while many take advantage of it for telephone networks that span the globe. But what is this thing called VoIP, and why has it proven so appealing to the masses? These two questions will be answered in this chapter. In addition, we'll explore the demands that VoIP will place on your network. The voice quality information provided in this chapter is essential knowledge for the CCNA (Cisco Certified Network Associate) Voice candidate, whether you plan to take the IIUC (Implementing Cisco IOS Unified Communications) or the CVOICE (Cisco Voice) exam, because both exams demand that you understand voice quality issues.

In fact, this voice quality information is the very knowledge that allows us to effectively implement VoIP on a large scale. Without it, back in the 1990s, many said this new thing called IP telephony would never take off. However, what was a new idea in the 1990s is commonplace today thanks to better quality management. So, with Mark Twain supporting us, let's begin our exploration of this new realm of communications.

# VoIP Defined

Voice over IP (VoIP), also called *IP telephony,* uses IP data networks to transfer audio- or sound-based communications. While traditional telephony networks convert voice to electrical signals and then pass these signals along the wires, VoIP networks convert voice to data first. The data is still converted to electrical signals that are passed on either wired or wireless networks, but the added step of converting the voice to data (specifically, IP packets) is the new factor introduced by VoIP networks.

In this section, you will read about the technologies used to build a VoIP network and the benefits and applications of VoIP. If you are using this book as a preparation tool for the CCNA Voice certification, some of this information will be a review from your earlier CCNA studies. If you are using this book as a learning tool to understand VoIP in Cisco networks, this information will be foundational to your learning process.

# Technologies Used for VoIP

VoIP networks depend on two primary technologies: traditional data networking and VoIP-specific protocols. Both technologies will be reviewed in the following sections; however, they are covered in more detail in Chapters 2 through 8, which provide the VoIP foundations required to fully understand Cisco's VoIP solutions.

## Traditional Data Networking

A *network* is a *group of connected or interconnected people or things*. When those of us working as technology professionals hear the term "network," we tend to immediately think of a computer network, but this is only one type of network. The popular web site known as LinkedIn (www.linkedin.com) is a networking site that allows people to form connections with one another based on shared likes, dislikes, experiences, or simply the desire to connect. "Network marketing" is a phrase that has been used for years to reference a form of marketing that takes advantage of an individual's network of connections with other people, which is similar to the networks that have been built on the LinkedIn web site. The point is, networks are groups of connected entities and are not limited to modern computer networks.

In fact, the public telephone system is a perfect example of a network different from the typical computer networks we implement as local area networks (LANs) and wide area networks (WANs) in our organizations. It is sometimes called the public switched telephone network (PSTN), and it is a network that consists of the telephone endpoints and the cables and devices used between these endpoints. This network allows us to use traditional land-line telephones to place calls to our friends across town or to our extended families several states away.

When two networks combine or connect in some way, these networks are said to have *converged*. Many years ago we modulated TCP/IP (Transmission Control Protocol/Internet Protocol) communications (data communications) over an analog phone line using the PSTN that was designed to carry the human voice and not data (some people still do this in rural areas of the United States and even in small businesses). The purpose of this modulation was to implement a connection that allowed communications on the Internet using a standard phone line. Today, we digitize the human voice over an IP network that was designed to carry computer data and not the human voice. Ultimately, when implementing VoIP, the IP network eventually connects to the PSTN (in many cases) to route calls outside of the IP network and to connect to other telephones that are simply connected to a standard land line. This connection point between the IP network and the traditional telephone network is one way in which we say the networks have converged.

Additionally, the fact that voice data is now traveling on a network that was designed for computer data also suggests convergence. We could say that the two data types have converged. The computer data may consist of a word processor document or an e-mail; voice data is a digitized version of the human-generated sound waves. In the end, both data types become IP packets, which become Ethernet frames (on Ethernet networks), which become 1's and 0's on the communications medium that is utilized—either wired or wireless.

At least two points of convergence are in the areas of voice and data. The first is the point where our IP networks connect to traditional telephone networks. The second is the unification of upper-level data such as voice and computer data into shared lower-level communications such as IP packets. This will all become clear as you read through this book. You will see why it's so important for a modern network engineer or for administrators to understand both data networking and telephony as the two have converged.

Let's explore the historical development of information networks. A brief overview of the major developments along the way will help you understand why things work the way they do today and how to best take advantage of the available technologies.

The electric telegraph was the precursor to modern electronic or digital information networks. While other networks, like the Pony Express or Claude Chappe's nonelectric telegraph, existed before the electric telegraph, they required complete involvement of humans on an ongoing basis either from end to end or at each end. The electric telegraph was a revolutionary leap forward in that it eventually allowed messages to be sent to a remote location and recorded onto paper tape as raised dots and dashes matching up with Morse code.

It is interesting to note that tests were performed over many years to validate the potential of electricity in communications. In 1746 Jean-Antoine Nollet asked about 200 monks to form a long snaking line. He had each one hold the end of a 25-foot iron wire connecting him to the next monk in the line. Then, without warning, he injected an electrical current into the line. The fact that monks in a line nearly one mile long all exclaimed their literal shock at the same time showed that electricity travels long distances very rapidly. Of course, we have much more humane methods of testing today, but these early tests did indeed reveal the knowledge that eventually led to the implementation of high-speed electric telegraphs.

By 1861 the United States was implementing the transcontinental telegraph, which allowed nearly instant communications across the country. Much as we are implementing IPv6 alongside our IPv4 networks, the transcontinental telegraph wire was placed alongside the existing Pony Express route. Once the telegraph was in place, the Pony Express became obsolete and was dissolved. Some of us look forward to the day when IPv6 does the same to IPv4.

In a quick jump to the peak of the era of the telegraph, within 30 years of its beginning, over 650,000 miles of wire were in place, and some 20,000 towns were connected to the network. You could send messages from London to Bombay or from New York to Sacramento in just a few minutes. Previously, such communications would have taken weeks or months. The telegraph showed that electronic communications were indeed the way to send information over long distances.

The use of electricity in sending telegraph messages eventually led to the use of electronic voice communications. The telephone was invented in the late 1800s; it converted sound waves into electronic signals on the sending end and then converted electronic signals into sound waves on the receiving end. Sound travels at an average speed of about 1,130 feet (344 meters) per second, while electromagnetic waves travel at about 186,400 miles (300,000 kilometers) per second. This means that a message sent electronically could travel around the Earth more than seven times in a second. By converting sound waves to electromagnetic waves and back, we can transmit the human voice very rapidly, and this is why you can have a conversation with someone on the other side of the globe with little delay.

The telephone system continued to evolve into the public switched telephone network that we utilize today. In the same way, new forms of information delivery were also being developed, and nearing the end of the 20th century two distinct networks had evolved: voice networks and data networks. Voice networks allowed the transfer of human conversations, and data networks allowed the transfer of all other kinds of information. At times our data networks connected to one another using the voice networks as the infrastructure, and at times our voice networks crossed over our data networks in the form of packet delivery; however, with the new millennium also came much greater interest in the convergence of voice and data networks.

**on the** 
**Job**

*If you would like to learn more about the history of the telegraph and telephone, I suggest the book* The Victorian Internet *by Tom Standage (Walker & Company, 2007) as a starting point. Studying these historical developments can help you better understand the technologies we use today and why convergence is important and beneficial to the future of data networks.*

## VoIP Protocols

The "IP" in "VoIP" stands for "Internet Protocol." The Internet Protocol (IP) is the foundation on which all modern networks operate. The most popular protocol suite in use today is the only suite that I will cover in this chapter. That suite is the TCP/IP protocol suite.

It's important to remember that there is really no such thing as the TCP/IP protocol. TCP is a protocol and IP is a protocol (though they were the same

Transmission Control Protocol from 1974 to 1978, when the single TCP solution was split into TCP for host-to-host communications and IP for network routing). The name "TCP/IP" indicates that the TCP segments travel as IP packets over the network. TCP travels over IP just like FTP (File Transfer Protocol) travels over TCP and SNMP (Simple Network Management Protocol) travels over UDP (User Datagram Protocol). We're dealing with layering concepts here that are very similar to the OSI (Open Systems Interconnection) model. For this reason, it's important to understand the TCP/IP model as opposed to the OSI model (the OSI model will be reviewed in Chapter 2 just in case you've forgotten it since your CCNA or other studies).

Unlike the OSI model's seven layers, the TCP/IP model contains only four layers. The four layers of the TCP/IP model are:

- Application layer
- Transport layer
- Internet layer
- Link layer

The *TCP/IP Application layer* can be said to encompass the OSI model's Application and Presentation layers. Layer 4 of the TCP/IP model performs the services required of Layer 6 and Layer 7 of the OSI model. RFC 1122 specifies two categories of Application layer protocols: user protocols and support protocols. User protocols include common protocols like FTP, SMTP (Simple Mail Transfer Protocol), and HTTP (Hypertext Transfer Protocol). These protocols are all used to provide a direct service to the user. FTP allows the user to transfer a file between two machines. SMTP allows the user to send an e-mail message. HTTP allows the user to view web pages from a web site. Support protocols include common protocols like DNS (Domain Name System), DHCP (Dynamic Host Configuration Protocol), and BOOTP (Bootstrap Protocol). DNS provides name resolution for user requests. For example, if a user requests to browse the home page at www.TomCarpenter.net, the DNS support service resolves the web site's domain name to an IP address for actual communications. Because this is an indirect service for the user, it is considered a support service as opposed to a user service. DHCP and BOOTP are both used to configure the IP protocol—and possible other TCP/IP parameters—without user intervention.

The *TCP/IP Transport layer* provides host-to-host or end-to-end communications. Transport layer protocols may provide reliable or non-guaranteed data delivery. TCP is an example of a Transport layer protocol that provides reliable delivery of data (usually called *segments*), and UDP is an example of a protocol that provides non-guaranteed delivery of data (usually called *datagrams*). Notice that I did not say that TCP provides guaranteed delivery of data. This is because no network protocol can provide guaranteed delivery of data; however, reliable protocols do provide notice of undelivered data, and UDP does not provide such notice. Later in this chapter I'll explain why a non-guaranteed data delivery model is very useful and how it plays an important role in Voice over IP networks.

The next layer is the *TCP/IP Internet layer*. The Internet layer is where host identification is utilized to route TCP segments and UDP datagrams to the appropriate end device. The protocol that all Application and Transport layer protocols use within the TCP/IP model is the Internet Protocol (IP). The IP provides the routing functionality that enables the implementation of very large LANs and communications across the Internet. You'll learn much more about this protocol in the IP section coming up next. In addition to IP, the Internet Control Message Protocol (ICMP) is considered an integral part of IP even though it actually uses IP for communications just like TCP and UDP. So ICMP is considered an Internet layer protocol because of its integral use in IP-based communications.

The final or bottom layer of the TCP/IP model is the *Link layer*. This is where the upper-layer TCP/IP suite interfaces with the lower-layer physical transmission medium. Some have said that the Link layer is equivalent to the Data Link layer of the OSI model and, of the TCP/IP layers, this is probably the most accurate linkage of all. In fact, when TCP/IP runs over Ethernet, there is no real Link layer provided by TCP/IP; instead the MAC (Media Access Control) and PHY (Physical Layer Protocol) of the IEEE 802.3 protocol provide the functionality of the TCP/IP Link layer to the TCP/IP suite. It is also interesting to note that protocols such as ARP (Address Resolution Protocol) and RARP (Reverse Address Resolution Protocol) that actually service the IP protocol are not actually Link layer protocols themselves. Instead, they seem to exist in some mysterious land between the Link layer and the Internet layer. I would suggest that they are simply part of the Internet layer and that you could represent the Internet layer as having an upper-management layer (ICMP, IGMP, etc.), a routing layer (IP), and a routing service layer (ARP and RARP); however, this is only my thinking and not really part of the standard TCP/IP model.

It has been much debated over the years whether ARP exists at Layer 2 or Layer 3 of the OSI model or at the Link layer or Internet layer of the TCP/IP model. I suggest that this debate exists because ARP really works between these layers. In fact, ARP is used to resolve the MAC address (a Layer 2 address) when the IP address (a Layer 3 address) is known. It could be said that ARP provides a service *between* these two layers, and this may be the point of debate. Wherever you decide to place the protocol, know that you will likely meet opposition to your view.

**FIGURE I-I**

TCP/IP model
mapped to the
OSI model

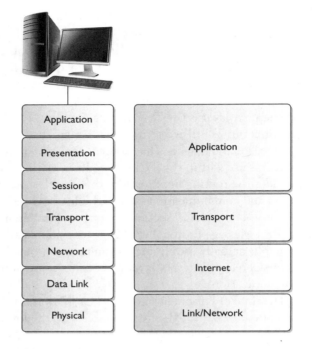

Figure 1-1 shows a common mapping of the TCP/IP model to the OSI model. Again, keep in mind that this is a mapping for understanding purposes only and that the TCP/IP suite of protocols makes no attempt or claim to mapping in this way. It is simply a helpful way of thinking about the functionality of the suite.

**exam**
**Watch**
It is important that you know the details of TCP/IP for the CCNA Voice exams regardless of which exam you choose to take for your certification path. While TCP/IP is not listed as one of the direct objectives, remember that the CCNA certification is a prerequisite and that the CCNA certification covers TCP/IP in depth. I've included a summary of the TCP/IP protocol suite here to help you refresh your memory for the CCNA Voice exams.

To fully understand the working of TCP/IP, it is essential to investigate the core protocols. In the following sections, I'll explain the basic functionality of IP, TCP, and other important TCP/IP protocols for our purposes.

On Ethernet networks, addresses are used to identify each node on the Ethernet. These addresses are called MAC addresses and are physical addresses usually burned into the device; however, some devices, such as wireless LAN adapters, do support configurable MAC addresses. Another address that each node possesses on a modern network is a Layer 3 address known as an IP address. MAC addresses are Layer 2 addresses, and IP addresses are Layer 3 addresses. This will become very important in a moment.

The Internet Protocol (IP) is the Network layer (OSI) or Internet layer (TCP/IP) solution to node identification. This protocol is responsible for addressing, data routing, and servicing the upper layers in the TCP/IP suite. The question is this: why do I need a Layer 3 address in addition to a Layer 2 address?

To understand the answer to this question, you must understand the concepts of network congestion, network segmentation, and network routing. *Network congestion* occurs when the bandwidth on the network is insufficient to meet the demands placed on the network. In other words, you can have too many nodes on a single network. This congestion can be detrimental to VoIP networks, causing calls to fail or suffer in quality.

Consider a network with only three computers connected to a 100-Mbps (megabits per second) switch. These computers will be able to communicate with each other very rapidly. Now, imagine that you add three more computers to double the size of the network. Each computer will now have an average of half the throughput available to it as was available with only three computers on the network. The guideline is that for every doubling of communicating nodes on the network segment (I'll define this in a moment), you halve the average throughput for each node. If we doubled our network four more times, we would have 96 nodes on the network. Each node would have an average of about 1 Mbps of throughput available. This may or may not be enough, and it could indeed lead to network congestion problems since it is now more likely that a number of nodes will use more than their "fair share" of network bandwidth.

So what can you do when you have too many nodes on a network segment? Create more segments. *Network segmentation* is the act of separating the network into reasonably sized broadcast domains. A *broadcast domain* is a shared medium where all devices can communicate with each other without the need for a routing or bridging device. The most commonly implemented network segmentation protocol is the IP protocol. It can be used, in conjunction with routers, to split any network into smaller and smaller segments, even down to a single node on each segment—which would not be practical or beneficial.

Of course, if you're implementing network segmentation, you must implement *network routing*. Network routing is the process of moving data from one network segment to another to allow that data to reach an intended node on a network or network segment separate from the originating node. IP is responsible for the routing of this data. There is a concept known as a routing protocol, but this should not be confused with routing itself. *Routing protocols* are used to dynamically create *routing tables* that allow routing to take place. It is IP that uses these routing tables to actually perform the routing. Remember: routing protocols like RIP (Routing Information Protocol) and OSPF (Open Shortest Path First) create the routing tables, and IP uses the routing tables to determine the best route available to get a data packet to its destination. These routing tables are stored in memory on devices called *routers*. A router may be a computer with multiple network interface cards (NICs) acting as a router, or it may be a dedicated routing device.

## e x a m
### w a t c h

*Remember that routers often introduce delay into the communications process. While vendors such as Cisco may claim line speed switching or routing, the truth is that you cannot "do extra steps" without introducing delay. The processor has to take at least a few milliseconds to process the incoming frames and forward them to the next hop along the way. Having too many routers between communicating devices can cause problems in VoIP communications.*

The IP address itself is a 32-bit address divided into four octets or four groups of 8 bits. For example, the following bits represent a valid IP address:

00001010.00001010.00001010.00000001

This is sometimes called "binary notation," but it is the actual form that an IP address takes. To understand this notation, you'll need to understand how to convert binary bits to decimal; I'm sure you're used to seeing the previous IP address shown as 10.10.10.1. These IP addresses comprise four octets and can contain decimal values from 0 to 255. Let's look at how you would convert an 8-bit binary number into the decimal version that we're used to.

Ethernet frames use bits to represent both the payload data and the Ethernet header information. The reality is that any data can be represented by binary bits. Someone simply has to devise how many bits there should be and what those bits should represent.

The smallest information element that can be transmitted on any network is a *bit*. A bit is a single value equal to 1 or 0. When you group these bits together, they form *bytes*. An 8-bit byte is the most commonly referenced byte and is the base of most networking measurements. An 8-bit byte is specifically called an *octet* in most standards, even though the vendors and networking professionals have leaned more toward the term "byte." For example, one kilobyte is 1,024 bytes, and one megabyte is 1,048,576 bytes. You will often see these numbers rounded to say that 1,000 bytes is a kilobyte or 1 million bytes is a megabyte. The term "octet" could also be used in these statements; for example, one kilobyte is 1,024 octets.

You might be wondering how a simple bit, or even a byte, can represent anything. This is an important concept to understand; otherwise, you may have difficulty truly understanding how a network works. Let's consider just an 8-bit byte. If you have one bit, it can represent any two pieces of information. The *1* can represent one piece of information, and the *0* can represent another. When you have two bits, you can represent four pieces of information. You have the values 00, 01, 10, and 11 available to use as representative elements. When you have three bits, you can represent eight pieces of information, and for every bit you add, you effectively double the amount of information that can be represented. This means that an 8-bit byte can represent $2^8$ pieces of information or 256 elements. You have now received a hint about why the numbers *0* through *255* are all that can be used in an IP address octet. (Remember, IP addresses are four octets or four 8-bit bytes grouped together.)

Standard mapping systems map a numeric value to a piece of information. For example, the ASCII system maps numbers to characters. Since I can represent up to 256 elements with an 8-bit byte, I can represent 256 ASCII codes as well. A quick Internet search for ASCII codes will reveal a number of sites that provide tables of ASCII codes. For example, the ASCII codes for 802.11 (one of my absolute favorite IEEE standards) are 56, 48, 50, 46, 49, and 49 in decimal form. Since I can represent any number from 0 to 255 with an 8-bit byte, I can represent these numbers as well. Table 1-1 shows a mapping of characters to ASCII decimal codes to 8-bit bytes.

| TABLE 1-1 | Character | ASCII Decimal Codes | 8-Bit Byte |
|---|---|---|---|
| | 8 | 56 | 00111000 |
| Representing | 0 | 48 | 00110000 |
| Characters with | 2 | 50 | 00110010 |
| Bytes | . | 46 | 00101110 |
| | 1 | 49 | 00110001 |
| | 1 | 49 | 00110001 |

For all this to work, both the sender and the receiver of the bytes must agree on how the bytes will be translated. In other words, for information to be meaningful, both parties must agree to the meaning. This is the same in human languages. If I speak a language that has meaning to me, but you do not understand that language, it is meaningless to you, and communication has not occurred. When a computer receives information that it cannot interpret to be anything meaningful, it sees the information as either noise or corrupted data.

To understand how the binary bits, in an octet, translated to the ASCII decimal codes, consider Table 1-2. Here you can see that the first bit (the rightmost bit) represents the number *1*, the second bit represents the number *2*, the third bit represents the number *4*, and so on. The example in the table is 00110001. Where there is a *0*, the bit is off. Where there is a *1*, the bit is on. We add up the total values in the translated row, based on the represented number for each bit, and find the result of 49 because we only count the values where the bit is equal to 1. This is how the binary octet of 00110001 represents the ASCII decimal code of 49, which represents the number *1* in the ASCII tables.

So how does all this apply to IP addressing? IP version 4 addresses comprise four 8-bit bytes or four octets. Now, you could memorize and work with IP addresses like *00001010.00001010.00001010.00000001*, or you could work with addresses like *10.10.10.1*. I don't know about you, but the latter is certainly easier for me; however, the former is not only easier for your computer to work with, but it is also the only way your computer thinks. Therefore, IP addresses can be represented in *dotted decimal* notation to make it easier for humans to work with. The dotted decimal notation looks like this: *10.10.10.1*.

IP version 4 (which is the current widely used implementation) addresses cannot just have any number in each octet. Remember that only 8 bits are available, so the number in each octet must be an 8-bit number. This means it will be a decimal value

**TABLE 1-2**   Converting Bytes to Decimal Values

| Bit Position | 8 | 7 | 6 | 5 | 4 | 3 | 2 | 1 |
|---|---|---|---|---|---|---|---|---|
| Represented decimal number | 128 | 64 | 32 | 16 | 8 | 4 | 2 | 1 |
| Example binary number | 0 | 0 | 1 | 1 | 0 | 0 | 0 | 1 |
| Translated | 0 | 0 | 32 | 16 | 0 | 0 | 0 | 1 |

from 0 to 255 for a total of 256 valid numbers. There is no IP address that starts with 0. In other words, you'll never see an address like 0.0.0.1 assigned to a device. In fact, the address 0.0.0.0 is reserved to indicate the *default network* and/or the *default device*. In this context, the term "default" should be understood according to context. For example, the IP address of 0.0.0.23 would refer to host identification 23 in the current (default) network and, flipping the numbers, the IP address of 192.168.12.0 refers to the entire network as a collective. Similarly, 255.255.255.255 is reserved to indicate all nodes or hosts. Of course, on the Internet, 255.255.255.255 would actually refer to every one of the millions of connected devices, and it is never used for any practical purpose.

Another special address that is important for you to know about is the *loopback* address. This is IP address 127.0.0.1. For example, if you use the PING command to communicate with 127.0.0.1, you are actually communicating with your own TCP/IP network stack or protocol implementation. This is sometimes called *pinging* yourself and is used to troubleshoot the local TCP/IP implementation and to ensure that it is working properly.

An organization known as the Internet Assigned Numbers Authority (IANA) manages the public IP address space. RFC 1166 briefly describes how the IP address space should be partitioned for distribution. It specifies three classes of addresses that are important to our discussion: class A, class B, and class C. Class D addresses are used for multicast implementations, and class E addresses are reserved for testing purposes. Table 1-3 shows the breakdown of the three primary classes of addresses.

The IP addressing, however, has been moving from classfull addressing to classless addressing over the past decade. In fact, the IANA even references the classes as "former class B" and "former class C" in many of their web pages, indicating that the age of classfull IP addressing is quickly passing. By doing away with the classes, the IP address space is more usefully managed and distributed. In addition, many companies now use private IP addresses internally and have only a few real Internet addresses for external communication. This is accomplished through something called Network Address Translation (NAT).

| TABLE 1-3 | IP Address Class | Decimal Representation | Number of Networks |
|-----------|------------------|------------------------|--------------------|
| IP Address Classes | A | 1.0.0.0–126.255.255.255 | 126 |
| | B | 128.0.0.0–191.255.255.255 | 16,384 |
| | C | 192.0.0.0–223.255.255.255 | 2,097,152 |

These private IP addresses fall into three different ranges that were originally set aside according to the A, B, and C classes. These address ranges are:

- 10.*x.x.x*
- 172.16.*x.x*–172.31.*x.x*
- 192.168.*x.x*

The class A private address space ranges from 10.0.0.1 to 10.255.255.254, provides about 16.7 million IP addresses, and can be divided into thousands of networks using classless subnetting. The class B private address space ranges from 172.16.0.0 to 172.31.255.254, provides about 1 million IP addresses, and can be divided into hundreds of networks. Finally, the class C private address space ranges from 192.168.0.1 to 192.168.0.254, provides 65,556 addresses, and can be divided into hundreds of networks as well.

You'll notice that the class B private address range is the only one that provides more than one starting set of decimal values. For example, all of the class A private addresses start with 10, and all of the class C private addresses start with 192.168. The class B private address range can start with any numbers from 172.16 to 172.31.

Ultimately, there's a big difference between a globally assigned IP address and a private IP address. Globally assigned addresses are assigned by the IANA or one of the agencies serving the IANA. Private addresses can be assigned by an organization in any way they desire as long as they have implemented a network infrastructure that can support them. The benefit of private addresses is that they are set aside by the IANA and are guaranteed to never be the destination of an actual "on-the-Internet" host. This means that you'll be able to use the same IP addresses on your network as those being used on mine, and we'll still be able to communicate with each other across the Internet as long as we both implement a NAT solution, and possibly port forwarding, depending on the scenario.

As you can imagine, a private network that uses the "ten space" (a phrase for referencing the private IP addresses that are in the 10.*x.x.x* range) can be rather large. To reduce network traffic on single segments, we can subnet our network and increase performance. To do this, you will need to implement the appropriate subnetting scheme with subnet masks.

A *subnet mask* is a binary-level concept that is used to divide the IP address into a network identifier (ID) and a host ID. The network ID identifies the network on which the host resides, and the host ID identifies the unique device within that network. The two basic kinds of subnetting are classfull and classless.

*Classfull* (also written "classful") subnetting simply acknowledges the class of the IP address and uses a subnet mask that matches that class. For example, a class-A IP address would use the first 8 bits for the network ID, and therefore the subnet mask would be:

11111111.00000000.00000000.00000000

Notice that the portion of the IP address that is the network ID is all 1's, and the portion that is the host ID is all 0's. For example, if the IP address were 10.12.89.75 and we were using classfull subnetting, the subnet mask would be 11111111.00000000. 00000000.00000000, which is represented as 255.0.0.0 in dotted decimal notation. As one more example, consider a class C IP address of 192.168.14.57. What would the classfull subnet mask be? Correct. It would be 11111111.11111111.11111111 .00000000. This is because a class-C IP address uses the first 24 bits to define the network ID and uses the last 8 bits to define the host ID. This would be represented as 255.255.255.0 in dotted decimal notation.

Most configuration interfaces allow you to enter the IP address in dotted decimal notation and also the subnet mask. This make configuration much easier; however, if you want to perform classless subnetting, you will need to understand the binary level where we now reside in our discussion.

*Classless Inter-Domain Routing (CIDR)* is the standard replacement for classfull addressing and subnetting. Classless subnetting allows you to split the network ID and the host ID at the binary level and, therefore, right in the middle of an octet. For example, you can say that 10.10.10.1 is on one network and 10.10.10.201 is on another. How would you do this? Let's look at the binary level. Here are the two IP addresses in binary:

00001010.00001010.00001010.00000001 (10.10.10.1)

00001010.00001010.00001010.11001001 (10.10.10.201)

To use CIDR and indicate that the final octet should be split in two so that everything from 1 to 127 is in one network and everything from 128 to 254 is in another, we would use the following subnet mask:

11111111.11111111.11111111.10000000

You might be wondering how this subnet mask works. To understand it, consider it in Table 1-4. The first row (other than the bit position identifier row) of the table is the IP address of 10.10.10.1, and the third row is the IP address of 10.10.10.201. The second row is the CIDR subnet mask. If you count the columns carefully, you'll see that the first 25 positions have a *1* and the last 7 positions have a *0*. Where there is a *1*, the IP addresses must match, or they are on different network IDs. As you read across the rows and compare the first row with the third row, you'll notice that they are identical until you read the 25th bit position. In the 25th bit position, the first row has a *0* and the third row has a *1*. They are different and therefore are on different network IDs. This is CIDR in action.

| TABLE 1-4 | | | | | | Subnetting with CIDR | | | | | | | | | |

| B 1 | B 2 | B 3 | B 4 | B 5 | B 6 | B 7 | B 8 | B 9 | B 10 | B 11 | B 12 | B 13 | B 14 | B 15 | B 16 |
|---|---|---|---|---|---|---|---|---|---|---|---|---|---|---|---|
| 0 | 0 | 0 | 0 | 1 | 0 | 1 | 0 | 0 | 0 | 0 | 0 | 1 | 0 | 1 | 0 |
| 1 | 1 | 1 | 1 | 1 | 1 | 1 | 1 | 1 | 1 | 1 | 1 | 1 | 1 | 1 | 1 |
| 0 | 0 | 0 | 0 | 1 | 0 | 1 | 0 | 0 | 0 | 0 | 0 | 1 | 0 | 1 | 0 |

| B 17 | B 18 | B 19 | B 20 | B 21 | B 22 | B 23 | B 24 | B 25 | B 26 | B 27 | B 28 | B 29 | B 30 | B 31 | B 32 |
|---|---|---|---|---|---|---|---|---|---|---|---|---|---|---|---|
| 0 | 0 | 0 | 0 | 1 | 0 | 1 | 0 | 0 | 0 | 0 | 0 | 0 | 0 | 0 | 1 |
| 1 | 1 | 1 | 1 | 1 | 1 | 1 | 1 | 1 | 0 | 0 | 0 | 0 | 0 | 0 | 0 |
| 0 | 0 | 0 | 0 | 1 | 0 | 1 | 0 | 1 | 1 | 0 | 0 | 1 | 0 | 0 | 1 |

Because CIDR subnetting allows subnet masks that mask part of an octet, you will see subnet masks like 255.255.255.128 (which is the decimal equivalent of the subnet mask row in Table 1-4). Instead of representing the subnet mask in decimal notation, it is often simply appended to the end of the IP address. For example, the IP address and subnet mask combination in Table 1-4 could be represented as 10.10.10.1/25. This representation, which is sometimes called Variable Length Subnet Mask (VLSM) representation or CIDR representation, is becoming more and more common. It indicates that the IP address is 10.10.10.1 and the network ID (sometimes called the "subnet" or "subnetwork") is the first 25 bits of the IP address.

At this point you're probably beginning to wonder why all this subnetting really matters. Other than the fact that it can be used to reduce the size of a network segment, which may or may not be a benefit depending on the infrastructure type you've implemented, it allows IP routing to function. To simplify the process down to the level that you really need to know to work with converged networks, the local TCP/IP implementation on a device needs a method for determining if it can send the data directly to the end IP address or if it needs to send it through a router.

Going back to the example in the subnet masks discussion, imagine that IP address 10.10.10.1 is attempting to send a packet to IP address 10.10.10.201. How does the machine at 10.10.10.1 know if it needs the router (also called the "default gateway")? The answer is that it determines the network ID of its own address and looks at the destination address to see if it has the same network ID. If the network IDs match, the Address Resolution Protocol (ARP) can be used to discover the MAC address of the destination IP address because they are on the same network. If the network IDs do not match, ARP is used to discover the MAC address of the router, and the IP packet is sent to the router. The local device assumes that the router knows how to get to any IP address in the world.

Inside the router, it must find the best path to the destination IP. Once this is determined, the router discovers the MAC address of the nearest router in that path and forwards on the IP packet. This process continues until the target end node is reached. However, it all started when that first device evaluated the IP address against the subnet mask and determined that it needed the help of the local router or default gateway. Figure 1-2 shows this process as described.

While IP is used to move data around on internetworks until that data reaches its intended target, the Transmission Control Protocol (TCP) is used both to provide reliability in those deliveries and to determine the application that should process the data on the receiving device. The reliability is provided by segmenting, transmitting, retransmitting, and aggregating upper-layer data. The application determination is accomplished through the use of TCP ports.

The TCP protocol takes data from the upper layers and segments that data into smaller units that can be transferred and managed. Because IP sometimes drops IP packets due to congestion and because packets can travel different routes to the destination, some TCP segments (which are sent across IP) may arrive at the destination out of order or may not arrive at all. For this reason, TCP provides resequencing when data arrives out of order and resends data that doesn't make it to the destination. This provides reliable delivery of data and makes TCP very useful for such solutions as file transfers, e-mail, and NNTP (Network News Transfer Protocol). Each of these applications needs reliable delivery, and this means TCP is a prime candidate.

In addition to reliable delivery, TCP uses ports to determine the upper-level applications that should receive the arriving data. Some port numbers are well-known, others are registered, and still others are unassigned or private. Common ports include 21 for FTP, 80 for HTTP, and 25 for SMTP. Knowing which port a service uses has become very important in modern networks due to the heavy implementation of firewalls. Firewalls often block all internetwork traffic except certain ports. If you don't know the port number the service is attempting to utilize, you won't know what exception to create in your firewall.

**FIGURE 1-2**

IP routing

10.10.10.1       Router       10.10.10.201

Interface 1: 10.10.10.100
Interface 2: 10.10.10.200
Subnet Mask: 255.255.255.128

## INSIDE THE EXAM

### Why Is TCP/IP Important?

TCP/IP is the foundational protocol of the Internet. Modern private networks primarily use this protocol as well. If you do not know the basics of IP, TCP, and other protocols in this suite, you will not be able to administer a modern network.

The success of TCP/IP has been largely due to its utilization on the Internet. If you wanted to browse web pages, download from FTP sites, or read text at gopher sites, you had to be running the TCP/IP protocol. Many early networks ran TCP/IP as well as some other protocol like IPX/SPX (Internetwork Packet Exchange/Sequenced Packet Exchange) or Banyan Vines. First, network vendors began by supporting TCP/IP alongside their proprietary protocols, and eventually they moved their systems not only to support the TCP/IP suite, but also to rely upon it. Today, Novell, Microsoft, Unix, Linux, and Apple computers all use TCP/IP as the primary communication protocol.

A very gradual transition is happening in relation to the IP protocol. IPv6 has been available for a number of years, and operating systems have slowly incorporated it into their available protocols. Windows Vista has integral support of IPv6 as does Windows Server 2008. Unix and Linux machines have supported it for some time, and Apple's Mac OS X also supports it. Once IPv6 support is available on the vast majority of computers, we'll likely see it used more and more on our networks; however, the CCNA Voice exams will not test your knowledge of this protocol, according to the stated objectives as of late 2010.

Oh, and TCP/IP is the foundation for all VoIP communications. Of course, that's what this book and the CCNA Voice exams are all about.

The *Real-time Transport Protocol (RTP)* is a protocol designed for moving audio and video data on internetworks running IP. Unlike TCP, RTP is focused not on reliability but rather on rapid transfer. It is used when the data being transferred must arrive in a timely fashion or it provides little value. For example, an e-mail message can take two or three minutes to arrive, and once it has arrived you can read it just fine; however, a five-second statement made into a VoIP phone cannot take two or three minutes to arrive. That five-second statement would have been broken into many packets, and they must arrive very quickly. If there are large gaps in their arrival, either the call will be lost, or the listener will not be able to intelligibly hear the message. RTP runs over UDP, which is discussed in a later section.

The *Real-time Transport Control Protocol (RTCP)* is used with RTP. It is used to gather and report on performance information about the network communications. Administrative applications have been developed that allow support professionals to monitor media communications issues like latency, jitter, and packet loss. These issues will all be addressed in later chapters.

Since RTP and RTCP use UDP, it would be a good idea to know what this protocol does. UDP is responsible for connectionless communications. Remember that TCP is a connection-oriented protocol. UDP is different; it just drops the data on the wire and says, "I hope you get there." At first glance, you might think there would be no use for such a protocol; however, this protocol is very important to our converged networks because it allows for timely delivery of information and ignores reliability completely. UDP doesn't care if the data gets there and doesn't even expect an acknowledgment from the receiver.

Here's why this is a good thing. Since UDP does not have to process an acknowledgment, it can just keep the stream of data flowing. The receiving end doesn't have to pause to acknowledge receipt either. The end result is that there is less processing for both the sender and the receiver. Another benefit is that network congestion is reduced since fewer packets are being transmitted. Finally, the packets that are transmitted are smaller since the UDP header is smaller than the TCP header. The UDP header is 8 bytes, and the TCP header is 24 bytes. This means that 16 bytes of extra information have to be transferred with TCP, which would be detrimental to voice communications where latency and packet loss must be kept to a minimum.

**e x a m**

**ᗯ a t c h**
*UDP is a connectionless protocol, which is good for VoIP communications. Streaming voice data will not allow for the delay required to resend packets. UDP datagrams are send-it-and-forget-it packets, and the receiver will simply generate the voice audio from whatever packets it receives.*

Additional protocols used in VoIP networks include:

- **SIP**  The Session Initiation Protocol is a protocol used for streaming data communications and is commonly used to place VoIP calls.

- **H.323**  H.323 is a protocol used for streaming voice or multimedia (such as video) and is also commonly used to place VoIP calls.

- **MGCP**    The Media Gateway Control Protocol is a protocol used to connect circuit-switched networks with IP-based networks.
- **SCCP**    The Skinny Client Control Protocol is a Cisco proprietary protocol used for VoIP calls and for video or audio conferencing over IP networks.

These additional protocols will be covered in detail in Chapters 6 through 8.

## Benefits and Applications of VoIP

Finally, we come to the benefits and applications of VoIP. First, I will address the benefits, and then I'll cover the applications.

The benefits of VoIP over traditional PBX (Private Branch Exchange)-based telephony systems are many. Here are just a few:

- Upgrades do not require hardware replacement.
- VoIP can scale much better than traditional PBX solutions.
- VoIP can operate across the Internet with no extra service charges with many service providers.
- VoIP solutions can be purchased from vendors or selected free from the open source community on the Internet.
- In smaller implementations, VoIP can operate on existing hardware, such as Cisco integrated service routers (ISRs), without requiring additional hardware.
- VoIP never locks you into a specific vendor as long as you select all standards-based VoIP client phones and software.

Of course, the most commonly cited benefit of VoIP is the reduction in cost that it offers. Indeed, many organizations can save thousands—if not hundreds of thousands—of dollars on their phone bills by using VoIP. In addition, the cost for implementing your internal telephony network using VoIP instead of PBX-based systems is usually far less. This cost reduction is typically based on the fact that you are using the same cables and routers and switches for the telephone network as you use for the data network.

The applications provided by VoIP are equally impressive. You can use VoIP for any of the following tasks:

- Place calls around the world using the Internet as your carrier. All you need is a VoIP "server" at both ends of the connection.

- Implement conferencing (both audio and video) on your internal network without requiring special hardware. All you need is the right software on existing laptop computers.

- Manage voice mail and on-hold systems using whatever technology or software you desire. All you need is a router that can forward calls to the appropriate processing IP address.

- Locate users regardless of their current physical location. Users can receive calls destined to their number while traveling, while in a conference room, or even at home.

And these are just a few examples of the benefits VoIP provides. While many of these features can be provided by PBX-based systems or the PSTN, remember that VoIP allows you to implement them without monthly charges or additional licenses in most cases. Clearly, VoIP can provide benefits to your organization whether you use Cisco hardware or some other solution. Of course, this book focuses on Cisco solutions; however, the knowledge you gain from this book and your CCNA Voice certification will be applicable to any vendor—only the specific commands and step-by-step actions will change—the underlying technology will remain the same.

## CERTIFICATION OBJECTIVE 1.01

# 640-460: Identify the Factors that Impact Voice Quality

To wrap up our grand tour of the VoIP market and the protocols used to implement VoIP, we must discuss the major concern that VoIP introduces to our voice communications. That concern is voice quality. It's not uncommon to hear a telephony engineer talk about something called toll quality. A *toll quality* call is a call that offers quality comparable to the PSTN. Because users are accustomed to the quality of the PSTN phone system, matching this quality with a VoIP call is considered acceptable. We now have to answer an important question. How do we achieve toll quality? While you'll learn much more about quality of service in VoIP networks in Chapters 4 and 17, I'll introduce the concepts here so that you are well on your way to understanding the reasons for our concern with quality that will crop up again and again throughout this book.

# Why Quality Is a Concern in VoIP Networks

Quality is a major concern in VoIP networks for two reasons. First, users expect their telephone calls to sound a certain way. They expect the quality they're used to. This is a perceived quality and, thankfully, we can match it or even beat it with modern VoIP protocols and quality of service (QoS) solutions within the TCP/IP protocol suite. Second, we do not want the productivity of our users to suffer. If calls have poor quality, the users will continually find themselves asking the other party to repeat information, which can be time-consuming and frustrating. Additionally, poor quality can cause calls to be dropped, which requires redialing. If quality is even worse, calls may simply not be completed. All of these outcomes result in a loss in productivity for our users and, therefore, a cost to our organizations.

## Quality Defined

Now, before we get ahead of ourselves, let's explore what is meant by quality. Voice quality for telephony networks means that the users can complete calls, maintain call sessions, and clearly understand the communications taking place in those sessions. If any of these three factors suffers, we do not have quality.

The VoIP industry has several methods for analyzing and defining quality. One common method is known as the Mean Opinion Score (MOS) rating. For example, VoIP encoding methods may be assigned an MOS rating. Table 1-5 shows the different scores for the different common encoding methods (codecs, or coder-decoders).

In Table 1-5 the codecs with a higher MOS (such as G.711 and G.726) have a higher level of voice quality. The MOS is determined by asking a group of people to listen to the audio and to rate it on a scale of 1 to 5, with 5 being best. Typically, an MOS of 4.0 or higher is considered toll quality. The key is to notice that, while G.729 has a lower MOS than G.711, it consumes one-eighth of the bandwidth. It is for this reason that G.729 is used for the vast majority of VoIP phone calls today. It provides toll quality calls and does it with less bandwidth consumption than either G.711 or G.726.

| TABLE 1-5 | Codec | Bit Rate | MOS |
|---|---|---|---|
| Codecs, Bit Rates, and MOS | G.711 | 64 kbps | 4.3 |
| | G.726 | 32 kbps | 4.0 |
| | G.728 | 16 kbps | 3.9 |
| | G.729 | 8 kbps | 4.0 |

## Causes of Poor Quality

*Delay* is the measurement of the time required to move data from one point to another across a network. For useful purposes, delay is usually measured from endpoint to endpoint. In a VoIP implementation, it would be a measurement of the delay in transmitting the VoIP packet from the sending phone to the receiving phone—whether that phone is a hardware-based or software-based phone. This delay is also known as *propagation delay*, because it is a measurement of the time that it takes for the data signal to propagate from one endpoint to the other.

Delay is impacted by a number of factors. These factors include bandwidth, efficiency, and utilization. Bandwidth affects delay because it limits the amount of total data that may transit the network. When more data can move across the network in a given window of time, delay usually decreases for each transfer.

Efficiency has a tremendous impact on delay because a slow router or switch can cause major increases in delay even though very high–bandwidth cabling and signaling technologies are used. Ultimately, all gigabit switches and routers are not created equal. For example, I have a router that is classified as an enterprise router by its vendor, and this router does not perform nearly as well as an inexpensive Netgear router that was manufactured during the same time according to the same signaling standards (100-Mbit Ethernet). You cannot assume that all devices by all manufacturers perform the same just because they support the same standards. This dilemma is why testing is so important to those who actually have to implement the technology.

Of course, utilization impacts delay through the simple math of large numbers. Think of it as being like a highway. If you have a specific route that you travel to work and you've traveled that route for a few years, you've probably noticed that congestion is getting worse (at least, if you're in a larger city). Why is this congestion happening? It's the math of large numbers. More cars are trying to get to the same relative area today than were a few years ago. Assuming that the number of lanes has not changed, the cars must either move more efficiently or take longer to get to their destinations. The point is simple: as more cars travel the same route you travel to get to work, your delay increases. We've seen four practical solutions implemented:

- Install more generic lanes.
- Flag one or more lanes as high-occupancy lanes.
- Teach people to drive better.
- Direct traffic along an alternative route.

Installing more generic lanes will increase the lane width (similar to network bandwidth) and reduce your delay. However, this solution is a very expensive one and can slow down traffic while the extra lanes are being installed. If we apply this concept to the data network, we face the same negative factors. It can be very expensive to rip out a 100-Mbps infrastructure and install a 1-Gbps infrastructure if the cabling that is already installed cannot handle the faster speeds. Additionally, major disruptions in service may occur during the upgrade. These factors must be considered.

The second option, of flagging a lane for high-occupancy vehicles (HOV lanes), will not have the same impact as adding more lanes, but it will be far less expensive and should not result in as many delays during initial implementation. Installing HOV lanes is analogous to implementing QoS on a network. QoS cannot increase the available bandwidth, but it can indicate that specific traffic types have a higher priority.

The third option is probably the most difficult in real life. Teaching people to drive better is a coded way of saying that we want to teach people to work together so that all drivers arrive at their destination in a window of time that is relatively acceptable to all drivers. In other words, one driver is not gaining an advantage while delaying other drivers even more. Ultimately, we're talking about implementing better collaborative driving algorithms. Thankfully, while this task is very difficult with human drivers on the highway, it is fairly simple to accomplish with data that is driven across our networks.

The fourth and final option may work well, but without rules or laws to require them to drive a different route, the drivers may simply ignore the suggestion. Thankfully, using dial peers (which are configuration elements within the Cisco gateways that indicate paths to VoIP destinations), we can dictate the route that calls should travel. This technique can be used to direct VoIP communications away from otherwise heavily trafficked areas of our networks.

Consider the fact that wireless IEEE 802.11g standard provides a higher throughput and data rate than IEEE 802.11b, even though they use the same 22 MHz of frequency bandwidth. You could say that both 802.11g and 802.11b use 22 lanes for data transfer, but 802.11g gets nearly five times more data through. How is this difference in throughput possible? The answer is that 802.11g drives better.

I'm sure you're beginning to see how these different terms relate to one another. Bandwidth or data rate provides the upper boundary of data throughput, and the actual throughput is a factor of bandwidth, overhead, and efficiency. Delay is impacted by bandwidth and efficiency. Utilization of the network also has a large impact on delay. In the end, these three (bandwidth, throughput, and delay) are interrelated, and you can seldom impact one without affecting one of the others. For example, if you want to decrease delay, the actions you take will likely also increase throughput—even if bandwidth is not changed; however, if you increase bandwidth, both throughput and delay will usually be impacted as well.

VoIP implementations must address delay from multiple perspectives. Effectively, delay is broken into components, and the delay is considered at this component level. For this reason, you'll want to be aware of delay from three perspectives:

- Encoding delay
- Packetizing delay
- Network delay

The concepts I've described up to this point are network and packetizing delay, with the greatest emphasis on network delay. In a VoIP system, we must remember that the real delay that is measured is the delay that occurs between when one user speaks the words into the phone and when the other user hears the words from her speakers (desktop speakers, handset speakers, headphones, etc.). For this reason, we must also consider encoding delay. The time it takes to encode a G.711 audio stream is different than the time it takes to encode a G.729 audio stream. However, the G.729 audio stream sends the same sound waves through the VoIP network with smaller packet sizes. Therefore, we see an increased encoding delay for G.729 and a reduced network delay. The reality is that the reduced network delay is usually far greater than the increased encoding delay, so G.729 is going to be a better VoIP protocol from a delay perspective.

Packetizing delay, which I've only hinted at before now, is the delay incurred by putting the voice data into UDP and IP packets. You can and usually do have more than one voice frame in a single IP packet (remember the HOV lane analogy?). When you have more voice frames in a single IP packet, packetizing delay increases; however, network delay decreases due to reduced bandwidth consumption, with fewer UDP and IP headers traveling the network for the same amount of audio data. When you have fewer voice frames in a single IP packet, packetizing delay decreases, but network delay may increase with more UDP and IP headers required.

While delay is a measurement of the time it takes for data to travel from endpoint to endpoint, *jitter* is the variance that occurs in this delay. There will always be jitter in any network that is not an exclusive, dedicated network between two endpoints. For this reason, jitter must be considered and addressed. I've defined jitter as the variation in delay; however, others frequently define jitter as the variation in the time between packets in a stream arriving at a receiving endpoint. We are basically saying the same thing. I focus on the delay, and the alternate definition focuses on the actual time span between arriving stream packets. If there is a variation in the time span between packets in a stream, it is because there is a variation in delay. If there is a variation in delay, it will result in a variation in the time span between arriving packets in a stream.

Why is jitter a problem? Jitter is a problem in VoIP networks because it can cause calls to drop (if the variation is too great), and it can lead to poor quality. Have you ever been listening to someone on the telephone while waiting for your opportunity to talk? If so, you've probably had the experience of interrupting someone accidentally. You thought they were finished talking because of an unusually long pause, but they were actually just catching their breath or trying to think of the right word. The same thing can happen on a VoIP network because of jitter. The jitter could cause a break in the audio stream that results in an artificial pause. The outcome is that you begin talking over the other party.

*Packet loss* or simply *loss* is the term used to describe packets that are missing in a stream. At the receiving end, lost packets can be detected through the analysis of sequence numbers. Packet loss can result in poor voice quality or even dropped calls. As an example, if a wireless user is located in an area with poor signal coverage or higher interference, many packets may be lost. Regardless of the quality of service measures you may employ, a poor wireless signal will still degrade the VoIP communications. These packet losses will result in broken communications, and retransmissions on the wireless link will result in delays.

## CERTIFICATION OBJECTIVE 1.02

# 642-436: Describe Voice Quality Considerations

In the following section, you will explore the solutions to the problems introduced in the previous section. These solutions can help to improve the quality of service for VoIP on your network.

## Methods for Improving Voice Quality

To achieve voice quality, we must counter delay, jitter, and packet loss. The following sections provide an overview of the methods we have available for addressing these issues.

### Delay Solutions

*Quality of service (QoS)*, in the domain of computer networking, can be defined as "the tools and technologies that manage network traffic in order to provide the performance demanded by the users of the network." As Andre Godin stated, "The quality of expectations determines the quality of our action." I will pour a different meaning into this statement. Here is a paraphrase of the quote: "The accuracy of your requirements determines the benefits of your efforts." If the quality requirements are not accurate, the QoS solutions that you implement are not likely to prove beneficial to your users. In fact, a poorly designed QoS solution can cause more trouble than it solves. Therefore, successful QoS implementation begins with quality requirements development.

Once you have a clear picture of the quality requirements in your network, you can begin to consider the different QoS tools that may assist you in meeting those requirements. These tools will be targeted at reducing latency, jitter, and delay, and they may accomplish these tasks through the use of prioritization, queuing, and dedicated connections. You can think of QoS tools as a collection of technologies that allow you to use any physical network more efficiently. QoS tools cannot make the network faster, but they can enforce or suggest better use of the network.

Several QoS types are available and will be covered in-depth in Chapters 4 and 17. For now, just know that QoS solutions can solve the problem of delay on most modern networks. You simply have to enable it and properly configure it to prioritize voice data. If your current network is a computer data-only network, it is highly unlikely that any QoS solutions have been implemented or configured.

## Jitter Solutions

*Jitter buffers* work at the receiving endpoint in most cases. Rather than sending the voice frames immediately up for processing, the jitter buffer holds the incoming voice frames for a very short time and then begins sending them up for processing at regular intervals, resulting in a smooth stream of audio projected through the speaker. The hold time or delay is very short, usually well under 200 milliseconds (ms). More often than not, the jitter buffer will be 100 ms or less.

Figure 1-3 illustrates the concept of a jitter buffer. Notice that the incoming packets have variable delays. The delay between the first packet coming into the buffer and the second packet is 30 ms, while the delay between the second and third packets is 15 ms. Within the jitter buffer, the packets are stored and sent out at 20-ms intervals.

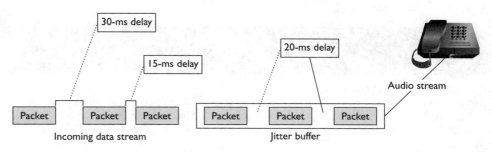

| FIGURE 1-3 |
|---|

Jitter buffer

30-ms delay

15-ms delay

20-ms delay

Audio stream

Packet    Packet    Packet          Packet    Packet    Packet

Incoming data stream          Jitter buffer

It's very important to understand the difference between a static jitter buffer and a dynamic jitter buffer. *Static* jitter buffers are of a fixed size. This fixed size means that the buffer is vulnerable to underruns—meaning that there are too few packets in the buffer to service the needed upstream rate to the telephone or software. Using a dynamic jitter buffer may resolve this issue. A *dynamic* jitter buffer evaluates the incoming delays and adjusts the jitter buffer size accordingly. While the dynamic jitter buffer may utilize more processing power on the receiving device, it is usually preferred due to its ability to function best in a network with variable utilization levels.

## Packet Loss Solutions

When packet loss occurs, different techniques can be used to address it. These techniques include:

- **Ignoring packet loss**  This solution is actually what most VoIP implementations do. Rather than trying to accommodate for lost packets or retransmit them, the lost packets are simply ignored up to a specified threshold.

- **Interpolating lost packets**  Interpolation is the process of estimating unknown values based on known values and patterns. Interpolation can be very processor intensive and can increase delay. Depending on the codec used, interpolation may not be an option.

- **Retransmitting packets**  Retransmission is very common with standard data transfers; however, it is not very useful with VoIP streams, since the retransmitted data would likely arrive too far out of synchronization. The receiver would have to send a request for the sender to retransmit the data, since UDP is used. This solution means that the sender would have to buffer transmitted packets for some time, and it also means that the delay between the sender and receiver would have to be phenomenally low. For these reasons retransmission is seldom used with lost packets in VoIP systems.

- **Transmitting redundant packets initially**  An alternative to retransmission is to transmit multiple copies of the same data all the time. The problem with

# SCENARIO & SOLUTION

| You are experiencing dropped calls. It appears to be happening because of varying delay rates in packet delivery. What technology could help with this scenario? | A jitter buffer can help with this scenario. A jitter buffer is used to counter the impact of variable delay (jitter) in network communications. It attempts to stream the arriving packets to the audio processor at regular intervals rather than at varying rates. |

this solution is that it will unnecessarily utilize network bandwidth when there are no dropped or lost packets.

■ **Using codecs with higher compression**   Implementing codecs that compress the audio to smaller sizes, and therefore smaller packets, may reduce packet loss to an acceptable level. For example, implementing G.729 instead of G.711 can have a big impact on reducing packet loss.

■ **Upgrading the network**   Of course, when all else fails, you can upgrade the network infrastructure to be able to handle VoIP better. Sometimes this solution means installing a faster standard, and sometimes it just means installing specialized equipment that can better handle VoIP.

■ **Tuning the network**   In this case, you are not changing the hardware, but you're fine-tuning the configuration. For example, you may adjust output power settings on wireless access points to tune the coverage area size.

In Cisco VoIP solutions, packet losses resulting in the loss of 20–50 milliseconds (ms) of audio data can typically be reconstructed. The Packet Loss Concealment (PLC) algorithm is used to regenerate the missing audio. The PLC algorithm cannot regenerate audio beyond 50 milliseconds of lost audio, and the user will hear this lost data as gaps in the audio stream. Since Cisco systems encode 20 ms of audio in each payload, you can see that any more than two to three lost chunks will result in audio gaps for the listener. The end result is that a loss of one to two packets in every ten will produce poor quality conversations. For this reason, many VoIP administrators aim for a packet loss of 10 percent or less to achieve quality.

In Exercise 1-1, you will explore packet loss using the Windows-based PATHPING command.

## EXERCISE 1-1

### Using the PATHPING Command to Simulate Packet Loss

In this exercise, you will use the PATHPING command to simulate packet loss. PATHPING is available on any Windows XP or later Windows-based operating system.

#### Open a Command Prompt and View PATHPING Help

1. Click Start | All Programs | Accessories | Command Prompt.
   Note: On Windows Vista and later systems, you may need to right-click the Command Prompt icon and select Run As Administrator to perform many tasks.

2. Type **PATHPING /?** and press ENTER.

When you view the help, you will notice that you can use the `-w` switch to determine the amount of time to wait for a reply. Once this time is expired, the `PATHPING` command assumes no reply is coming and will consider the non-reply as a dropped packet.

### Use the PATHPING Command

1. Type **`PATHPING -w 50 www.sysedco.com`** and press ENTER.
2. Type **`PATHPING www.sysedco.com`** and press ENTER.

You should see results similar to those in Figure 1-4. Notice in Figure 1-4 that the first time, 19 packets were dropped, but the second time, no packets were dropped. This is because we entered a very low wait time of just 50 ms the first time. However, this shows one simple way that you can look for dropped packets, by specifying the wait time that you can accept. For example, you may want to try the same command again with a wait time of 150 ms, which is closer to what we want for VoIP communications.

**FIGURE 1-4** Running the `PATHPING` command to simulate dropped packets

```
Administrator: Command Prompt

C:\Users\Tom>pathping -w 50 www.sysedco.com

Tracing route to www.sysedco.com [64.71.229.252]
over a maximum of 30 hops:
  0  ACER7 [192.168.10.222]
  1  64.71.229.252

Computing statistics for 25 seconds...
            Source to Here   This Node/Link
Hop  RTT    Lost/Sent = Pct  Lost/Sent = Pct  Address
  0                                           ACER7 [192.168.10.222]
                               19/ 100 = 19%   |
  1   82ms    19/ 100 = 19%     0/ 100 =  0%  64.71.229.252

Trace complete.

C:\Users\Tom>pathping www.sysedco.com

Tracing route to www.sysedco.com [64.71.229.252]
over a maximum of 30 hops:
  0  ACER7 [192.168.10.222]
  1  64.71.229.252

Computing statistics for 25 seconds...
            Source to Here   This Node/Link
Hop  RTT    Lost/Sent = Pct  Lost/Sent = Pct  Address
  0                                           ACER7 [192.168.10.222]
                                0/ 100 =  0%   |
  1   82ms     0/ 100 =  0%     0/ 100 =  0%  64.71.229.252

Trace complete.

C:\Users\Tom>
```

# CERTIFICATION SUMMARY

In this chapter, you began your journey to mastery of VoIP. You learned about the benefits of VoIP and the applications it provides to your users. You also reviewed the basics of TCP/IP networking as a refresher, since this information is assumed knowledge for the CCNA Voice exams. Finally, you explored the quality factor as it relates to VoIP communications. You learned why VoIP makes special demands on the quality of network communications and how to address common hindrances to this quality. In the next chapter, you will review fundamental networking technologies from the perspective of a VoIP professional.

✓ **TWO-MINUTE DRILL**

### 640-460: Identify the Factors that Impact Voice Quality

❑ Delay is the time it takes for data to go from one point to another on your network.

❑ Jitter is the variance in delay on your network.

❑ Jitter can cause poor voice quality and even dropped calls.

### 642-436: Describe Voice Quality Considerations

❑ Jitter buffers can help to counter the impact of jitter on VoIP calls.

❑ Packet loss must be addressed in order for your VoIP network to function properly.

❑ Retransmission of dropped packets is not a viable solution for packet loss in VoIP communications.

❑ Quality of service (QoS) solutions must be used on IP networks that also service VoIP calls.

# SELF TEST

The following questions will help you measure your understanding of the material presented in this chapter. Read all the choices carefully because there might be more than one correct answer. Choose all correct answers for each question.

## 640-460: Identify the Factors that Impact Voice Quality

1. What is the term used to define the variance in delay on IP-based networks?
   A. Packet loss
   B. Jitter
   C. RTT
   D. Quantization

2. What technology can be used to counter the impact of jitter on voice communications?
   A. 802.1X
   B. 802.1Q
   C. Jitter buffer
   D. Delay buffer

3. What is the term used to define the time it takes for an IP packet to go from one point to another on a network?
   A. Delay
   B. Jitter
   C. Variance
   D. Packet loss

4. What solution can help to improve the throughput for highly prioritized data packets on an IP network?
   A. Quality of service
   B. Jitter buffers
   C. Packet regenerators
   D. Digital signal processors

### 642-436: Describe Voice Quality Considerations

5. What is the upper limit on the audio data loss that the PLC algorithm can correct in Cisco systems?
   A. 20 ms
   B. 10 ms
   C. 40 ms
   D. 50 ms

6. What packet loss percentage is usually considered acceptable for VoIP implementations?
   A. Less than 10 percent
   B. More than 10 percent
   C. Less than 20 percent
   D. Less than 25 percent

7. Which of the following is not a viable solution for excessive packet loss in VoIP communications?
   A. QoS
   B. PLC
   C. Retransmission
   D. Ignoring

8. Which one of the following is not a benefit of VoIP when contrasted with PBX-based telephony?
   A. Upgrades without hardware replacement
   B. Not locked to a specific vendor for upgrades
   C. Uses a separate network from your computer data
   D. Provides potential cost savings in toll charges

# LAB QUESTION

Mark is implementing a network solution that provides Voice over IP. He is running a Voice over IP client phone software package that works on Windows XP and Windows 7 as well as on Linux clients. The application specifications state that the computer should be connected to the network with a 100-Mbps connection if any other network applications such as e-mail are to be used during phone conversations. Your network environment currently consists of 1-Gbps connections between routers, 100-Mbps connections from switches to routers, and 100-Mbps connections from switches to client nodes.

In addition to the met requirement of 100 Mbps, what else could you enable and configure on the network in order to improve the performance of the VoIP client application?

# SELF TEST ANSWERS

## 640-460: Identify the Factors that Impact Voice Quality

**1.** ☑ **B** is correct. Jitter references the variance in delay of arriving packets. For example, if the first packet in a stream arrives, then the second arrives 32 ms later, and then the third arrives 38 ms later, the jitter was 6 ms.

☒ **A, C,** and **D** are incorrect. Packet loss refers to dropped packets that do not make it to the destination. RTT is round-trip time and refers to the time it takes to go from point A to point B and back again. Quantization has nothing to do with data delivery on IP networks.

**2.** ☑ **C** is correct. A jitter buffer attempts to counter the jitter on the network by queuing up a few packets before beginning the audio stream.

☒ **A, B,** and **D** are incorrect. 802.1X is a security protocol. 802.1Q is a bridging and VLAN protocol. Delay buffers are not defined in VoIP systems.

**3.** ☑ **A** is correct. Delay defines the time it takes for a packet to traverse the network, and it is quantified in milliseconds (ms).

☒ **B, C,** and **D** are incorrect. Jitter is the variance in delay. Variance is the difference between two values. Packet loss is a reference to dropped packets.

**4.** ☑ **A** is correct. Quality of service (QoS) can help improve throughput. It does not increase bandwidth, but it uses it more effectively.

☒ **B, C,** and **D** are incorrect. Jitter buffers help to counter the impact of jitter. Packet regenerators, such as the PLC algorithm in Cisco systems, can attempt to regenerate missing audio. Digital signal processors (DSPs) are used within Cisco ISRs to encode audio streams.

## 642-436: Describe Voice Quality Considerations

**5.** ☑ **D** is correct. The PLC can correct 20–50 ms of lost audio; therefore, the upper limit is 50 ms.

☒ **A, B,** and **C** are incorrect. Because 50 ms is the upper limit, 20, 10, and 40 are incorrect.

**6.** ☑ **A** is correct. Less than 10 percent packet loss is usually considered acceptable.

☒ **B, C,** and **D** are incorrect. More than 10 percent, which includes less than 20 or 25 percent, would be unacceptable.

7. ☑ **C** is correct. Retransmission is not a viable solution. In voice communications, the data stream must be continuous. For this reason, waiting on retransmitted data is not possible.

    ☒ **A**, **B**, and **D** are incorrect. QoS, PLC, and ignoring the packet loss are all possible solutions, assuming the packet loss is less than 10 percent.

8. ☑ **C** is correct. VoIP actually uses the same network as your computer data.

    ☒ **A**, **B**, and **D** are incorrect. All of the listed items in answers **A**, **B**, and **D** are valid benefits of VoIP when contrasted with PBX-based solutions.

# LAB ANSWER

While answers may vary, you will likely implement quality of service (QoS). By implementing QoS, you further optimize the network to allow for voice traffic. It's always important to remember that, when you implement VoIP on a network, the existing network applications and traffic have to allow for the VoIP communications. This may require greater network segmentation, but it will nearly always require the implementation and configuration of QoS solutions.

# 2

# Networking from a VoIP Perspective

> *In times of change, learners inherit the Earth, while the learned find themselves*
> *beautifully equipped to deal with a world that no longer exists.*
>
> —Eric Hoffer

In this chapter, you will review some information from your CCNA studies, but you will also consider this information from the perspective of a VoIP administrator. First, you'll explore the functions of the network infrastructure in a unified communications and VoIP environment. Next, you'll uncover the functionality of VLANs related to VoIP, and finally, you'll learn to configure voice and data VLANs on Cisco switches. This information will be essential to understanding the rest of this book and gaining the ability to actually implement and support Cisco VoIP solutions.

## CERTIFICATION OBJECTIVE 2.01

# 640-460: Describe the Functions of the Infrastructure in a UC Environment

A unified communications (UC) environment demands a well-designed network infrastructure. Cisco's routers, switches, and gateways can be used to implement such an infrastructure, and it is important for you to understand how this infrastructure functions for VoIP networks. In this section, you will review the OSI model and networking technologies you first learned about in your CCNA studies. It may have been awhile since you learned this information, and the CCNA Voice and CVOICE exams simply assume you know it. For this reason, you'll review the fundamentals here. Then you'll explore the VoIP-specific infrastructure components from a high level, including gateways and gatekeepers.

## OSI Model

To help you understand how the various networking components work together to form a converged network, I will first explain the Open Systems Interconnection (OSI) model. While this model is not directly implemented in the TCP/IP networks that are most common today, it is a valuable conceptual model that helps you to relate different technologies to one another and to implement the right technology in the right way. You will find references to the OSI model throughout vendor literature from Cisco and from other vendors as well, so it is important to understand what these references mean.

According to document ISO/IEC 7498-1, which is the "OSI Basic Reference Model" standard document, the OSI model provides a "common basis for the coordination of standards development for the purpose of systems interconnection, while allowing existing standards to be placed into perspective within the overall reference model." The model is useful for new standards as they are developed and for thinking about existing standards. One common way of using the OSI model is to relate the TCP/IP protocol suite to the layers of the OSI model. Even though TCP/IP was developed before the OSI model, it can be *placed in perspective* in relation to the model.

on the job

**You can download the "OSI Basic Reference Model" document at the ECMA web site located at http://www.ecma-international.org/activities/Communications/TG11/s020269e.pdf.**

The OSI model allows us to think about our network in chunks or layers. You can focus on securing each layer, optimizing each layer, and troubleshooting each layer. This allows you to take a very complex communications process apart and evaluate its components. To understand this, you'll need to know that the OSI model is broken into seven layers. The seven layers are (from top to bottom):

- Application
- Presentation
- Session
- Transport
- Network
- Data Link
- Physical

Each layer is defined as providing services to and receiving services from the layers above and below. For example, the Data Link layer provides a service to the Physical layer and receives a service from the Physical layer. How is this? In a simplified explanation, the Data Link layer converts packets into frames for the Physical layer, and the Physical layer transmits these frames as bits on the chosen medium. The Physical layer reads bits off of the chosen medium and converts the bits into frames for the Data Link layer.

The layered model allows for abstraction. The higher layers do not necessarily have to know how the lower layers are doing their jobs. In addition, the lower layers do not necessarily have to know what the upper layers are actually doing with the results of the lower layers' labors. This abstraction means that you have the ability to use the same web browser and HTTP protocol to communicate on the Internet whether the lower-layer connection is a dial-up modem, a high-speed Internet connection, or somewhere in between. The resulting speed or performance will certainly vary, but the functionality will remain the same.

Figure 2-1 illustrates the concept of the OSI model. As you can see, data moves down through the layers, across the medium, and then back up through the layers on the receiving machine. Remember, most networking standards allow for the substitution of nearly any Data Link and Physical layer. While this example shows a wired Ethernet connection between the two machines, it could just as easily have been a wireless connection using the IEEE 802.11 and IEEE 802.2 standards for the descriptions of the Data Link and Physical layers. This example uses the IEEE 802.3 Ethernet standard and the IEEE 802.2 LLC standard (a layer within the Data Link layer) for the lower layers. The point is that the most popular upper-layer protocol suite, TCP/IP, can work across most lower-layer standards such as IEEE 802.2 (Logical Link Control), 802.3 (Ethernet), 802.5 (Token Ring), 802.11 (Wireless LANs), and 802.16 (WiMAX).

To fully understand the OSI model and be able to relate to it throughout the rest of this book, it is important that we evaluate each layer. You will need to understand the basic description of each layer and the services it provides to the networking process. I will define each layer and then give examples of its use, starting with the topmost layer, which is the Application layer, since this is the order in which they are documented in the standard.

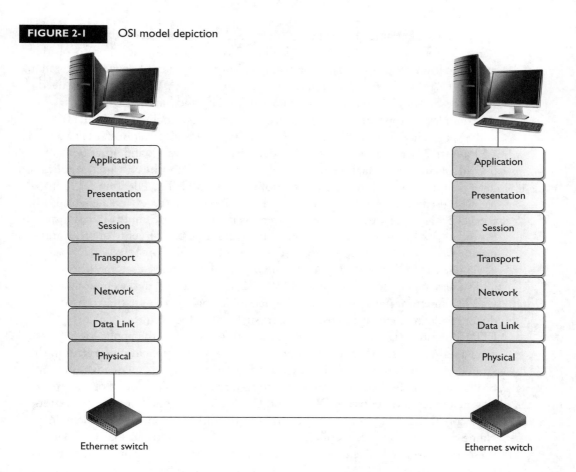

**FIGURE 2-1**  OSI model depiction

## Application Layer

The seven layers of the OSI model are defined in Clause 7 of the document ISO/IEC 7498-1. The Application layer is defined in Subclause 7.1 as the highest layer in the reference model and as the sole means of access to the OSIE (Open System Interconnection Environment). In other words, the Application layer is the layer that provides access to the other OSI layers for applications and to applications for the other OSI layers. Do not confuse the Application layer with the general word "applications," which is used to reference programs like Microsoft Excel, Corel WordPerfect, and so on. The Application layer is the OSI layer that these applications communicate with when they need to send or receive data across the network. You could say that the Application layer is the higher-level protocols that an application needs to talk to. For example, Microsoft Outlook may need to talk to the SMTP protocol in order to transfer e-mail messages. A VoIP phone may need to talk to SIP or H.323 interfaces in order to initiate and handle a call.

Examples of Application layer protocols and functions include HTTP, FTP, and SMTP. The Hypertext Transfer Protocol (HTTP) is used to transfer HTML, ASP (Active Server Pages), PHP (PHP: Hypertext Processor), and other types of documents from one machine to another. HTTP is the most heavily used Application layer protocol on the Internet, and possibly, in the world. The File Transfer Protocol (FTP) is used to transfer binary and ASCII files between a server and a client. Both the HTTP and FTP protocols can transfer any file type. The Simple Mail Transport Protocol (SMTP) is used to move e-mail messages from one server to another and usually works in conjunction with other protocols for mail storage.

Application layer processes fall into two general categories: user applications and system applications. E-mail (SMTP), file transfer (FTP), and web browsing (HTTP) functions fall into the user application category, because they provide direct results to applications used by users such as Outlook Express (e-mail), WS_FTP (file transfer), and Firefox (web browsing). Notice that the applications or programs used by the user actually take advantage of the application services in the Application layer, or Layer 7. In other words, Outlook Express takes advantage of SMTP. Outlook Express does not reside in Layer 7, but SMTP does. For examples of system applications, consider DHCP and DNS. The Dynamic Host Configuration Protocol (DHCP) provides for dynamic TCP/IP configuration, and the Domain Name Service (DNS) protocol provides for name-to-IP-address resolution. Both of these are considered system-level applications because they are not usually directly accessed by the user (this is open for debate, since administrators are users too, and they use command-line tools or programs to directly access these services quite frequently).

According to the OSI model standard, the processes operating in the Application layer are known as *application-entities*. An application-entity is defined in the standard as "an active element embodying a set of capabilities which is pertinent to OSI and which is defined for the Application Layer." In other words, application-entities are the services that run in Layer 7 and communicate with lower layers while exposing entry points to the OSI model for applications running on the local computing device. SMTP is an application-entity, as are HTTP and other Layer 7 protocols.

We'll use e-mail as a simple demonstration of the OSI model in this chapter. At this point, you may not be fully aware of VoIP technologies, but you should understand basic e-mail operations from your CCNA and other networking studies and work. Imagine that you are sending an e-mail using the Simple Mail Transport Protocol (SMTP), which is the most popular method of sending an e-mail message. Your e-mail application will connect to an SMTP server to send the e-mail message. Interestingly, from the e-mail application's perspective, it is connecting directly to the SMTP server and is completely unaware of all the other layers of operation that allow this connection to occur. Figure 2-2 shows the e-mail as it exists at Layer 7.

**FIGURE 2-2**   SMTP e-mail being sent through Layer 7

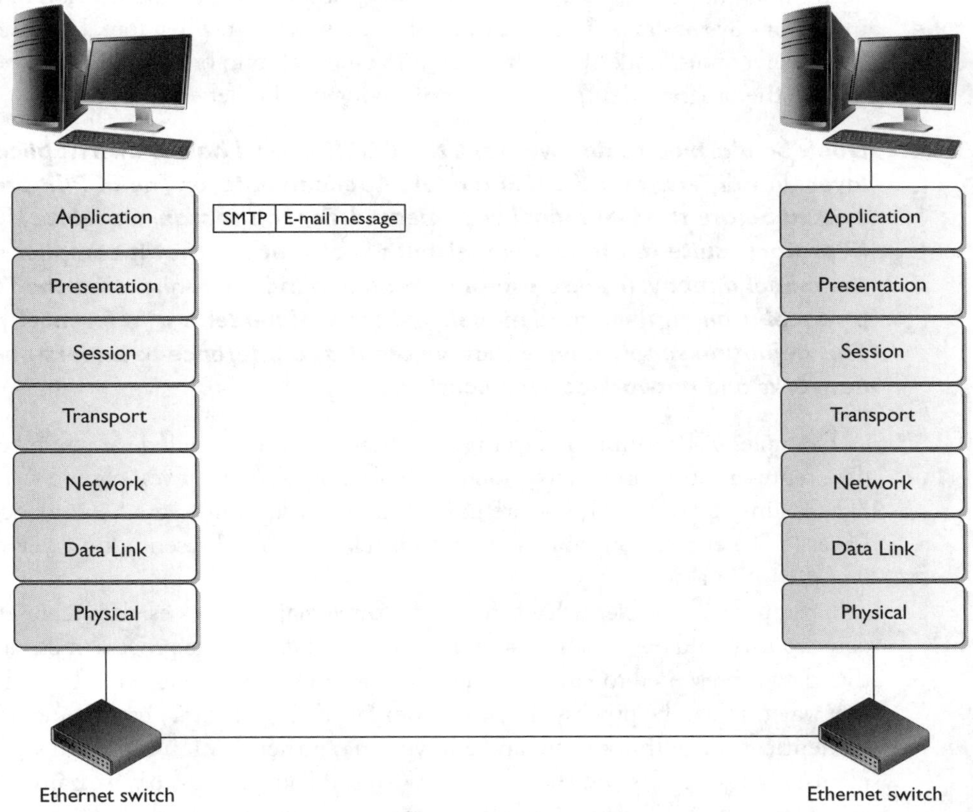

## Presentation Layer

The Presentation layer is defined in Subclause 7.2 of the standard as the sixth layer of the OSI model, and it provides services to the Application layer above it and the Session layer below it. The Presentation layer, or Layer 6, provides for the representation of the information communicated by or referenced by application-entities. The Presentation layer is not used in all network communications, and it, as well as the Application and Session layers, is similar to the single Application layer of the TCP/IP model. The Presentation layer provides for syntax management and conversion as well as encryption services. Syntax management refers to the process of ensuring that the sending and receiving hosts communicate with a shared syntax or language. When you understand this concept, you will realize why encryption is often handled at this layer. After all, encryption is really a modification of the data in such a way that must be reversed on the receiving end. Therefore, both the sender and receiver must understand the encryption algorithm in order to provide the proper data to the program that is sending or receiving on the network.

on the

**Job**

*Don't be alarmed to discover that the TCP/IP model has its own Application layer that differs from the OSI model's Application layer. The TCP/IP protocol existed before the OSI model was released. For this reason, we relate the TCP/IP protocol suite to the OSI model, but we cannot say that it complies with the model directly. It's also useful to keep in mind the reality that the TCP/IP protocol is an implemented model, and the OSI model is a "reference" model. This definition simply means that we use it as a reference to understand our networks and network communications.*

Examples of Presentation layer protocols and functions include any number of data representation and encryption protocols. For example, if you choose to use HTTPS instead of HTTP, you are indicating that you want to use Secure Sockets Layer (SSL) encryption. SSL encryption is related to the Presentation layer, or Layer 6 of the OSI model.

Layer 6 is responsible, at least in part, for three major processes: data representation, data security, and data compression. *Data representation* is the process of ensuring that data is presented to Layer 7 in a useful way and that it is passed to Layer 5 in a way that can be processed by the lower layers. *Data security* usually includes authentication, authorization, and encryption. Authentication is used to verify the identity of the sender and the receiver. With solid authentication, we gain a benefit known as *non-repudiation*. Non-repudiation simply means that the sender cannot deny the sending of data. This differentiation is often used for auditing and incident-handling purposes. *Authorization* ensures that only valid users can access the data being accessed, and *encryption* ensures the privacy and integrity of the data as it is being transferred.

The processes running at Layer 6 are known as presentation-entities in the OSI model documentation. Therefore, an application-entity is said to depend on the services of a presentation-entity, and the presentation-entity is said to serve the application-entity.

As your e-mail message moves down to the Presentation layer, and since it uses SMTP, it is sent as clear text by default. This transfer is accomplished today using the Layer 6 Multipurpose Internet Mail Extensions (MIME) representation protocol that allows for binary attachments to SMTP messages. This means that the Presentation layer is converting your e-mail message, whatever its origination, into the standard MIME format or syntax. If you wanted to secure the message, the Secure/MIME (S/MIME) protocol could also be used. The S/MIME protocol, still operating at Layer 6, uses encryption to secure the data as it traverses the network. This encrypted data is sometimes said to be enveloped data. You can see the e-mail now as it exists at Layer 6 in Figure 2-3.

| FIGURE 2-3 | SMTP e-mail after reaching Layer 6 |
| --- | --- |

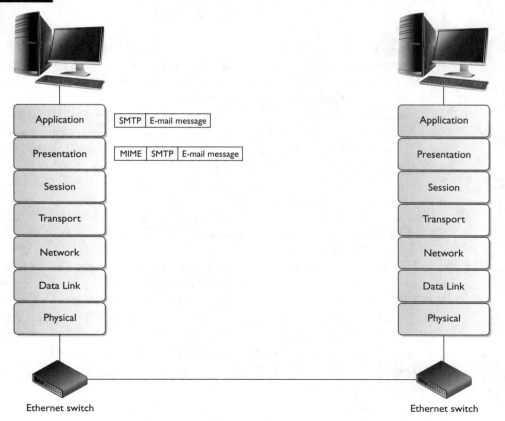

## Session Layer

The Session layer is defined in Subclause 7.3 of the standard as "providing the means necessary for cooperating presentation-entities to organize and to synchronize their dialog and to manage their data exchange." This exchange is accomplished by establishing a connection between two communicating presentation-entities. The result is simple mechanisms for orderly data exchange and session termination.

A session includes the agreement to communicate and the rules by which the communications will transpire. Sessions are created, communications occur, and sessions are destroyed or ended. Layer 5 is responsible for establishing the session, managing the dialogs between the endpoints, and conducting the proper closing of the session.

Examples of Session layer protocols and functions include the iSCSI (Internet small computer systems interface) protocol, RPC, and NFS. The iSCSI protocol provides access to SCSI devices on remote computers or servers. The protocol allows a SCSI command to be sent to the remote device. The Remote Procedure Call (RPC) protocol allows subroutines to be executed on remote computers. A programmer can develop an application that calls the subroutine in the same way as a local subroutine. RPC abstracts the Network layer and allows the application running above Layer 7 to execute the subroutine without knowledge of the fact that it is running on a remote computer. The Network File System (NFS) protocol is used to provide access to files on remote computers as if they were on the local computer. NFS actually functions using an implementation of RPC known as Open Network Computing RPC (ONC RPC) that was developed by Sun Microsystems for use with NFS; however, ONC RPC has also been used by other systems since that time. Remember that these protocols are provided only as examples of the protocols available at Layer 5 (as were the other protocols mentioned for Layers 6 and 7). By learning the functionality of protocols that operate at each layer, you can better understand the intention of each layer.

The services and processes running in Layer 5 are known as session-entities. Therefore, RPC and NFS would be session-entities. These session-entities will be served by the Transport layer.

At the Session layer, your e-mail message can begin to be transmitted to the receiving mail server. The reality is that SMTP e-mail uses the TCP protocol from the TCP/IP suite to send e-mails, and the analogy is not perfect at this point. This imperfection in the comparison of models is because the TCP/IP protocol does not map directly to the OSI model, as you will learn in the next chapter. For now, know that Layer 5 is used to establish sessions between these presentation-entities. In Windows, the Winsock API provides access to the TCP/IP protocol suite. We could, therefore, say that your e-mail is passed through to the TCP/IP suite using Winsock here at Layer 5. Figure 2-4 shows the e-mail as it is passed through the Winsock API at Layer 5.

## Transport Layer

Layer 4, the Transport layer, is defined as providing "transparent transfer of data between session entities and relieving them from any concern with the detailed way in which reliable and cost effective transfer of data is achieved." This definition simply means that the Transport layer, as its name implies, is the layer where the data is segmented for effective transport in compliance with quality of service (QoS) requirements and shared medium access.

| FIGURE 2-4 | SMTP e-mail at Layer 5 |

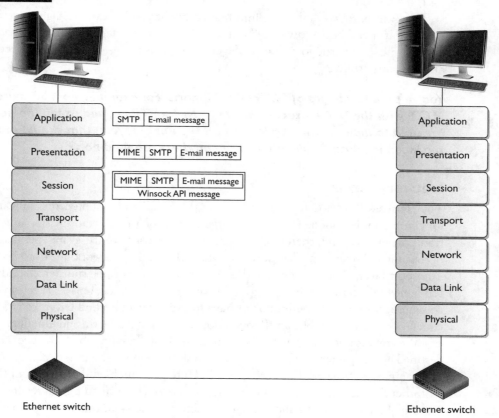

Examples of Transport layer protocols and functions include TCP and UDP. The Transmission Control Protocol (TCP) is the primary protocol used for the transmission of connection-oriented data in the TCP/IP suite. HTTP, SMTP, FTP, and other important Layer 7 protocols depend on TCP for reliable delivery and receipt of data. The User Datagram Protocol (UDP) is used for connectionless data communications. For example, when speed of communications is more important than reliability, UDP is frequently used. Because voice data either has to arrive or not arrive (as opposed to arriving late), UDP is frequently used for the transfer of voice and video data.

TCP and UDP are examples of transport-entities at Layer 4. These transport-entities will be served by the Network layer. At the Transport layer, the data is broken into segments if necessary. If the data will fit in one segment, then the data becomes a single segment. Otherwise, the data is segmented into multiple segments for transmission.

The Transport layer takes the information about your e-mail message from the Session layer and begins dividing (segmenting) it into manageable chunks (packets) for transmission by the lower layers. Figure 2-5 shows the e-mail after the processing at the Transport layer.

on the
job

*You've probably heard of TCP and UDP ports. For example, port 80 is used for HTTP with the TCP protocol, port 21 is used for Telnet, and so on. The ports are used to indicate the application (at the upper layers) that should process the incoming data. Applications listen on these assigned ports.*

### Network Layer

The Network layer is defined as providing "the functional and procedural means for connectionless-mode (UDP) or connection-mode (TCP) transmission among transport-entities and, therefore, provides to the transport-entities independence of routing and relay considerations." In other words, the Network layer says to the Transport layer, "You just give me the segments you want to be transferred and tell me where you want them to go. I'll take care of the rest." This segregation of communication is why routers do not have to expand data beyond Layer 3 to route the data properly. For example, an IP router does not care if it's routing an e-mail message or voice conversation. It only needs to know the IP address for which the packet is destined and any relevant QoS parameters in order to move the packet along.

Examples of Network layer protocols and functions include IP, ICMP, and IPSec (Internet Protocol Security). The Internet Protocol (IP) is used for addressing and routing of data packets to allow them to reach their destination. That destination

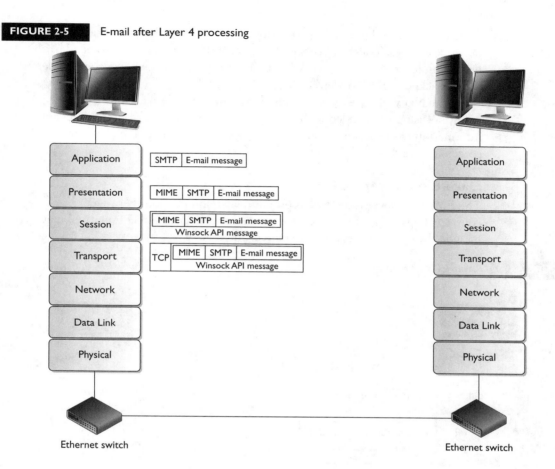

**FIGURE 2-5**     E-mail after Layer 4 processing

can be on the local network or a remote network. The local machine is never concerned with this, with the exception of the required knowledge of an exit point, or default gateway, from the local machine's network. The Internet Control Message Protocol (ICMP) is used for testing the TCP/IP communications and for error-message handling within Layer 3. Finally, IP Security (IPSec) is a solution for securing IP communications using authentication and/or encryption for each IP packet. While security protocols such as SSL, TLS (Transport Layer Security), and SSH (Secure Shell) operate at Layers 4 through 7 of the OSI model, IPSec sits solidly at Layer 3. The benefit is that, since IPSec sits below Layer 4, any protocols running at or above Layer 4 can take advantage of this secure foundation. For this reason, IPSec has become more and more popular since it was first defined in 1995.

The services and processing operating in the Network layer are known as network-entities. These network-entities depend on the services provided by the Data Link layer. At the Network layer, Transport layer segments become packets. These packets will be processed by the Data Link layer.

At the Network layer, your e-mail message that was broken into segments at Layer 4 is now appended with appropriate destination and source addressing information to ensure that it arrives at the destination. The results of Layer 3 processing are shown in Figure 2-6.

## Data Link Layer

The Data Link layer is defined as providing communications between connectionless-mode or connection-mode network entities. This method may include the establishment, maintenance, and release of connections for connection-

**FIGURE 2-6**    Layer 6 SMTP e-mail

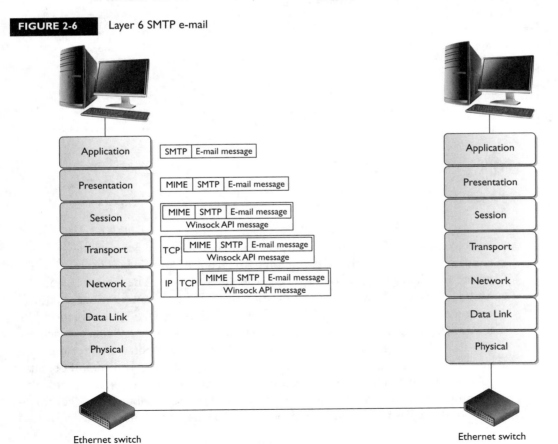

mode network entities. The Data Link layer is also responsible for detecting errors that may occur in the Physical layer. Therefore, the Data Link layer provides services to Layer 3 and Layer 1. The Data Link layer, or Layer 2, may also correct errors detected in the Physical layer automatically.

Examples of Data Link layer protocols and functions include Ethernet, PPP (Point-to-Point Protocol), and HDLC (High-Level Data Link Control). Ethernet is the most widely used protocol for local area networks (LANs) and will be the type of LAN you deal with when using most modern LAN technologies. Ethernet comes in many different implementations from 10 Mbps (megabits per second or million bits per second) to 1,000 Mbps in common implementations. Faster Ethernet technologies are being developed and implemented on a small scale today. The Point-to-Point Protocol (PPP) is commonly used for wide area network (WAN) links across analog lines and for other tunneling purposes across digital lines. The High-Level Data Link Control (HDLC) protocol is a solution created by the ISO for bit-oriented synchronous communications. It is a very popular protocol used for WAN links and is the default WAN link protocol for many Cisco routers.

The IEEE has divided the Data Link layer into two sublayers: the Logical Link Control (LLC) sublayer and the Medium Access Control (MAC) sublayer. The LLC sublayer is not actually used by many transport protocols such as TCP. The varied IEEE standards identify the behavior of the MAC sublayer within the Data Link layer and the PHY layer as well. The IEEE has defined several MAC layers of importance:

- **IEEE 802.3**  This is the Ethernet MAC layer specification. It is used for wired networking from 10 Mbps all the way up to several gigabits per second (Gbps).
- **IEEE 802.11**  This is the Wi-Fi or wireless MAC layer specification. As of the 802.11n ratification in September 2009, this standard is used for wireless networking from 1 Mbps all the way up to the potential of 600 Mbps.
- **IEEE 802.15**  This is the MAC layer standard for wireless personal area networks. It is commonly used for ZigBee implementations.
- **IEEE 802.16**  This is the famous MAC layer standard also known as WiMAX, and it is used for wireless metropolitan area networking protocol.

The results of the processing in Layer 2 are that the packet becomes a frame (or it may become multiple frames on a wireless network with a low fragmentation threshold) that is ready to be transmitted by the Physical layer, or Layer 1. So the segments became packets in Layer 3, and now the packets have become frames. Remember, this is just the collection of terms that we use; the data is a collection of 1's and 0's all the way down through the OSI layers. Each layer is simply manipulating or adding to these 1's and 0's to perform that layer's service. As in the other layers before it, the services and processes within the Data Link layer are named after the layer and are called data-link-entities.

The Data Link layer adds the necessary header to the e-mail packets received from Layer 3, and your e-mail message, in its one or many parts, is now a frame or set of frames. The frames are ready to be transmitted by the Physical layer. In Figure 2-7 we see the e-mail message after the Data Link layer processing is complete.

## Physical Layer

The Physical layer, sometimes called the PHY, is responsible for providing the mechanical, electrical, functional, or procedural means for establishing physical connections between data-link-entities. The connections between all other layers

**FIGURE 2-7**    Layer 2 e-mail results

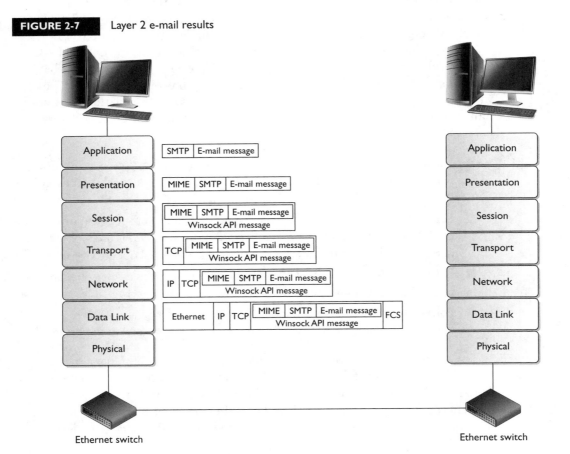

are really logical connections, because the only real physical connection that results in true transfer of data is at Layer 1—the Physical layer. For example, we say that the Layer 7 HTTP protocol on a client creates a connection with the Layer 7 HTTP protocol on a web server when a user browses an Internet web site; however, the reality is that this connection is logical, and the real connections happen at the Physical layer.

It is really amazing to think that my computer—the one I'm using to type these words—is connected to a wireless access point (AP) in my office, which is connected to my local network, which is in turn connected to the Internet. Through connections— possibly both wired and wireless—I can send signals (that's what happens at Layer 1) to a device on the other side of the globe. To think that there is a potential electrical connection path between these devices and millions of others is really quite amazing.

Layer 1 is responsible for taking the data frames from Layer 2 and transmitting them on the communications medium as binary bits (1's and 0's). This medium may be wired or wireless. It may use electrical signals or light pulses (both actually being electromagnetic in nature). Whatever you've chosen to use at Layer 1, the upper layers can communicate across it as long as the hardware and drivers abstract that layer so that it provides the services demanded of the upper-layer protocols.

Examples of Physical layer protocols and functions include Ethernet, Wi-Fi, and DSL. You probably noticed that Ethernet was mentioned as an example of a Data Link layer protocol. This is because Ethernet defines both the MAC sublayer functionality within Layer 2 and the PHY for Layer 1. Wi-Fi technologies (IEEE 802.11) are similar in that both the MAC and PHY are specified in the standard. Therefore the Data Link and Physical layers are often defined in standards together. You could say that Layer 2 acts as an intermediary between Layers 3 through 7 so that you can run IPX/SPX (though hardly anyone uses this protocol today) or TCP/IP across a multitude of network types (network types being understood as different MAC and PHY specifications such as 802.3 and 802.11).

Your e-mail is finally being transmitted across the network. First a *1* and then a *0*, then maybe another *1* or *0*, and on and on until the entire e-mail message is transmitted. Figure 2-8 shows the final results with the e-mail, now broken into frames, being transmitted on the medium.

The example of the e-mail transmission has been simplified in comparison to what really takes place. For example, each packet (from Layer 3) will be transmitted by Layer 1 (after being converted to frames by Layer 2), and then the next packet may be sent, or the network interface card (NIC) may need to process incoming data. That incoming data may be a confirmation of a past outgoing packet that was part of the e-mail message, it may be a retry request, or it may be completely unrelated data. Due to the nature of varying underlying Layer 1 technologies, the actual transfer may differ from network to network. However, this example illustrates, in a simple manner, how the data is modified as it passes down through the OSI model.

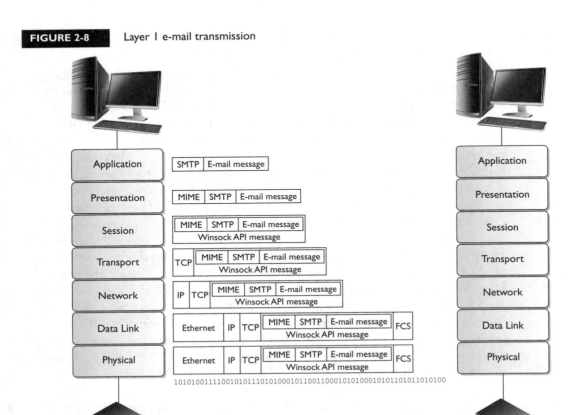

**FIGURE 2-8**    Layer 1 e-mail transmission

## SCENARIO & SOLUTION

| | |
|---|---|
| You are sending a file to an FTP server. The data that is to be transmitted needs to be encrypted. Which layer of the OSI model is the likely area where this will happen? | The Presentation layer. This is because encryption, compression, and syntax are frequently applied at this layer. It is important to keep in mind the possibility that encryption may also occur at other layers. For example, IPSec encrypts data at Layer 3. |
| Information about the source and destination MAC addresses is being added to a packet. Which layer of the OSI model is performing this operation? | The Data Link layer. Packets are created at the Network layer and are sent down to the Data Link layer, where MAC addresses are added in the frame's header for both the source and the destination. |

Now, on the receiving machine, exactly the opposite would transpire. In other words, frames become packets, which become segments, which become the data that may need to be represented, decompressed, or decrypted before being forwarded upstream to the user's program. When the data is sent, it is formatted, chunked, and transmitted. On the receiving end it is received, aggregated, and possibly reformatted. This sequence is what the OSI layers do for us. It is also what many actual network protocols do for us, such as TCP/IP.

## INSIDE THE EXAM

### Why Is the OSI Model Important?

The OSI model is more than a set of facts that you memorize for certification exams. It has become the most common method for referencing all things networking. Many resources assume that you understand this model and reference it without explanation. You may read statements like the following:

"Web authentication is a *Layer 3* security feature that causes the controller to not allow IP traffic (except DHCP-related packets) from a particular client until that client has correctly supplied a valid username and password. When you use web authentication to authenticate clients, you must define a username and password for each client. When the clients attempt to join the wireless LAN (WLAN), their users must enter the username and password when prompted by a login window."

This statement is quoted from an article at Cisco's web site. The article does not explain what is meant by *Layer 3*. It assumes that you know what this means. The OSI model, therefore, has become required foundational knowledge for anyone seeking to work in the computer or data networking industry. Many certification exams will not test you on the OSI model directly, but will phrase questions in such a way that you will have to understand the OSI model—as well as some other set of facts—to answer the question correctly.

For example, it is not uncommon to see questions like this: "You are a network administrator working for a manufacturing company. You want to enable secure Voice over IP communications at Layer 3. What technologies can you use to implement this security?"

The possible answers will, of course, be a list of protocols. You'll have to know which of these protocols both provide security and operate at Layer 3 of the OSI model. While you will not see an exact question such as this on the CCNA Voice or CVOICE examinations, you will be greatly benefited by learning the OSI model in greater depth than required by the CCNA for both your certification examination and everyday workload. Not to mention the fact that you'll actually be able to understand all those articles, white papers, and books that refer to various layers of the OSI model.

## OSI Model Communications Process

Now that you understand the layers of the OSI model, it is important for you to understand the communications process utilized within the model. Each layer is said to communicate with a peer layer on another device. This process means that the Application layer on one device is communicating with the Application layer on the other device. In the same way, each layer communicates with its peer layer. This virtual communication is accomplished through segmentation and encapsulation.

*Segmentation* is the process of segmenting or separating the data into manageable or allowable sizes for transfer. As an example, the standard Ethernet frame can include a payload (the actual data to be transferred) of no more than 1,500 octets. An *octet* is eight bits and is usually called a *byte*. Therefore, data that is larger than 1,500 bytes will need to be segmented into chunks that are 1,500 bytes or smaller before they can be transmitted. This segmentation begins at Layer 4, where TCP segments are created, and may continue at Layer 3, where IP fragmentation can occur to reduce packet sizes so that they can be processed by Layer 2 as Ethernet frames.

*Encapsulation* is the process of enveloping information within headers so that the information can be passed across varied networks. For example, IP packets (also called *datagrams*) are encapsulated inside of Ethernet frames to be passed on an Ethernet network. This encapsulation means that the IP packet is surrounded by header and possibly footer information that allows the data to be transmitted. Ethernet frames consist of a header that includes the destination and source MAC addresses and the type of frame in the header. The frames also have a footer that consists of a frame check sequence (FCS) used for error correction. Figure 2-2 through Figure 2-8 depict the way the data changes as it travels down through the OSI model; notice how encapsulation begins to occur at Layers 5–7 in an almost vague way (because there is no direct mapping of TCP/IP to the OSI model) and then becomes very clear as we approach Layers 1–4.

The most important thing to remember about all of this is that, in actuality, the Application layer on one device never talks directly to the Application layer on another device, even though they are said to be peers. Instead, the communications travel through many intermediaries (OSI layers) on the way to the final destination. This layered effect is really no different than human communications. Layering is seen in human interactions as well.

Notice, in Figure 2-9, that we have two humans communicating. Behind the communications is an initial thought that needs to be transferred from Fred to Barney. This thought may or may not already be in a language that Fred and Barney know. In this case, we assume that Fred's native speaking language is French and

Barney's is English. The result is that Fred's thought is in French, and he must translate it into English before he speaks it. After the thought is translated into English, his brain must send signals to the vocal chords and mouth to transmit the signals of sound that result in English enunciation. Now the signals (sound waves) travel through the environment in which they are spoken until they reach Barney's ears. The eardrums receive these signals and send the received information to the brain. Here the information is interpreted and may or may not have been received correctly. Barney can send back a signal (verbal, visual, or kinesthetic) to let Fred know his understanding so that Fred can be sure Barney received the communication properly.

Do you see the similarities? Much as the Session layer represents data in a way that the remote machine can understand it, Fred's brain had to translate the original French thought into a shared language. Much as the Physical layer has to transmit electrical signals on a wired network, the vocal cords and mouth had to transmit signals as sound waves to Barney's ears. The point is that we could break human communications into layers that are similar to those defined in the OSI model. Additionally, the goal here is to provide peer communications from the "thought area" of the brain to another person's "thought area."

The most important thing for you to remember is that the OSI model is a reference and not an actual implementation. It is also useful to remember that data travels down through the OSI model on the sending machine and up through the OSI model on the receiving machine. Finally, remember that every device on a network will not need to extract everything within the encapsulated data to do its job. For example, a Layer 3 router can extract only to the point of the Layer 3 data and still route the data packets just fine.

**FIGURE 2-9**

Layering in human communications

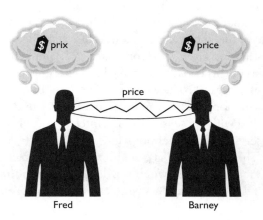

*You will hear of many different techniques for memorizing the layers of the OSI model. While these techniques can be helpful, I encourage you to fully understand the communications process that occurs within the OSI reference model. When you remember what each layer does, you'll remember almost automatically the layers in the proper order. This correlation is because communications should occur in the order in which the layers define them. It's really easy to remember a story, so think of the story of an e-mail message traveling down the stack and across the network to its destination.*

## Switches

In VoIP infrastructures, the two primary technologies are switches and routers. Switches are used to provide communications among devices on the same subnet or network, and routers are used to provide communications among devices on different subnets or networks. The following information provides a brief overview of these technologies.

Telecommunications networks can implement two primary kinds of switching: circuit switching and packet switching. *Circuit switching* is used to reserve a route or path between the two endpoints that need to communicate. Because a circuit is reserved, the entire communication is sent in sequence, and there is no rebuilding of the data at the receiver, as it is certain to arrive in order. Of course, this reservation means the bandwidth cannot be utilized by any other devices that may need it and can make circuit switching rather costly in today's packet-switched world. The benefit of circuit switching is that the connection is always there, and the bandwidth is guaranteed as long as the connection exists. The older public switched telephone network (PSTN) communications used circuit switching entirely.

*Packet switching* (also called "datagram switching") is used to segment a message into small parts and then send those parts across a shared network. The first part may actually travel a different route than the second part and could arrive at the destination after the second part. VoIP implementations, which are the primary focus of this book, rely on packet switching as opposed to circuit switching. This design does introduce concerns because the voice data must arrive quickly at the destination, or calls can be dropped and sound quality can suffer. You will learn how to deal with those issues in Chapters 4 and 17, which provide information on quality of service (QoS) technologies.

The term *switching* can also represent the actions carried out by a network switch. In fact, a network switch is a device that performs packet forwarding for packet-switched networks. A switch can forward packets from an incoming port to the necessary outgoing port or ports to enable the packet to reach its destination. It is inside of these switches—as well as the routers I'll talk about next—that much of the QoS processing is performed. The switch can extract a frame and determine if it has QoS parameters and, if it does, treat it accordingly. You'll learn about Cisco switches in more detail in Chapter 10.

To help you understand the benefit an Ethernet switch brings to your network, let's review the method used to access the medium in Ethernet networks. Remember from your CCNA studies that Ethernet uses CSMA/CD, or Carrier Sense Multiple Access with Collision Detection. Just as we have rules of etiquette for human communications (though they are sometimes assumed and not really taught), Ethernet networks have rules for communicating.

Every Ethernet device complies with the rules of CSMA/CD. These devices need to be able to detect activity on the medium before they attempt to use it for their own communication. This method is like being in a meeting and using your ears to listen for other conversations before you begin speaking yourself. In addition, the Ethernet device needs to have a method for detecting a collision even if it begins communicating. In other words, it is possible for two Ethernet devices connected to the same medium to begin communicating at exactly or almost exactly the same moment. This situation will result in a collision. When this collision happens, a jam signal is sent on the medium letting all the devices know that a collision has occurred and that they should all begin the backoff operation before attempting to communicate again. Relating again to our meeting of humans, this event is like you beginning to speak at the same moment as one of the other attendees. You will both sense this "collision," and according to many possible parameters, one of you will back off and let the other speak.

Here's the question: If there are 200 people in a room, is it more likely that two people will begin talking at the same moment, or is it less likely? The answer is clearly that it is more likely. This scenario is also true on your Ethernet network. When you have more nodes connected to a shared medium, you are more likely to see collisions on that medium. The goal is to reduce the number of nodes on the medium. This task can be done by using routers to implement smaller collision domains, but there is also another way.

What if you could implement a network where there were never any collisions? You can, and that network is a network that uses switches. This desire is why hubs have all but been removed from enterprise-class networks and why switches have been implemented in their place. A *switch* is defined as a network device that filters, forwards, or floods Ethernet frames based on the destination MAC address of each frame. To best understand switches, you should understand the differences between unicast, multicast, and broadcast traffic:

■ *Unicast* traffic is traffic that moves from one point (the source) to another point (the destination). The traffic or frame is intended for a single endpoint.

■ *Multicast* traffic is traffic that moves from one point to multiple specified points. The traffic or frame is intended for multiple endpoints that are defined or listed.

■ *Broadcast* traffic is traffic that moves from one point to all other points in a broadcast domain. The traffic or frame is intended for all endpoints rather than a list of endpoints or a single defined endpoint.

It is essential that you understand these three types of traffic, as they are all processed by switches. Switches can handle broadcast and multicast traffic, but their great power is in how they handle unicast traffic. A hub, now an outdated device, receives frames on each port and floods those frames out all other ports. Some devices known as switching hubs were created, but they were really simple switches for which—for some reason—people felt a great need to keep the term "hub" in the name. A switch receives frames on each port and then analyzes the frame to see if it is a unicast, multicast, or broadcast frame.

I'll explain what happens next in the following section, "Functionality"; however, it is important that you understand this one guideline: a switch implements a number of segments (at the Data Link layer) equal to the number of ports it provides, and these segments experience no collisions. Of course, this guideline assumes that you are using full-duplex communications. This assumption is because full-duplex communications use one pair of wires to send data to the switch and another pair of wires to receive data from the switch. Since this configuration is a pair of one-way streets, there will be no collisions and CSMA/CD is not used. This design greatly improves actual data throughput as opposed to management overhead. It also allows you to grow network segments (though they are logical, since each full-duplex connection is like a segment in itself as far as unicast data is concerned) much larger. Many enterprise networks have segments as large as 500 nodes on the segment. I certainly wouldn't recommend segment sizes any larger than that.

Figure 2-10 shows an example Cisco switch series. The 3560V2-24PS and 3560V2-48PS models support Power over Ethernet (PoE), which can be used to power Cisco IP phones. Cisco switches and devices are the focus of this book; other popular switch vendors include 3COM, HP, Nortel, and Foundry Networks. Even though you are studying for a Cisco certification, in the real world, you're likely to encounter environments with a mixture of switches from different vendors.

Cisco 3560-X
switch series
(Courtesy of
Cisco Systems,
Inc. Unauthorized
use not
permitted.)

## Functionality

So how does the switch work its magic? The first thing that you need to know is that a switch is a learning device. As data comes in and out of the switch, it notices the MAC address of the sending device as it transmits data through a particular port. Since the device sent data to the switch through that port, the switch knows that it can reach the device (or its MAC address) through that same port. This learning process is repeated again and again, and it forms a database in memory that tracks the various MAC addresses and the ports through which they can be reached.

Now when a frame comes into the switch destined for a known MAC address, the switch forwards that frame to the appropriate port. When a frame comes into the switch destined for an unknown MAC address, the switch floods the frame to all ports. In the end, a switch is effectively a multiport bridge. The traditional and now obsolete bridge had two ports in most implementations. One port existed on one network, and the other port existed on another. Each port learned the MAC addresses on that side of the bridge, and the bridge only forwarded frames from one side to the other that were actually destined for a device on the other side. Switches implement the same basic functionality; only multiple "virtual bridges" are within the switch. In fact, most switches state that they support the IEEE 802.1D standard, which is not a switching standard, but is rather a bridging standard. Cisco switches implement the IEEE 802.1D Spanning Tree Protocol (STP).

Just like routers, and all other computing devices, a switch is a computer.

## Common Features

Network switches support many common features, of which the most common are listed here:

- Autosensing
- Autonegotiating
- ASICS processors
- LEDs
- Managed/unmanaged
- VLANs

An *autosensing* switch is a switch that automatically determines the speed for each port. Some switches are 10/100, and others are 10/100/1000, while still others are only 100/1000. The point is that any port can accept any of the valid speeds. Most switches do not fall back to the slowest connected device, but some do and this is an important consideration.

When a switch is *autonegotiating*, it means that the switch can determine if communications are to be half-duplex or full-duplex. Half-duplex communications use the same pair of wires to both send and receive, and the result is a reduction in data throughput. Full-duplex communications use two wires to send and two wires to receive, resulting in potential full use of the available throughput. In a full-duplex installation, CSMA/CD is not used and management overhead is therefore reduced. The switch basically creates a single LAN between each endpoint and the switch port.

Application-Specific Integrated Circuits (ASICs) are special processors designed for specific purposes. The routers tend to use general-purpose processors just like a desktop PC. Switches may use general-purpose processors, but most of them use ASICs processors. Since the processor is actually created for the purpose of switching, it is much faster at what it does. In fact, many switches are able to offer line-speed switching. What this ability means is that—assuming there are not other operations being performed in the switch that would delay processing—the frame can come in the port, be processed, and be sent out the proper port at the same speed as it would have traveled in a direct crossover cable from node to node. Of course, line-speed switching is a concept and rarely a reality, since multiple frames may be coming into the switch from multiple ports concurrently.

Most switches also have *light emitting diodes (LEDs)* that indicate the operation of the switch. Each port may have an LED that indicates communications, speed, duplex, and other parameters. Additionally, there is usually a collection of LEDs that can be used to determine many factors about the health and utilization of the switch.

For example, you can usually see how much of the switch's capacity is actually being utilized by simply looking at the LEDs.

However, the greatest management and administrative power comes through the switch management interface. Some switches are *managed* and others are *unmanaged*. Consumer-grade switches that you would buy at the local computer store are traditionally unmanaged switches. This difference simply means that there are no configuration options for the switch other than a possible uplink or duplex toggle button on the physical unit itself. Indeed there is rarely a software-based configuration interface. There are exceptions to this rule, but as a general guideline, the less expensive switches do not have management features.

Enterprise-class switches are usually managed switches. This function means that they have software-based management interfaces. This interface may be a web-based interface that is accessed through a standard web browser, or it may be a custom management application. Some switches also support centralized management through a custom application. These switches can usually be managed en masse and can sometimes even be grouped together to form one extremely large (hundreds or thousands of ports) virtual switch for management purposes.

Managed switches also support QoS tagging, which is essential for proper VoIP operations. Cisco switches support a QoS feature known as AutoQoS that greatly simplifies the configuration of QoS for your network.

Finally, *virtual LANs*, or *VLANs*, may be supported. A VLAN is a logical LAN that exists only in the memory of the switches and/or routers. They can exist independently of the physical LAN implementation. For example, a node that physically exists in one building and is three routers away from a node that physically exists in another building can be on the same VLAN as that other node. They will have the same IP network ID and have different host IDs. VLANs are used for management purposes. You can apply policies, restrictions, and more to VLANs. For example, you can say that a user that exists on a particular VLAN can only access the Internet but cannot access any internal servers. This ability to contain traffic is very useful for guests on your network. VLANs will be discussed in more detail in a later certification objective of this chapter titled "Describe the Purpose of VLANs in a VoIP Environment."

## Physical Installation Options

Switches are installed in much the same way as routers. They usually exist in the Distribution and Access layers of a tiered network model, though they may exist at the Core layer, since the distinction between switches and routes is being blurred by modern Layer 3 and Layer 4 (or higher) switches.

### Configuration Process

Configuring a switch can be very simple or equally complex. In a simple installation, you just plug the cables into the right ports and power on the switch. You're done. In a complex installation, you'll need to configure access control lists, policies, VLANs, quality of service, and other parameters. You'll learn about these different parameters in more detail in later chapters.

## Routers

*Routing* is the process of moving data packets from one network to another. A data packet that is transmitted from a computing device may be able to move directly to another device on the same network, or it may need to be forwarded to another network by a router. This is the primary job of a router: to connect otherwise-disconnected networks.

Here's a good way to remember the difference between a switch and a router: If you connect multiple switches together, you're just creating a bigger physical network segment. The same is not true with routers. In fact, you should really think of routers as being connected together. Instead routers have two or more interfaces. As seen in Figure 2-11, one interface will be connected to one network, and the other interface will be connected to another. This demarcation allows the router to be used as a packet-routing device when a device in Network A wants to send a packet to a device in Network B. You'll learn more details about Cisco-specific routers as well as switches and other infrastructure devices in Chapter 10.

A *router* is a network device that is capable of moving data from one network to another using different algorithms, depending on the network protocols implemented. The most common type of router used within LANs is an IP router. Additionally, routers are used as interfaces to WAN service providers so that they have an interface operational on the LAN and another interface operational on the WAN. When data needs to traverse to the remote network, it will pass in through the LAN interface and out through the WAN interface. On the remote network, the

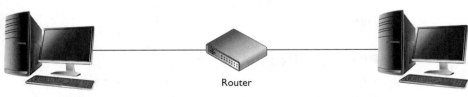

**FIGURE 2-11**

Routers routing packets

Router

10.10.10.1

Interface 1: 10.10.10.100
Interface 2: 10.10.10.200
Subnet Mask: 255.255.255.128

10.10.10.201

data will pass in through the WAN interface and out through the LAN interface. Of course, when the communications are reversed, so is the interface utilization.

To help you better understand routers, I will document them from four perspectives:

- ■ Functionality
- ■ Common features
- ■ Physical installation options
- ■ Configuration process

In addition to these perspectives, I'll provide information about routing protocols, since they are so important to the functionality of routers. At the same time, the basics of IP routing will be presented.

### Functionality

To help you understand what a router really is and does, consider that a router is nothing more than a computer. If you were to install two NICs in a single computer and then connect one NIC to one network and the other NIC to another network, your computer could be configured to route between the two networks. The Windows operating system has had routing capabilities in it since the early Windows NT days, and Linux systems have this capability as well. In fact, there are a few routers on the market that actually run a scaled-down version of the Linux operating system.

While most computers have hard drives, memory chips (RAM, or random access memory), and a processor, most routers have non-volatile RAM (NVRAM), memory chips (RAM), and a processor or set of special processors. Computers use the hard drive to store permanent information that needs to be retained between boots, and routers use the NVRAM for this purpose. This difference allows the routers to boot quickly and, probably more important, reboot quickly. It also reduces moving parts and therefore common points of failure. In comparison to computers, network routers very rarely fail. Even a consumer-grade router, such as one from Linksys, will usually work for well over ten years; however, most computers do well if they make it four or five years without needing a hard drive replaced at a minimum. Notice what is most likely to fail: the hard drive. This problem is why the NVRAM is so beneficial.

on the **job**

*The reality is that things are changing somewhat. Hard drives seem to be outlasting processors and memory these days. I'm not sure if it's just an illusion of my experience or if it's true, but it seems that the great heat in the average computer case is causing failures in areas less frequently seen in the past.*

You can also use a computer to perform the functions of a router. This is possible for one simple reason: all routers are simply computers. If you take a Cisco router apart, you will see a processor, memory, and sometimes even a hard drive (for example, a hard drive used for voice mail storage). The computer may be running Windows 2000 Server, and routing may be enabled across two networks by using two network cards. When the computer with the IP address of say, 10.10.1.5, needs to communicate with the computer at say, 10.10.2.7, it must communicate through the computer. The Windows 2000 Server receives the communication on the NIC at 10.10.1.1 and sends it out of the NIC at 10.10.2.1 so that it can reach the destination of 10.10.2.7. Because this routing process is taking place on a computer running Windows 2000 Server, the routing may be slower, since the server is not likely to be a dedicated router. This server may be providing DHCP services, DNS services, domain services, or any other service supported by the Windows Server. This additional overhead is why we usually use dedicated devices as routers.

A dedicated device has at least two major benefits. First, the processing will most likely be faster, since it is dedicated to the process of routing. Second, the uptime will most likely be greater, since you will have to perform fewer upgrades and you will experience fewer hardware failures (remember, nonmoving parts). On the first point, the processing will be faster not only because the entire device is dedicated to routing, but also because the software is optimized for that purpose. With a regular PC running an operating system that supports routing, the operating system is most likely doing many unnecessary things not related to routing.

Routers, in most cases, route IP traffic. Where does the IP protocol operate in the OSI mode? At Layer 3 or the Network layer. This tells you that a router is a Layer 3 device. Routers are most commonly used to connect switches, which are Layer 2 devices in most implementations, together to form larger networks than could be otherwise created. It is important to know that some routers can perform switching with added components, and some switches can perform routing. However, for our purposes here, we'll treat the two as completely separate devices, and ignore the customized modern routers and switches offered by today's vendors.

## Common Features

Regardless of the vendor, routers share a common set of features, which include:

- CPU
- Memory
- NVRAM
- ROM or BIOS

- Operating system
- Interfaces
- Management methods

**CPU**   Processor speeds vary in routers from less than 100 MHz to greater than 1 GHz. Keep in mind that the router is dedicated to routing, so a speed of say, 266 MHz, is not as slow as it sounds by today's standards. However, enterprise-class routers will have both faster processors and more memory than consumer-grade routers in most cases. Additionally, many consumer-grade routers are hard-coded to disallow data from the Internet that is not based on a previous internal request, and this feature simply cannot be disabled. This feature is unacceptable in enterprise networks.

**Memory**   The newest routers support 1 gigabyte (GB) or more of RAM for massive processing capabilities. Again, keep in mind that these dedicated devices do not have the 100–500 megabytes (MB) being consumed by the operating system as a PC does. Most of this RAM is being utilized for the work of routing. Older and consumer-grade routers may have as little memory as a few megabytes. Those with less than 1 MB of memory are of little use today.

**NVRAM**   The NVRAM in routers and other network devices is usually used to store the configuration settings for the device. In addition to storing the configuration in NVRAM, you can usually upload the configuration to an FTP or TFTP server, or you can save the configuration to a local PC when connected via the console port on the router or an HTTP web-based configuration interface.

**ROM or BIOS**   Just like in a computer, the ROM or BIOS in a router contains the bootstrap program used to get the device up and running. This may include initial system checks known as the power on self test (POST), and it may include features related to customizable components in the router. The ROM or BIOS is often updated using a flash mechanism and downloaded modules from the router vendor's web site.

**Operating System**   Again, like a PC, a router has an operating system. The famous Cisco Internetwork Operating System (IOS) is used on most all newer Cisco routers (and other Cisco devices for that matter) and is probably the most well-known router OS in the world. However, each vendor typically uses its own proprietary OS, since that gives the vendor a competitive advantage. Even consumer-grade routers have an OS; it's usually just much less powerful than those in the enterprise-class routers. In fact, sometimes the only difference between a consumer device and an enterprise device is the software that it's running. This difference is similar to the way that home PCs ran Windows 98 in the late '90s while many enterprise computers ran Windows NT Workstation. The consumer PCs could well have run the enterprise operating system, but it simply offered more complexity than the average home user desired.

**Interfaces**    Routers typically come with one or more built-in interfaces and the ability to add more interfaces through add-on modules. Each vendor refers to these add-on modules with differing terminology, but you can think of them as PCI (Peripheral Component Interconnect) cards for a desktop computer. Just as you can add a PCI wireless network card to a computer and—poof—the computer now has wireless capabilities, you can add a new card to a router and provide additional capabilities. Cisco typically refers to the modules as network modules or interface cards.

These add-on interfaces are usually used to route between Ethernet and some other serial technology such as HDLC, PPP, or ISDN (Integrated Services Digital Network). You may, for example, need to route between your local network and the EVDO (evolution data optimized) network provided by a cell provider. You can usually purchase an add-on to a router that will allow it to route internal users onto the Internet across the EVDO provider's network. Some routers come with two Ethernet ports and have no feature available for exchanging or upgrading ports. In these cases, you'll be forced to use the router as is, which means you can only use it to route from one Ethernet subnet to another. In many cases, these types of routers are used to route from your local network to the Internet using business-class DSL or cable Internet service. I use a TP-LINK TL-R480T router in my home office. With street prices of less than $120, this device is a very powerful router for SOHO (small-office/home-office) installations with anywhere from 5 to 50 nodes. This device is both a router and a switch. It has a four-port switch for a local LAN and a single Ethernet port for the WAN. This inexpensive router is not upgradeable and has limited configuration options. Most Cisco devices, however, are upgradeable and have nearly limitless configuration options depending on the Internetwork Operating System (IOS) you are running.

**Management Methods**    When it comes to managing routers, the options are nearly endless. You can manage most enterprise routers in any of the following ways:

■ **Console**    This connection uses a serial interface and a terminal emulation program allowing for command-line management of the router.

- **Telnet**  This application gives you the same options as the console (as long as Telnet is enabled), only you manage your router across the network.
- **Web-based**  Using a web browser, you can connect to the router and configure it using a graphical management interface.
- **Custom Applications**  Some vendors provide custom applications that run on Windows, Linux, or the Mac OS and that can be used to configure the router. Third-party companies also sometimes provide such applications.
- **SNMP**  The Simple Network Management Protocol can be used with some routers to configure them on a large scale.

The reality is that these are just the most common configuration and management options. You may also be able to use SSH, SFTP (Secured File Transfer Protocol), and other methods with the routers that you implement. The key is to know the most secure and efficient methods. If you implement an insecure management solution such as Telnet across an unencrypted channel, the administrative account will be exposed, and hackers can find their way easily into your network. You'll learn more about this in the last two chapters of this book when you study security.

You should consider downloading the manuals for two or three routers from two or three vendors to expose yourself to the various configuration options available. Usually, just reading the sections on initial installation and configuration are enough to expose you to the basics of how you would interact with that device. When selecting your reading materials, make sure you get the documents from enterprise hardware vendors, as their configuration options are very different from those for consumer-grade devices. Most consumer-grade routers are really broadband Internet routers, and they are very limited in their configurability and in their management interfaces. In most cases, if you want to experience a command-line interface (CLI) to the router, you'll need to use enterprise-class routers.

## Physical Installation Options

Most enterprise-class routers are designed to fit into rack mounts, since rack mounts are commonly used in data centers and wiring closets. SOHO-class routers may simply be shelf devices, meaning that they rest on a shelf, but even these devices usually come with mounting hardware (or it can be purchased separately) to mount them to the wall or even in a rack. The big items to consider when installing them are:

- **Distance**  The distance from the router to the switches or Internet connections or other routers. You must ensure that you can run a cable without incurring signal loss because of increased length.

■ **Power source**   There must be a source of power where the router is installed. Some devices may accept PoE (Power-Over-Ethernet), but most routers will not, since they are core infrastructure devices.

■ **Ease of access**   If you need to test a port, change a cable, or replace an interface, you will want to be able to access the router easily.

Figure 2-12 shows a typical Cisco router. This is a Cisco 3825 series router, which has been a very popular device for many years. It is not powerful enough for the most intensive modern operations, such as voice QoS and Gigabit Ethernet data rates, but it is still one of the most commonly used examples of a router.

## Configuration Process

The complete details for configuring a Cisco router are beyond the scope of this book, and they were covered in your CCNA studies. However, there is a basic process that should be followed when installing and configuring any infrastructure device, including a router. That is to configure it offline and then connect it to the network. Here's the basic flow:

1. Unpack the router and place it on a stable surface for initial configuration.
2. Connect the router to a power source.
3. Connect to the router using the appropriate mechanism (console, Ethernet, etc.).
4. Power on the router.
5. Update the router's software if necessary.
6. Perform the basic configuration of the interfaces so that they will function appropriately on your network.
7. Perform any security configuration steps required.

**FIGURE 2-12**

Cisco 3800 series router (Courtesy of Cisco Systems, Inc. Unauthorized use not permitted.)

8. Save the configuration.

9. Power off the router.

10. Install the router in the production location and power it on.

At this point, you have configured and installed the router, and it should be performing as configured for your network. You'll want to test the network and ensure that this is correct. Can you reach the network on the other side of the router from each side? Can only the nodes that should be able to pass through the router indeed do so? These and other factors should be verified.

## IP Routing and Routing Protocols

As I stated previously, routers perform their most important tasks at Layer 3. This layer is where the IP protocol operates, and in today's networks, IP routing is the primary function of a Layer 3 router. It is very useful for you to understand how a router works its magic. It all begins at Layer 1 and it ends at Layer 1 as well. To understand this concept, consider Figure 2-13.

**FIGURE 2-13**

The router at work

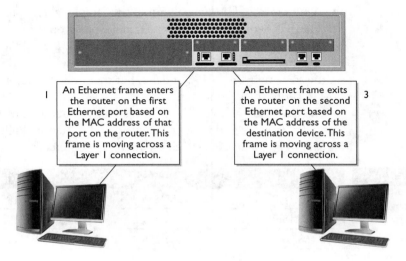

2 | The router receives the frame on the physical interface and decapsulates the MAC frame, which results in an IP packet. The router determines the outbound interface based on the IP header, which includes the destination IP address.

1 | An Ethernet frame enters the router on the first Ethernet port based on the MAC address of that port on the router. This frame is moving across a Layer 1 connection.

An Ethernet frame exits the router on the second Ethernet port based on the MAC address of the destination device. This frame is moving across a Layer 1 connection. | 3

The work of a router can be summarized as follows:

1. Receive incoming frames on each interface.
2. Extract the IP packet from the incoming frame.
3. Evaluate the IP header in order to determine the destination of the packet.
4. Look in the routing table to determine the best route to the destination.
5. Encapsulate the IP packet inside a new frame, and transmit it on the interface that connects to the next step in the route.
6. Process the next received frame.

As you can see, the process is really quite simple. The router must remove the preamble and MAC frame header and the FCS from the Ethernet frame, which results in the original IP packet. This original IP packet will remain the same as it moves from source to destination as long as no dynamic tagging is used. The header of the IP packet contains the destination address as well as the source address. The router can use the destination address to determine the best way to reach that network on which that destination address exists. To do this task, it will use its routing table.

The router's *routing table* is a listing of known networks and the routes to those networks. The simplest routing table may look something like Table 2-1. Each entry will contain an IP address and a subnet mask. These two values are used to determine a destination network. The same IP address can be listed multiple times with different subnet masks and would result in different networks based on the subnet masks. The Via column in the sample table represents the "way to the destination" network or host. For example, based on this routing table, if the router received an IP packet destined for 192.168.15.73, it would forward that packet on to 192.168.5.2. Now, considering the subnet mask, we know that 192.168.15.73 is not on the same network as 192.168.5.2, but that node (which is another router) knows how to get to the destination address.

These routing tables can be built manually or automatically. If they are built manually, they are said to be *static routes*, and if they are built automatically, they are said to be *dynamic routes*. Static routes are entered by an administrator who

| TABLE 2-1 | IP Address | Subnet Mask | Via |
|---|---|---|---|
| | 192.168.13.0 | 255.255.255.0 | 192.168.5.1 |
| IP Routing Table Sample | 192.168.15.0 | 255.255.255.0 | 192.168.5.2 |
| | 192.168.20.0 | 255.255.255.0 | 192.168.5.2 |

understands the structure of the network. The benefit of static routes is that they give you, the administrator, full control over the routing process. The problem with static routes is that they must be manually modified anytime the network changes. This task can become time-consuming and burdensome.

This point is where routing protocols come into the picture. Don't get confused about the term "routing protocol." A *routing protocol* is a protocol that discovers the neighbor networks around a router and dynamically builds the routing table for IP to utilize in routing decisions. The key is to remember that a routing protocol does not perform routing. IP is in charge of the actual routing, but the routing protocol provides the information to IP so that it can make the best decision.

There are many routing protocols, but the most popular are

- BGP
- IS-IS
- OSPF
- IGRP
- EIGRP
- RIP

Routing protocols are often categorized as either interior or exterior. Of those listed, only the Border Gateway Protocol (BGP) is considered an exterior routing protocol. BGP is used for routing on the Internet and is a distance-vector routing protocol. Distance-vector protocols choose the best route based on how many hops or routers the packet will have to pass through to reach the destination.

IS-IS (Intermediate System to Intermediate System) is an interior routing protocol (interior routing protocols are used within local networks) and is a link-state protocol as opposed to a distance-vector protocol. Link-state protocols actually look at the state of a connection. For example, is the link up or down? Additionally, link-state protocols can usually measure the quality of the link and the speed of the link to truly find the best route. For this reason, in enterprise networks, link-state protocols are often preferred over distance-vector protocols.

Consider the following scenario. Imagine that three routers are interconnected such that router A is connected to both routers B and C, and routers B and C are both connected to each other. This design forms a logical triangle. Now, further assume that all three routers are connected to local subnets on another interface. This configuration is represented in Figure 2-14. Notice that the link between routers A and B is a 128-kbps link. Now notice that the links between A and C, and C and B are actually 1.5-Mbps links. When a user on subnet A wants to communicate with a user on subnet B, what is the fastest route? The distance-vector would say to use the link from router A straight to router B because the hop count is the lowest; however, the reality is that the fastest route is to add hops on much faster connections going through router C to get to router B. A link-state routing protocol may catch this and give appropriate preference to that route entry in the routing tables.

OSPF (Open Shortest Path First) is another link-state interior routing protocol. It borrows some of its features from IS-IS and is probably the most popular link-state protocol in use on modern networks.

Both IGRP (Interior Gateway Routing Protocol) and EIGRP (Enhanced IGRP) are distance-vector routing protocols that were developed by Cisco. IGRP was created in the 1980s by Cisco to overcome some of the limitations of the RIP protocol, which was and is limited to having 16 hops in a route. This limitation affected the overall size of the network. Additionally, RIP supported only a single metric: hop count. IGRP added new metrics such as internetwork delay and load. This addition makes the route calculation similar to a link-state protocol. EIGRP is simply an enhanced version of IGRP that was created in the 1990s to improve efficiency. The biggest change is in the fact that EIGRP does not send out a periodic update to all neighboring routers of its routing table. It instead discovers neighbors and communicates with them directly, greatly improving network efficiency.

RIP, the Routing Information Protocol, is one of the oldest distance-vector routing protocols still in use today. RIP and RIPv2 are excellent solutions for small networks with two or three routers. The big problem with using them in larger

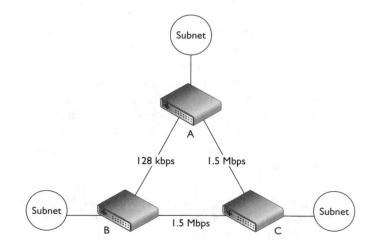

**FIGURE 2-14**

Example network for routing protocol analysis

networks is that they do send broadcasts to all neighboring routers, whether or not anything has changed in the routing tables. This design is not very efficient. Also, both versions are limited to 16 hops in a route. This number limits the size of the network to medium-sized organizations anyway. Those medium-sized organizations would be much better served by OSPF or EIGRP and should avoid RIP.

## VoIP Infrastructure Solutions

Now that you've explored the two core components that make up a network infrastructure, it's time to look at the specific VoIP components you'll need on your network. These components include:

- Gateways
- Gatekeepers
- Call Managers
- VoIP Phones

### Gateways

If you need to provide telephone calls only between internal endpoints, you will have no need for a *gateway*. Such implementations are rare, however, and it is more common to interface your local VoIP network with another telephony provider. This telephony provider may also use VoIP, or it may use traditional PSTN technology. Either way, the device that allows you to communicate with this other telephony network is a gateway. Gateways provide off-network calling (calls within your VoIP network are considered on-network calls). In the Cisco world, a voice gateway is a router that converts VoIP packets into traditional phone network signals and traditional phone network signals into VoIP packets. Chapter 14 covers gateways in depth.

*Gateways are used to connect your VoIP network to both the PSTN and PBX-based phone networks. If a PBX system is used in your organization, a Cisco router can be configured to act as a gateway between the PBX telephone network and your VoIP network. This is very useful during the transition from traditional PBX systems to new VoIP systems.*

## Gatekeepers

Gatekeepers serve two purposes in H.323 networks. First, they allow entry by endpoints (IP phones) into the network. H.323 gatekeepers use Registration, Admission, and Status (RAS) messages for network admission. Second, gatekeepers perform address translation. For example, the gatekeeper can convert Tom.Carpenter@sysedco.com to 192.168.12.14. Chapter 14 also covers gatekeepers in greater depth.

## Call Managers

A call manager is used to initiate a call, manage the call, and terminate that call in a VoIP network. Cisco call managers include the Cisco Unified Communications Manager (CUCM) and Cisco Unified Communications Manager Express (CME). Additionally, the small-office/home-office (SOHO) market product is the Unified Communications 500 (UC500) series, which includes call management capabilities. In Chapters 9, 12, and 13, you will explore these call managers in depth.

## VoIP Phones

You may be wondering why VoIP phones are listed in an infrastructure section. The reason is simple: many Cisco VoIP phones act as both a client and an access point to the network. The phone is a client to the network when it acts as a phone. The phone is an access point when it acts as a switch port for a client device. The phone implements a VLAN trunk for the client computers that connect to the phone's switch port. This allows the client computer to exist on one VLAN while the VoIP phone itself exists on another VLAN. A Cisco phone has three ports:

- The external Ethernet port for connection to a Cisco switch, which provides the actual infrastructure network connectivity
- The external Ethernet port for connection to a PC, which provides networking functionality to the PC in the work area of the VoIP phone
- The internal Ethernet port for VoIP traffic, which is a virtual port within the phone allowing for differentiation between the VoIP traffic and the PC traffic

The Cisco VoIP phones support 802.1Q tagging for VLAN identification. They do not support Inter-Switch Link (ISL) encapsulation. Additionally, some Cisco phones do not support a PC Ethernet port. If this feature is important to your implementation, be sure to select a phone model that implements the PC port. The 7940G, 7960G, and 7970G models all support the PC port. They also support inline power for PoE power solutions. The 7910G model does not support the PC port; however, the 7910G+SW model does, with the *+SW* signifying a switch is integrated into the model. Additionally, the 7905G model does not support the PC switch port, but the 7912G model does. As you can see, there is a lot of variety in the Cisco phones. Cisco sells and supports both wired and wireless IP phones, which are covered in more detail in Chapter 10.

**CERTIFICATION OBJECTIVE 2.02**

# 640-460: Describe the Purpose of VLANs in a VoIP Environment

Cisco switches, as well as most enterprise switches, support VLANs. VLANs are useful in a VoIP environment, and you'll need to understand why for the CCNA Voice and CVOICE exams. You should understand what a VLAN is, how the VLAN trunking protocol works, and the use of VLANs in VoIP networks.

## VLANs and VoIP

VLANs provide multiple broadcast domains within a single switch or within a switch environment with multiple connected switches. Normally, without VLANs, if a broadcast is sent into a switch port, it is forwarded out on all other switch ports. VLANs allow you to break these ports apart into logical switches. The beauty of this feature is that the VLANs can even span multiple switches using VLAN trunking protocols.

As an example, imagine you have a small 12-port switch. You want six of the ports to be configured with IP addresses from 10.10.10.14 through 10.10.10.19. You want the other six ports to be configured with IP addresses from 10.10.11.14 through 10.10.11.19. While you could statically configure the IP addresses without the requirement of a VLAN, this would not result in separate broadcast domains. The best way to implement this configuration is as follows:

- Create one VLAN for the 10.10.10.x network and another for the 10.10.11.x network.
- Assign the appropriate switch ports to each VLAN.
- Configure the IP addresses appropriately using DHCP or static configurations.

This method results in both separate IP networks and separate broadcast domains. Now, if a broadcast IP message is sent to the switch from the PC at 10.10.10.17, it will only be forwarded to the 10.10.10.14, 15, 16, 18, and 19 addresses. It will not be forwarded to the six ports in the 10.10.11.x network.

In addition to this broadcast domain isolation, which can greatly increase network performance, VLANs can improve manageability and security. The logical grouping of devices based on function rather than location can make for simpler management. This logical group occurs because you are no longer restrained to a single switch acting as a broadcast domain. Instead you can have three ports on one switch, five ports on another, and four ports on another, all participating in the same VLAN.

VLANs can improve security in that they can provide confinement or separation within your network. For example, when an insecure client connects, it can be placed on a VLAN with limited access to the rest of the network (via ACLs in routers or simply because of the lack of routing configuration). You can also create "Internet-only" VLANs for guests so they can access the Internet but nothing else.

But how does all this help with VoIP networks? VLANs allow the voice communications to be separated from and treated differently than the standard data communications. In fact, newer Cisco switches support a specific type of VLAN known as a voice VLAN. VLANs work based on VLAN tagging. For the VLANs to work properly, all devices in the path of communications from the initiating VLAN tag point to the drop-off point must use the same tagging protocol such as 802.1Q.

In a Cisco network, the Cisco Discovery Protocol (CDP) is used by the VoIP phones to determine the proper voice VLAN during startup. When the Cisco phone includes an Ethernet switch, it will tag the voice communications with the voice VLAN tag and leave the PC-originating frames untagged. The actual infrastructure switch may still tag these PC frames for normal VLAN operations.

## CERTIFICATION OBJECTIVE 2.03

# 640-460: Configure Switched Infrastructure to Support Voice and Data VLANs

In the end, if you want to support Cisco VoIP networks, it's not enough to know the theory. You'll need to understand how to actually configure the network to support VoIP. This section provides instructions for creating voice VLANs in Cisco switches. Don't worry, the process is simple and painless.

| | | |
|---|---|---|
| **w a t c h** *Cisco switches have a default VLAN known as VLAN 1. By default, all switch ports are in this VLAN. If you* | *do not specify another VLAN, all data communications will occur across this VLAN.* | |

## Configuring Voice VLANs

Before you can actually configure any VLANs, you'll have to do some planning. You must determine the VLAN IDs that you'll use on your network. You may have only two VLANs: a voice VLAN and a data VLAN. However, you may have several VLANs for different purposes. For example, consider the following possibility:

- A VLAN for voice
- A VLAN for authenticated Ethernet data users
- A VLAN for authenticated wireless data users
- A VLAN for guests

In this simple example, we've already got four VLANs. In Cisco switches, you can configure both the VLAN ID and a name for the VLAN. Let's assume our network will use the simple VLAN configuration in Table 2-2.

| TABLE 2-2 | Name | Purpose | ID |
|---|---|---|---|
| VLAN Configuration Example | Data | Standard data communications | 20 |
| | Voice | VoIP communications | 30 |

To implement this configuration, you would execute the following commands on a Cisco switch:

```
Switch# configure terminal
Switch(config)# vlan 20
Switch(config-vlan)# name DATA
Switch(config-vlan)# exit
Switch(config)# vlan 30
Switch(config-vlan)# name VOICE
Switch(config-vlan)# exit
Switch(config)# exit
Switch# show vlan brief
```

The last command is used to view the VLAN configuration in the switch. You should see that a VLAN named DATA and another named VOICE exist and that the DATA VLAN is VLAN 20, while the VOICE VLAN is VLAN 30. Now that the VLANs exist, you can assign ports to the appropriate VLANs. For example, assume that port Fa0/2 should be configured to support a VoIP phone with an integrated switch for PC connectivity. You would configure the switch port as follows:

```
Switch# configure terminal
Switch(config)# interface fa0/2
Switch(config-if)# switchport mode access
Switch(config-if)# switchport access vlan 20
Switch(config-if)# switchport voice vlan 30
```

Now, when the phone is connected to the switch port and powered on, the phone will be placed in VLAN 30 for VoIP communications, and the PC connected to the phones Ethernet switch port will be placed in VLAN 20 by the switch.

You should also know that you can assign a range of ports to a VLAN with the **interface range FA0/2 - 4** command structure. For example, to configure interfaces FA0/5 through FA0/12 at the same time with the same configuration we previously applied only to FA0/2, execute the following commands:

```
Switch# configure terminal
Switch(config)# interface range fa0/5 - 12
Switch(config-if)# switchport mode access
Switch(config-if)# switchport access vlan 20
Switch(config-if)# switchport voice vlan 30
```

# CERTIFICATION SUMMARY

In this chapter, you reviewed the infrastructure technologies that allow for VoIP communications. You explored the important OSI model from a reference perspective and reviewed the basic operations of switches, routers, gateways, gatekeepers, call managers, and VoIP phones. Next you learned about VLANs and their importance in VoIP networks, and finally, you learned to configure voice VLANs on Cisco switches.

✓ # TWO-MINUTE DRILL

## 640-460: Describe the Functions of the Infrastructure in a UC Environment

❑ Switches provide Ethernet connectivity for VoIP phones and may provide power to the phones as well.

❑ Power over Ethernet (PoE) is the technology used to power Cisco phones from the newer Cisco switches and is based on the 802.3-2005 standard.

❑ Routers provide network communications for the IP layer so that devices on different networks may communicate with each other.

❑ Gateways allow different types of networks to communicate.

❑ VoIP gateways interface with the PSTN and PBX-based phone networks.

❑ Many different Cisco integrated services routers can act as VoIP gateways.

❑ Gatekeepers provide access to the VoIP network and address translation for communications.

❑ Gatekeepers are used in H.323 networks.

❑ Call managers initiate, manage, and terminate calls. Cisco Unified Communications Manager and Cisco Unified Communications Manager Express are the two primary Cisco call manager solutions.

❑ The Unified Communications 500 (UC500) series is provided for integrated communications management in SOHO deployments.

## 640-460: Describe the Purpose of VLANs in a VoIP Environment

❑ VLANs provide separate broadcast domains within switches or switched environments.

❑ VLANs provide enhanced management as devices are represented based on groupings or functions rather than physical connection points.

❑ VLANs provide enhanced security since one VLAN cannot communicate with another without routing configurations enabled.

❑ VLANs are commonly used to separate voice and data traffic on modern converged networks.

### 640-460: Configure Switched Infrastructure to Support Voice and Data VLANs

❑ The IOS **vlan** command is used to create VLANs from within configure mode on Cisco switches.

❑ The **name** command is used from the configure vlan mode to provide a VLAN name.

❑ Ports are assigned to VLANs with the **switchport** command.

❑ The **show vlan brief** command can be used from enable mode to view the current VLAN database on a switch.

# SELF TEST

The following questions will help you measure your understanding of the material presented in this chapter. Read all the choices carefully because there might be more than one correct answer. Choose all correct answers for each question.

## 640-460: Describe the Functions of the Infrastructure in a UC Environment

1. What infrastructure device may provide power to Cisco IP phones?
   A. Router
   B. Call manager
   C. Switch
   D. Gatekeeper

2. What infrastructure device allows devices on different subnets to communicate with each other?
   A. Router
   B. Call manager
   C. Switch
   D. Gatekeeper

3. What standard defines PoE?
   A. 802.2
   B. 802.1Q
   C. 802.1X
   D. 802.3

4. What device is used in small offices and home offices for all-in-one unified communications?
   A. CUCM server
   B. CME ISR
   C. UC500 device
   D. Cisco 3560 switch

5. What two primary functions does a gatekeeper provide for H.323 networks? (Choose two.)
   A. Address resolution
   B. Call initiation
   C. Call termination
   D. Admission control

6. What types of networks may be interfaced with through a VoIP gateway? (Choose all that apply.)
   A. PSTN
   B. IP
   C. PBX-based
   D. Banyan Vines

7. At what highest layer of the OSI model do standard Ethernet switches operate?
   A. Application
   B. Data Link
   C. Physical
   D. Network

## 640-460: Describe the Purpose of VLANs in a VoIP Environment

8. What is created by a VLAN?
   A. A broadcast domain
   B. An IPSec subnet
   C. An OSPF server
   D. A collision domain

9. Which of the following are benefits provided by VLANs? (Choose all that apply.)
   A. Improved management
   B. Improved security
   C. Improved SSL encryption
   D. Improved performance

## 640-460: Configure Switched Infrastructure to Support Voice and Data VLANs

10. What IOS command is used to assign a port to a VLAN?
    A. vlan
    B. show vlan
    C. switchport
    D. name

**11.** What IOS command is used to create a VLAN?

   A. vlan

   B. show vlan

   C. switchport

   D. name

**12.** What feature of many Cisco IP phones allows the phone to provide connectivity for a desktop or laptop PC?

   A. Integrated wireless AP

   B. Integrated switch

   C. Integrated router

   D. Integrated DHCP server

# LAB QUESTION

You work in a small organization with a single 48-port Cisco switch. You want to configure a voice VLAN on the switch with VLAN ID 50. You will use the default VLAN for all non-voice communications. Ports FA0/6 through FA0/10 should be configured to allow for automatic placement of Cisco IP phones into the voice VLAN. At this point, no VLANs have ever been created. What commands will you type on the switch to enable this configuration?

# SELF TEST ANSWERS

## 640-460: Describe the Functions of the Infrastructure in a UC Environment

1. ☑ **C** is correct. Switches may provide power to Cisco IP phones. The switches that provide power support PoE or Cisco proprietary power solutions. All newer Cisco phones and switches support PoE standards, and it is recommended that the standards-based power solution be utilized.

   ☒ **A, B,** and **D** are incorrect. Routers do not provide power. Call manager software runs on a dedicated server or on an integrated services router (ISR) and also cannot provide power. Gatekeepers also run on ISRs or dedicated servers and cannot provide power.

2. ☑ **A** is correct. Routers provide communications at the Network layer. When a device on one IP subnet needs to communicate with a device on another IP subnet, a router is used.

   ☒ **B, C,** and **D** are incorrect. Call managers, switches, and gatekeepers do not perform routing as a function of these specified roles. Call managers and gatekeepers may also function as routers, but that is not the intent of the call manager or gatekeeper function.

3. ☑ **D** is correct. As of the 802.3-2005 rollup, the PoE standard is defined in the 802.3 specification as Clause 33.

   ☒ **A, B,** and **C** are incorrect. 802.2 is the definition for the logical link control (LLC) layer. 802.1Q defines VLAN tagging. 802.1X defines port-based security for wired and wireless networks.

4. ☑ **C** is correct. The UC500 device series provides all-in-one service solutions for VoIP, wireless, and wired networking.

   ☒ **A, B,** and **D** are incorrect. CUCM servers, CME ISRs, and Cisco 3560 switches are used in larger environments and do not provide all-in-one solutions.

5. ☑ **A** and **D** are correct. Gatekeepers provide address resolution and admission control in H.323 networks.

   ☒ **B** and **C** are incorrect. Call initiation and call termination are the responsibility of a call manager such as CUCM or CME.

6. ☑ **A** and **C** are correct. Cisco ISRs acting as VoIP gateways can interface with PSTN networks and PBX-based telephony systems.

   ☒ **B** and **D** are incorrect. VoIP gateways are not required to communicate with IP networks because standard IP routing will work. VoIP gateways were not produced to interface with the old Banyan Vines protocol.

**7.**  ☑  **B** is correct. Switches operate below the Network layer (think IP) and therefore work at the Data Link layer at the highest. Of course, they also operate at the Physical layer.

☒  **A**, **C**, and **D** are incorrect. Layer 3 switches may operate at the Network layer, but most switches stop at the Data Link layer.

## 640-460: Describe the Purpose of VLANs in a VoIP Environment

**8.**  ☑  **A** is correct. A VLAN implements a unique broadcast domain.

☒  **B**, **C**, and **D** are incorrect. A VLAN does not implement an IPSec subnet, an OSPF server, or a collision domain.

**9.**  ☑  **A**, **B**, and **D** are correct. Management is improved through groupings. Security is improved through segregation. Performance is improved through the implementation of broadcast domains that may be smaller than the available switch port count.

☒  **C** is incorrect. SSL encryption is not impacted by VLANs as it operates at a layer above the Data Link and Network layers where VLANs have impact.

## 640-460: Configure Switched Infrastructure to Support Voice and Data VLANs

**10.**  ☑  **C** is correct. The **switchport** command is used to assign a port to a VLAN.

☒  **A**, **B**, and **D** are incorrect. The **vlan**, **show vlan**, and **name** commands are used for different functions.

**11.**  ☑  **A** is correct. The **vlan** command is used to create a VLAN on a Cisco switch.

☒  **B**, **C**, and **D** are incorrect. The **show vlan**, **switchport**, and **name** commands are used for different functions.

**12.**  ☑  **B** is correct. The integrated switch allows the phone to be on one VLAN while the connected PC is on another.

☒  **A**, **C**, and **D** are incorrect. Cisco IP phones do not provide integrated wireless APs, integrated routers, or DHCP servers.

# LAB ANSWER

While answers may vary, you will likely implement the desired configuration with commands similar to the following:

```
Switch# configure terminal
Switch(config)# vlan 50
Switch(config-vlan)# name VOICE
Switch(config-vlan)# exit
Switch(config)# exit
Switch# show vlan brief
Switch# configure terminal
Switch(config)# interface range fa0/6 - 10
Switch(config-if)# switchport mode access
Switch(config-if)# switchport access vlan 1
Switch(config-if)# switchport voice vlan 50
```

Notice that we did not create a data VLAN because the default VLAN (VLAN 1) already exists, and the lab assumes that the default VLAN is used for data.

# 3

# Traditional
# Telephony

> *Mr. Watson, come here, I want you.*
>
> *—Alexander Graham Bell*

The public switched telephone network (PSTN) is the primary method we've used to place phone calls for nearly 100 years. While things are certainly changing today, as organizations large and small move over to more and more VoIP solutions, we still usually have to interconnect with the PSTN to place calls to other organizations or possibly to other locations within our organization. This chapter introduces you to the PSTN and the features it offers. You'll also learn about the North American Numbering Plan. The differences between PBX systems and key systems are covered. You'll also learn about trunk lines and tie lines that are used to connect PBX systems together to form a telephony WAN of sorts.

## CERTIFICATION OBJECTIVE 3.01

# 640-460: Describe the Services Provided by the PSTN

To understand the PSTN and services it provides, we need to begin by learning about how the human voice becomes a signal on the telephone wires. In this section, you'll learn how sound becomes signal, and you'll learn about the features offered by the PSTN.

## Telephones and Human Speech

Before you can understand the telephone and modern IP telephony, you must understand sound waves and the way they are generated by human beings when they talk. This knowledge will allow you to better understand the way in which telephone systems are implemented. Once you've mastered the basics of sound waves and vocal communications, you'll learn how we convert sound waves into electrical waves (or signals) and back again. By the end of this section, you'll understand how the telephone cooperates with the laws of physics in order to provide us with a long-distance communications device.

## A Brief Introduction to Sound Waves

To fully understand voice communications, you must have a basic understanding of wave theory, and specifically, of sound waves. A *wave* is defined as an *oscillation* (a back-and-forth motion or an up-and-down motion) traveling through space or matter. Another way of defining a wave is to say that it is a disturbance that travels through space or matter without permanently changing the conveying medium. Matter or empty space may be the medium through which the waves travel.

For example, consider a wave in the ocean. Imagine a ball floating on the ocean surface. As the waves pass by, you'll notice that the ball does not travel with the waves. The ball travels with the current, which is another discussion altogether; however, we do see that the waves pass under the ball and that they leave it in place. Sound waves also may be said to pass through space or matter without actually displacing the matter. The sound waves travel through "it," but do not take "it" with them. The reality is that the waves may move the ball in one direction or another over time, but the ball does not latch onto a single wave and pass along with it.

The observance of waves in water was what led to the theory that sound also travels in similar wave forms. Sound waves, like ocean waves, pass through space and matter; however, they make no permanent change to the matter. When you hear a sound, you are hearing the disturbances in the air around you. Your ears are transducers that convert the air pressure changes into signals that your brain can process as sound. A microphone works in much the same way. A microphone, using varying technologies, converts the sound waves into electrical signals, and acts as a transducer. A *transducer* is any device that converts energy from one form to another, such as sound waves into electrical signals. Amazingly, the human ear has an eardrum that processes the sound waves by vibrating small bones in the ear, and these bones convert the vibrations into what could be called electrical impulses— though we call them nerve impulses in the human body. So the ear acts as a transducer in that it converts sound waves into nerve impulses.

The process of converting sound waves into electrical signals is what allows us to communicate over great distances. For example, imagine that you live in New York and your first child has been born. Your parents live in California, and you want to tell them about it. If you were to attempt this using sound waves without any transduction, you would have to generate tremendous volume, and you would cause great suffering to everyone between New York and California. In fact, these sound waves would likely become nothing more than a rumble by the time they reached California anyway. Assuming a 70°F day with dry weather all over the country, it would take these sound waves approximately 3.5 hours to travel from New York to California. Obviously, this time would create a tremendous delay in a conversation, even if it were possible.

What if we convert these sound waves to electrical signals, transmit them from New York to California as electrical signals, and then convert them back to sound waves once they arrive? This method works much better. First, there is no suffering for those in between. Second, the electrical signal can travel from New York to California in about 0.013 second. This is faster than the blink of an eye or a speeding bullet. This amazing result is based on the fact that light waves and electromagnetic waves travel at approximately 300 million meters per second. Sound waves travel much more slowly. By converting the sound wave to an electrical signal, we accomplish very rapid transfer. The question becomes: How do we convert sound waves into electrical signals? To answer that, I'll begin by explaining how the human sound-generation system known as the voice actually works.

## The Human Instrument

The three major components of the human voice besides air are the larynx, vocal tract, and articulators. Figure 3-1 is borrowed from Homer Dudley's 1940 paper, "The Carrier Nature of Speech." This diagram shows the vocal cords or larynx as a backward Pac Man–type entity. Of course, we know that they open and close more like a mouth as they let the air pass through, but they also vibrate. It is at this point that sound begins to develop as the air passes through the vocal cords.

It is important to note that the amplitude of the sound is based on the air pressure pushed from the lungs through the vocal cords. When someone yells, for example, he or she pushes harder from the diaphragm in order to expel more air from the lungs more rapidly. This action results in a sound with a greater amplitude. However, you can yell as loud as you want, but if you keep your mouth closed, the sound will be attenuated by the vocal tract and articulators so that the volume is very low in spite of the greater amplitude at the point of passage through the vocal cords.

The point is simple: the end sound that is produced by the human voice is a unique combination of the air pressure on the vocal cords, the shape of the vocal cords, the shape of the vocal tract leading up to the articulators, and the individual's manipulation by his or her articulators. For example, to experience the impact of the articulators (lips, teeth, and tongue), form an "s" sound and lower your tongue while still expelling the same air pressure from the vocal tract. You'll notice that the "sssss" sound quickly becomes an "uhhhh" or "ahhhh" sound. This is because the resulting sound is greatly impacted by the articulators.

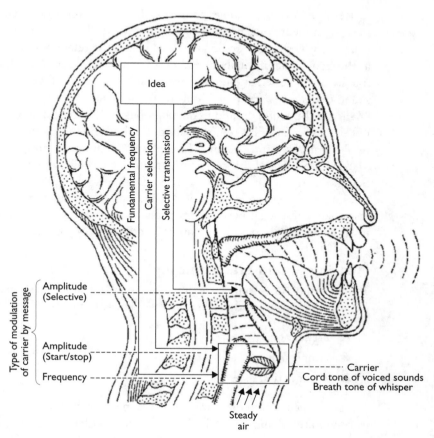

**FIGURE 3-1**

The human
instrument

Here's an interesting exercise:

1. Form a "ck" sound while paying close attention to the position or relationship to one another of your articulators (remember, the teeth, lips, and tongue).

2. Now, try to form an "s" sound while placing your articulators in the position for the "ck" sound.

What happened? No matter how hard you tried, you could not create an "s" sound while your articulators were in the "ck" position. But why does all this movement matter to a VoIP technology professional? The answer is that you must understand how the human voice produces sound in order to fully understand why voice systems work the way they do. For example, why does the telephone network only look at the frequencies from about 300 Hz to 3,400 Hz? Because the human voice can usually be processed and understood by another human's ears, if we capture these sound frequencies. However, limiting the frequencies to this range does reduce the quality of the sound. Sound frequencies below 300 Hz and above 3,400 Hz are simply not processed, and this removal causes the low and high sounds to be removed, resulting in the "tinny" sound of telephone communications.

You'll understand this concept better after reading the next section, "Hearing Sound Electronically." For now, just know that sound waves are produced by air pressure, the vocal cords, the vocal tract, and the articulators. The result is a disturbance in the air between the human emitting the sound and the receiving instrument, which may be human or mechanical, as you'll see in the next section.

## Hearing Sound Electronically

To understand how sounds are processed mechanically, you should be aware of a number of terms related to sound theory. These terms are

- Frequency
- Amplitude
- Attenuation

The *frequency* of a sound wave is the number of cycles per second that a sound wave vibrates. A higher-pitched sound or tone vibrates at a higher frequency rate, and a lower-pitched sound vibrates at a lower frequency rate. This difference is why the piano keyboard keys have higher frequency rates on higher notes, as depicted in Figure 3-2. You'll notice that a piano tuned to standard pitch has a frequency of 261 Hz for middle C. This number simply means that the sound generated by that key on the piano vibrates or passes through a wave cycle 261 times each second.

**FIGURE 3-2**

Piano key
frequencies

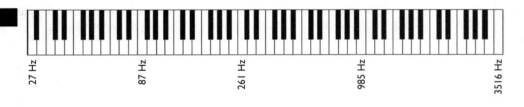

27 Hz      87 Hz      261 Hz      985 Hz      3516 Hz

The result of this cycle is that frequency over time equals a sound. While most sounds we hear, including those produced by the human voice, are a complex combination of multiple frequencies, this concept remains true that each of those independent sounds is a vibration at a given rate within a given time frame.

A sound wave of a simple sound (a single frequency sound) can be represented with a traditional sine wave, as in Figure 3-3. In this figure the vertical scale represents the amplitude of the sound wave, and the horizontal scale represents the time. Point A represents the first crest of the sound wave, and point B represents the second crest. A complete cycle of the wave includes the first crest—the upward arch—and the first trough or downward arch. Therefore, middle C on a standard tuned piano would cycle through 261 of these crests and troughs in a single second.

When I grew up in West Virginia, many of my uncles and aunts played musical instruments. As far as I know, they all claimed that they "played them by ear." What did this statement mean? It meant that they reproduced the sounds that they heard in one source on their chosen instrument. For example, my uncle Bob could play most any instrument with a string on it. He could listen to a song on the radio and then play it on his guitar. He did not need sheet music telling him which chord to play when.

According to physics and human biology, what was Uncle Bob actually doing? He was hearing the sound waves, or more specifically, the frequencies of the sound waves, and then reproducing similar or compatible sound waves with his guitar, banjo, or mandolin. These musicians often talked about the need to train your ears. They meant that you had to learn to link a frequency from one instrument—like a trumpet—to another instrument—like a guitar. They could hear when the two sounds were compatible and did not need music notation to tell them where to place their fingers.

**FIGURE 3-3**

A single-frequency sound wave

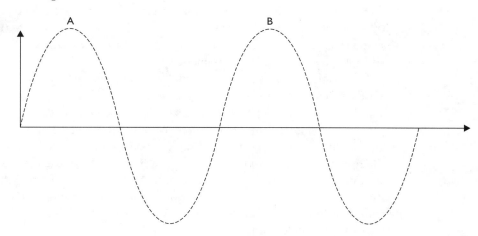

In a similar way mechanical devices can be tuned to accept only certain frequencies or to reject certain frequencies. They can also be programmed to compare and contrast frequencies. This latter ability is the core of many active noise-cancellation technologies in microphones and headsets.

While frequency may describe the pitch of the sound, *amplitude* determines the volume of the sound. One of Uncle Bob's favorite pastimes was that of connecting his electric guitar to an amplifier and playing his most cherished tunes. The amplifier took the electrical signal from the guitar and increased the volume as it re-created it through the built-in speaker. The guitar listened for the sound waves with built-in microphones, and these microphones converted the sound waves into electrical signals for the amplifier. This conversion is an example of active amplification. The sound wave is converted to an electrical signal, and the signal is amplified and then converted back to sound waves through the speaker.

Uncle Bob also liked to play his Gibson Hummingbird guitar. This guitar had a hollow body with a hole in the front. The sound generated by the guitar strings entered the hollow body of the guitar through the hole and echoed throughout the body before being thrust back out of the guitar. The result was a passive amplification of the sound wave. If you have access to a hollow-body guitar like this, place a thick piece of cardboard in front of the hole behind the strings and then strum the guitar. You'll notice that the volume is greatly diminished, and you'll experience just how powerful passive amplification of sound waves can be.

What this passive amplification really does is redirect the sound energy. Normally, sound waves travel out from the sound-emitting entity in all directions if the air or space around the emitting entity is open. By creating an echo chamber behind the strings, a hollow-body guitar takes many of the backward sound waves and thrusts them back out the front of the guitar. The result is both increased perceived amplitude (though the original sound waves are not really increased in this case) and a melodic sound (because sound at the same frequency is hitting your eardrums more than once and with somewhat different ambience).

Why is this information important? It is important when selecting headsets for VoIP implementations, and it is important when considering whether to actively amplify signals on telephone networks. When you amplify the signal at the source, you are less likely to amplify interference or environmental noises. When you amplify the signal nearer the destination, you are more likely to amplify noises in the results. The major consideration, however, will be in the microphones that you use in the headsets (if headsets are used) for your VoIP communications. Figure 3-4 shows the impact of amplification and attenuation on a simple sound wave without consideration for interference (which would effectively result in a complex sound instead of a simple sound).

**FIGURE 3-4**

Sound waves with
amplitude and
attenuation

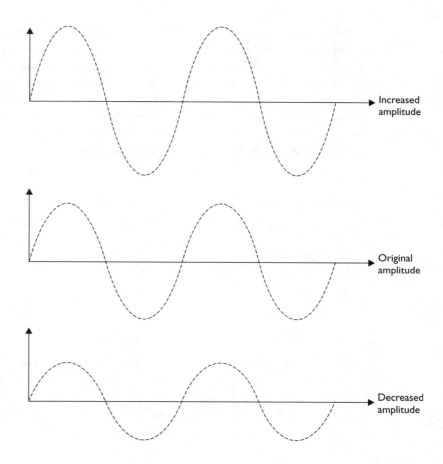

Increased
amplitude

Original
amplitude

Decreased
amplitude

When a sound wave is attenuated, the amplitude is decreased. Sound waves are attenuated as they pass through the air, and they can be heavily attenuated as they pass through more solid materials. This attenuation is why closing a door can quiet a room. The door attenuates the sound waves more than the open air. Sound waves do not travel in a vacuum because they need a medium to disturb in order to travel. The wonderful explosions you hear in outer-space sci-fi movies would never take place, since there would be no medium through which the sound waves could travel. The old question, "If a tree falls in the woods, but no one is there to hear it, does it make a sound?" could be answered, "Yes," but the question, "If a spaceship fires a phaser blast against another spaceship, but no one is there to hear it, does it make a sound?" would be answered, "No!"

Technically, you could argue that the tree makes only a disturbance if no one is there to hear it fall, but the disturbance is a compression and rarefaction wave regardless of how it is perceived. We are now to the point where we can understand how a sound becomes an electrical signal. If sound waves are disturbances or vibrations that pass through a medium, we should be able to create mechanical devices that can detect these sound waves based on how they impact (disturb) the mechanical device. This detection is exactly what a telephone does. It detects the disturbance and converts it into an electrical signal. Let's see how the telephone works its magic.

## The Telephone

The traditional telephone is composed of five major components:

- A microphone
- A speaker
- A ringer
- A switch hook
- A dialing device

These components, with the exception of the ringer, are indicated in Figure 3-5. The first element is the microphone, or transmitter. This component converts the sound waves into electrical signals. The way it performs this operation varies depending on the type of microphone used, but I'll explain the traditional carbon-based method that is still used in some telephones today.

**FIGURE 3-5**

A traditional telephone

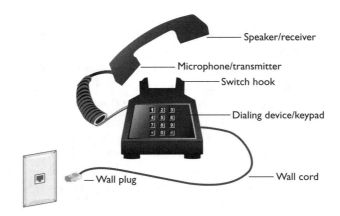

Speaker/receiver

Microphone/transmitter

Switch hook

Dialing device/keypad

Wall plug

Wall cord

Inside the handset of the telephone is a diaphragm that is very sensitive to the changes in air pressure caused by sound waves. This diaphragm moves in relation to the sound wave. The movement of the diaphragm compresses and expands the space behind it where carbon particles are located. These carbon particles conduct electricity differently, depending on the compression caused by the diaphragm. The end result is that we can pass electrical current through the carbon particles at a constant input rate, but the output rate will vary depending on the compression caused by the sound waves hitting the diaphragm. When the output is the same as the input, we can trust that there is silence. When the output is different than the input, there is sound.

Since the transmitter (microphone) detected the sound as a vibration against the diaphragm and converted it to electrical signals, the receiver (speaker) must do the opposite. It must take the electrical signal (a varying frequency of electrical energy) and convert it back to sound waves. This task is done by passing the electrical signals to a magnet that vibrates a diaphragm at the rate represented by the electrical signals. This diaphragm creates disturbances in the air instead of being disturbed by the sound waves in the air. The result is that the human brain perceives sound entering through the ears.

If you had two phones connected directly to each other, this would be enough; however, in the real world, we connect our phones to a network known as the public switched telephone network (PSTN), and we have to have a way to indicate to that network that we wish to make a call. That point is where the switch hook comes into play. The switch hook indicates to the PSTN that you are about to dial a number with the intention of creating a connection to the device represented by that number.

When your telephone detects an 80-volt alternating current (AC) at 20 Hz coming in on the phone line, it rings using whatever mechanism the phone has implemented as a ringer. Whether it plays music, says your name, or uses the traditional ring is irrelevant. The phone must simply be configured to ring when the 20-Hz signal comes in. While some systems may use different frequencies and voltages for signaling, the concept remains the same. A particular frequency indicates that the phone should ring.

The switch hook basically completes a circuit when you lift the handset, and it breaks a circuit when you replace the handset. If the circuit is closed, the PSTN detects this circuit as an active connection and the central office (CO) returns a dial tone. This connection happens so quickly that the dial tone is seemingly instantaneous, but a microsecond delay occurs during this task. Remember that the electrical signals are traveling at roughly the speed of light, so the communications occur very rapidly. When you replace the handset, the circuit is broken and the CO can end the connection.

Finally, the dialing device or keypad is used to indicate to the PSTN the actual identification of the target phone that is being requested. The dialing devices in most phones today are digital, and they send signals at particular frequencies (tones) to the telephone network to indicate the target. This feature is why you can hear the tones when you're dialing the connection.

The modern touch-tone phones use a dual-tone multifrequency (DTMF) dialing method. Each number on the phone generates two simultaneous tones. For example, the number *1* generates both a 1,209-Hz tone and a 697-Hz tone concurrently, and the number 6 generates both a 1,477-Hz and a 770-Hz tone concurrently.

The older pulse-dialing systems used rotary-dial telephones to create pulses or interruptions of the circuit in order to indicate the target device. This system worked in a simple way, but it was time-consuming. You could transmit ten pulses per second, and this time meant that it would take more than five seconds to transmit a ten-digit number. This transmission didn't include the actual dial time, which added even more time to the sequence. The reality is that it took most people longer than ten seconds to dial a long-distance number. Since the other party often did not answer or was on the line, this system became frustrating to many customers. Particularly since there was no inexpensive way to store commonly dialed numbers.

Tone dialing did provide an excellent solution. You can enter the number more quickly, and you can store frequently dialed numbers for speed dial. For this reason, it has become very popular, and you rarely see a rotary phone in the United States or Europe these days.

## Types of Systems

The two general categories of telephone systems are public systems and private or local systems. The public system is run by either private organizations or the government, depending on the country in which the system operates. The private system is run by individual organizations. It is important that you understand both types. Additionally, you should understand the differences among legacy, IP telephony, and hybrid systems that may be used as private systems.

### The Public Telephone System

In most cases, the public system is referred to as the public switched telephone network (PSTN), although it is also sometimes called the plain old telephone system (POTS). The major components of the PSTN are the local exchange and the PSTN interoffice network. The local exchange is often analog, and the interoffice network is mostly digital today.

# INSIDE THE EXAM

## How Does a Telephone Indicate the Target for a Connection?

The answer to this question varies, depending on the type of telephone. A rotary telephone uses pulses, a touch-tone telephone uses frequency combinations, a cell phone uses digital packets, and an IP phone may use IP addresses when connecting to another IP phone. The rotary telephones worked by breaking and completing the circuit a specified number of times for each digit in the target address or target phone number. I won't go into more detail about them here, since they are being used less and less.

The touch-tone telephones use the dual-tone multifrequency (DTMF) tones over the analog network. The DTMF tones are combinations of tones or frequencies. The combinations are as follows:

- 1 = 1,209 Hz and 697 Hz
- 2 = 1,336 Hz and 697 Hz
- 3 = 1,477 Hz and 697 Hz
- 4 = 1,209 Hz and 770 Hz
- 5 = 1,336 Hz and 770 Hz
- 6 = 1,477 Hz and 770 Hz
- 7 = 1,209 Hz and 852 Hz
- 8 = 1,336 Hz and 852 Hz
- 9 = 1,477 Hz and 852 Hz
- * = 1,209 Hz and 941 Hz

- 0 = 1,336 Hz and 941 Hz
- # = 1,477 Hz and 941 Hz

As you can see, the top row of digits on a standard dial pad all use the same horizontal frequency of 697 Hz. Additionally, the left column of digits all use the same vertical frequency of 1,209 Hz. The intersection of 1,209 Hz and 697 Hz is the digit 1, and the intersection of 1,209 Hz and 941 Hz is the asterisk (*).

When you press the button for the asterisk, the tones at frequency 1,209 and 941 are both generated simultaneously. Only seven tones are needed to represent all 12 buttons, since the tones are paired with each other in horizontal and vertical fashion. Additionally, rarely if ever do the tones used occur in nature as pure tones. Remember that the human voice usually operates at 50–100 Hz on the low end to 4,000–5,000 Hz on the high end, but the sounds emitted are complex combinations of frequencies. They are not pure tones perfectly placed on a unique frequency.

In the end, the CO detects these tones as indicating the phone number of the target node on the PSTN. Once enough digits are received to place a call (possibly seven for local calls in the United States, or ten for long distance), the CO switch can use the SS7 network to determine the location of and route to the destination.

**Local Exchange** The *local exchange* includes everything from the customer location to the CO. This service includes the cable plant and the cable vault at the CO. The phrase *cable plant* is usually used to reference the cabling or aerial connections, the structures that connect or link them, and any other components involved in connecting customers to the PSTN. The network interface device (NID) is that box on the side of your house that connects to the cable plant. In fact, that box is owned by the local exchange in most cases. Of course, the NID is much more complex and supports more lines in a business setting, but the concept is the same.

The wires from the NID to the cable plant will run either underground or, more commonly, overhead to a telephone pole. The wires from all the houses come together in terminal boxes and then run back to the CO. Along the way, the wires are spliced together as needed using what are called "splice cans." These are simply containers that protect the splice points from exposure to weather.

In a commercial installation for a business or organization, the wires come into the customer's building and are usually connected directly to the organization's telephone switch (PBX system).

The CO is where all the cable plants come together. The wires come into the CO through the cable vault. The cable vault is where the power systems or batteries are located that allow the local exchange to operate. For example, they provide the power for signaling on the network.

To help you understand how all these components work within the local exchange, consider the flow of a call placed between two telephones connected to the same local exchange. When you pick up the handset and dial the number, the switch determines if that number is in the local exchange or not. In this case, it is in the local exchange, so the switch sends the ring signal to the target telephone. Assuming the target telephone is answered, the switch creates a virtual circuit between the two nodes. At this point, voice communications begin. As long as both nodes keep the circuit open, the switch maintains the circuit. In most modern networks, either node can break the circuit and thereby break the connection.

In addition to intra-exchange calls like the one highlighted in the preceding paragraph, you can also place inter-exchange calls. These calls pass from one local exchange to another. These calls may be handled by multi-exchange switches, or they may require communications between different COs. Either way, the difference is that there will now be a route that your voice communications must travel that is usually more complex than the intra-exchange phone call. The voice signal, which is analog on the local exchange, may be converted to a digital signal in order to traverse the PSTN network. It will then have to be converted back to an analog signal when it arrives at the remote local exchange. This conversion takes extra time, but due to powerful processors and other modern technologies, the latency is usually so low that the delay is not noticed by the communicating parties. This latency may be greater with a cell tower, since there are more conversions involved. To see this latency in action, you can call yourself using your cell phone and your land line. If you do this test, you'll be able to perceive the delay that occurs between the time you speak something into your cell phone and the time you hear it in your land line. This delay, again, is mostly because of the conversions that must take place along the way and less because of the speed of the actual signals. The signals move at the speed of light, but the conversion and queuing systems are not quite so fast yet.

**Interoffice Switching**   As was stated previously, most connections from the CO to the subscriber are analog; however, the connections between COs are mostly digital today. These CO-to-CO networks are built on optical fiber lines in a ring structure. Calls are passed from CO to CO through switches that are connected to the fiber ring. These switches are connected via trunk units (TUs) to the ring. When a call is connected from one CO to another, the virtual circuit is created from the subscriber to the CO, from the CO to the ring, from the ring to the destination CO, and finally from the destination CO to the destination subscriber.

The switches at the CO and the TUs use the Signaling System 7 (SS7) system to discover which network should be used based on the subscriber's long-distance provider selection and the needed path to the destination subscriber.

## INSIDE THE EXAM

### How Does a Call Actually Work Across the PSTN?

Let's walk through a telephone call placed across the PSTN from start to finish. The first step in placing a call is the creation of an off-hook condition. This means that the telephone handset is lifted. When you lift the handset, the circuit of the local loop with the CO is closed, and current flows through your local loop. The CO switch detects this current almost immediately and returns a dial tone (this tone is an electrical signal that is converted to sound waves by the receiver or speaker in your telephone) on your line.

In actuality, the CO switch may perform line tests before sending back the dial tone in order to ensure that the line is in a condition that will support a voice call. This test happens quickly, though, and you will rarely if ever pick up a phone that is operational and connected to the local loop and not receive a dial tone immediately.

Now that you have a dial tone, you can begin entering the phone number for the node you wish to call. As you press the buttons, the DTMF signals are sent across the local loop back to the CO switch. Keep in mind that these signals are sound waves in your earpiece, but they are electrical signals

## INSIDE THE EXAM

sent to the switch. The switch disables the dial tone as soon as it detects the first signal indicating that you are dialing a number. This action is why the dial tone goes away when you begin the actual dialing process.

Modern CO switches are very intelligent and may interrupt the dialing process if they detect an error. For example, if I am dialing from area code 937 to area code 614 and I must dial a 1 before the ten-digit phone number, the switch may detect that I've dialed 614-555-12 and immediately understand that I've dialed incorrectly. It can send a recorded message to my phone indicating that I need to dial a 1 before a long-distance number. If I've dialed the number correctly, however, the next step for the CO switch is to determine how it will create the connection to the target node on the PSTN.

From here, the call proceeds differently depending on whether the target phone is connected to the same switch or a different switch. If it is connected to the same switch, the switch simply connects the call and reports to an administrative module that the call has been placed in case billing must be performed. If the call is targeting a phone connected to another switch at another CO, the call is routed through a tandem switch to the appropriate switch at the other CO, which connects the call to the end node.

Finally, if the call is targeting a phone in a completely different region, such as another state or country, the call is routed up to higher-level COs until eventually a route is determined for the connection. This routing all happens in a matter of a few seconds at most, and once the circuit is established, the voice communications can travel across it very quickly (remember, the signals travel at roughly the speed of light).

Before any voice communications travel across the circuit, the target phone must be answered. This task means that the target human (the person who owns or answers that phone) must be notified that a call is coming in. To notify the target of a call request, the CO sends a ring signal to the phone, and it sends a ring sound back to the calling receiver. Assuming the person on the target end picks up the phone, the off-hook condition exists and voice communications can ensue. Of course, the traditional "hello" message is optional from the target to the initiator, but it is quite courteous.

### Private Telephone Systems

When an organization desires to implement a private telephone system, they will implement a *Private Branch Exchange (PBX)*. PBX systems can be hardware devices that operate as stand-alone equipment. They can be software applications that run on computers and control hardware, and they can be IP-based PBX systems.

When an organization implements a PBX, they must connect to the PSTN in some way. These connection points to the PSTN or CO are called *trunks*. The trunks are typically either analog FXO lines or digital T1 or ISDN lines, and can be configured to support incoming, outgoing, or two-way calls. The number of incoming trunks needed depends on the number of lines that must be supported. For example, a telemarketing company would need many more outbound lines than a customer service department; however, the customer service department would likely need more incoming lines than the telemarketing company.

The good news is that a single inbound or two-way line can usually support multiple actual internal phones. This support is possible because users are not on their phones all the time (with the possible exception of the telemarketing company mentioned previously). For example, you may have 1,000 users at a location that have telephones in their offices. However, you may determine that at any given time only 125 of them are using the telephone. You may further determine that a peak call volume would be around 400 active connections. This ratio means that you do not need the bandwidth capabilities between your PBX and the CO to support 1,000 concurrent calls. You only need to support 400 concurrent calls.

It's also important to keep in mind that you will not have to have bandwidth to the CO for internal calls. Calls between internal users (those among the 1,000 in this case) can be routed internally by the PBX.

## Voice Transmission

To transmit voice across the PSTN, there must be methods for setting up calls, routing calls, and managing calls. These methods are known as *signaling*. The two primary signaling areas you need to be aware of are the local loop and the digital PSTN network. The local loop is the connection between you and the CO. The digital PSTN network uses the SS7 signaling system for communications. I'll provide you with an overview of both here.

e x a m
w a t c h
*PSTN network signaling can be broken into three categories. The first is address signaling for endpoint location. The second is supervisory signaling for access to and termination of the connection with the network. The final is informational signaling, which includes things like the dial tone, busy signal, and call-waiting notifications for information feedback.*

## Local-Loop Signaling

Earlier in this chapter, you learned about the basic process used to create a phone call. You learned about the closing of the circuit to create an off-hook condition. This circuit is the first signal used to establish a phone call. The closing of the circuit signals the CO switch that you are about to attempt a call. The switch, in turn, sends back the dial tone, which could be called a signal, since it does indicate to you that you can begin dialing the target phone number.

In addition to this step, you'll remember that the dial pad or keypad sends DTMF signals back to the CO switch in order to connect to the target phone. The switch may send the ring signal to the target if the target is connected to the same switch. The switch may also send the ringing sound back to the dialing phone. These are all signals that happen in the local loop.

## SS7

When you need to connect to a telephone outside of your switch and certainly when you need to connect to one outside of your region, the PSTN uses the Signaling System 7 (SS7) switching standard that was developed in 1981 by the ITU-T (International Telecommunication Union–Telecommunication), formerly known as the CCITT (*Comite Consultatif International de Telegraphique et Telephonique* [International Telegraph and Telephone Consultative Committee]). SS7 is an out-of-band signaling architecture. This architecture means that the signals are sent in a different frequency range than the voice data. It can also mean that the signals are sent on a different wire than the voice data. In-band signaling, like the local-loop signaling, is actually sent using the limited available bandwidth in the channel. In the case of the SS7 system, a separate line is used, or an entirely separate network is used.

## e x a m

### ⓦatch

*Remember that SS7 is used between network elements in the PSTN and not between your telephone and the CO. Remember that SS7 uses out-of-band signaling in that it sends the signals on one channel and routes the call on another. Finally, don't forget that SS7 is digital and packet-based.*

In North America, a unique architecture has been developed for SS7 signals. This architecture is known as the North American Signaling Architecture. The North American Signaling Architecture stipulates a separate signaling network. The network is built out of the following three components and is connected through signaling links:

■ Signal switching points (SSPs)
■ Signal transfer points (STPs)
■ Signal control points (SCPs)

The SSPs are responsible for the communications between the CO and the SS7 network. The STPs are the packer routers that allow SSPs to communicate with each other. Finally, the SCPs are basically databases of call-processing features and capabilities. As with the Internet, for the network to function, there must be redundancy. For this reason, the hardware that acts as the STPs and SCPs is redundant and therefore fault tolerant.

To understand how these different SS7 components interoperate, consider the diagram in Figure 3-6. As you can see, local loops are connected into the SSP, which is a CO switch capable of talking to the STPs in the SS7 network. When the user in area code 937 attempts to call the user in area code 206, the call is routed through the SS7 network.

**FIGURE 3-6**

Call routing through the SS7 network

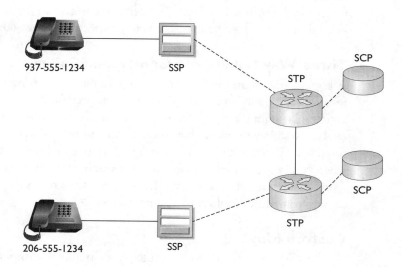

# PSTN Calling Features

In North America and most other parts of the world, the telephone networks offer many calling features or line features. These features include call waiting, conference calling, custom ringing, caller ID, and blocking.

## Call Waiting

The *call waiting* feature that is available in most areas provides you with the ability to be notified when a call comes in while you are on the line. If you are currently connected to someone's phone and are involved in a phone conversation when another call comes in destined for your line, the CO switch sends a tone on your line that you can hear. This tone indicates that another call is coming in. If you want to take the call, you can press a particular button or take the specified action that sends the signal to the CO switch to allow the call in. Most of these services allow you to switch to the incoming call and then switch back to the original call.

When call waiting is enabled on a line, it can usually be turned off before dialing a phone number. This task is usually accomplished in the United States with the *70 prefix. When you pick up the phone and receive a dial tone, if you dial *70, it tells the CO switch that you want to disable call waiting during the call that you are about to make. This feature is useful if you are about to participate in a conference call or some other communication where you want to ensure that you are not interrupted. In the days of using modems to connect to the Internet, it was very helpful in ensuring you didn't lose your connection when someone called you.

## Three-Way Calling and Conference Calling

A popular feature in small businesses and home offices is *conference calling*. This feature was called three-way calling early on because it allowed you to create a conference among three different telephone connections; however, the technology evolved to allow for more than three connections, and many telephone companies provide conference calling as an optional or included part of the package you get when you become a subscriber. Three-way and conference calls effectively create a private circuit network among the involved subscribers and broadcast the audio signals from all subscribers to all subscribers.

## Custom Rings

To allow subscribers to have multiple phone numbers without the need for multiple lines, many service providers offer *custom rings* or distinctive rings. This feature causes the phone to ring differently depending on the incoming number dialed. For example, you could have both 555-1234 and 555-4321 as valid numbers for a single land line. When someone calls your land line by using the number 555-1234, the phone may ring twice quickly and then pause before ringing twice quickly again, and so on. When someone calls the 555-4321 number, the phone may simply ring once and then pause as a normal phone ring does. You will know which number was dialed from the ring. This difference allows you to answer the phone as one logical entity when it rings one way and as another logical entity when it rings another way.

## Caller ID

You are able to identify the phone number and usually the name of the calling party when you subscribe to the *caller ID* feature. If you've been around long enough to have used a 1,200-baud modem, then you've experienced the technology that allows caller ID to work. Telephone line modems use an encoding mechanism known as frequency shift keying (FSK), where one frequency represents a 1 and another frequency represents a 0. This allows the modems to transmit any binary or digital data they desire. The caller ID technology uses exactly the same FSK algorithm as the old 1,200-baud modems. This message that is encoded with FSK is sent between the first and second rings. This placement is why you will usually notice that the caller ID information does not show up until shortly before the second ring, or sometimes it appears to show up at the same time as the second ring. For caller ID to work across different carriers, the carriers must be connected by SS7. Luckily, the vast majority of the telephone service providers are connected this way. Caller ID is also known as Calling Number Delivery (CND).

## Blocking

Two kinds of blocking are important for you to understand. The first is *caller ID blocking*, and the second is *number blocking*. The first protects your location identity when you are the caller, and the second protects you from calls that originate at a specific location or number.

Blocking caller ID, like disabling call waiting, is achieved by dialing a special code assigned by your telephone service provider before dialing the target phone number. This code is usually *67. Effectively, caller ID blocking simply does not allow the phone number to be sent by the modem technology that was described in the preceding section on caller ID.

With the number-blocking feature, you can specify that you do not want to receive calls from particular phone numbers. When individuals at the specified numbers attempt to call you, your phone does not ring, and instead they receive a recorded message in most cases. In addition to this service, many telephone service providers now offer a *privacy manager* service. This service will give you the option to disallow any unknown, anonymous, or blocked calls. Instead, the caller will receive a message telling them to unblock their call if they want to get through. It may also give them the opportunity to enter a special access code to get through anyway.

## CERTIFICATION OBJECTIVE 3.02

# 640-460: Describe Numbering Plans

With a little thought, it becomes clear that there must be some structure to the numbering plans used on the PSTN. If not, numbers would be reused and the PSTN would be unable to route calls appropriately. In the United States, the North American Numbering Plan (NANP) is used. The following section describes this numbering plan.

## North American Numbering Plan

The North American Numbering Plan Administration (NANPA) is responsible for managing the phone numbers available in North America. I'll briefly cover their numbering plan as an example of how one might work. The North American Numbering Plan (NANP) consists of Numbering Plan Areas (NPAs), Central Office Codes (COCs), and Caller Identification Codes (CICs).

The NPAs, more commonly known as area codes, are three digits long. Some specific area codes are not allowed to be used for general purposes, and they are as follows:

- **N11** The N11 area code or prefix is set aside for specific purposes. Certainly the most well-known implementation in the United States is the 911 code. In the N11 code, N can be any number from 2 to 9. The FCC only recognizes 211, 311, 511, 711, 811, and 911, but 411 has been implemented as directory information and 611 is usually implemented as a repair request line. Note that 611 is specific to the carrier that owns the circuit you are using to connect to the PSTN and will connect you to their service center.

- **N9X** The N9X code is reserved for future expansion. The N can be any number from 2 to 9, and the X can be any number from 0 to 9. Of course, the 9 is only a 9. This is why you never see area codes like 497 or 598.

- **37X and 96X** These two blocks of ten NPAs are set aside in case they are needed for some undefined reason in the future. The X, again, can be any number from 0 to 9.

COCs take on the format of *NXX*. This means that a COC can have any number from 2 to 9 in the first position and then have any number from 0 to 9 in the second and third positions. This means that 218 is a potentially valid COC, but 187 is not. The COC is also often called the "local exchange number."

Finally, the CICs are the last four digits of the phone number and can contain any numbers from 0 to 9. Therefore, the format for the NANP numbering plan is NPA-NXX-XXXX, where *NPA* is a valid code based on the constraints specified earlier.

In some parts of North America, you may be required to enter the NPA even for local calls. You will usually not be required to include the country code in these scenarios. The Country Code (CC) for the United States and Canada is 1, and the CC for Mexico is 011. In other areas of the country, the NPA may be added for you automatically. This feature is known as *digit translation*. Digit translation alters dialed numbers according to predefined rules and is mostly used to convert internal numbers on private networks to compatible external numbers on the PSTN.

When placing international calls, you may be required to enter the country code. Exceptions do exist, such as dialing between Canada and the United States, because they both use the NANP numbering system. The International Numbering Plan is managed by the International Telecommunication Union (ITU) as document E.164. The E.164 numbering plan identifies the country codes to be used. The E.164 numbering plan identified three components within its structure:

- Country Code (CC): 1–3 digits
- National Destination Code (NDC): 0–15 digits (optional)
- Subscriber Code (SC): 1–15 digits

While the ITU manages the CC list, the NDC and CC databases are managed within the countries or regions covered, such as those regions covered by the NANP. To see the country code list, visit http://www.itu.int/publ/T-SP-E.164D-2009.

## CERTIFICATION OBJECTIVE 3.03

# 640-460: Describe PBX, Trunk Lines, Key-Systems, and Tie Lines

The Private Branch Exchange (PBX) is, in large part, to telephony what Network Address Translation is to IP networking. While they are not exact equivalents, the PBX systems do allow you to run a private network of telephones with features similar to those of the PSTN or POTS networks. You will need to understand the basic features and components of TDM, IP, and Hybrid PBX systems for the CCNA Voice and CVOICE examinations.

In addition to the PBX systems, another telephone system type known as a key system is available. A *key system* uses telephones with multiple buttons, or "keys," and lights that indicate which lines are in use. Someone who wants to place a call just presses a button to select a line and begins dialing. Each line will connect the user directly with the telephone company's central office for a dial tone. The Hybrid PBX solution refers to a TDM-and-IP-combined PBX and not to a key system/PBX combination. Table 3-1 provides a comparison of PBX systems and key systems.

# TDM

Time-division multiplexing (TDM) refers to the signaling and transmission method used in the phone system. Traditional PBX units use TDM for the transmission of voice and signals and interconnect with the PSTN using the TDM solution. These TDM-only PBX systems are often called legacy PBX systems today; however, there are still many thousands of them in production environments, though the sales of new legacy PBX systems have dropped significantly over the past decade.

TDM requires the use of specialized switches that route calls and that are designed specifically for telephony purposes. TDM is a process that provides the appearance of running multiple signals on a single channel by segmenting the different signals and sending the segments in short bursts. By giving some time to each of the signals (time division), TDM can provide for both the transfer of the voice communications and the signaling related to those communications across one line (multiplexing).

At one end of the link is a multiplexer, which is the device that joins the signals before sending them as segments across the TDM link. In addition to signaling, the TDM link may contain voice communications from multiple conversations. The signal that is sent across the link is sometimes called a "composite signal" because

**TABLE 3-1**   PBX Compared with Key Systems

| PBX Systems | Key Systems |
| --- | --- |
| Digital or analog telephones | Digital or analog telephones |
| Used in larger organizations (≥50 users) | Used in smaller organizations (≤50 users) |
| Works like a CO switch | Shared lines |
| Key code for outside line (like 9) | Uses the line button for outside lines |
| Provides advanced user features (call forwarding, conferencing, contact center) | Provides basic user features (call hold, Music on Hold, intercom) |

it is a composition of multiple original signals. On the receiving end of the link, a demultiplexer will separate the signals into their original individual signals based on timing. In reality, each end of the link will have a multiplexer and a demultiplexer to provide two-way communications.

TDM links are usually implemented as T-lines or E-lines and allow for multiple calls to be placed across the link simultaneously. Traditional or legacy PBX systems use these T- and E-lines to link to the PSTN and use TDM for communications across the links. Internally, direct dedicated lines usually run from the endpoints (telephones) to the central PBX, and the TDM communications occur across the trunk lines that are either connected to the PSTN for telephone calls outside the organization's network or are connected to other PBX systems within the organization for internal telephone calls.

TDM has also been called *time-domain multiplexing* because it multiplexes within the time domain, whereas *frequency-division multiplexing*, also called "frequency-domain multiplexing," multiplexes in the frequency domain.

The central office (CO) has a connection to the larger network of telephony devices around the world. The TDM PBX or legacy PBX is used to connect to the traditional telephone network. It is connected through a CO trunk, and the PBX system acts much like the CO for your company while connecting to the CO for outside communications. Each phone or endpoint device is connected to the PBX and has its own ID or extension. In most cases these internal phones will be digital phones using 1's and 0's for communications with the PBX.

However, if one of the phones dials the number indicating the need for an outside line (frequently the 9 digit), the PBX will grab an available line and return the dial tone to the user again, or the user will simply be expected to continue dialing. If one user within the organization wants to communicate with another user within the organization, the connection can be made through the PBX and will not require an outside line.

You can also connect PBX systems in different offices using what are called *tie lines*. By connecting PBX systems with tie lines, you enable a user in one city to call a user in another city by simply dialing that user's internal PBX-assigned extension. These tie lines usually route through the CO and may interconnect through different providers, but they provide dedicated channels for direct communications between the PBX systems at the various locations.

## IP Only

Many modern PBX systems are IP only. These systems convert all voice signals to IP packets and route them through optimized IP networks. They usually provide the same traditional features such as call waiting and voice mail that the TDM PBX systems have, and they usually provide enhanced features as well. Many service providers now support pure IP routing of voice packets, enabling the entire enterprise infrastructure to use IP telephony while only converting calls that must be routed across the PSTN to traditional voice calls.

## Hybrid

By combining TDM and IP, you can create a hybrid PBX system. The vast majority of hardware devices on the market today are hybrid PBX systems. It is becoming increasingly difficult to locate a pure TDM PBX or at least one that cannot be expanded to support IP telephony. Companies like Avaya and Nortel have protected customer investments by providing upgrades to hybrid systems through new line cards. This upgrade option prevents the need for forklift implementations (a forklift upgrade or implementation occurs when the entire system must be replaced).

Hybrid PBX systems usually support connecting to the PSTN through both TDM trunks and lines dedicated to running IP telephony. These IP telephony lines may be used to connect different sites of the same enterprise. Ultimately, a hybrid PBX system is a traditional TDM PBX system with a Voice over IP gateway that provides for the IP telephony support, or the system uses a special processor card instead of the TDM processor. The special processor card allows the phones to run as traditional digital sets, but the brains of the PBX are now based on IP instead of on traditional telephony.

## Common PBX Features

Some features are common to most PBX systems, and then a few features, or ways in which the features are implemented, help to differentiate one vendor's offering from another's. The following list includes the most common features offered by PBX solution providers:

- Auto attendant
- Automated directory assistance
- Automatic ring back

- Call accounting
- Call forwarding
- Call through
- Call transfer
- Call waiting
- Call return/call back
- Conference calling
- Extension dialing
- Follow-me
- Music on Hold (MOH)
- Voice mail
- Voice recognition

## Auto Attendant

The *auto attendant* feature provides the capability to have a single number that outside callers dial and then allows those callers to choose from a predefined selection of options. The caller may choose to enter the extension of the target individual and be connected directly to that extension. If the PBX system supports directory services, the caller may choose to look up an individual's or department's extension in the directory. Also, other options may include listening to prerecorded messages, and so on.

## Automated Directory Assistance

When a caller doesn't know a specific extension number, he or she can be given access to a company directory. This service is usually a dial-by-name directory where the customer begins entering the letters in the target's name until a match is found or until a sufficient limitation is imposed that results in fewer potential targets than some upper threshold. For example, if you have 5 people with the last name of Carpenter and 6 people with the last name of Carrel, this would result in 11 people matching the first three letters of "Car" as they are keyed in. As soon as the letter *p* is added to the sequence, the total number has been limited to 5 people. We can now assign each of the five Carpenters to the keypad numbers *1* through *5*, and ask the caller to select the intended target from that list. The caller may also be informed of the actual extension, once the name is selected, for future reference.

A few PBX systems will handle this task automatically. When users set up the telephone for the first time, they are asked to key in their name and to record an audio file of their name. This way, when an individual calls in and attempts to spell a name, the user's name will be in the list. The caller will actually hear the user stating his or her name instead of some electronically generated voice. It is much more pleasant, and the caller may recognize the recipient's voice.

## Automatic Ring Back

Automatic ring back is the answer to that common dilemma of trying to reach an individual who is on his or her line. Instead of trying to call again and again, you can simply choose to have the PBX system ring you back when the line becomes free. This service saves a tremendous amount of time and greatly increases user productivity.

## Call Accounting

It is very important to many departments that they have the ability to track the actual time spent on the telephone. Sales managers like to see how many calls their salespeople make. Customer service managers like to see how many calls their customer service representatives take. Every organization needs to be able to perform cost management by watching what calls are placed and ensuring that the telephone system is not being abused. For example, I remember working in one organization in the 1990s where an individual from another country was placing long-distance calls back home that were costing the company more than $300 every month. This example is just one reason that call accounting is very important. It can also be used to audit the service provider to ensure that you are not being overcharged for the services to which you have subscribed.

## Call Forwarding

Call forwarding, just like in our home telephone systems, is used to forward a call that comes into a particular extension to another extension. For example, you may need to work outside of your office for some period. You may have a land line in your office, but you may also have a mobile VoWLAN (Voice over Wireless Local Area Network) phone. You could have the system forward all calls placed to your land line over to your VoWLAN phone with this feature. It is also very common to forward a phone to a conference center when you are in meetings for long periods and you are expecting an important call to come in during that time.

## Call Through

Some organizations provide the call-through feature to traveling salespeople and others to whom they want to be able to place calls by first dialing into the PBX. A toll-free number will frequently be used for this purpose. So, traveling employees can call into the 1-800 number and then enter an authorization code that gives them an outside line. Now they can call any number that is allowed by the PBX. The end result is that they are calling through the PBX.

## Call Transfer

I'm sure you've experienced receiving that call that was not intended for you. In the early days of PBX systems, you often had to ask the caller to call back to reach the proper extension; however, most modern PBX systems will allow you to transfer the call (though, in my experience, the average user is not very good at doing it, at least not if the times I've been "hung up on" are any indication).

## Call Waiting

This PBX feature is much like the call-waiting feature you might have at home. When you are on the line, the telephone will provide you with a specified tone to indicate that another call is coming in. In addition, most phone systems will also show the telephone number and any other caller ID information on the telephone's LCD so that you can make a better decision as to whether you should answer the call.

## Call Return/Call Back

This feature allows you to redial the number that last called your extension. This may work both internally and externally, or it may only work internally, depending on the implementation method. This is very useful if you've just received a message from someone who asked you to call back, but did not leave his or her number. Many phone systems will also allow you to scroll back through the list of previous calls, but this is usually a feature of the telephone endpoint and not the PBX system itself. This is why you have this feature in your caller ID on your home phone. The CO is not keeping this list for you. The list is stored in the memory of your telephone. This is also why the list will disappear if your telephone loses power.

## Conference Calling

The reality is that we can rarely accomplish big things in business with just two people involved. Sometimes it's easier to get everyone involved in a problem or a solution on the telephone at the same time. This is particularly true when they are in different physical areas. Conference calling has been the answer for the last couple of decades, and most modern PBX systems will support this feature. Depending on the PBX system, you may be able to include only extensions within your PBX system's control, or you may be able to include a PSTN number in the conference call. The latter is true for most modern PBX solutions.

## Extension Dialing

PBX systems will allow users who are connected to the system to dial other users connected to the system by entering a simple four- or five-digit number. This both keeps the call within the PBX system and makes for more efficient dialing.

## Follow-Me

The *follow-me* feature of phone systems is a little different than call forwarding. Whereas call forwarding forwards the phone call to one other specified number, follow-me includes a list of numbers, and the PBX continues to ring the numbers down the list until either it exhausts the numbers or you answer one of them. While you could accomplish a similar feat by forwarding your phone to another phone, which is forwarded to another, which is forwarded to another, you would not be accomplishing quite the same thing. In the latter scenario, the only phone that would actually ring—in most implementations—is the very last phone in the forwarding chain. With follow-me, all the phones in the list will ring, and you can answer where you are.

## Music on Hold (MOH)

Of course, what is a PBX system worth if it can't play music and other messages while the caller is on hold? Some organizations use MOH to simply act as a notice to the caller that he or she is indeed still connected. Other organizations use it very strategically. For example, I called an ISP in the late 1990s and still recall the on-hold message. It went something like this, "We appreciate your business and want to help you get the most out of your Internet connection. For this reason, we thought you'd rather get some tips about how to get more out of the Internet instead of hearing music that you do not find particularly appealing. Your call will be answered within the next five minutes, but here's your first tip while you wait…." I thought this was brilliant, and more and more organizations are realizing that this is something that they should take advantage of. Of course, you'll have to be careful. I know that I don't want a company to try to sell me something while I'm on hold with a complaint about what I've already purchased from them. I suppose it's about balance in the end, but this is just an example of what MOH can be used for other than simply playing music.

### Voice Mail

No list of PBX features would be complete without voice mail. Other than e-mail, and voice mail has been around longer, voice mail is probably one of the most important business tools in use today. I'm not suggesting that it's always used well, but many of us have come to rely on it for many of our daily routines. Modern PBX systems not only provide you with voice mail, but many of them also allow you to have the voice mail messages sent to your e-mail as either links to audio files or embedded audio files. Internal voice mail messages from your peers can usually be responded to by simply pressing the right key to respond and then speaking your response into the telephone. This keeps you from having to write down extensions or other information when it's not needed.

Of course, a PBX with a voice mail system is a PBX with a hard drive. This audio data has to be stored somewhere, and this means that you're dealing with a more complex PBX solution. In some cases PBX systems link to external voice mail applications rather than providing their own voice mail solution, but I don't know of a modern PBX solution that does not in some way provide for voice mail services.

### Voice Recognition

Some PBX systems either come with or allow for expansions to include voice recognition. This provides the feature you may have encountered where the automated attendant allows you to "press or say one," just as a simple example. Needless to say, these systems are not infallible, but they have really come a long way. Ten or fifteen years ago, you would never have been able to implement flexible voice recognition technology on the scale that it has been implemented today. The ability to understand a single human's voice was hard enough, but today the recognition systems do pretty well at recognizing hundreds of humans when they speak particular words or phrases. I'm still impressed that I can read my entire credit card and the company can process it—not that I would, since someone may be listening nearby, but it's still impressive.

## Special PBX Features

In addition to the common features, special demands are placed on PBX systems for unique scenarios. For example, a call center may need automatic call distribution (ACD) that maps a single incoming number to any number of internal representatives. Such a system will likely need a queue as well to reduce the total number of employees needed to handle the call volume. I remember my first job in information technology was that of a help desk technical support staff member. Probably 20 of us answered incoming calls, and we could see the number of calls waiting in the queue on our telephones' LCDs. These features have obviously been with us for some time now in the traditional PBX solutions.

## Hardware Components of a PBX

If you're going to work with PBX systems, it's important that you understand the hardware and software components that form a PBX. In addition to the phone lines, specialized components are used in these systems. A PBX will have line cards and trunk cards. The line cards provide connectivity to your phones, and the trunk cards are used to connect to the CO. Hybrid PBX solutions will also have network interface cards for connectivity to the data network.

The control complex of the PBX is the logic-processing section of the system. This is where the real controlling power of the PBX is. This intelligent component provides features such as call waiting, call forwarding, and more. In addition, the PBX will have a switch backplane that is used to make the connections between the telephone endpoints. Keep in mind that you will likely be required to use telephones from the same vendor that manufactured your PBX in order for them to communicate with the PBX appropriately. The newer IP PBX solutions may be an exception to this, since they communicate using many standardized protocols.

Of course, the PBX will have to have a power supply and cooling fans, since it is basically a computing device, whether it is a TDM PBX, an IP-only PBX, or a hybrid PBX.

In summary, you could say that a PBX provides all the components of a CO on a smaller scale. The end result is that you're able to implement your telephone system as a stand-alone system, but it will also be able to connect to the CO for PSTN connectivity.

# CERTIFICATION SUMMARY

In this chapter, you learned about three important topics related to the CCNA Voice exam. First, you learned how a traditional telephone works by converting analog sound waves to electrical signals and back again. You also learned how a telephone signals the network that it needs to acquire a line and place a call. Next, you learned about numbering plans through the example of the North American Numbering Plan. Finally, you learned about PBX and key systems and the features they provide for traditional internally managed telephony. In the next chapter, you'll begin to learn how the traditional PSTN and the new VoIP networks can work together.

# TWO-MINUTE DRILL

### 640-460: Describe the Services Provided by the PSTN

❑ The PSTN or POTS provides the network through which public calls are routed.

❑ The PSTN uses SS7 signaling within its network.

❑ Loop-start signaling occurs when a user takes a PSTN telephone handset off hook.

❑ Three types of signaling are identified in analog telephone networks such as the PSTN: address signaling, supervisory signaling, and informational signaling.

### 640-460: Describe Numbering Plans

❑ Numbering plans are used to standardize the addressing systems used within a region or internationally.

❑ The ITU E.164 numbering plan defines country codes used to dial internationally.

❑ The ITU E.164 system defines three codes: Country Code (CC), National Destination Code (NDC), and Subscriber Code (SC).

❑ The NANP numbering system is used in Canada and the United States.

❑ International calls between Canada and the United States do not require a country code.

❑ The North American Numbering Plan (NANP) consists of Numbering Plan Areas (NPAs), Central Office Codes (COCs), and Caller Identification Codes (CICs).

### 640-460: Describe PBX, Trunk Lines, Key-Systems, and Tie Lines

❑ Small businesses or organizations may choose to install a key system. Key systems allow each phone to use all PSTN lines available to the system.

❑ With a key system, users press the button for the line they wish to answer or to use to place a call.

❑ Larger organizations use PBX systems. PBX systems share multiple PSTN lines with users by using a switching infrastructure.

❑ With a PBX system, the user indicates the need for an outside line (typically by pressing 9), and the PBX system selects an available PSTN line or rejects the call if no line is available.

❑ Trunk lines are used to provide one or more connections to the PSTN from a PBX or key system.

❑ Tie lines or trunk tie lines are used to directly connect two locations, which are operated by the same organization, together for internal calling.

# SELF TEST

The following questions will help you measure your understanding of the material presented in this chapter. Read all the choices carefully because there might be more than one correct answer. Choose all correct answers for each question.

## 640-460: Describe the Services Provided by the PSTN

1. What is a name for the public network used for telephone communications? (Choose all that apply.)
   - A. PBX
   - B. POTS
   - C. Key system
   - D. PSTN

2. What signaling system is used within the PSTN, but not usually between residential phones and the PSTN?
   - A. SS7
   - B. Local-loop signaling
   - C. Morse code
   - D. RJ-45

3. What signaling occurs when a PSTN phone is taken off hook?
   - A. Loop stop
   - B. Loop start
   - C. Hook stop
   - D. Hook start

4. Which one of the following is not one of the three types of signaling identified in analog telephones?
   - A. Resolution
   - B. Address
   - C. Supervisory
   - D. Informational

5. What type of PSTN analog signaling directly enables dial tones and busy signals?
   - A. Supervisory
   - B. Address
   - C. Informational
   - D. SS7

## 640-460: Describe Numbering Plans

**6.** What numbering plan identifies international country codes?
A. H.323
B. NANP
C. E.174
D. E.164

**7.** What three codes are identified in the ITU E.164 numbering plan? (Choose three.)
A. CC
B. NDC
C. NPA
D. SC

**8.** What PSTN telephone numbering system is used in Canada and the United States?
A. NANP
B. Base 10
C. Hexadecimal
D. NAPN

**9.** The NANP comprises what identified numbers or codes? (Choose all that apply.)
A. COC
B. NPA
C. NDC
D. CC

**10.** What component of traditional telephony is used to standardize the addressing system used within a region?
A. SS7
B. Loop start
C. Numbering plan
D. Carbon fibers

## 640-460: Describe PBX, Trunk Lines, Key-Systems, and Tie Lines

**11.** Which one of the following businesses is most likely to implement a key system?
A. A company employing approximately 25 employees
B. A company employing approximately 250 employees
C. A company employing approximately 2,500 employees
D. A company employing approximately 1,250 employees

**12.** What internal telephone system uses phones that have direct access to each available PSTN line?

    **A.** PBX

    **B.** VoIP

    **C.** Key system

    **D.** Cellular telephones

**13.** What kind of PBX system supports IP telephony and traditional analog telephony at the same time?

    **A.** TDM-only

    **B.** IP-only

    **C.** TDM-over-IP

    **D.** Hybrid

# LAB QUESTION

You work for a small organization located in the southwestern United States. You must provide telephone service for 12 users. The users have informed you that as many as five may need to use the phones for external calls at any given time. An additional line should always be open for incoming calls. What kind of traditional telephony system might you recommend and why?

# SELF TEST ANSWERS

## 640-460: Describe the Services Provided by the PSTN

1. ☑ **B and D are correct.** The public telephone network is known as the public switched telephone network (PSTN) or plain old telephone system (POTS).

   ☒ **A and C are incorrect.** PBX and key system refer to types of internal telephone systems.

2. ☑ **A is correct.** The Signaling System 7 (SS7) is used for internal signaling within the PSTN.

   ☒ **B, C, and D are incorrect.** Local-loop signaling is used between the CO and the endpoints. Morse code is not used anywhere in the phone system and RJ-45 is a cable connector type.

3. ☑ **B is correct.** When a phone is taken off hook, the loop-start signaling occurs.

   ☒ **A, C, and D are incorrect.** Loop stop, hook stop, and hook start are not signaling methods defined in the telephone networks.

4. ☑ **A is correct.** Resolution is not a known signaling type for telephony networks.

   ☒ **B, C, and D are incorrect.** Address, supervisory, and informational are valid signaling types.

5. ☑ **C is correct.** Dial tones and busy signals are part of informational signaling.

   ☒ **A, B, and D are incorrect.** Supervisory signaling is about call setup and tear down. Address signaling is used to indicate dialed numbers. SS7 is used within the PSTN network.

## 640-460: Describe Numbering Plans

6. ☑ **D is correct.** The ITU E.164 numbering plan identified the country codes.

   ☒ **A, B, and C are incorrect.** H.323 is not a numbering plan and neither is E.174. NANP identifies the telephone addresses within North America.

7. ☑ **A, B, and D are correct.** The Country Code (CC), the National Destination Code (NDC), and the Subscriber Code (SC) are all defined in E.164.

   ☒ **C is incorrect.** The Numbering Plan Areas (NPAs) are defined in the NANP.

8. ☑ **A is correct.** The North American Numbering Plan (NANP) is used in Canada and the United States.

   ☒ **B, C, and D are incorrect.** None of these are numbering plans.

9. ☑  **A** and **B** are correct. The Central Office Codes and Number Plan Area (NPA) are defined in the NANP numbering system.

☒  **C** and **D** are incorrect. The NDC is defined in E.164 and the CC is also defined in E.164.

10. ☑  **C** is correct. The numbering plan is used to standardize the addresses or phone numbers used in a telephone system.

☒  **A**, **B**, and **D** are incorrect. SS7 is a signaling solution used within the PSTN network. Loop start is a signaling system used from the endpoints to the PSTN. Carbon fibers are used within traditional telephones to convert sound waves to electrical signals.

## 640-460: Describe PBX, Trunk Lines, Key-Systems, and Tie Lines

11. ☑  **A** is correct. Smaller businesses are more likely to implement a key system telephony solution because they require fewer lines.

☒  **B**, **C**, and **D** are incorrect. All of these organizations are more likely to implement a PBX because they will need many lines.

12. ☑  **C** is correct. A key system provides users with direct access to each available line. Users press a button to choose the line they wish to use or to answer a ringing line.

☒  **A**, **B**, and **D** are incorrect. A PBX system is used as a switch to allow fewer lines to be dynamically shared with internal phones. A VoIP system allows for a theoretically unlimited number of phones, but would not provide direct access to PSTN lines for users. A cellular telephone does not connect to the traditional PSTN directly, but rather passes through the assigned cellular networks first.

13. ☑  **D** is correct. A hybrid PBX can support both IP telephony (VoIP) and TDM or traditional telephony.

☒  **A**, **B**, and **C** are incorrect. TDM-only and IP-only would support one or the other, but not both. TDM-over-IP does not exist.

# LAB ANSWER

While answers may vary, you will most likely implement a key system. With a network this small, the PBX solution would be too expensive. A key system, with six lines or more, will meet the need. Five users can be on the line while keeping a sixth line free. To allow room for increased future demand, a ten-line system may be selected instead, and the appropriate PSTN connections can be purchased in the future as needed.

# 4

# They Meet— Data and Voice Converged

> *Switching to Voice over IP—especially in an enterprise environment—is wrought with perils that you won't experience on a non-VoIP network.*
>
> —Ted Wallingford, VoIP Hacks, O'Reilly, 2006

**T**his chapter explains how voice communications work on a data network. If you do not understand the basics presented in this chapter, you are more likely to run into those perilous problems Ted Wallingford mentions in this chapter's opening quotation. To prevent such problems, you begin by learning about how voice is transmitted over data networks and how voice (or sound in general) is converted to data streams through the process of packetization. Next, you explore the concept of a codec and learn about the different codecs in use today. Finally, you'll learn to choose the appropriate codec for your needs.

## CERTIFICATION OBJECTIVE 4.01

# 640-460: Describe the Process of Voice Packetization

For voice to travel over a data network, it must be converted into a data format. This section explains the concept and processes used to accomplish this goal. We first look at the general concept of running voice over data networks and then dive deeper into the conversion and encoding processes.

## Voice over Data Networks

You've learned about data networks and telephone networks, but how do we get telephone conversations to travel over data networks? The answer is a simple one: convert the audible telephone conversation into digital data packets. This conversion is accomplished with encoding standards, and the voice data packets are then transferred using standard or proprietary voice communication protocols. It's really no different than any other data communications process as to its technical nature; however, voice data packets do come with demands that are not seen in traditional data packets.

For example, if you are sending a file to a server using FTP, it doesn't matter if a few packets arrive out of order or if a delay occurs between the arrival of one packet and the arrival of the next packet that is greater than a particular threshold. Of course, an extended delay will slow down the communications, but the data will eventually arrive at the destination. Voice traffic will not tolerate such occurrences. If there is an extended delay, the call will be dropped or quality will suffer. If you think about it for a moment, you'll understand why this low tolerance is true.

Humans are at both ends of a Voice over IP (VoIP) communications link. They will both talk and listen, and their expectations have been set by the analog telephone network. If they do not hear any sound for some variable length of time, they will assume that the call has been dropped or the person on the other end has disconnected. If the sound quality is inferior, particularly to the point where they cannot understand one another, they may give up on the conversation. Expectations of quality must be met with VoIP data that have not traditionally been required of other data types. In fact, we often refer to "carrier grade" or "carrier quality" VoIP communications. This term means that we have accomplished a quality of sound and communication speed that is, at least, equivalent to the traditional PSTN.

Since we are transmitting the VoIP packets over the same physical network as our traditional data packets (think e-mail, database access, file transfer, printing, etc.), we can say that we are layering voice over the data network. We are using the same network devices, cables, and software that are used for our traditional data to transfer our voice data. This layering places a new demand on the network. The demand is that the data network must be able to differentiate between different packet types and give priority to voice data so that the quality expectations of the VoIP users are met. The needed technology is known as quality of service (QoS). QoS provides queue management and prioritization of traffic to allow the most important traffic through first.

Since voice traffic must move rapidly across the network and would not benefit from being corrupted or lost in transmission, we use UDP to send most VoIP data packets. You'll remember from previous chapters that UDP is a connectionless protocol, unlike TCP. TCP has far too much overhead to transmit voice packets as rapidly as they must be transmitted.

You may wonder why there is no benefit to resending corrupted or lost voice packets. The reason is simple. Think about how long it takes you to say the word "don't." If you're like me, it will take you far less than a second. Now, imagine you're having a conversation on a VoIP phone and you say the following sentences, "Don't push the button. Pull the lever." Further imagine that the word "don't" was lost in transmission, and the system decided to resend it. Because of the sequencing problem, the user on the other end hears the following, "Push the button. Don't pull the lever." This reordering could theoretically happen because the phrase "push the button" made it through while the word "don't" didn't make it through. When the word "don't" was retransmitted, it was placed before the phrase "pull the lever." The result is a complete opposite of the intended message. Do you see why retransmitting lost audio packets would be useless and possibly damaging?

Instead, the listener would just not hear the word "don't"; however, the reality is that it all gets a bit more complex. More than likely the listener would hear something like, "D---t pu--the ---ton. Pu-- --- --ver." All the dashes represent either sounds that are unintelligible or complete silence. The point is that the network doesn't usually drop exact words but rather drops portions of audio much less than a complete word, resulting in what we usually call a "bad connection."

## Converting Voice to Data

The process used to convert voice to data is really a five-step process. The steps can be described as follows:

1. Convert the sound waves to analog electrical signals.
2. Convert the analog electrical signals to digital signals.
3. If required, compress the digital signal.
4. Create packets from the signal data.
5. Transmit the packets on the data network.

The following sections explore each step in the process.

### Converting Sound Waves to Electrical Signals

In Chapter 3, you learned how devices can "hear sound" electrically by using a microphone. In that chapter, you learned about carbon-based microphones that have been used in telephones for over a century. Additional microphone types exist and may be used in modern telephones.

From what you learned in Chapter 3, you know that sounds are really pressure differences in the air. These pressure variations are picked up by the human ear and converted to nerve impulses, which are perceived as sound by the brain. Just as the human ear detects these pressure variations, a microphone uses various technologies to detect the same variations. Instead of creating nerve impulses, the microphone generates electrical signals that vary in relation to the detected pressure variations in or around the microphone. Of course, microphones are important because they are the first element used in converting sound waves to voice over IP packets.

The very first microphone was a simple metal diaphragm attached directly to a needle, which made impressions in another piece of malleable metal. The impressions varied according to the pressure differences on the diaphragm. When you ran the needle back over the impressions, a sound similar to the original sound—but greatly lacking in quality—was produced. If you're familiar with the old vinyl long-playing records, this may all seem familiar to you. Today, we have several different types of microphones, many of which are used in telephones:

- **Carbon fiber**   The carbon fiber microphone uses carbon fibers to change the conductivity of electricity and therefore the signal coming out of the microphone. The diaphragm presses on the carbon fibers as sound pressure variations occur, resulting in different levels of conductivity. Stated in the negative, the compression changes the resistance of the carbon fibers, which changes the flow of electricity resulting in a signal that represents the sound around the microphone.

- **Condenser**   The condenser microphone uses a capacitor to detect changes in air pressures around the microphone. Condenser microphones require power from a battery or another power source. The condenser microphone works by using two plates with voltage existing between them. One plate acts as the diaphragm, and as the sound waves strike it, it moves closer to or farther from the other plate, changing the charges and discharges, which results in a signal.

- **Dynamic**   A dynamic microphone uses a wire coil and a magnet behind a diaphragm to generate an electrical signal. When the coil, which is attached to the diaphragm in some way, moves near the magnet, it generates an electrical change. This electrical change is the signal representing the sound picked up by the microphone.

You may have noticed a pattern in each of these microphones. Each type generates an electrical signal using a diaphragm. The movement of the diaphragm, which is the only way we can detect sound waves (even our ears use the same basic concept with tiny bones), causes changes in electrical current, voltage, or some other electrical factor, and these changes act as a signal. The Cisco 7960G VoIP telephone pictured in Figure 4-1 uses a condenser microphone.

The microphone is usually located in one or both of two locations. The first is in the telephone handset, and the second is in the base unit for speakerphone capabilities. Additionally, most Cisco phones support an external headset connector, which would allow the use of a microphone built into the headset. This microphone is the first element used to generate VoIP data. The electrical signals leave the microphone and are passed to the Cisco VoIP phone for the next stage of processing.

Cisco 7960G telephone implements a condenser microphone (Courtesy of Cisco Systems, Inc. Unauthorized use not permitted.)

## Converting Electrical Signals to Digital Signals

Now that the microphone has generated electrical signals, the VoIP phone can convert these analog electrical signals to digital signals or information. This is accomplished through a process known as sampling and quantization. *Sampling* refers to the process of selecting enough value readings from the electrical signal to effectively represent it digitally. Remember that an electrical signal from a microphone is analog—think smooth and very gradual changes (though occurring in nanoseconds) over time—and we must convert this analog information to digital information. Because the analog signal is smooth, we could sample to practical infinity, which means that some better method is needed. This is where the Nyquist theorem comes into play.

Harry Nyquist and Claude Shannon developed the theory that you can represent an analog signal in digital format as long as you capture twice as many samples per second as the highest frequency in the signal. For example, if the highest frequency is 4,000 hertz (Hz) or 4,000 cycles per second, you can represent the signal digitally with 8,000 samples per second. The PSTN has set the standard for voice quality, which is usually called toll quality today, by establishing the signal transfer at about 4,000 Hz. Therefore, if we sample at 8,000 times per second, we can generate a VoIP stream that roughly equates to the quality of the PSTN. Keep in mind that the PSTN intentionally reduces the frequency to 4,000 Hz to save on bandwidth. The human voice generates frequencies up to approximately 9,000 Hz. With the greater potential bandwidth provided by VoIP, in the future we may actually be able to communicate with people over better quality connections. We would simply have to sample at 18,000 samples per second or greater. Table 4-1 lists common frequencies related to sounds and sound processing for telephony and other audio recording and conversion processes.

| TABLE 4-1 | Frequencies, Ranges, and Applications | |
|---|---|---|
| **Frequency Description** | **Frequency Range** | **Application** |
| Human speech | 200–9,000 Hz | Telephony; audio recording; AM and FM radio |
| PSTN channels | 300–3,400 Hz | Telephony; conferencing |
| Human ear (biological microphone) | 20–20,000 Hz | Listening |
| Nyquist theorem | 300–4,000 Hz | Telephony and other audio capture scenarios |

**on the** *You may have noticed the impact of reducing the supported frequency to*
**job** *4,000 Hz. Have you ever been in a webinar or online virtual class and noticed that the speaker sounds like he or she is on an AM radio station? This is usually because the speaker is dialing into the conference using a land-line (PSTN) phone.*

*Quantization* is the process of matching the samples to a voltage scale. In every second, for voice communications, 8,000 samples must be matched to voltage levels. Most telephony networks use pulse code modulation (PCM), which assigns each sample to an 8-bit value. Therefore, 8,000 samples times 8-bits equals 64,000 bits or 64 kilobits. Since this happens each second, we say that the bandwidth is 64 kbps (kilobits per second). Just remember that quantization is the process used to convert the samples into actual bits of data.

**exam**
**watch** *Quantization is the process of converting the samples taken from an analog electrical signal into digital data. Most telephony networks use PCM and generate one bit of data for each sample, equaling a data rate of 64 kbps.*

Codecs are fully defined later in this chapter; however, for now, just know that they are the factor that defines how the voice signals are quantized and compressed. One of the most common codecs used, G.711, uses the PCM system. Other codecs may use different quantization or encoding techniques. G.711 is covered more in the later sections of this chapter titled "Codecs Defined" and "Codec Complexity." Another quantization technique is Adaptive Differential PCM (AD-PCM), and it only requires 32, 24, or 16 kbps. The AD algorithm takes advantage of the predictability of human voice patterns and uses less data to represent the same analog electrical signals. AD-PCM will not be as accurate as PCM, but the bandwidth is reduced. In many cases, you may not be able to perceive a quality difference between G.711 and G.726, but more on that concept in the later section of this chapter titled "Selecting the Best Codec."

### Compressing the Digital Signal

Compression of the generated digital signal is an optional step. Some codecs perform compression, while others do not. For example, G.711 does not compress the data, while G.729 does. Based on human speech patterns, compression-based codecs can reduce network bandwidth required. The simplest way to understand this compression is to consider an example. Imagine you want to say the word "horse" to someone across a VoIP telephone link. If you speak at a normal rate, it probably takes about one second for you to say "horse." Now, remember, that word spoken in one second must be broken into 8,000 different samples. But how many sounds are really in that word (from a hearing and understanding perspective)? First, we have the "hhhh" sound, followed by the "or" sound, and then ending with the "sss" sound. Three basic sounds. Of course, there is more complexity than this, but you can see the concept. Now, the compression method in the G.729 codec can simply say to the remote end, "Please play the 'hhhh' sound for .2 second, and then play the 'or' sound for .6 second, and finally play the 'sss' sound for .2 second." Can you see how this saves on data transfer? Instead of sending 64 kb (kilobits) of data, we can send possibly 2 kb of data for each sound, with 1 kb of data for playing instructions, equaling only 9 kb of total data. Now, this is a simplification of what really happens, but you can see from this how the compression can work to your benefit.

### Creating Voice Data Packets

The next step in the voice-to-data process is the creation of voice data packets. As you'll see in the next section, voice packets are transmitted as UDP packets on the network; however, we must consider several factors that impact how much data is in each packet that is transmitted. The sample size, codec selected, and number of samples in each packet will impact the total packet size transmitted on the network. The packet size will impact dropped packets and delay in larger networks where the packets must traverse multiple routers and switches along the way to the destination.

In a Cisco VoIP implementation, the voice is packetized using digital signal processor (DSP) resources on VoIP gateways. Additionally, Cisco IP phones packetize the voice as it leaves the phone and enters the switched network. The VoIP phones perform the *packetization* and send the voice packets across the network. Voice gateways packetize analog data from FXO and FXS ports and convert VoIP packets to analog signals for those ports. Voice gateways may also repacketize the VoIP packets. For example, a G.711 stream from a Cisco VoIP phone may have to be transcoded (repacketized) by the gateway into a G.729 stream for an Internet telephony service provider connection. In a Cisco world, the integrated services routers (ISRs) are usually the voice gateways.

The packetization process can be broken into three basic steps:

1. Capture the digital data.
2. Aggregate the data, if necessary.
3. Place the data into packets.

In the first step, the digital data is captured, which was performed when the electrical signals were converted to digital data and then compressed (if a compression-based codec is used). The next step is to aggregate this data together. With Cisco DSPs, the voice information is digitized for 10 milliseconds (the sampling period) and stored as a collective voice sample. By default, two of these 10-millisecond blocks are sent together in a single packet resulting in 20 milliseconds of information per packet.

You will remember that the G.711 codec, for example, uses 8,000 samples per second. Since 10 milliseconds is 1/100 of a second, the result is 80 samples per sampling period. Each sample is 8 bits or 1 byte, which results in 80 bytes of data for each sample period. Since two blocks are combined together, each packet contains 160 bytes of voice information.

In addition to the 160 bytes of voice information, the packet will require RTP (Real-time Transport Protocol) header information, which requires 12 bytes of data. At this point, we have a voice container that equals 172 bytes of data ready to be placed into a UDP packet. The UDP header is 8 bytes, bringing us to a total of 180 bytes of data at the Transport layer or Layer 4 of the OSI model.

Now that we have a UDP packet ready, we can send it using the IP Layer 3 protocol. This requires an IP header, which is 20 bytes in size. If you've done the math, you know that we're now at 200 bytes total, and we still have to go to the Data Link layer or Layer 2 of the OSI model. Assuming we use Ethernet to transfer the IP datagram, we must add 18 bytes of extra overhead. In the end, our grand total is 218 bytes to send 20 milliseconds of voice information. Clearly, we need to send 50 of these packets every second to keep up with the demands of the voice information. The result is 50 times 218 bytes or 10,900 bytes per second or roughly 10 KBps (kilobytes per second). Remember that Ethernet and Wi-Fi networks operate at much higher speeds than this. The result is that you can handle more than one call on the network at a time. However, time also exists between the individual packets and, for this reason, you may need 50–60 percent more bandwidth per call than this 10 KBps rate.

on the job

*When you see tables that report on the bandwidth required for a codec, such as 64 kbps (or 8 KBps) for G.711, keep in mind that this does not include overhead for UDP, IP, and Ethernet or Wi-Fi.*

If you choose to implement compressed RTP (cRTP), you can reduce the overhead and the total bandwidth required for the voice packets. cRTP can be used with or without UDP checksums. Without UDP checksums, which is the Cisco default, the 40 bytes of overhead required by the IP, UDP, and RTP headers is reduced to only 2 bytes. With UDP checksums, the overhead is still reduced to only 4 bytes. If cRTP is implemented using the Cisco defaults, we can reduce the required data rate by 1,900 kbps to only 9 KBps total, which can have a significant impact on network performance for large-scale implementations.

## Transmitting the Voice Data Packets

VoIP networks use the User Datagram Protocol (UDP) to transmit the actual voice packets. UDP is a connectionless protocol, unlike Transmission Control Protocol (TCP). A connectionless protocol is a send-it-and-forget-it protocol. Consider that voice packets cannot be retransmitted in a useful manner like data packets can. If a packet is lost, the time it takes to notify the sender, retransmit the packet, and receive it at the receiver would be far too long. By the time the packet was retransmitted, the moment would have passed, and the voice data would no longer be useful.

While UDP is used to transmit the packets, special management communications may also be used. These management communications are used to establish a call, track the call, and ultimately terminate the call when it is completed. The protocols that allow for these voice communications will be covered in detail in Chapters 5 through 8.

## Converting Data to Voice

In the preceding pages, you learned how voice becomes data; now you must understand how data becomes voice again. Once the data traverses the network and reaches the destination phone, the voice packets must be converted back into analog signals that can vibrate a speaker and generate the same original sound waves—or very close to the same at the least. Ultimately the concept is no different than recording sound onto CDs and then playing it back again. The only difference is the real-time nature of the VoIP telephone conversation.

On the receiving end, the VoIP phone must replay the audio as a steady stream. To accomplish this, a buffer is typically used. This buffer, known as the jitter buffer, caches the first few packets and then begins streaming the audio. If a few packets are lost during the transfer, audio quality may suffer, but the call can continue. If too many packets are lost, the telephone may terminate the call. An example of a VoIP endpoint with a jitter buffer is the Cisco 7920 wireless IP phone shown in Figure 4-2. This phone supports an adaptive jitter buffer.

**FIGURE 4-2**

Cisco 7920 phone with adaptive jitter buffer (Courtesy of Cisco Systems, Inc. Unauthorized use not permitted.)

# 642-436: Describe Codecs and Codec Complexity

In the preceding section, the word "codec" came up several times. It is difficult to discuss the conversion of analog sound into digital packets without mentioning codecs. Codecs are one of the more important concepts related to VoIP networks, and the remainder of this chapter will focus on the information you need to know related to these codecs. In this section, you'll learn what a codec is and all about the topic of codec complexity.

## Codecs Defined

The word "codec" comes from the words "coder" and "decoder," and these words represent what a codec does. A codec encodes information and then decodes that information. Ultimately, it's not much different from a compression program, an encryption program, or a modem. A compression program compresses and decompresses data. The purpose is space reduction. An encryption program encrypts and decrypts data. The purpose is data privacy. A modem modulates information onto an analog telephone line and demodulates the information off the line. The purpose is digital communications across analog carriers. A codec encodes audio information for transmission or storage and decodes audio information for reception or playback. The purpose is sound information transfer or storage.

Several different codecs exist, and you must choose the appropriate codec for your needs. Codecs have the following characteristics:

- **Bandwidth**   The codec bandwidth is usually represented in kbps. For example, the G.711 codec works at 64 kbps, and the G.729 codec works at 8 kbps.

- **Sample size**   The codec sample size is usually represented in bytes. G.711 may use 160-byte or 240-byte sample sizes in Cisco equipment. G.729 may use 40-byte or 20-byte sample sizes.

- **Mean Opinion Score (MOS)**   The MOS represents the perceived quality of the call when a codec is used. The highest score is a 5.0, and a score of 4.0 or higher is considered equal to the PSTN or toll quality. The G.711 codec has an MOS of 4.1, and the G.729 codec has an MOS of 3.92.

- **Compression**   Some codecs support compression. For example, the G.729 codec uses compression to reduce the bandwidth from 64,000 kbps to 8,000 kbps, while only reducing the MOS from 4.1 to 3.92. The G.711 codec does not use compression.

| TABLE 4-2 | Cisco-Supported Codecs and Features | | | | |
|---|---|---|---|---|---|
| **Codec** | **Bandwidth (kbps)** | **Sample Size (ms)** | **MOS** | **Compression** | **Packets Per Sec** |
| G.711 | 64 | 240 | 4.1 | No | 33 |
| G.711 | 64 | 160 | 4.1 | No | 50 |
| G.726r32 | 32 | 120 | 3.85 | Yes | 33 |
| G.726r32 | 32 | 80 | 3.85 | Yes | 50 |
| G.726r24 | 24 | 80 | N/A | Yes | 25 |
| G.726r24 | 24 | 60 | N/A | Yes | 33 |
| G.726r16 | 16 | 80 | N/A | Yes | 25 |
| G.726r16 | 16 | 40 | N/A | Yes | 50 |
| G.728 | 16 | 80 | 3.61 | Yes | 13 |
| G.728 | 16 | 40 | 3.61 | Yes | 25 |
| G.729 | 8 | 40 | 3.92 | Yes | 25 |
| G.729 | 8 | 20 | 3.92 | Yes | 50 |
| G.729a | 8 | 40 | 3.7 | Yes | 25 |
| G.723r63 | 6 | 48 | 3.9 | Yes | 16 |
| G.723r63 | 6 | 24 | 3.9 | Yes | 33 |
| G.723r53 | 5 | 48 | 3.65 | Yes | 17 |
| G.723r53 | 5 | 24 | 3.65 | Yes | 33 |

Table 4-2 lists the Cisco-supported codecs and the applicable features for each codec.

In addition to the codecs in Table 4-2, Cisco devices also support the Internet Low Bit Rate Codec (iLBC). However, only a select group of Cisco devices support this codec. The iLBC provides a bandwidth of 13.33 kbps at a 30-ms sample rate and 15.20 kbps at a 20-ms sample rate. iLBC is supported on Cisco AS5400XM and AS5350XM Universal Gateways. The gateways must have a Voice Feature Card (VFC) or use an IP-to-IP gateway without transcoding or conferencing. One key feature of iLBC is the built-in error correction features. These features allow for use in high packet-loss networks.

**ⓦatch** **Be sure to understand the different codec features before exam day. You may be asked to select the best codec for a given scenario, and you'll need to know these features to accomplish the task.**

## Codec Complexity

Different codecs require more or less processing power to accomplish their results. The least intensive is the G.711 codec because it performs no compression. Other codecs perform different levels of compression and error correction, and these actions increase codec complexity. With increased codec complexity come increasing demands on the CPU in the device performing the encoding and decoding. In Cisco ISR hardware, the digital signal processor (DSP) is responsible for this encoding and decoding. The DSPs look a lot like traditional desktop memory trips and typically come as PVDM modules for the ISRs. The older DSPs came as packet voice/data modules (PVDMs), and the newer DSPs are generation 2 modules represented by the acronym PVDM2. When you must process more calls or implement greater codec complexity, you will require more DSP resources, which means more PVDMs and potentially more ISRs once your ISR reaches its call-volume limit.

on the
**job**

*Your life will be much simpler if you use the DSP calculator provided at Cisco's web site. Visit http://www.cisco.com/cgi-bin/Support/DSP/dsp-calc.pl to use this calculator. It will tell you the number of DSPs needed and the PVDM or PVDM2 modules that will provide the resources. You must have a valid CCO (Cisco Connection Online) account to access this resource.*

The codec complexity is configured with the Cisco IOS **codec complexity** command. You must first access the voice card within configuration mode. Then you can set the codec complexity to one of two options with C549 DSPs:

- **High**   High complexity is required for G.728, G.723, and G.729.
- **Medium**   Medium complexity is used for G.711, G.726, and G.729a.

When using the newer C5510 DSPs, you can set the codec complexity to high or medium and also two additional levels:

- **Flex**   Flex complexity allows the DSP resources to be used as needed depending on the type of call. Call volume can be from 6 to 16 per DSP depending on the codec. More complex codecs reduce call volume.
- **Secure**   Secure complexity uses secure RTP (sRTP) to authenticate and encrypt the voice calls and the voice data streams.

To configure the codec complexity, at the Cisco IOS command prompt, type the following commands:

```
Router(config)#voice-card 1
Router(config-voicecard)#codec complexity high
```

The preceding commands would set the complexity to **high** for voice-card number one. To set the complexity to one of the other three options, simply change the keyword **high** to **medium, flex,** or **secure.** You can view the current codec settings with the **show voice dsp** command within enable mode.

*Voice companding* refers to the process of compressing the audio on the transmitting end and expanding the audio on the receiving end. "Compressing" and "expanding" equals "companding." I know, it sounds like something my 6-year-old would create, but it's an important part of IP telephony.

G.711 defines two different companding algorithms. Each is based on mathematical formulas or laws, and each is named for this law. The first is *μ-law* (pronounced *mu-law*), and the second is *a-law.* Here, μ-law is a mathematical algorithm used for pulse code modulation (PCM). The algorithm represents analog amplitude values as compact digital codes. Three binary bits represent one of eight different ranges of amplitude values. Four more bits are used to represent an amplitude value within the range specified by the first three bits. The μ-law algorithm is used in T1 lines in the United States and J1 lines in Japan.

A-law is also a mathematical algorithm. The specifications are the same as for μ-law in that the first three bits represent the range, and the last four bits represent an amplitude in that range. A-law companding is used primarily on E1 lines in Europe.

**e x a m**

**ⓦatch**  **When configuring the G.711 codec, you should know that it uses two different encoding methods known as μ-law and a-law. μ-law is used in the** **United States and Japan, and a-law is used everywhere else. They simply encode differently—in fact, they encode in an exact opposite way.**

**CERTIFICATION OBJECTIVE 4.03**

# 640-460: Describe the Function of and Differences between Codecs

In this section, you'll explore the similarities and the differences among the many codecs. You'll explore the benefits of the features mentioned in the preceding section so that you can best select the appropriate codec as covered in the later section of this chapter titled "Selecting the Best Codec."

## Codecs Compared

The major differences between the codecs have to do with the balancing of quality and bandwidth. Without compression, the G.711 codec provides the best quality. Cisco hardware devices use the G.711 codec for this reason. It is recommended that you use the G.711 codec for LAN VoIP communications; however, even on a LAN, the network can get very busy, and you may find improved performance of the VoIP functions by using a codec with compression. For now, let's look at each feature of the codecs as represented in Table 4-2 and discuss the impact of that feature.

The first feature is bandwidth. Each codec has a different requirement for bandwidth, and within a codec, multiple bandwidths may be supported. The G.711 codec supports only one bandwidth, and that bandwidth is 64 kbps. Other codecs, through the use of compression or simply reduced sample rates, use lower bandwidth levels. Lower bandwidth means less traffic on the network to carry the same voice information; however, it also means reduced quality as is seen in the MOS values in Table 4-2.

The second feature of importance is the sample size. The sample size impacts the number of transmitted packets required each second on the network. A larger sample size means fewer packets and larger packets. A smaller sample size means more packets and smaller packets. The option of adjusting the sample size is useful because networks with higher collision rates can benefit from smaller packets, and networks with lower collision rates can take advantage of larger packets with less management overhead. Remember, each packet has the payload and overhead information. If you can deliver more of the payload in each packet, you can reduce overall throughput consumption on the network.

The third and final feature we'll consider here is the MOS. The MOS or Mean Opinion Score is used to measure the quality of the codec. A higher value equates to improved quality. The quality measurement of MOS is purely perceptual, which means that humans give their opinion about the quality of the audio, and the average (the mean) of these opinions is taken to reach the MOS. Even though the MOS is subjective, it is still a valuable way to measure codec quality because, after all, it is humans who will be listening to all of the VoIP calls that use the codec you select.

In general, an MOS of 4.0 or better is considered *toll quality*. This phrase, "toll quality," simply means that the VoIP system provides a quality equal to or better than the PSTN. It does not indicate that it is the best quality possible. According to the ITU-T, in recommendation P.800, the following MOS value interpretations can be used:

- 1 = Bad
- 2 = Poor
- 3 = Fair
- 4 = Good
- 5 = Excellent

Reflecting back on Table 4-2, you'll recall that the G.711 codec has an MOS of 4.1. This MOS is the highest value in the table and for good reason: the G.711 codec doesn't compress the VoIP data, but it does limit the frequency range to a range that captures the majority of the sound waves from the majority of human voices. The other codecs limit the frequency range in a similar way, but they also compress the data.

MOS values are calculated by using surveys of human participants. A group of usually 30 or more individuals will listen to a telephone conversation and then rate the quality of the connection on the 5-point scale used by the MOS system. A mean score is calculated based on the results of these user surveys. Remember from your school days that the mean average is the one calculated by adding all the values together and then dividing by the total number of inputs. For example, assume that you were performing an MOS test and you had 37 people listening to a connection that uses your new codec. Your goal is to calculate an MOS for the codec. Table 4-3 represents the breakdown of the participant's ratings. Based on these ratings, you determine that the MOS value for your codec is approximately 3.65.

As you can probably imagine, some vendors may desire to inflate the scores for their chosen codecs and deflate the scores for the codecs chosen by their competitors. The reality is that one independent test may result in a score of 4.2, while another will result in a score of 4.0. This variation can be the result of unseen variables such as participants with hearing difficulties on the day of the test that they were not aware of or undetected problems in the network connection. The moral of the story is simple: MOS values are very useful, but they are not absolute.

**TABLE 4-3**   MOS Ratings in an MOS Test

| Rating on the Five-Point Scale | Number of Participants |
|---|---|
| 5 | 4 |
| 4 | 18 |
| 3 | 14 |
| 2 | 0 |
| 1 | 1 |

While G.729 has a good MOS score, it is important to remember that the MOS score only ensures good voice quality. If Music on Hold (MoH) is to be used, the quality will be very poor with G.729. The compression used is aimed at voice communications and not at the variety found in musical sounds. In addition, fax communications will usually fail when the information travels across a standard G.729-encoded connection.

**CERTIFICATION OBJECTIVE 4.04**

# 642-436: Choose the Appropriate Codec for a Given Situation

In this final chapter section, you'll take the information learned so far and use it to select an appropriate codec for a given scenario. This ability is key to implementing a well-performing VoIP network.

## Selecting the Best Codec

With the information provided in this chapter, you are well-prepared to choose the appropriate codec for a given environment. Several factors must be considered when choosing a codec, including:

- **Device support** All devices on the network must support the codec, or you must provide a gateway for conversion between the differing devices. Using gateways throughout your network for this purpose can cause latency and certainly increases cost. It's usually best to choose a codec that is supported by all of your hardware. G.711 and G.729 are supported by all Cisco voice equipment.

- **Network activity** You must consider the activity on the network before VoIP is introduced. If the network is already busy, the VoIP traffic will only add to the current load. A codec with compression may be a good choice in congested networks that cannot be upgraded. The preference, of course, is to upgrade the network.

- **Network packet loss** Packet lost must also be considered. Some networks lose packets even though the entire network is not congested or busy. This can happen because a network *choke point* exists (a point where the different network segments converge, such as a single router connecting all segments). In this case, you can use a lower bandwidth codec, but, again, the preference is to eradicate the choke point through hardware upgrades or replacements.

■ **Sample sizes** You must consider the sample size used by the codec. In addition to compression, the sample size impacts the packet size and the number of packets needed to transmit one second of voice data. Networks with higher packet loss may be better configured with a codec using more but smaller packets.

It's important to discuss the last bullet point in more depth. The impact of the packet size on network communications is an important factor to understand when selecting codecs for your VoIP infrastructure.

Multimedia data packets come in varying sizes. We generally speak of a long packet or a short packet, and each packet type has its benefits and drawbacks. Since management information is related to each frame or packet, longer packets incur less overhead. This conclusion is simple math. If you have a total amount of data that you wish to transmit and you transmit that data with short packets, you will incur more overhead. That same amount of data sent with long packets incurs less overhead, since there are fewer packets. To clearly understand this concept, consider the fictional packet sizes in this table:

| Total Data | Packet Size | Management per Packet | Total Packets | Total Management |
|------------|-------------|------------------------|----------------|-------------------|
| 100 KBps | 10 KBps | 1 KBps | 10 | 10 KBps |
| 100 KBps | 2 KBps | 1 KBps | 50 | 50 KBps |

As the table shows, a packet size of 10 KBps results in 10 KBps of management overhead, assuming a fictional 1k measurement for management data per useful data packet. However, a 2k packet size increases the management overhead by five times (interestingly, the same factor by which it reduced the packet size). The resulting principle is that long packets usually incur less management overhead than short packets.

Long packets also reduce the packet-processing load. The devices that forward the packets on the network must de-encapsulate the packets from the frames and re-encapsulate them to send them on to their destination. The result of using long packets is that there are fewer iterations of the de-encapsulation and re-encapsulation process per total data payload. Think back to the table that listed management overhead for a long packet as opposed to a short packet. The same factor applies here. The long packet configuration would demand only 10 iterations of the packet processing, and the short packet would require 50 iterations.

Another possible benefit of long packets is that you achieve greater network loading. More time is spent sending data as opposed to determining where to send data. This greater loading capability means that the network bandwidth may be more evenly consumed and that the network performance may be more predictable.

The negative aspects of long packets become the positive benefits of short packets. Long packets do create more problems when packets are lost. Since there is so much data in an individual packet, the loss of just one packet can greatly impact the quality of a video or audio stream. Shorter packets are less harmful in such situations. In fact, some scenarios where a packet is lost will hardly be noticeable to the user.

When longer packets are used, latency is increased. Latency is a measure of the difference in time from when a packet is transmitted to when the same packet arrives. Most streaming video and audio technologies, as well as VoIP in general, have upper boundaries that must be imposed on latency variables. One way to reduce latency is to shorten the packet size. Smaller packets move through the network faster because of smaller bits to transmit, and QoS processing can "fit" the smaller packets in more easily.

Finally, short packets have less need for fragmentation. Upper-layer (OSI) data must be chunked or fragmented if it is too large for the lower TCP, UDP, or IP layers. Fragmentation incurs extra processing for both the sender and the receiver and can cause unnecessary delay. A simple method for removing much of the fragmentation is to set your application to send data chunks that result in smaller packets, and therefore, less fragmentation.

Ultimately, a simple formula can be used to help you determine network bandwidth and the best codec to use from a bandwidth perspective. The formula is used to determine the bandwidth is as follows:

```
Bytes_Per_Second = Packet_Size_Bytes(sample_size * samples_in_packet *
codec_bit_length / 8 + mgt_overhead) * Packets_Second(1 / sample_size
/samples_in_packet)
```

You may have noticed that I said it is a simple formula and then delivered quite a long formula. When you break the formula into its components, it is rather simple. Let's look at each part, starting with the Packet_Size_Bytes formula:

```
Packet_Size_Bytes(sample_size * samples_in_packet * codec_bit_length / 8 +
mgt_overhead)
```

This portion is very simple. We take the sample size (for example, 10 ms or .01 second) and multiply it by the samples in a packet (for example, 2) and multiply that by the codec bit length (for example, 64,000 in G.711) and finally divide by 8 (this action converts bits to bytes) to get the payload bytes. The math works like this:

```
Payload = .01 * 2 * 64,000 / 8
Payload = .02 * 64,000 / 8
Payload = 1280 / 8
Payload = 160 bytes
```

Now we need only to add the management overhead to the payload to determine the packet size in bytes. The management overhead differs from network to network. For example, Ethernet is 20 bytes, Frame Relay is 4 to 6 bytes, PPP is 6 bytes, and so on. The IP header adds another 20 bytes, and the UDP header adds 8 bytes. Finally, the RTP header adds another 12 bytes. Assuming we're using Ethernet, the final result is as follows:

```
Packet_Size_Bytes = 160 + 20 (Ethernet) + 20 (IP) + 8 (UDP) + 12 (RTP)
Packet_Size_Bytes = 220
```

Now you understand the first part of the original formula. The second part is very easy:

```
Packets_Second(1 / sample_size /samples_in_packet)
```

Assuming the G.711 codec with a 10-ms sample size and 2 samples per packet, the formula works out like this:

```
Packets_Second = 1 / .01 /  2
Packets_Second = 100  / 2
Packets_Second = 50
```

Finally, we have the two components of our bandwidth formula. The result is as follows:

```
Bytes_Per_Second = 220 * 50
Bytes_Per_Second = 11,000
```

As you can see, the result is 11,000 bytes per second or roughly 11 KBps. This is the throughput needed per call, so you must determine the number of concurrent calls in order to calculate the total bandwidth needed. Also, you must consider additional bandwidth factors in certain scenarios. For example, VPNs can add additional overhead.

# CERTIFICATION SUMMARY

In this chapter, you learned about the way in which voice (sound waves) is converted into digital data for VoIP networks. You learned that a codec is used to encode the voice data and decode it. You also learned about the differences between the codecs and the factors that must be considered when selecting a codec for your environment.

✓ # TWO-MINUTE DRILL

### 640-460: Describe the Process of Voice Packetization

❑ Sampling is the process used to gather numeric data that represents the electrical signals received from a microphone.

❑ The Nyquist theorem specifies that twice the number of samples must be taken as the highest frequency in the sound.

❑ Most human speech comprises frequencies up to 4,000 Hz or 4 KHz. For this reason, 8,000 samples per second work well for human speech sampling.

❑ Quantization is the process used to assign the samples to codes representing the audio information in the samples.

### 642-436: Describe Codecs and Codec Complexity

❑ A codec is used to encode and decode audio information for storage or transmission.

❑ Codec complexity is a reference to the processing power required to perform the operations demanded by a codec.

❑ More complex processes such as compression and error corrections increase codec complexity.

❑ Increased codec complexity demands increased DSP resources, but reduces network bandwidth consumption.

❑ The Cisco IOS **codec complexity** command is used to set the complexity level.

❑ The **codec complexity** command can be used to set the complexity level to high, medium, flex, and secure.

### 640-460: Describe the Function of and Differences between Codecs

❑ The G.711 codec operates at 64 kbps, and the G.729 codec operates at 8 kbps.

❑ The G.711 codec does not use compression and is a medium complexity codec in Cisco hardware.

❑ The Mean Opinion Score (MOS) is a common rating used to measure the quality of codecs.

❑ The G.711 codec has an MOS of 4.1 or higher.

❑ The G.729 codec has an MOS of 3.92.

### 642-436: Choose the Appropriate Codec for a Given Situation

❑ The available network bandwidth must be considered when choosing a codec.

❑ The network latency must be considered when choosing a codec.

❑ You must ensure that all devices support the chosen codec; otherwise, you will be required to implement gateways for conversion between the differing devices.

# SELF TEST

The following questions will help you measure your understanding of the material presented in this chapter. Read all the choices carefully because there might be more than one correct answer. Choose all correct answers for each question.

## 640-460: Describe the Process of Voice Packetization

1. What is the first step in converting speech to IP packets on a VoIP phone conversation?
   A. Converting the sound waves to analog electrical signals
   B. Converting the analog electrical signals to digital signals
   C. Creating packets from the sound waves
   D. Compressing the sound waves

2. Why do most telephony networks process only frequencies up to 4,000 Hz?
   A. Because the processes cannot process higher frequencies
   B. Because most human speech falls between 300 Hz and 3,400 Hz
   C. Because the PSTN supports up to 4,000 Hz
   D. Because the DSPs in a Cisco ISR cannot be designed to support higher frequencies

3. What is the name of the process used to convert samples into digital data?
   A. Sampling
   B. Compression
   C. Quantization
   D. Encryption

## 642-436: Describe Codecs and Codec Complexity

4. Which of the following factors may increase the complexity of a codec? (Choose all that apply.)
   A. Compression
   B. MOS
   C. Error correction
   D. Jitter buffer

5. Which codec has an MOS of 3.92 while requiring one-eighth the bandwidth of G.711?
   A. G.726
   B. G.723
   C. G.728
   D. G.729

## 640-460: Describe the Function of and Differences between Codecs

**6.** Which one of the following codecs supports compression and may use 32-kbps bandwidth?

A. G.711

B. G.726

C. G.729

D. G.728

**7.** Which one of the following codecs is among the medium complexity codecs in Cisco hardware implementations?

A. G.729

B. G.728

C. G.729a

D. G.723

**8.** What is the Cisco IOS command used to set the complexity of a codec to allow for dynamic selection of codec complexity?

A. codec complexity high

B. codec complexity medium

C. codec complexity dynamic

D. codec complexity flex

**9.** You want to use a codec with smaller packets even though it will result in more packets for one second of audio. What feature should the codec support?

A. Smaller sample sizes

B. Larger sample sizes

C. Higher MOS

D. Lower MOS

**10.** How is the MOS for a codec calculated?

A. By averaging the ratings assigned by humans who listen to audio rendered by the codec

B. By using a complex mathematical algorithm that assures accuracy of the rating

C. By comparing the volume levels (dB values) of the codec against a known high-quality codec

D. By calculating the bandwidth required for the codec

### 642-436: Choose the Appropriate Codec for a Given Situation

**11.** Which of the following are important considerations when selecting a VoIP codec? (Choose all that apply.)

    **A.** Device support

    **B.** Network packet loss

    **C.** User training

    **D.** Network activity

**12.** What formula is used to calculate the number of packets required per second for a given codec?

    **A.** 1 / sample_size / samples_in_packet

    **B.** Packet_Size * Packets_Per_Second

    **C.** sample_size * samples_in_packet * codec_bit_length / 8 + mgt_overhead

    **D.** 100 / 5 * 6

**13.** What formula is used to calculate the size of each packet for a given codec?

    **A.** 1 / sample_size / samples_in_packet

    **B.** Packet_Size * Packets_Per_Second

    **C.** sample_size * samples_in_packet * codec_bit_length / 8 + mgt_overhead

    **D.** 100 / 5 * 6

# LAB QUESTION

You have chosen the G.729 codec for your Cisco VoIP network. Up to seven calls may be made on the network at any given time. You must calculate three values: the number of packets required per second, the size of each packet, and the total bandwidth consumed with a maximum call load. All default settings are in use for sampling on the Cisco equipment in the environment. What are your answers to these questions assuming that cRTP is not used and Ethernet is the Layer 1 and 2 technology in use?

# SELF TEST ANSWERS

## 640-460: Describe the Process of Voice Packetization

1. ☑ **A is correct.** Just as with the PSTN on an analog PBX system, you must always convert the sound waves (speech) to electrical signals first. The electrical signals are measured to create the digital representation of the sound waves.

   ☒ **B, C, and D are incorrect.** You can convert analog electrical signals to digital signals only after the sound waves have been converted to analog electrical signals. You cannot create packets directly from sound waves. The sound waves must first be converted to a measurable state, such as analog electrical patterns or signals. Compressing is performed against digital data and not against sound waves directly.

2. ☑ **B is correct.** Most human speech falls between 300 Hz and 3,400 Hz, and the PSTN uses this range too.

   ☒ **A, C, and D are incorrect.** The processors could process higher frequencies if it were beneficial. The PSTN supports up to 3,400 Hz. DSPs could be designed to support differing frequencies if the human voice demanded it.

3. ☑ **C is correct.** Quantization is used to convert samples into digital data.

   ☒ **A, B, and D are incorrect.** Sampling is used to gather the samples for quantization. Compression is used to reduce the space required to represent the data. Encryption is used to provide data privacy.

## 642-436: Describe Codecs and Codec Complexity

4. ☑ **A and C are correct.** Compression and error correction can increase the complexity of a codec as they increase processing demands.

   ☒ **B and D are incorrect.** MOS is a measurement of a codec's quality and does not create anything within the codec. In fact, G.711 has a higher MOS than G.723, and yet G.723 is considered more complex. The jitter buffer has nothing to do with the codec directly, but it is used to buffer incoming packets for more consistent processing.

5. ☑ **D is correct.** The G.711 codec requires 64 kbps, and the G.729 codec only requires 8 kbps, yet the G.729 codec still has an MOS of 3.92.

   ☒ **A, B, and C are incorrect.** G.726 has an MOS of 3.85 at best. G.723 has an MOS of 3.9, and G.728 has an MOS of 3.61.

## 640-460: Describe the Function of and Differences between Codecs

**6.** ☑ **B** is correct. G.726, specifically G.726r32, uses a 32-kbps bandwidth rate and supports compression.

☒ **A, C,** and **D** are incorrect. G.711 uses a 64-kbps bandwidth rate and does not support compression. G.729 uses an 8-kbps bandwidth rate and does support compression. G.728 uses a 16-kbps bandwidth rate and does support compression.

**7.** ☑ **C** is correct. G.729a is a medium complexity codec.

☒ **A, B,** and **D** are incorrect. G.729 is not a medium complexity codec; it is a high complexity codec. G.723 and G.728 are also high complexity codecs.

**8.** ☑ **D** is correct. The **codec complexity flex** command is used to enable dynamic complexity selection based on the codec used to place the call.

☒ **A, B,** and **C** are incorrect. High complexity and medium complexity are fixed to allow only high complexity or medium complexity codecs. Dynamic complexity does not exist in Cisco IOS equipment.

**9.** ☑ **A** is correct. Smaller sample sizes result in smaller packet sizes and more packets per second.

☒ **B, C,** and **D** are incorrect. Larger sample sizes result in larger packets and fewer packets per second. Higher and lower MOS scores are not based on packet numbers or sizes, but rather on the quality of the end-rendered audio stream.

**10.** ☑ **A** is correct. The MOS score is subjective and is calculated through the mean average of a group of listening users.

☒ **B, C,** and **D** are incorrect. Complex mathematical algorithms are not used in determining the MOS. Volume levels are not relevant to the MOS. The bandwidth required is not relevant to the MOS.

## 642-436: Choose the Appropriate Codec for a Given Situation

**11.** ☑ **A, B,** and **D** are correct. The devices must all support the codec you chose; otherwise, you will be required to implement gateways to convert (transcode) from one codec to another. Network packet loss should be considered. On a high packet loss network, smaller packet sizes may be preferred. Network activity should also be considered because it will impact the settings chosen for a given codec.

☒ **C** is incorrect. User training is not important when selecting a codec because the codec is used within the VoIP network, and the user is not required to configure or manage the codec in any way.

**12.** ☑ **A** is correct. By dividing 1 second by the sample size and dividing that result by the number of samples placed in a packet, you can determine the number of packets required per second for a codec.

☒ **B, C,** and **D** are incorrect. These formulas do not determine the number of packets required per second for a given codec.

**13.** ☑ **C** is correct. A single packet size can be calculated by multiplying the sample size by the number of samples in a packet and then multiplying this value by the codec bit length (such as 64,000 bits for G.711) and then dividing by 8 to convert to bytes. Finally, add in the management overhead to determine the total size on the network.

☒ **A, B,** and **D** are incorrect. These formulas do not help you determine the size of a single packet.

# LAB ANSWER

In this lab, answers should not vary. Cisco equipment uses 10-ms samples and places two of these samples in each packet. The packet size should be calculated first. To do this, we process the following formula:

```
Payload_Bytes = .02 * 8000 / 8 = 20
```

We get the value 8,000 from the bandwidth of the G.729 protocol, as shown in Table 4-2 of this chapter. The result is 20 bytes of payload information. We need to add in management overhead to determine the packet size:

```
Packet_Size = Payload_Bytes (20) + Ethernet(20) + IP(20) + UDP(8) + RTP(12) = 80
```

The result is an 80-byte packet size. The first part of our lab is complete.

Next, we should calculate the packets required per second. This is accomplished with the following formula:

```
Packets_Per_Second = 1 / .02 = 50
```

We will need 50 packets per second to transfer one second of audio. The second part of our lab is complete.

Finally, we need to calculate the total bandwidth consumed if a maximum call load (7 calls) is in place. This value could be represented in several ways, but we'll look at the kbps rating here. To determine this rating, we use the following formula:

```
Max_Bandwidth = Packet_Size (80) * Packets_Per_Second(50) * Max_Load(7) = 28,000
```

This number is 28,000 bytes per second. To convert it to bits per second (bps), we simply multiply by 8 to reach 224,000 bps or 224 kbps.

# 5

# Real-time Transport Protocol

> *Telegraphing, in this country, has reached that point, by its great stretch*
> *of wires and great facilities for transmission of communications, as to*
> *almost rival the mail in the quantity of matter sent over it.*
>
> —*Laurence Turnbull*, The Electro-Magnetic Telegraph, *published in 1852*

As with the telegraph and its competition with the mail service, VoIP now rivals the PSTN in many ways. Some are already pronouncing traditional telephony dead, and others are predicting its quick demise. Whenever analog telephony dies and even now while the two technologies abide side-by-side, something has to carry all the voice traffic across the data networks. That something is the Real-time Transport Protocol for most VoIP implementations today, and it is the topic of this chapter.

The protocol used to carry the voice traffic is often confused with the protocols used to manage the call setup, reporting, and teardown. For example, H.323 and SIP set up calls and report call termination. They do not carry the voice itself. The voice is carried using a very simple protocol called Real-time Transport Protocol (RTP). In addition, a management protocol called the Real-time Transport Control Protocol (RTCP) provides management information for the RTP connections. Newer technologies allow for encryption and compression, which can secure the communications and protect them from eavesdropping. These last two features are provided by the secure RTP (sRTP) and compressed RTP (cRTP) protocols. All four protocols are covered in this chapter with sufficient depth to allow you to understand them and use them within a Cisco VoIP implementation. This chapter is the first of four chapters that focus on the protocols that allow VoIP to work.

## CERTIFICATION OBJECTIVE 5.01

# 640-460: Describe RTP and RTCP

The CCNA Voice exam (exam 640-460) is focused on small VoIP implementations. For this reason, it only requires that you understand RTP and RTCP. This first section will address these two protocols. Later in this chapter, you'll read about cRTP and sRTP, which are required for the CVOICE exam (exam 642-436). In this section, you'll first learn about the purpose of the RTP protocol and its implementation. You'll then learn about the structure of an RTP payload. Finally, you'll learn about the RTCP protocol with its features and benefits.

# RTP

RTP is, as its name implies, a transport protocol. Unlike FTP and many other protocols, RTP is usually implemented with the UDP protocol instead of TCP. TCP is connection oriented and has more overhead than UDP. UDP is normally a send-it-and-forget-it protocol, which is perfect for the transmission of voice information. Resending voice packets is not only useless, but it can also cause unnecessary network consumption. So RTP is used to transfer the stream of information that is the voice data in a phone conversation.

RTP was first published in 1996 as RFC 1889; however, RFC 3550 supersedes RFC 1889 and defines the current standard for RTP. RFC 3550, published in July 2003, defines a standardized packet format used for the delivery of audio and video over internetworks. The focus of RTP is on real-time applications. According to the RFC:

> RTP provides end-to-end network transport functions suitable for applications transmitting real-time data, such as audio, video or simulation data, over multicast or unicast network services. RTP does not address resource reservation and does not guarantee quality-of-service for real-time services.

Contained in this quote are two key facts you should know. First, RTP is used between two or more endpoints. The term *end-to-end* indicates that it is used for the real-time transfer of data between these endpoints. Second, RTP has no internal QoS mechanisms and does not ensure the required resources for its operation. However, RTP layers over the IP protocol, which does offer QoS capabilities. RTP can take advantage of the QoS capabilities in the IP protocol implementation.

RFC 3550 provides four basic services for the delivery of real-time information:

- **Payload type identification** Because RTP can carry any real-time information, the RTP header provides a field for payload identification. The field can identify the codec used and the sample rate. It is a 7-bit field.

- **Sequence numbering** The sequence number for each RTP packet is stored in a two-octet (two-byte) field within the packet header. The sequence number allows for detection of dropped packets or out-of-order packets.

(Note that the sequence number is not for retransmissions because RTP does not offer a reliable service since retransmissions are not useful in VoIP data streams.)

■ **Timestamping**   The timestamp is a 32-bit field, which is used to determine the timing of the current packet's data within a stream. This allows for proper sequencing of packets that are encoded out of sequence (for example, the sequence numbers do not reflect the actual required order of playback).

■ **Delivery monitoring**   Delivery monitoring and all other monitoring is provided through the RTCP component defined in RFC 3550. RTCP is covered later in this section.

You should be familiar with the following bulleted terminology, as defined in RFC 3550, to fully understand the functionality of RTP and RTCP. The definitions have been extracted directly from the RFC (with permission), and any references to sections are in reference to the RFC itself and not to this book. (Copyright © The Internet Society 2003. All Rights Reserved.)

❑ **RTP payload**   The data transported by RTP in a packet, for example audio samples or compressed video data. The payload format and interpretation are beyond the scope of this document.

❑ **RTP packet**   A data packet consisting of the fixed RTP header, a possibly empty list of contributing sources (see below), and the payload data. Some underlying protocols may require an encapsulation of the RTP packet to be defined. Typically one packet of the underlying protocol contains a single RTP packet, but several RTP packets MAY be contained if permitted by the encapsulation method (see Section 11).

❑ **RTCP packet**   A control packet consisting of a fixed header part similar to that of RTP data packets, followed by structured elements that vary depending upon the RTCP packet type. The formats are defined in Section 6. Typically, multiple RTCP packets are sent together as a compound RTCP packet in a single packet of the underlying protocol; this is enabled by the length field in the fixed header of each RTCP packet.

❑ **Port**   The "abstraction that transport protocols use to distinguish among multiple destinations within a given host computer. TCP/IP protocols identify ports using small positive integers." [12] The transport selectors (TSEL) used by the OSI transport layer are equivalent to ports. RTP depends upon the lower-layer protocol to provide some mechanism such as ports to multiplex the RTP and RTCP packets of a session.

❑ **Transport address** The combination of a network address and port that identifies a transport-level endpoint, for example an IP address and a UDP port. Packets are transmitted from a source transport address to a destination transport address.

❑ **RTP media type** An RTP media type is the collection of payload types which can be carried within a single RTP session. The RTP Profile assigns RTP media types to RTP payload types.

❑ **Multimedia session** A set of concurrent RTP sessions among a common group of participants. For example, a videoconference (which is a multimedia session) may contain an audio RTP session and a video RTP session.

❑ **RTP session** An association among a set of participants communicating with RTP. A participant may be involved in multiple RTP sessions at the same time. In a multimedia session, each medium is typically carried in a separate RTP session with its own RTCP packets unless the encoding itself multiplexes multiple media into a single data stream. A participant distinguishes multiple RTP sessions by reception of different sessions using different pairs of destination transport addresses, where a pair of transport addresses comprises one network address plus a pair of ports for RTP and RTCP. All participants in an RTP session may share a common destination transport address pair, as in the case of IP multicast, or the pairs may be different for each participant, as in the case of individual unicast network addresses and port pairs. In the unicast case, a participant may receive from all other participants in the session using the same pair of ports, or may use a distinct pair of ports for each. The distinguishing feature of an RTP session is that each maintains a full, separate space of SSRC identifiers (defined next). The set of participants included in one RTP session consists of those that can receive an SSRC identifier transmitted by any one of the participants either in RTP as the SSRC or a CSRC (also defined below) or in RTCP. For example, consider a three-party conference implemented using unicast UDP with each participant receiving from the other two on separate port pairs. If each participant sends RTCP feedback about data received from one other participant only back to that participant, then the conference is composed of three separate point-to-point RTP sessions. If each participant provides RTCP feedback about its reception of one other participant to both of the other participants, then the conference is composed of one multi-party RTP session. The latter case simulates the behavior that would occur with IP multicast communication among the three participants. The RTP framework allows the variations defined here, but a particular control protocol or application design will usually impose constraints on these variations.

❏ **Synchronization source (SSRC)**    The source of a stream of RTP packets, identified by a 32-bit numeric SSRC identifier carried in the RTP header so as not to be dependent upon the network address. All packets from a synchronization source form part of the same timing and sequence number space, so a receiver groups packets by synchronization source for playback. Examples of synchronization sources include the sender of a stream of packets derived from a signal source such as a microphone or a camera, or an RTP mixer (see below). A synchronization source may change its data format, e.g., audio encoding, over time. The SSRC identifier is a randomly chosen value meant to be globally unique within a particular RTP session (see Section 8). A participant need not use the same SSRC identifier for all the RTP sessions in a multimedia session; the binding of the SSRC identifiers is provided through RTCP (see Section 6.5.1). If a participant generates multiple streams in one RTP session, for example from separate video cameras, each MUST be identified as a different SSRC.

❏ **Contributing source (CSRC)**    A source of a stream of RTP packets that has contributed to the combined stream produced by an RTP mixer (see below). The mixer inserts a list of the SSRC identifiers of the sources that contributed to the generation of a particular packet into the RTP header of that packet. This list is called the CSRC list. An example application is audio conferencing where a mixer indicates all the talkers whose speech was combined to produce the outgoing packet, allowing the receiver to indicate the current talker, even though all the audio packets contain the same SSRC identifier (that of the mixer).

❏ **End system**    An application that generates the content to be sent in RTP packets and/or consumes the content of received RTP packets. An end system can act as one or more synchronization sources in a particular RTP session, but typically only one.

❏ **Mixer**    An intermediate system that receives RTP packets from one or more sources, possibly changes the data format, combines the packets in some manner and then forwards a new RTP packet. Since the timing among multiple input sources will not generally be synchronized, the mixer will make timing adjustments among the streams and generate its own timing for the combined stream. Thus, all data packets originating from a mixer will be identified as having the mixer as their synchronization source.

❑ **Translator** An intermediate system that forwards RTP packets with their synchronization source identifier intact. Examples of translators include devices that convert encodings without mixing, replicators from multicast to unicast, and application-level filters in firewalls.

❑ **Monitor** An application that receives RTCP packets sent by participants in an RTP session, in particular the reception reports, and estimates the current quality of service for distribution monitoring, fault diagnosis and long-term statistics. The monitor function is likely to be built into the application(s) participating in the session, but may also be a separate application that does not otherwise participate and does not send or receive the RTP data packets (since they are on a separate port). These are called third-party monitors. It is also acceptable for a third-party monitor to receive the RTP data packets but not send RTCP packets or otherwise be counted in the session.

❑ **Non-RTP means** Protocols and mechanisms that may be needed in addition to RTP to provide a usable service. In particular, for multimedia conferences, a control protocol may distribute multicast addresses and keys for encryption, negotiate the encryption algorithm to be used, and define dynamic mappings between RTP payload type values and the payload formats they represent for formats that do not have a predefined payload type value. Examples of such protocols include the Session Initiation Protocol (SIP) (RFC 3261 [13]), ITU Recommendation H.323 [14] and applications using SDP (RFC 2327 [15]), such as RTSP (RFC 2326 [16]). For simple applications, electronic mail or a conference database may also be used. The specification of such protocols and mechanisms is outside the scope of this document.

To help you better understand how the RTP protocol works, let's look at the RTP header and discuss the functions of each part. Figure 5-1 shows the structure of the RTP header in ASCII representation as it is displayed in the RFC.

If you've never read an RFC, RFC 3550 might be a good first read. It is an easy read in comparison to many other RFCs. However, whether you read it or not, most RFCs use formats like the one in Figure 5-1 when they need to represent the frame formats or packet structures for networking protocols.

**FIGURE 5-1**

RTP header
as defined in
the RFC

```
 0                   1                   2                   3
 0 1 2 3 4 5 6 7 8 9 0 1 2 3 4 5 6 7 8 9 0 1 2 3 4 5 6 7 8 9 0 1
+-+-+-+-+-+-+-+-+-+-+-+-+-+-+-+-+-+-+-+-+-+-+-+-+-+-+-+-+-+-+-+-+
|V=2|P|X|  CC   |M|     PT      |       sequence number         |
+-+-+-+-+-+-+-+-+-+-+-+-+-+-+-+-+-+-+-+-+-+-+-+-+-+-+-+-+-+-+-+-+
|                           timestamp                           |
+-+-+-+-+-+-+-+-+-+-+-+-+-+-+-+-+-+-+-+-+-+-+-+-+-+-+-+-+-+-+-+-+
|           synchronization source (SSRC) identifier            |
+=+=+=+=+=+=+=+=+=+=+=+=+=+=+=+=+=+=+=+=+=+=+=+=+=+=+=+=+=+=+=+=+
|            contributing source (CSRC) identifiers             |
|                             ....                              |
+-+-+-+-+-+-+-+-+-+-+-+-+-+-+-+-+-+-+-+-+-+-+-+-+-+-+-+-+-+-+-+-+
```

The first thing I want to address about the RTP frame structure is true of all networking frames. This truth is that all frames are a series of bits. The frames are a collection of organized 1's and 0's. The payload is just a collection of 1's and 0's itself, but the carrying protocol (in this case RTP) doesn't really need to interpret the payload data in any way. The carrying protocol provides the information needed to properly transport and process the payload information. The RTP header, as defined in the RFC and depicted in Figure 5-1, provides this needed information.

**Remember the different RTP header fields and their purposes for exam day. You may encounter** **questions about this information in RTP data packets.**

The following descriptions address each field in the RTP header:

■ **Version (V)**   This first 2-bit field is used to indicate the version of RTP in use. Currently, version 2 is the newest version. Version 1 was the draft standard, and version 0 was a more proprietary solution. Because the field is 2 bits, it can contain any number from 0 to 3 in decimal.

■ **Padding (P)**   This 1-bit field is set when the packet contains padding bytes at the end. The padding bytes are not part of the payload and are used with encryption algorithms requiring fixed block sizes. Padding bytes may also be needed when carrying multiple RTP packets in a lower-layer protocol. Because the field is 1 bit, it can contain the value of 0 (no padding octets) or 1 (padding octets included).

- **Extension (X)** The extension bit is a 1-bit field. When the extension bit is set (the value is 1 and not 0), the header must be followed by a header extension. An RTP header extension is used to allow customizations to the RTP header for specific-use profiles.

- **CSRC Count (CC)** The CC field specifies the number of CSRC identifiers that come after the fixed header. This is a 4-bit field.

- **Marker (M)** The marker field is interpreted differently depending on the profile. RTP works based on profiles, and the profiles identify different use scenarios (such as VoIP or video streaming). The marker field is 1 bit and is used to identify significant events like frame boundaries in the packet stream.

- **Payload Type (PT)** The PT field is 7 bits and is used to indicate the format of the RTP payload and how that payload should be processed by the receiving application. RFC 3551 identifies default mappings for audio and video payloads. For example, RFC 3551 suggests that G.729 should be PT 18 and G.723 should be PT 4. Table 5-1 provides a listing of the default PT values for different protocols based on RFC 3551. If a receiver is unaware of a defined PT, the standard dictates that the packet must be ignored, which provides better security.

- **Sequence Number** The sequence number is a field in the RTP header, and it is a 16-bit value. The sequence number increments by one for each RTP packet sent. The receiver can use this number to detect lost packets or to restore the packet sequencing if they arrive out of order. The standard recommends that the initial sequence number value be determined by a random algorithm.

| TABLE 5-1 | Codec | PT Value |
|---|---|---|
| RFC 3551 Payload Type (PT) Mappings | GSM | 3 |
| | G.723 | 4 |
| | G.728 | 15 |
| | G.729 | 18 |
| | G.726(16) | dynamic |
| | G.726(24) | dynamic |
| | G.726(32) | dynamic |
| | G.726(40) | dynamic |
| | H.263 | 34 |

- **Timestamp**   The timestamp field is 32 bits. The timestamp reflects the sampling instant of the first octet in the RTP data packet. The sampling instant must be derived from a clock that increments monotonically and linearly in time to allow synchronization and jitter calculations.

- **Synchronization Source (SSRC)**   This 32-bit field defines the synchronization source. The source is identified randomly so that no two sources within the same RTP session will have the same SSRC identifier. Because random algorithms can generate the same value (though it is less likely with 32-bit numbers), the RTP protocol must implement algorithms to detect and resolve collisions. Section 8 of RFC 3550 provides a mechanism for collision detection and resolution and indicates that the probability of two sources having the same identifier is roughly $10^{-4}$. The code listing following this RTP header field list is the algorithm suggested by RFC 3550.

- **Contributing Sources (CSRCs)**   The CSRC field may contain from 0 to 15 items of 32-bits each. The list defines the contributing sources for the payload in the packet and is applicable in conferencing scenarios where multiple audio streams are combined. When more than 15 CSRCs are included, only 15 may be identified. The CSRCs are added by mixers (conferencing servers), and the individual SSRCs are used.

```
if (SSRC or CSRC identifier is not found in the source identifier table)
{
create a new entry storing the data or control source
transport address, the SSRC or CSRC and other state;
}
/* Identifier is found in the table */
else if (table entry was created on receipt of a control packet
        and this is the first data packet or vice versa)
{
store the source transport address from this packet;
}
else if (source transport address from the packet does not match
        the one saved in the table entry for this identifier)
{
/* An identifier collision or a loop is indicated */
if (source identifier is not the participant's own)
{
        /* OPTIONAL error counter step */
        if (source identifier is from an RTCP SDES chunk
          containing a CNAME item that differs from the CNAME
          in the table entry)
        {
```

```
                count a third-party collision;
        }
        else
        {
                count a third-party loop;
}
        abort processing of data packet or control element;
        /* MAY choose a different policy to keep new source */
        }
    /* A collision or loop of the participant's own packets */
    else if (source transport address is found in the list of
            conflicting data or control source transport
            addresses) {
        /* OPTIONAL error counter step */
        if (source identifier is not from an RTCP SDES chunk
        containing a CNAME item or CNAME is the
        participant's own) {
            count occurrence of own traffic looped;
        }
        mark current time in conflicting address list entry;
        abort processing of data packet or control element;
    }
/* New collision, change SSRC identifier */
    else
    {
        log occurrence of a collision;
        create a new entry in the conflicting data or control
        source transport address list and mark current time;
        send an RTCP BYE packet with the old SSRC identifier;
        choose a new SSRC identifier;
        create a new entry in the source identifier table with
        the old SSRC plus the source transport address from
        the data or control packet being processed;
}
}
```

Because RTP is used to transfer the data packets and provides no session setup or management, another protocol is needed for the monitoring of a data stream. This is where the RTCP protocol comes in.

## RTCP

The RTP Control Protocol (RTCP) is used to provide four basic functions. The first and primary function is providing feedback on the quality of data distribution. The information provided may be used for control of dynamic or adaptive encoding solutions, and it is critical for fault detection within the distribution system (such as frame loss, jitter, and delay). The second function is the transfer of a persistent transport-level ID for each RTP source known as the canonical name or CNAME. The CNAME is similar to DNS names on the Internet. The SSRS may change due to conflicts; however, the CNAME will remain the same. This construct is similar to the way an IP address may change while the DNS host name remains the same. These first two functions of RTCP are critical to the operations of a media-transport network and are most important in a multicast environment such as conferencing or multicast audio and video streaming.

The third function of RTCP is the management of rate so that all participants can send RTCP packets. The rate at which packets are sent depends directly on the number of participants in the communication. The fourth function, which is optional, is used to convey session control information. This information may include participant identification. The methods by which session control information are generated are beyond the scope of this book or RFC 3550.

Five major RTCP packet types are defined in RFC 3550. These five types are

- **Sender report (SR)**   The sender report includes transmission and reception statistics from active participants in the communication. The RTCP header identifies an SR packet with the PT field set to 200.

- **Receiver report (RR)**   The receiver report includes reception statistics from non-active participants in the communication (such as listeners of an audio stream who cannot talk). The RTCP header identifies an RR packet with the PT field set to 201.

- **Source description (SDES)**   Source description items such as the CNAME. While the CNAME is mandatory, other optional items may be included. These items include the NAME (a personal name), the EMAIL (the e-mail address of the participant), the PHONE (the participant's phone number), the LOC (user's geographic location), the NOTE (notice or status information), the TOOL (the application or tool name generating the stream), and PRIV (private extensions for application-specific SDES values). The RTCP header identifies an SDES packet with the PT field set to 202.

- **BYE**   Used to end participation in an RTP session. The RTCP header identifies a BYE packet with the PT field set to 203.

- **APP** Provides for application-specific functions. The RTCP header identifies an APP packet with the PT field set to 204.

RTCP packets, like RTP packets, begin with a fixed header and then end with flexible lengths depending on the RTCP packet type. All RTCP packets must be divisible by 32 bits. This constraint is imposed so that multiple RTCP packets can be stacked and placed into a compound RTCP packet.

exam
ⓦatch
*Be sure to remember that RTCP sender and receiver reports are used to monitor RTP data streams, and applications may use this information to dynamically adjust codecs and other parameters of the RTP data stream.*

The most important of these RTCP packets are the sender and receiver reports. These reports are used to make adjustments to the RTP streams to accommodate actual operations on the network. They can also be used to locate the source of a problem (on your local network, on the WAN, etc.). The sender reports include the following useful information:

- **NTP timestamp** The actual time (wall-clock time) when the report was sent. Used with RTP timestamps to calculate round-trip times and other values.
- **RTP timestamp** Relates to the NTP timestamp, but is defined in the same units and random offset as the RTP timestamps in the monitored data packets.
- **Sender's packet count** The total number of RTP data packets sent since starting the transmission.
- **Sender's octet count** The total number of octets (bytes) sent in the payload of RTP packets since starting the transmission.
- **Fraction lost** The number of RTP data packets lost since the previous sender report or receiver report.
- **Cumulative number of packets lost** The total number of lost packets since the transmission began.
- **Interarrival jitter** An estimation of the variance in RTP data packet arrival times.

The receiver report contains the same information minus the NTP and RTP timestamps and the sender's packet and octet counters. According to RFC 3550 several calculations may be valuable and processed against the sender and receiver reports. The following text is quoted from RFC 3550 with permission. (Copyright © The Internet Society 2003. All Rights Reserved.)

It is expected that reception quality feedback will be useful not only for the sender but also for other receivers and third-party monitors. The sender may modify its transmissions based on the feedback; receivers can determine whether problems are local, regional or global; network managers may use profile-independent monitors that receive only the RTCP packets and not the corresponding RTP data packets to evaluate the performance of their networks for multicast distribution.

Cumulative counts are used in both the sender information and receiver report blocks so that differences may be calculated between any two reports to make measurements over both short and long time periods, and to provide resilience against the loss of a report. The difference between the last two reports received can be used to estimate the recent quality of the distribution. The NTP timestamp is included so that rates may be calculated from these differences over the interval between two reports. Since that timestamp is independent of the clock rate for the data encoding, it is possible to implement encoding- and profile-independent quality monitors.

An example calculation is the packet loss rate over the interval between two reception reports. The difference in the cumulative number of packets lost gives the number lost during that interval. The difference in the extended last sequence numbers received gives the number of packets expected during the interval. The ratio of these two is the packet loss fraction over the interval. This ratio should equal the fraction lost field if the two reports are consecutive, but otherwise it may not. The loss rate per second can be obtained by dividing the loss fraction by the difference in NTP timestamps, expressed in seconds. The number of packets received is the number of packets expected minus the number lost. The number of packets expected may also be used to judge the statistical validity of any loss estimates. For example, 1 out of 5 packets lost has a lower significance than 200 out of 1000.

From the sender information, a third-party monitor can calculate the average payload data rate and the average packet rate over an interval without receiving the data. Taking the ratio of the two gives the average payload size. If it can be assumed that packet loss is independent of packet size, then the number of packets received by a particular receiver times the average payload size (or the corresponding packet size) gives the apparent throughput available to that receiver.

In addition to the cumulative counts which allow long-term packet loss measurements using differences between reports, the fraction lost field provides a short-term measurement from a single report. This becomes more important as the size of a session scales up enough that reception state information might not be kept for all receivers or the interval between reports becomes long enough that only one report might have been received from a particular receiver.

The interarrival jitter field provides a second short-term measure of network congestion. Packet loss tracks persistent congestion while the jitter measure tracks transient congestion. The jitter measure may indicate congestion before it leads to packet loss. The interarrival jitter field is only a snapshot of the jitter at the time of a report and is not intended to be taken quantitatively. Rather, it is intended for comparison across a number of reports from one receiver over time or from multiple receivers, e.g., within a single network, at the same time. To allow comparison across receivers, it is important the jitter be calculated according to the same formula by all receivers.

Because the jitter calculation is based on the RTP timestamp which represents the instant when the first data in the packet was sampled, any variation in the delay between that sampling instant and the time the packet is transmitted will affect the resulting jitter that is calculated. Such a variation in delay would occur for audio packets of varying duration. It will also occur for video encodings because the timestamp is the same for all the packets of one frame but those packets are not all transmitted at the same time. The variation in delay until transmission does reduce the accuracy of the jitter calculation as a measure of the behavior of the network by itself, but it is appropriate to include considering that the receiver buffer must accommodate it. When the jitter calculation is used as a comparative measure, the (constant) component due to variation in delay until transmission subtracts out so that a change in the network jitter component can then be observed unless it is relatively small. If the change is small, then it is likely to be inconsequential.

**CERTIFICATION OBJECTIVE 5.02**

# 642-436: Describe RTP, RTCP, cRTP, and sRTP

In addition to the RTP and RTCP protocols, you should be aware of two special additions to these protocols that provide improved communications efficiency and improved security. Compressed RTP (cRTP) provides improved efficiency, and secure RTP (sRTP) provides improved security.

## cRTP

The RTP communications stream is all about getting audio and/or video data from one node to another on the network as quickly as possible. The problem is that the header is 40 bytes by itself when you include the triple header of IP, UDP, and RTP. The RTP header is 12 bytes by itself. The UDP header is 8 bytes, and the IP header is a minimum of 20 bytes. When you consider that hundreds of RTP packets may be needed for a few seconds of voice conversion, you realize that this header overhead can be significant. cRTP can reduce this 40-byte header to as little as 2 bytes (with no UDP checksums) or 4 bytes (with UDP checksums).

In the real world, cRTP causes overhead in processing on your routers. For this reason, you must consider its value carefully. In most cases, cRTP is used for WAN links and is not used for internal links. The internal bandwidth is usually sufficient to allow for the extra 36–38 bytes required by uncompressed RTP.

on the **job**

*Because cRTP can cause processor utilization on your Cisco routers, it might be a good idea to check the utilization levels of your processor in your routers. You can view processor utilization on a Cisco router with the show processes CPU IOS command from privileged exec mode. When routers are over 70 percent utilized, you should avoid cRTP.*

The method used for compression is simple. Much of the data in IP, UDP, and RTP headers is static. To say that the data is static simply means that it does not change from packet to packet. Since this data remains the same, there is no reason to repeat it within each packet once a stream begins. The header compression techniques used in cRTP are based on TCP/IP header compression, which was defined in RFC 1144. cRTP is defined in RFC 2508.

## SCENARIO & SOLUTION

| | |
|---|---|
| You are configuring RTP for use on a WAN link. The WAN link is trusted from a security perspective, but it has limited bandwidth. Should you enable cRTP, sRTP, or both? | Since the WAN link is trusted, sRTP will not be required; however, cRTP can be utilized to reduce the bandwidth consumed by RTP communications. |

cRTP should be differentiated from algorithmic compression techniques like the ZIP algorithm developed by PKware or the JPEG algorithm used to compress images. ZIP is a mathematical compression algorithm that is lossless, but is achieved through very complex mathematical computations. JPEG is a lossful algorithm that permanently destroys data to reduce the size of images. cRTP is neither lossful nor mathematically intensive. For example, several fields may be removed from the IP header. In fact, only the packet ID must be included. With the UDP header, the checksum must be communicated when it is used, but most other fields are either redundant with IP fields or static. In the RTP header, the SSRC ID is constant in a given communications stream, so it can be removed. Typically, only the sequence number and timestamp change in the RTP headers from packet to packet.

As you can see, from the brief summary in the preceding paragraph, compression of the IP/UDP/RTP header chain can be achieved with no loss of data at all. It is not computationally intensive; however, if a router must do the extra work of caching full headers for the rebuilding of future compressed headers, this does introduce overhead. It is for this reason that cRTP is usually used only on WAN connections.

### exam
#### Watch

*Remember that cRTP compresses RTP, UDP, and IP headers by removing redundant information and not by implementing some kind of algorithmic compression scheme such as those used in PKZip, Arj, and other compression applications.*

You enable RTP header compression (cRTP) on Cisco routers in interface configuration mode. For example, you can enable cRTP on a serial interface by first entering the interface configuration mode and then executing the following command:

```
ip rtp header-compression
```

Optionally, you may add the **passive** keyword to the end of the command (making the command **ip rtp header-compression passive**) to change the behavior of cRTP. In passive mode, the router only compresses outgoing RTP when the incoming packets on the same interface are also compressed. When the **passive** keyword is omitted, all RTP communications are compressed when sent on the configured interface.

The Cisco IOS also allows you to control the number of compressed connections allowed on an interface. This configuration can help limit the impact on processor utilization. The default number of cRTP connections allowed is 16. Use the following command to modify this value:

```
ip rtp compression connections number
```

The variable number represents the number of allowed connections. For example, to set the number of allowed cRTP connections to 20, execute the following command from interface configuration mode for the appropriate interface:

```
ip rtp compression connections 20
```

# sRTP

Secure RTP (sRTP) is used to secure the RTP data payloads. Normally, RTP data is sent in clear text (unless transmitted within a VPN tunnel) and is easily readable using a protocol analyzer or specialty VoIP hacking tools. sRTP allows for the encryption of this RTP data. Additionally, sRTP provides authentication and the avoidance of replay attacks. RFC 3711, which defines sRTP, states the goals of the protocol as follows:

- The confidentiality of RTP and RTCP payloads
- The integrity of the entire RTP and RTCP packets, together with protection against replayed packets

Of course, in the world of computer and network security, anytime you see the word "confidentiality," you know that encryption is in play. When you see references to integrity, hashing algorithms or checksums are likely used.

You may remember that RTP is designed to allow for profiles that provide specific use scenarios for RTP. sRTP is actually a standardized profile for RTP that specifies security solutions. Secure RTCP (sRTCP) is also defined, and it provides security services to RTCP in the same way that sRTP provides the services to RTP. The standard indicates that sRTP and sRTCP act as a "bump in the stack" so that RTP packets are intercepted on the sending side and an equivalent sRTP packet is sent to the receiver. The receiver intercepts the sRTP packet and strips off the security, sending a standard RTP packet up the layers to the application. The same behavior is true for sRTCP. The benefit is that existing application could potentially work with sRTP without awareness of its utilization.

The RFC 3711 standard included the use of AES (Advanced Encryption Standard) as the block cipher algorithm. Hash Message Authentication Code Secure Hashing Algorithm version 1 (HMAC-SHA1) may be used for integrity and authentication.

| | |
|---|---|
| **Remember that sRTP provides more than just encryption. It** | **provides authentication, encryption, and protection against replay attacks.** |

## CERTIFICATION SUMMARY

In this chapter, you learned about the Real-time Transport Protocol (RTP) and the supporting protocols it requires and utilizes. RTP is used to transfer data streams. The RTP Control Protocol (RTCP) is used to monitor those RTP data streams. The compressed RTP (cRTP) may be used to increase efficiency by removing redundancy from RTP headers. The secure RTP (sRTP) may be used to encrypt RTP data streams. All four protocols are defined as RFC standards and commonly implemented in VoIP solutions such as those from Cisco.

# ✓ TWO-MINUTE DRILL

## 640-460: Describe RTP and RTCP

❑ The Real-time Transport Protocol (RTP) uses UDP to transport time-sensitive data such as voice and video.

❑ RTP is a flexible protocol that can be extended through the use of profiles.

❑ The RTP Control Protocol (RTCP) is used to monitor RTP communications.

❑ The RTCP sender report (SR) and receiver report (RR) are used to report on important issues such as jitter, delay, and lost packets.

❑ RFC 3550 defines both RTP and RTCP. RFC 3551 defines the mappings for payload type (PT) values used in RTP headers.

## 642-436: Describe RTP, RTCP, cRTP, and sRTP

❑ cRTP provides header compression for RTP data streams.

❑ With UDP checksums, the cRTP header can be reduced to 4 bytes.

❑ Without UDP checksums, the cRTP header can be reduced to 2 bytes.

❑ The **ip rtp header-compression** command is used to enable cRTP on an interface.

❑ When in passive mode, a Cisco interface only compresses outgoing RTP packets when the incoming packets are compressed on that same interface.

❑ The **ip rtp compression connections** command is used to limit the number of allowed cRTP connections on an interface.

❑ sRTP provides security for RTP data streams.

❑ The default sRTP encryption algorithm is AES.

❑ The default sRTP integrity and authentication algorithm is HMAC-SHA1 (sometimes simply called SHA1) with a 160-bit hash length.

❑ sRTP provides confidentiality, authentication, and the avoidance of replay attacks.

# SELF TEST

The following questions will help you measure your understanding of the material presented in this chapter. Read all the choices carefully because there might be more than one correct answer. Choose all correct answers for each question.

## 640-460: Describe RTP and RTCP

1. What protocol is used to transport real-time data in VoIP networks?
   A. H.323
   B. SIP
   C. RTP
   D. RTCP

2. What protocol is used to monitor the transport of real-time data in VoIP networks?
   A. SCCP
   B. RTP
   C. cRTP
   D. RTCP

3. What can be created to extend the use of RTP for application-specific scenarios?
   A. Profile
   B. Encryption algorithms
   C. Hashing algorithms
   D. Compression algorithms

4. What two RTCP packet types can be used to provide useful information about RTP data streams such as jitter and lost packets? (Choose two.)
   A. BYE
   B. SR
   C. RR
   D. SDES

5. What RTP packet type is used primarily for the transfer of the CNAME information, but may also include e-mail addresses, phone numbers, and other application-specific information?
   A. BYE
   B. SR
   C. RR
   D. SDES

6. What RTCP packet type is used to end participation in an RTP session?
   A. BYE
   B. SR
   C. RR
   D. SDES

7. What is the PT value for the G.729 codec in an RTP header PT field?
   A. 4
   B. 15
   C. 18
   D. 34

## 642-436: Describe RTP, RTCP, cRTP, and sRTP

8. What protocol is used to reduce the header sizes for RTP packets?
   A. cRTP
   B. sRTP
   C. RTCP
   D. RTSP

9. What is the size of a maximum compressed IP/UDP/RTP header series without UDP checksums?
   A. 2 bytes
   B. 4 bytes
   C. 12 bytes
   D. 40 bytes

10. How does cRTP compress the IP/UDP/RTP headers?
    A. Using ZIP algorithms provided by PKware, Inc.
    B. Using lossy algorithms, such as JPEG
    C. Using Arj algorithms, provided through open source
    D. Using static data–removal processes and basic value determination algorithms

11. You want to enable cRTP on a serial interface. You are in interface configuration mode. You want all traffic to be compressed. What single command should you execute to turn on cRTP?
    A. ip rtp compression connections 16
    B. rtp header-compression on

    C.  ip rtp header-compression

    D.  ip rtp header-compression passive

**12.** You want to enable cRTP compression on a serial interface. You want only 10 connections at a time to use compression. You want to compress streams only when the incoming connections use cRTP. What commands will you type to enable compression and limit the connections? (Choose two.)

    A.  ip rtp compression connections 10

    B.  ip rtp header-compression

    C.  ip rtp header-compression passive

    D.  ip rtp compression limit 10

**13.** What protocol is a profile extension to RTP that provides security for RTP communications?

    A.  cRTP

    B.  sRTP

    C.  RTSP

    D.  DES

**14.** What is the default encryption algorithm used by sRTP?

    A.  DES

    B.  RC4

    C.  AES

    D.  Blowfish

**15.** What security features are provided by sRTP to RTP data streams? (Choose all that apply.)

    A.  Confidentiality

    B.  Authentication

    C.  Physical security

    D.  Biometrics

# LAB QUESTION

You are configuring RTP for your network infrastructure and WAN connections. You want to enable the most efficient use of the protocols for your VoIP implementation. The network consists of two WAN connections (serial 0 and serial 1) and 12 Ethernet router interfaces. On what interfaces, if any, may you choose to implement? Explain your reason for the interfaces you have or have not chosen.

# SELF TEST ANSWERS

## 640-460: Describe RTP and RTCP

1. ☑ **C** is correct. The Real-time Transport Protocol (RTP) is used to transport data in VoIP networks. It is also used for video and multimedia streaming and conferencing.

   ☒ **A**, **B**, and **D** are incorrect. H.323 and SIP are call setup and management protocols and are not actually used to transfer the real-time voice data. RTCP is used to monitor RTP communications.

2. ☑ **D** is correct. The RTP Control Protocol (RTCP) is used to monitor and report on RTP data streams.

   ☒ **A**, **B**, and **C** are incorrect. SCCP is used to set up and manage voice calls. RTP is used to transfer data streams and is monitored by RTCP. cRTP is used to compress the headers for the RTP data streams.

3. ☑ **A** is correct. A profile is used to extend RTP for application-specific functions. For example, sRTP is a profile that enables security for RTP data streams and RTCP communications.

   ☒ **B**, **C**, and **D** are incorrect. Encryption algorithms provide confidentiality and may be specified within a profile, but they do not extend RTP themselves. This is also true for hashing algorithms and compression algorithms.

4. ☑ **B** and **C** are correct. The sender report (SR) and receiver report (RR) packets contain useful monitoring information on RTP streams. The information included is jitter, delay, lost packets, and other identifier type information.

   ☒ **A** and **D** are incorrect. The BYE packet is used to end an RTP stream participation. The SDES packet is used to communicate the CNAME and other optional information values unrelated to the actual monitoring data of the RTP streams.

5. ☑ **D** is correct. The source description (SDES) packet is used to transfer the canonical name (CNAME), personal name (NAME), geographic location (LOC), e-mail address (EMAIL), and phone number (PHONE) among a few other possible values.

   ☒ **A**, **B**, and **C** are incorrect. The BYE packet is used to end an RTP stream participation. The sender report (SR) and receiver report (RR) packets contain useful monitoring information on RTP streams.

6. ☑ **A** is correct. The BYE packet is used to end participation in an RTP stream. It is identified as packet type (PT) 203.

   ☒ **B, C,** and **D** are incorrect. The sender report (SR) and receiver report (RR) packets contain useful monitoring information on RTP streams. The source description (SDES) packet is used to transfer the canonical name (CNAME) among other informational values.

7. ☑ **C** is correct. The PT field will contain the value 18 when G.729 is used.

   ☒ **A, B,** and **D** are incorrect. The value of 4 in the PT field indicates G.723. The value of 15 in the PT field indicates G.728. The value of 34 in the PT field indicates H.263.

## 642-436: Describe RTP, RTCP, cRTP, and sRTP

8. ☑ **A** is correct. Compressed RTP (cRTP) is used to reduce the IP, UDP, and RTP header sizes and allow for more efficient communications on the network; however, it may result in increased CPU utilization on Cisco and other routers.

   ☒ **B, C,** and **D** are incorrect. sRTP provides security for RTP data streams. RTCP is the RTP Control Protocol and is used to monitor and report on RTP communications. RTSP is not defined in the RTP protocol suite.

9. ☑ **A** is correct. When UDP checksums are disabled, the headers can be compressed to as small as 2 bytes.

   ☒ **B, C,** and **D** are incorrect. 4 bytes is the value when UDP checksums are enabled. 12 bytes is the size of the uncompressed RTP header by itself. 40 bytes is the size of the IP/UDP/RTP header combination when uncompressed.

10. ☑ **D** is correct. The compression is based mostly on the fact that many header values are static (they remain the same from packet to packet). Additionally, some header values are redundant (for example, redundant between RTP and IP), and others can be recomputed instead of transferred.

    ☒ **A, B,** and **C** are incorrect. ZIP and Arj algorithms are not used. cRTP is lossless compression.

11. ☑ **C** is correct. The **ip rtp header-compression** command is used to enable cRTP. By default, all RTP traffic will be compressed with this command.

    ☒ **A, B,** and **D** are incorrect. The **ip rtp compression connections 16** command sets the number of allowed cRTP connections. No such **rtp header-compression on** command exists in the Cisco IOS. The **ip rtp header-compression passive** command would only compress RTP packets on interfaces where received packets are compressed, which is not the desired result.

**12.** ☑ **A** and **C** are correct. The **ip rtp compression connections** 10 command limits the number of cRTP connections to 10. The **ip rtp header-compression passive** command ensures that only RTP packets sent on interfaces that receive compressed packets will be compressed.

☒ **B** and **D** are incorrect. The **ip rtp header-compression** command would compress all packets going out the interface, which is not the desired result. The **ip rtp compression limit 10** command is not a valid Cisco IOS command.

**13.** ☑ **B** is correct. The secure RTP (sRTP) protocol is a profile extension enabling security for RTP data streams and RTCP communications.

☒ **A**, **C**, and **D** are incorrect. cRTP provides compression for RTP data streams. RTSP is not defined as relating to RTP, but is a streaming protocol for multimedia streaming. DES (the Digital Encryption Standard) is an encryption algorithm.

**14.** ☑ **C** is correct. The Advanced Encryption Standard (AES) is the default encryption algorithm used in sRTP communications.

☒ **A**, **B**, and **D** are incorrect. DES is not used by default in sRTP, though an application may extend the RTP protocol to use the DES encryption algorithm. RC4 and Blowfish are not used by default with sRTP either.

**15.** ☑ **A** and **B** are correct. Confidentiality is provided through encryption; however, the sRTP standard does allow for a null encryption algorithm, which would result in no confidentiality. Authentication is provided through the use of integrity checks with HMAC-SHA1.

☒ **C** and **D** are incorrect. Physical security is a reference to the measures you use to monitor and protect the physical environment within which your network operates. sRTP provides no measures to assist with physical security. Biometrics may be used to authenticate to a VoIP system, but sRTP provides no direct interaction with such security solutions.

# LAB ANSWER

Answers may vary, but in most networks cRTP would be used only on the WAN links. The reason for this decision is simple: while cRTP allows for more efficient network utilization, it causes processor overhead in the routers. On low-bandwidth WAN links the trade-off is worth it. On fast connections such as 100 Mbps or 1 Gbps it's usually not worth the processor cost.

# 6

# H.323

> *During the summer of 1968, representatives from the initial*
> *four sites met several times to discuss the HOST software and*
> *initial experiments on the network.*
>
> —RFC 1, *referencing the first four sites of the ARPA Network,*
> *which eventually became the Internet.*

While RTP is the core protocol behind all VoIP communications, it does not provide management features required to initiate a call, manage a call, or terminate a call. For these actions, another protocol must be used. The primary VoIP call management protocols are H.323, SIP, MGCP, and SCCP. This chapter presents the H.323 protocol suite, and the next two chapters will cover SIP, MGCP, and SCCP. The Internet has come a long way since the first four sites were connected to the tiny little ARPA (Advanced Research Projects Agency) Network, and now we can use protocols like H.323, SIP, MGCP, and SCCP to have a phone conversation across the Internet of thousands, even millions, of networks.

## CERTIFICATION OBJECTIVE 6.01

# 642-436: Describe H.323

Unlike RTP, which is defined in a single RFC and updated as a single protocol, H.323 is a standard that encompasses many protocols. Much as with TCP/IP, we often refer to H.323 as a protocol suite because multiple protocols are defined under the H.323 umbrella. H.323 is a standard that defines the components (roles and devices) and protocols for multimedia communications over IP or packet networks. The multimedia communications include VoIP as well as real-time video or data (such as video conferencing services). In this section, you will learn about the protocol suite and the devices that function on an H.323 network.

## H.323 Protocol Suite

The H.323 protocol suite includes protocols for three primary purposes. The first is endpoint or terminal control and management. These protocols allow you to set up a call and manage the features available for that call. The second is the audio and video protocols. These protocols include the codecs used to encode and possibly compress the call data. The third set of protocols is used for data communications, and they are not covered in detail here. These protocols allow for the transfer of data files and information, and they use their own proprietary Layer 4 solution (T.123). Figure 6-1 depicts the H.323 protocol suite in detail.

It is important that you understand the basic purpose of each protocol. The following list should help you remember what each protocol is used for and the role played in a VoIP network:

- ■ **IP**   The Internet Protocol (IP) is the Layer 3 protocol used on all VoIP networks; hence, the "IP" in "VoIP." IP is used to transport the TCP and UDP packets across the routed network or across the LAN segment. IP is used in both routed and non-routed networks.

- ■ **TCP**   When the upper-layer protocol requires delivery verification, the Transport Control Protocol (TCP) is used. For H.323, TCP is used for the initial call setup with H.225.0 (or H.225 for short) and H.245.

- ■ **UDP**   When the upper-layer protocol does not require delivery verification, the User Datagram Protocol (UDP) is used. For H.323, UDP is used for H.225 RAS messages, RTCP packets, and the actual data streams (audio or video encoded packets).

**FIGURE 6-1**

H.323 protocol suite

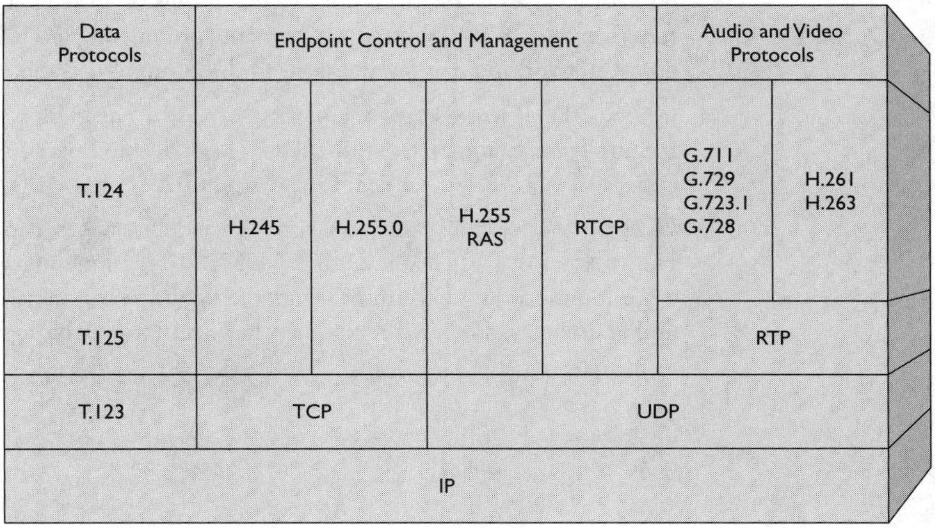

| Data Protocols | Endpoint Control and Management | | | | Audio and Video Protocols | |
|---|---|---|---|---|---|---|
| T.124 | H.245 | H.255.0 | H.255 RAS | RTCP | G.711 G.729 G.723.1 G.728 | H.261 H.263 |
| T.125 | | | | | RTP | |
| T.123 | TCP | | UDP | | | |
| IP | | | | | | |

- **H.245**   The control signaling between H.323 endpoints (terminals) is performed with H.245. Control signaling includes capabilities or features exchange, flow-control messaging, initiating and terminating of logical channels for media streams, and other general commands or notifications. In Cisco VoIP networks, the key utilization of H.245 is in feature communications.

- **H.225**   The initial connection between two H.323 endpoints is achieved using H.225. H.225 protocol messages are exchanged on the call-signaling channel that is opened between the endpoints or between the endpoint and a gatekeeper when H.323 gatekeepers are in use.

- **H.225 RAS**   The H.225 Registration, Admission, and Status (RAS) is used to transfer messages between endpoints and gatekeepers. Registration, admission control, status messages, bandwidth changes, and call-termination procedures are all handled by H.225 RAS. H.225 RAS is typically used only when an H.323 gatekeeper is present on the VoIP network.

- **RTP**   The Real-time Transport Protocol (RTP) is used to transport the actual voice data on an H.323 VoIP network. RTP uses UTP for communications. Payload identification, timestamps, delivering monitoring, and sequence numbering are all provided by RTP.

- **RTCP**   The Real-time Transport Control Protocol (RTCP) is used for control services in relation to RTP. The provision of feedback is the primary function of RTCP. Quality measurements provided by RTCP can be used to adjust networking communications for QoS improvements.

- **G.7xx**   The G.7xx series of codecs are specified as ITU-T standards. H.323 terminals must support at least the G.711 codec and may support additional codecs such as G.722, G.723, G.728, and G.729.

- **H.26x**   When H.323 terminals provide video services, they will use the H.26x series of ITU-T standards. The H.261 recommendation is required as a minimum for H.323 terminals supporting video communications. H.263 and H.264 are additional recommendations that may be supported by H.323 terminals.

In addition to these protocols, the H.323 VoIP network will use several different
device types. These devices are covered in the following section.

## H.323 Devices

Several devices may be used on an H.323 network. The H.323 standard suggests four
primary devices:

- Terminals
- Gateways
- Gatekeepers
- Multipoint Control Units (MCUs)

### Terminals

Terminals are the devices or software applications that communicate with each
other using the H.323 protocols. A terminal can be a unique device, such as a Cisco
IP phone, or it can be a desktop or laptop computer running a software-based H.323
terminal, such as a Cisco SoftPhone. H.323 terminals must support a minimum set
of requirements to qualify as a standards-based terminal. These requirements are

- H.245 support for terminal capability or feature exchange and the creation of
  media communication channels
- H.225 support for call signaling and call setup
- H.225 RAS support for registration, admission control, and bandwidth
  management when a gatekeeper is present

■ RTP/RTCP support for audio and/or video packet sequencing and transfer

■ G.711 codec support for audio encoding

The requirement for H.225 RAS is based on the fact that all H.323 terminals must use the H.323 gatekeeper when one is present on the network. H.323 is a peer-to-peer protocol that also supports centralized management and call setup through a gatekeeper. If the gatekeeper is used, an architecture more like a client/server model is in place for call setup (though the audio streams still travel directly from one terminal to another and do not pass through the gatekeeper). If a gatekeeper is not used, the H.323 terminals work in a pure peer-to-peer mode.

In addition to the minimum requirements, several optional items may be supported. Among these optional items are

■ Additional G.7xx codecs

■ T.120 data-conferencing solutions

■ Multipoint Control Unit support for conferencing

## Gateways

An H.323 gateway is intended to provide protocol translation for call setup and for communications with different networks. In general, gateways connect two different network types so that communications can occur between them. An H.323 gateway, for example, may connect a local VoIP network with the PSTN through T1, analog, or ISDN lines.

Gateways are covered in more detail in Chapter 14.

## Gatekeepers

Gatekeepers are like the central brain of an H.323 network. When you do not use a gatekeeper, all Cisco Communications Manager Express (CME) routers must know where all the other CME routers are located. When you use a gatekeeper, it keeps a central database of the CME routers and the extensions they can access. This greatly simplifies dial-peer configuration and the general VoIP network setup. However, it also introduces a potential central point of failure in the gatekeeper. For this reason, some form of redundancy should be provided so that the VoIP network can continue to function should a hardware or software failure occur.

Like gateways, gatekeepers are covered in more detail in Chapter 14.

### Multipoint Control Units

The MCU provides support for multiuser conferencing when three or more uses are involved in the conference. The MCU manages the resources used in a conference, and it also negotiates for the best codecs within a call setup. In the Cisco world, an MCU will require DSP (digital signal processor) resources in order to combine the audio signals. The MCU receives audio signals from all participants and combines them into a single outgoing audio signal. The result is a conference call.

While the gateway, gatekeeper, and MCU are defined as logically separate components within the H.323 specification, they may be implemented by a single device. For example, a single Cisco ISR can act as the gateway and the gatekeeper for your VoIP network. As VoIP networks grow larger, they are more likely to implement the different H.323 components as separate physical entities.

*Remember that the four key components of an H.323 network are the terminals, gateways, gatekeepers, and MCUs. Also remember that the gatekeeper is optional, but when it is implemented all terminals must use it for call processing.*

## CERTIFICATION OBJECTIVE 6.02

# 640-460: Describe H.323 Signaling Protocols

Now that you understand the parts that make up the whole of H.323, it's time to explore how H.323 calls are processed. In this section, you will learn about the way in which calls are processed using the H.225.0 protocol and the H.245 protocol. These two protocols form the core of H.323 VoIP networking.

## H.323 Call Setup

As a VoIP administrator, it's important that you understand how a call is actually set up and managed with the H.323 protocol suite. The process begins with the H.225 protocol. When you have a VoIP phone connected to a Cisco switch, which is connected to an H.323 gateway (a Cisco IOS router), which is connected to another switch, which is connected to another VoIP phone, some protocol must be utilized to start the communications. Just as you pick up your handset with your traditional PSTN line phone and place a call using PSTN signaling methods, you must have some method for signaling on the VoIP network. This is the role of H.225.

When you lift the VoIP phone handset and dial another VoIP phone, the H.225 protocol is used to send the ring notice to the remote phone and to send the response to the original phone. After this initial call is set up and the receiver picks up the handset, the H.245 protocol kicks in to negotiate the features or capabilities of the call. These features would include, most commonly, the codec to be utilized. Assuming both phones agree on the G.711 codec, the conversation can begin using this codec.

Now, it's important that you understand that all of this takes place very rapidly. Even though the features are not negotiated until the called party lifts the handset, this negotiation happens so rapidly that the called party can begin speaking immediately, and the audio will still get through the VoIP network to the calling party. This reality exists because our networks think in milliseconds (or nanoseconds) while we think in seconds or minutes.

---

### exam
### ⓦatch

*If the feature negotiation within H.245 fails, the Cisco IP phones may simply play a busy signal on the speakers of both the calling party and the called* *party. In most cases, the two phones are not properly configured to support a shared codec.*

---

## H.323 Call Signaling Phases

According to the H.323 recommendation (what the ITU-T calls a "standard"), call processing or signaling occurs in five phases. The five phases are referenced as Phase A through Phase E, with the final phase being call termination. The following list outlines what occurs in each of the five phases:

■ **Phase A: Call Setup** The call setup transpires using H.225.0. While bandwidth requests are not required at this phase, the H.323 standard suggests that they happen at the earliest phase. When no gatekeeper is present, a simple four-step process is used to establish channels for Phase B. When a gatekeeper is present, eight steps are required because the gatekeeper acts as an intermediary or proxy between the two parties.

- **Phase B: Initial Communication and Capability Exchange**   Phase A establishes an H.245 control channel, and that control channel is used for capability (feature) exchange during Phase B. Terminals communicate both transmit and receive capabilities. The receive capabilities limit what can be sent to that terminal. The transmit capabilities limit what can be sent from that terminal. The primary capabilities communicated are the codec or codecs supported for the call.

- **Phase C: Establishment of Audio/Visual Communication**   Once the capabilities are negotiated Phase C can begin, and the first step is to establish logical channels for the information streams. The standard specifies that the audio and video streams should be communicated using an unreliable protocol (such as RTP and UDP) and that the data transmitted using H.245 itself should be transmitted using a reliable protocol (such as TCP), as depicted in Figure 6-1.

- **Phase D: Call Services**   During the Call Services phase, the active VoIP call is taking place; however, administrative actions may still be required. For example, an endpoint may request a bandwidth change. If a new bandwidth is assigned, the endpoint will communicate this new allowance to the other endpoint using H.245. Additionally, H.225.0 Information Request/ Information Request Response messages may be sent for status updates in this phase.

- **Phase E: Call Termination**   The final phase is Call Termination. The H.323 specification defines two call-termination procedures. The first might be considered a dirty termination in that the closing of media channels is implied rather than explicitly requested. The second includes explicit requests for the closing of media channels. When a network includes a gatekeeper, the endpoints must send an H.225.0 Disengage Request message to the gatekeeper. The gatekeeper responds with a Disengage Confirm message.

In addition to the standard phases of H.323 call processing, failure handling is specified in the standard. If an endpoint detects a failure and wishes to determine if the remote endpoint is still functioning and connected to the network, it may use the H.245 roundTripDelayRequest message as a test. If the endpoint responds, it is still active. If a transport error occurs, the infrastructure may have failed, or the endpoint is no longer connected to the network.

In the end, H.323 can be a reliable protocol for your Cisco VoIP network. It provides both VoIP and Video over IP functionality and includes conferencing support as well. For more information about the H.323 protocol itself, consider visiting either of the following web sites:

- http://en.wikipedia.org/wiki/H.323
- www.itu.int/rec/T-REC-H.323-200606-S/en

## CERTIFICATION SUMMARY

In this chapter, you learned about the H.323 protocol and its various components and functions. You learned that H.323 is an umbrella protocol that includes the H.225 and H.245 protocols at its core. H.323 networks still rely on RTP for audio stream delivery and only provide the call setup and management within the H.225 and H.245 protocols respectively. You also learned about the four primary H.323 components: The terminal is the VoIP phone in an H.323 VoIP network. The gateway is a device that connects the H.323 network to other H.323 networks or to different network types, such as the PSTN. The gatekeeper is an optional component that centralizes much of the management of the H.323 network. The MCU is a device that allows for conference calls and video conferences to transport.

# TWO-MINUTE DRILL

### 642-436: Describe H.323

❑ H.323 is not a specific protocol definition as much as it is an aggregation of other protocols and a specification for how they can interoperate.

❑ H.323 specifies H.225.0 for call setup.

❑ H.323 specifies H.245 for feature negotiation and call management.

❑ H.323 still depends on RTP and RTCP for the voice data transfer.

❑ H.225.0 RAS is used to communicate with an H.323 gatekeeper.

❑ In H.323 terminology a VoIP phone is a terminal or an endpoint.

❑ A gateway may also be considered an endpoint on an H.323 network.

❑ H.323 gateways provide connectivity to different H.323 networks or to completely different network types.

❑ The H.323 gatekeeper is an optional component; however, if it is implemented, it must be used by all terminals on the network.

❑ The Multipoint Control Unit (MCU) is used to aggregate multiple incoming streams into a single outgoing stream for audio and/or video conferencing.

### 640-460: Describe H.323 Signaling Protocols

❑ When you first pick up a Cisco VoIP handset and dial another extension, the H.225.0 protocol is used to set up the call with the remote VoIP phone.

❑ When you pick up a ringing handset, the H.245 protocol is used to negotiate capabilities (features) between your phone and the calling phone.

❑ The H.323 call process is broken into five phases in the H.323 recommendation document.

❑ If an endpoint detects a failure, it may send an H.245 roundTripDelayRequest as a test.

❑ During Phase A, H.225.0 is used.

❑ During Phase B, H.245 is used

❑ During Phases C–E, both H.225.0 and H.245 may be used.

# SELF TEST

The following questions will help you measure your understanding of the material presented in this chapter. Read all the choices carefully because there might be more than one correct answer. Choose all correct answers for each question.

## 642-436: Describe H.323

1. What H.323 network device or software provides video and/or audio conferencing?
   A. Multipoint Control Unit
   B. Gatekeeper
   C. Gateway
   D. Terminal

2. What H.323 network device provides RAS services?
   A. Multipoint Control Unit
   B. Gatekeeper
   C. Gateway
   D. Terminal

3. What H.323 device is a VoIP telephone or a video conferencing endpoint?
   A. Multipoint Control Unit
   B. Gatekeeper
   C. Gateway
   D. Terminal

4. What is the primary function of an H.323 gateway?
   A. Directing H.323 calls to the proper endpoint or gatekeeper
   B. Providing RAS services to the H.323 network
   C. Providing audio conferencing services
   D. Acting as a VoIP telephone

5. What is the best description of the H.323 recommendation?
   A. H.323 is a protocol that defines the transport of VoIP data.
   B. H.323 is a specification that recommends the use of multiple other protocols for VoIP network signaling and management.
   C. H.323 is a protocol that allows for Internet e-mail.
   D. H.323 is the protocol that performs the RAS signaling when a gatekeeper is in use.

**6.** When a gatekeeper is installed in an H.323 network, what protocol is uniquely used to communicate with the gatekeeper?

A. H.245

B. H.225.0 RAS

C. RTP

D. RTCP

**7.** In addition to the VoIP phones, what other device may be considered an endpoint in an H.323 network?

A. MCU

B. Gatekeeper

C. Gateway

D. Switch

**8.** What protocol is used to transport the audio and video streams in an H.323 network?

A. H.225.0

B. H.245

C. H.225.0 RAS

D. RTP

**9.** What protocol is used for capability or feature negotiation in an H.323 network?

A. H.245

B. H.225.0 RAS

C. H.225.0

D. RTCP

**10.** You have implemented an H.323 gatekeeper. Which devices on the H.323 network must be able to communicate with this gatekeeper according to the H.323 recommendation?

A. All registered VoIP phones

B. All PBX systems

C. All PSTN phones

D. All analog phones

**11.** You are implementing an H.323 network. To what networks will H.323 gateways connect and route or receive calls? (Choose all that apply.)

A. Other H.323 networks

B. Non-H.323 voice networks

C. ARPA Network (ARPANET)

D. Commodore 64 networks

## 640-460: Describe H.323 Signaling Protocols

12. You pick up the handset on your Cisco VoIP phone. You hear a dial tone and dial the extension of another VoIP phone on the network. The network uses the H.323 protocol. What protocol is used to initiate the connection with the remote VoIP phone?

    A. H.245

    B. H.225.0

    C. RTP

    D. RTCP

13. Your Cisco VoIP phone rings. You pick up the handset. The network uses the H.323 protocol. What protocol is used to determine the codec that will be used for the call?

    A. H.245

    B. H.225.0

    C. RTP

    D. RTCP

14. If an H.323 endpoint detects a failure, what may it send on the H.323 network to test the connectivity of the remote terminal?

    A. H.245 roundTripDelayRequest

    B. H.225 roundTripDelayRequest

    C. H.245 roundTripPINGRequest

    D. H.225 roundTripPINGRequest

15. How many phases are involved in call processing according to the H.323 recommendation?

    A. 1

    B. 3

    C. 5

    D. 7

# LAB QUESTION

You are implementing an H.323 VoIP network using Cisco equipment. You want to ensure that all VoIP phones must be registered with the network in order to communicate with any other phones on the network. You want to avoid configuring all extensions on all Cisco ISRs acting as H.323 gateways. How can you implement this network with central management in the simplest way?

# SELF TEST ANSWERS

## 642-436: Describe H.323

1. ☑ **A** is correct. The MCU (Multipoint Control Unit) provides audio/video conferencing. The MCU receives multiple incoming audio streams and combines them into one outgoing stream. It may also generate video streams of combined incoming streams into quadrants or some other video layout method for video conferencing; however, video conferencing is beyond the scope of this book or the CCNA Voice exams.

   ☒ **B**, **C**, and **D** are incorrect. The gatekeeper provides H.323 network access and call routing information. The gateway provides connectivity to other networks. The terminal is the VoIP phone.

2. ☑ **B** is correct. The gatekeeper utilizes H.225.0 RAS messages and acts as a RAS service provider. The gatekeeper can provide H.323 network registration (R) services, admission (A) or access services, and call monitoring or status (S) services.

   ☒ **A**, **C**, and **D** are incorrect. The MCU provides audio/video conferencing services. The gateway provides connectivity to other networks. The terminal is the VoIP phone.

3. ☑ **D** is correct. The terminal is the VoIP phone. The terminal may be a hardware-based phone such as the Cisco 7960G, or it may be a software-based phone such as the Cisco IP SoftPhone for Windows.

   ☒ **A**, **B**, and **C** are incorrect. The MCU provides audio/video conferencing services. The gatekeeper provides RAS services to the H.323 network. The gateway provides connectivity to other networks.

4. ☑ **A** is correct. The gateway directs H.323 calls to the proper endpoint or gatekeeper on the same network or on another network. The primary purpose, then, is the direction or routing of calls.

   ☒ **B**, **C**, and **D** are incorrect. The gatekeeper provides RAS services to the H.323 network. The MCU provides audio conferencing services. The terminal acts as the VoIP phone.

5. ☑ **B** is correct. The H.323 recommendation (or standard) is not a protocol specification in and of itself. Instead, H.323 references other standards such as the H.225.0 recommendation for call setup and the H.245 recommendation for feature negotiation. It also recommends the use of RTP and RTCP for audio and video data transfer in media networks.

   ☒ **A**, **C**, and **D** are incorrect. H.323 does not define the transport of VoIP data; the transport is defined in the RTP and RTCP standards. H.323 is not a protocol for sending or receiving Internet e-mail; SMTP is a standard for such purposes. H.323 does not actually perform the RAS signaling; H.225.0 RAS performs the RAS signaling and is referenced by H.323.

6. ☑ **B** is correct. The H.225.0 RAS (Registration, Admission, and Status) protocol is used for communications with the gatekeeper.

   ☒ **A**, **C**, and **D** are incorrect. H.245 is used for feature negotiation and may be used between multiple components on the H.323 network; H.225.0 RAS, however, is uniquely used when a gatekeeper is on the network. RTP and RTCP are used between endpoints to transfer and monitor VoIP data streams.

7. ☑ **C** is correct. The H.323 gateway is also considered an endpoint on the network. In fact, Cisco ISRs, which often act as gateways, can even place a call to a VoIP phone for testing purposes.

   ☒ **A**, **B**, and **D** are incorrect. The MCU, gatekeeper, and switch are not considered endpoints because they facilitate communications but are not intended as the endpoint of the communication.

8. ☑ **D** is correct. The Real-time Transport Protocol (RTP) is used to transport the audio streams in VoIP networks regardless of the signaling protocol. With H.323, SIP, or SCCP, RTP is still used for the actual VoIP data transfer.

   ☒ **A**, **B**, and **C** are incorrect. H.225.0 is used for call setup and has no facility to transfer the data itself. It will create channels within which the RTP protocol can operate. H.245 provides the feature negotiation and will determine the codec used within the RTP stream, but RTP is still the transport protocol. H.225.0 RAS is used when a gatekeeper is on the H.323 network, but RTP is the data transport protocol for the voice data.

9. ☑ **A** is correct. H.245 is used for feature negotiation during Phase B of the five-phase H.323 call-processing structure.

   ☒ **B**, **C**, and **D** are incorrect. H.225.0 RAS is not used for feature negotiation, but for access to the H.323 network when a gatekeeper is installed on the network. H.225.0 is used to set up the call in Phase A of the five-phase process. The Real-time Transport Control Protocol (RTCP) is used to monitor the RTP communication streams.

**10.** ☑ **A** is correct. When an H.323 gatekeeper is enabled on the VoIP network, all registered VoIP phones must use the gatekeeper to establish entry to the network and to place calls on the network.

☒ **B**, **C**, and **D** are incorrect. PBX systems may operate within themselves without requiring access to the H.323 gatekeeper; though the gatekeeper may be used to gain entry to the H.323 network through an H.323 gateway. PSTN phones do not require access to the gatekeeper. Analog phones are either PSTN or PBX phones or are connected to FXS ports on Cisco gateways, and they can communicate with each other without requiring access to the gatekeeper.

**11.** ☑ **A** and **B** are correct. H.323 gateways may connect to other H.323 networks or to non-H.323 voice networks such as PBX systems or the PSTN.

☒ **C** and **D** are incorrect. H.323 gateways do not connect to the ARPANET, since no computers connect to it anymore, and it has evolved into the modern Internet. Because the author loves Commodore 64 computers, he has to find a place to mention them in each book. They are not valid networked computing devices on modern networks (sadly).

## 640-460: Describe H.323 Signaling Protocols

**12.** **B** is correct. The H.225.0 protocol is used to initiate the call. It sends a setup message to the remote phone (or the gatekeeper) to begin the call setup. The actions taken by the H.225.0 protocol represent Phase A of the five-phase H.323 call setup procedures.

☒ **A**, **C**, and **D** are incorrect. H.245 is used when the called party picks up the handset. RTP is used once the features are negotiated and the audio stream begins. RTCP is used alongside RTP to monitor the data stream.

**13.** ☑ **A** is correct. When you answer an incoming call, the H.245 protocol is used to establish features or capabilities. This action set represents Phase B in the five-phase H.323 call processing steps.

☒ **B**, **C**, and **D** are incorrect. H.225.0 is used to set up the call before the called party answers. RTP is used once the features are negotiated and the audio stream begins. RTCP is used alongside RTP to monitor the data stream.

**14.** ☑ **A** is correct. The H.245 roundTripDelayRequest can be sent as a test. If no response is received or a transport error is detected, the remote endpoint is assumed to be disconnected.

☒ **B**, **C**, and **D** are incorrect. No such messages exist in the H.225 protocol, and the roundTripPINGRequest message does not exist in the H.245 protocol either.

15. ☑ **C** is correct. The H.323 recommendation specifies five phases for call processing. Phase A provides the initial call setup using H.225.0. Phase B provides the feature negotiation using H.245. Phase C establishes the RTP streams for data transfer. Phase D monitors the call and provides services during the call. Phase E provides call-termination services.

☒ **A, B,** and **D** are incorrect. The H.323 call processing steps are broken into five phases; therefore, 1, 3, and 7 are incorrect.

# LAB ANSWER

The simplest solution is to implement an H.323 gatekeeper. When you implement a gatekeeper, all the gateways look to the gatekeeper for call-routing information. Without a gatekeeper, you must configure the extension blocks, such as 4... or 3..., on each of the gateways. If you have ten gateways, each gateway must know of the nine other gateways and the extension blocks they manage. The configuration can become quite large. To avoid this complexity, implement a gatekeeper and simply point the gateways to the gatekeeper for this information.

# 7

## SIP

> *The minimum length for a NWG [Network Working Group] note is one sentence.*
>
> —*Steve Crocker, RFC 3, 1969, when defining the documentation standards for RFCs*

T he Session Initiation Protocol (SIP) is an application layer control or signaling protocol used in media networks. It is a primary protocol used in modern VoIP implementations. Like H.323, SIP is a peer-to-peer protocol, and it may utilize a proxy server for communications with devices on different LAN segments or on entirely different networks. In this chapter, you'll learn about the basics of the SIP protocol and about the signaling procedures used when SIP is implemented. The beauty of SIP, like the beauty of RFC-based Internet standards in general, is that it is simple in its implementation, yet it achieves seemingly complicated results.

## CERTIFICATION OBJECTIVE 7.01

# 642-436: Describe SIP

The Session Initiation Protocol (SIP) is a modern alternative to H.323. While H.323 was first developed in 1996, SIP began development in that same year and was finalized in 1999. The current RFC for SIP (RFC 3261) was finalized in 2002. Because of SIP's later development, the authors were able to learn from H.323 and incorporate the good components already there. In this section, you will learn about the basics of the SIP protocol. You can read any RFC online at www.ietf.org. In fact, you can go directly to an RFC with the following URL syntax:

www.ietf.org/rfc/rfc####.txt

Just replace #### with the number of the RFC. For example, to view RFC 3261, navigate to www.ietf.org/rfc/rfc3261.txt.

SIP was created by the Internet Engineering Task Force (IETF). SIP is built from several other protocols and adds new features as well. For example, SIP builds on HTTP, SMTP, DNS, and RTP. In this section, you'll learn some key SIP definitions, investigate the features of SIP, and explore the common components in a SIP VoIP network.

# Key SIP Definitions

The SIP RFC provides several key definitions to assist in your understanding of the SIP protocol. The following definitions are provided in RFC 3261, which is the SIP standard document. As you read through the definitions, know that the 1*xx* and 2*xx* references (among other such notations) refer to response codes based on the HTTP/1.1 response codes. These same codes, where relevant, are used by the SIP protocols. The following text is quoted from RFC 3261 with permission. (Copyright © The Internet Society 2003. All Rights Reserved.)

❑ **Address-of-Record**   An address-of-record (AOR) is a SIP or SIPS URI that points to a domain with a location service that can map the URI to another URI where the user might be available. Typically, the location service is populated through registrations. An AOR is frequently thought of as the "public address" of the user.

❑ **Back-to-Back User Agent**   A back-to-back user agent (B2BUA) is a logical entity that receives a request and processes it as a user agent server (UAS). In order to determine how the request should be answered, it acts as a user agent client (UAC) and generates requests. Unlike a proxy server, it maintains dialog state and must participate in all requests sent on the dialogs it has established. Since it is a concatenation of a UAC and UAS, no explicit definitions are needed for its behavior.

❑ **Call**   A call is an informal term that refers to some communication between peers, generally set up for the purposes of a multimedia conversation.

❑ **Call Leg**   Another name for a dialog [31]; no longer used in this specification.

❑ **Call Stateful**   A proxy is call stateful if it retains state for a dialog from the initiating INVITE to the terminating BYE request. A call stateful proxy is always transaction stateful, but the converse is not necessarily true.

❑ **Client**   A client is any network element that sends SIP requests and receives SIP responses. Clients may or may not interact directly with a human user. User agent clients and proxies are clients.

❑ **Conference**   A multimedia session (see below) that contains multiple participants.

❑ **Core**   Core designates the functions specific to a particular type of SIP entity, i.e., specific to either a stateful or stateless proxy, a user agent or registrar. All cores, except those for the stateless proxy, are transaction users.

❑ **Dialog**   A dialog is a peer-to-peer SIP relationship between two UAs that persists for some time. A dialog is established by SIP messages, such as a 2xx response to an INVITE request. A dialog is identified by a call identifier, local tag, and a remote tag. A dialog was formerly known as a call leg in RFC 2543.

❑ **Downstream**   A direction of message forwarding within a transaction that refers to the direction that requests flow from the user agent client to user agent server.

❑ **Final Response**   A response that terminates a SIP transaction, as opposed to a provisional response that does not. All 2xx, 3xx, 4xx, 5xx and 6xx responses are final.

❑ **Header**   A header is a component of a SIP message that conveys information about the message. It is structured as a sequence of header fields.

❑ **Header Field**   A header field is a component of the SIP message header. A header field can appear as one or more header field rows. Header field rows consist of a header field name and zero or more header field values. Multiple header field values on a given header field row are separated by commas. Some header fields can only have a single header field value, and as a result, always appear as a single header field row.

❑ **Header Field Value**   A header field value is a single value; a header field consists of zero or more header field values.

❑ **Home Domain**   The domain providing service to a SIP user. Typically, this is the domain present in the URI in the address-of-record of a registration.

❑ **Informational Response**   Same as a provisional response.

❑ **Initiator, Calling Party, Caller**   The party initiating a session (and dialog) with an INVITE request. A caller retains this role from the time it sends the initial INVITE that established a dialog until the termination of that dialog.

❑ **Invitation**   An INVITE request.

❑ **Invitee, Invited User, Called Party, Callee**   The party that receives an INVITE request for the purpose of establishing a new session. A callee retains this role from the time it receives the INVITE until the termination of the dialog established by that INVITE.

❑ **Location Service**   A location service is used by a SIP redirect or proxy server to obtain information about a callee's possible location(s). It contains a list of bindings of address-of-record keys to zero or more contact addresses. The bindings can be created and removed in many ways; this specification defines a REGISTER method that updates the bindings.

❑ **Loop**   A request that arrives at a proxy, is forwarded, and later arrives back at the same proxy. When it arrives the second time, its Request-URI is identical to the first time, and other header fields that affect proxy operation are unchanged, so that the proxy would make the same processing decision on the request it made the first time. Looped requests are errors, and the procedures for detecting them and handling them are described by the protocol.

❑ **Loose Routing**   A proxy is said to be loose routing if it follows the procedures defined in this specification for processing of the Route header field. These procedures separate the destination of the request (present in the Request-URI) from the set of proxies that need to be visited along the way (present in the Route header field). A proxy compliant to these mechanisms is also known as a loose router.

❑ **Message**   Data sent between SIP elements as part of the protocol. SIP messages are either requests or responses.

❑ **Method**   The method is the primary function that a request is meant to invoke on a server. The method is carried in the request message itself. Example methods are INVITE and BYE.

❑ **Outbound Proxy**   A proxy that receives requests from a client, even though it may not be the server resolved by the Request-URI. Typically, a UA is manually configured with an outbound proxy, or can learn about one through auto-configuration protocols.

❑ **Parallel Search**   In a parallel search, a proxy issues several requests to possible user locations upon receiving an incoming request. Rather than issuing one request and then waiting for the final response before issuing the next request as in a sequential search, a parallel search issues requests without waiting for the result of previous requests.

❑ **Provisional Response**   A response used by the server to indicate progress, but that does not terminate a SIP transaction. 1xx responses are provisional, other responses are considered final.

❑ **Proxy, Proxy Server**   An intermediary entity that acts as both a server and a client for the purpose of making requests on behalf of other clients. A proxy server primarily plays the role of routing, which means its job is to ensure that a request is sent to another entity "closer" to the targeted user. Proxies are also useful for enforcing policy (for example, making sure a user is allowed to make a call). A proxy interprets, and, if necessary, rewrites specific parts of a request message before forwarding it.

❑ **Recursion**   A client recurses on a 3xx response when it generates a new request to one or more of the URIs in the Contact header field in the response.

❑ **Redirect Server**   A redirect server is a user agent server that generates 3xx responses to requests it receives, directing the client to contact an alternate set of URIs.

❑ **Registrar**   A registrar is a server that accepts REGISTER requests and places the information it receives in those requests into the location service for the domain it handles.

❑ **Regular Transaction**   A regular transaction is any transaction with a method other than INVITE, ACK, or CANCEL.

❑ **Request**   A SIP message sent from a client to a server, for the purpose of invoking a particular operation.

❑ **Response**   A SIP message sent from a server to a client, for indicating the status of a request sent from the client to the server.

❑ **Ringback**   Ringback is the signaling tone produced by the calling party's application indicating that a called party is being alerted (ringing).

❑ **Route Set**   A route set is a collection of ordered SIP or SIPS URI which represent a list of proxies that must be traversed when sending a particular request. A route set can be learned, through headers like Record-Route, or it can be configured.

❑ **Server**   A server is a network element that receives requests in order to service them and sends back responses to those requests. Examples of servers are proxies, user agent servers, redirect servers, and registrars.

❑ **Sequential Search**   In a sequential search, a proxy server attempts each contact address in sequence, proceeding to the next one only after the previous has generated a final response. A 2xx or 6xx class final response always terminates a sequential search.

❑ **Session**   From the SDP specification: "A multimedia session is a set of multimedia senders and receivers and the data streams flowing from senders to receivers. A multimedia conference is an example of a multimedia session." (RFC 2327 [1]) (A session as defined for SDP can comprise one or more RTP sessions.) As defined, a callee can be invited several times, by different calls, to the same session. If SDP is used, a session is defined by the concatenation of the SDP user name, session id, network type, address type, and address elements in the origin field.

❑ **SIP Transaction**   A SIP transaction occurs between a client and a server and comprises all messages from the first request sent from the client to the server up to a final (non-1xx) response sent from the server to the client. If the request is INVITE and the final response is a non-2xx, the transaction also includes an ACK to the response. The ACK for a 2xx response to an INVITE request is a separate transaction.

❑ **Spiral**   A spiral is a SIP request that is routed to a proxy, forwarded onwards, and arrives once again at that proxy, but this time differs in a way that will result in a different processing decision than the original request. Typically, this means that the request's Request-URI differs from its previous arrival. A spiral is not an error condition, unlike a loop. A typical cause for this is call forwarding. A user calls joe@example.com. The example.com proxy forwards it to Joe's PC, which in turn, forwards it to bob@example.com. This request is proxied back to the example.com proxy. However, this is not a loop. Since the request is targeted at a different user, it is considered a spiral, and is a valid condition.

❑ **Stateful Proxy**   A logical entity that maintains the client and server transaction state machines defined by this specification during the processing of a request, also known as a transaction stateful proxy. The behavior of a stateful proxy is further defined in Section 16. A (transaction) stateful proxy is not the same as a call stateful proxy.

❑ **Stateless Proxy**   A logical entity that does not maintain the client or server transaction state machines defined in this specification when it processes requests. A stateless proxy forwards every request it receives downstream and every response it receives upstream.

❑ **Strict Routing**   A proxy is said to be strict routing if it follows the Route processing rules of RFC 2543 and many prior work in progress versions of this RFC. That rule caused proxies to destroy the contents of the

Request-URI when a Route header field was present. Strict routing behavior is not used in this specification, in favor of a loose routing behavior. Proxies that perform strict routing are also known as strict routers.

❑ **Target Refresh Request**   A target refresh request sent within a dialog is defined as a request that can modify the remote target of the dialog.

❑ **Transaction User (TU)**   The layer of protocol processing that resides above the transaction layer. Transaction users include the UAC core, UAS core, and proxy core.

❑ **Upstream**   A direction of message forwarding within a transaction that refers to the direction that responses flow from the user agent server back to the user agent client.

❑ **URL-encoded**   A character string encoded according to RFC 2396, Section 2.4 [5].

❑ **User Agent Client (UAC)**   A user agent client is a logical entity that creates a new request, and then uses the client transaction state machinery to send it. The role of UAC lasts only for the duration of that transaction. In other words, if a piece of software initiates a request, it acts as a UAC for the duration of that transaction. If it receives a request later, it assumes the role of a user agent server for the processing of that transaction.

❑ **UAC Core**   The set of processing functions required of a UAC that resides above the transaction and transport layers.

❑ **User Agent Server (UAS)**   A user agent server is a logical entity that generates a response to a SIP request. The response accepts, rejects, or redirects the request. This role lasts only for the duration of that transaction. In other words, if a piece of software responds to a request, it acts as a UAS for the duration of that transaction. If it generates a request later, it assumes the role of a user agent client for the processing of that transaction.

❑ **UAS Core**   The set of processing functions required at a UAS that resides above the transaction and transport layers.

❑ **User Agent (UA)**   A logical entity that can act as both a user agent client and user agent server.

## SIP Features

SIP uses text-based communications. Stated differently, the ASCII character set is used to communicate SIP messages. Because of this format, SIP is easier to analyze and understand than most other networking protocols. Instead of worrying about the number of bits in a header that represent specific data, we are looking at plain text that clearly indicates the meaning. The messages are still said to have headers, but the headers are in ASCII text format instead of binary bit format.

SIP is a simplified protocol when compared with the H.323. This simplification comes from the fact that SIP includes everything needed to establish the VoIP call instead of using one protocol for call setup (H.225.0 in H.323 networks) and another for feature negotiation (H.245 in H.323 networks). Many assume this always makes SIP the better choice; however, it could be argued that H.323's componentized nature makes it more flexible for implementation. Regardless of the side of the argument you take, you must understand the basics of both protocols for the Cisco CVOICE and CCNA Voice exams.

When it comes to SIP addressing (locating SIP endpoints), the addresses may look very familiar to you. For example, an address for Tom Carpenter may look like this:

SIP://Tom.Carpenter@SysEdCo.com

This address format is technically known as a URI (Uniform Resource Identifier). URIs provide a standard way to reference a resource on an internetwork. Here are some other examples of URIs:

HTTP://www.SysEdCo.com

FTP://ftp.download.com

Do you recognize these? You probably do because they are used all over the Internet. URIs work for HTTP, FTP, SIP, and even Gopher (although Gopher is not as popular today as it once was). You can also access a SIP device securely by using the secure SIP protocol (which takes advantage of TLS) with a URI like the following:

SIPS://Tom.Carpenter@SysEdCo.com

As you can see, even the addressing used in the SIP world is based on Internet standards. The most important feature of the SIP protocol that has allowed it to catapult beyond its predecessors to success seems to be this use of existing Internet standards whenever possible.

## SIP Components

When considering the components used in a SIP network, you must first realize that the network infrastructure must exist to support the SIP-specific components. In other words, SIP doesn't define DNS, but it will rely on DNS for name resolution. DNS must already exist in your network infrastructure or at least be accessible by the infrastructure.

In addition to the network infrastructure, the following basic SIP components should be understood. These components were defined in the previous list of definitions from the RFC; however, I will address them here with simplified real-world definitions and references to actual Cisco hardware and software that will play the roles of these components.

- **User agent (UA)**    When SIP is used to implement VoIP, the UA is the VoIP phone on the network. The UA may be hardware when a Cisco 7960G phone is used, for example, or it may be software when the Cisco IP SoftPhone is used. Additionally, a gateway may be considered a SIP UA because it communicates using the SIP protocol. Cisco VoIP phones act as a UAC and a UAS. The SIP standard suggests that the UAC and UAS roles are independent entities within the UA.

- **User agent client (UAC)**    The UAC is the UA that sends a request message using the SIP protocol. For example, the UA sending an INVITE message to begin a call is the UAC. The practical example is the Cisco IP phone that dials the call or starts the call.

- **User agent server (UAS)**    The UAS is the UA that responds to a request message using the SIP protocol. The practical example is the Cisco IP phone that receives the call.

- **Server**    A server, in the SIP protocol terminology, can be one of several components. It can be the UA when it is acting as the UAS. It can be a registrar, a proxy, or a redirect server.

- **SIP proxy**    The SIP proxy is the component that acts as a server to one UA (or another proxy) and a client to another UA (or another proxy). In the Cisco world, the SIP proxy is a Linux-based server running specialized software provided by Cisco. Do not confuse the Cisco SIP Proxy Server with the Cisco IOS ISR routers. The ISR routers can point to the SIP Proxy Server, but they cannot play the role of a proxy server.

- **Registrar**   The registrar server manages the registration database. The registration database contains the UA to address mappings for the local network. The Cisco SIP Proxy Server performs this function as well.

- **Redirect server**   The redirect server is the SIP server capable of directing a UA to the appropriate server with the information about the target when the target is not managed in the location database (managed by the location service). This functionality is implemented in the Cisco SIP Proxy Server as well.

- **Location service**   The location service uses the Lightweight Directory Access Protocol (LDAP) as the directory source for UA location. Microsoft's Active Directory also uses LDAP. The location service runs in the Cisco SIP Proxy Server and may use the external LDAP directory for name resolution.

The key factor to take from these component definitions is that the Cisco SIP Proxy Server accommodates the entire server role set required by SIP. The Cisco phones, which support SIP, act as the UAs on this network. Cisco ISR routers can point to a Cisco SIP Proxy Server, but they cannot act as a proxy server.

**Make sure you remember that Cisco's SIP Proxy Server is a Linux-based server and is not integrated into** **the ISR routers in the way that the call manager and dial-peers are integrated.**

## Cisco IOS SIP Support

As of Cisco IOS 12.1(1)T, Cisco supports a SIP gateway function in their voice-enabled ISRs. The SIP features were enhanced in IOS 12.1(3)T and subsequent releases. The SIP gateway feature allows the ISR to act as a SIP UA (both a UAC and a UAS). The gateway allows the SIP VoIP network to connect to traditional telephony networks and other VoIP networks, such as H.323.

Several features are provided by the Cisco SIP gateway, including:

- Support for ISDN, PRI, and CAS signaling.

- Support for multiple hardware interfaces including FXS, FXO, T1, and E1 interfaces.

- Implementation of SIP over both TCP and UDP.
- Support for DNS SIP name resolution.
- Implementation of RTP and RTCP for media transport.
- Support for SIP redirection messages with interaction with SIP proxy servers.
- Multiple codecs are supported for SIP calls, including G.711, G.723, G.726, G.728, and G.729.
- SIP signaling messages can be secured using IP Security (IPSec).
- Several feature extensions are implemented, including call hold, call transfer, calling number hiding, and support for third-party call control.

## CERTIFICATION OBJECTIVE 7.02

# 640-460: Describe SIP Signaling Protocols

In the preceding section, you learned about the basics of the SIP protocol, including its features and components. In this section, you will learn about SIP call processing. Specifically, you will learn about the layered architecture used in the SIP standard, the SIP headers, the methods used to communicate, and the SIP response categories.

## SIP Call Processing

To understand how SIP calls are made, you'll need to understand four basic concepts. First, you must understand the SIP layered architecture. Second, you should be aware of the SIP headers and how they operate. Third, you'll need to know about the SIP methods or commands. And finally, you'll need to understand the SIP responses and the categories of responses. Once you've understood these concepts at a basic level, you're ready to explore a typical SIP call process.

### SIP Layered Architecture

According to RFC 3261, SIP is structured as a layered protocol. The layering allows for the SIP operations to be explained in chunks or mostly independent processing stages. The SIP standard defines four layers:

- Syntax and encoding
- Transport

- Transaction
- Transaction user (TU)

Each layer is described in the following sections.

**Syntax and Encoding**   The syntax and encoding layer is considered layer one or the lowest layer. The Backus-Naur Form (BNF) grammar is used for SIP encoding. The BNF grammar is also defined in RFC 2234. You will not be required to understand the BNF grammar for your Cisco certifications; however, you can find more information in the BNF RFC and in Section 25 of the SIP RFC. Ultimately, this layer simply defines the format of the messages and commands that can be transmitted within SIP dialogs.

**Transport**   The second layer is the transport layer. This layer defines how a client sends requests and receives responses as well as how servers receive requests and send responses over a given network. The transport layer is described in detail in Section 18 of the SIP RFC. The key fact in relation to the transport layer is the requirement for the implementation of UDP and TCP. While SIP may use other protocols, a standards-compliant implementation must use UDP and TCP.

**Transaction**   The transaction layer is the third layer in the SIP architecture. This layer is responsible for application-layer retransmissions, matching up responses to requests, and processing application-layer timeouts. All tasks performed by UAs take place in a series of transactions. The transaction layer does not exist in all SIP elements. A SIP element is a component of SIP such as a UA, a proxy, or a registrar. SIP proxies come in two forms: stateless and stateful. A stateful proxy maintains the state or session between the UA and the remote element. A stateless proxy does not maintain this state. Stateless proxies do not include a transaction layer because they simply forward messages and do not maintain state for transaction processing.

**Transaction User (TU)**   The fourth and final layer is the transaction user (TU) layer. The TU layer is the logical entity that creates transactions for transport using the syntax and encoding specified in the SIP RFC. All SIP entities or elements, with the exception of the stateless proxy, qualify as a TU.

## SIP Headers

If you've ever performed HTTP debugging or analysis, then you'll be well prepared for understanding the SIP headers. SIP headers are very similar to HTTP headers in that they are constructed as ASCII text and not as binary numbers. With SIP, each header field includes a field name followed by a colon and then one or more field values. Multiple values can be entered separated by commas. The standard recommends that the field name be immediately followed by the colon, which should be immediately followed by a space, and then the field values as in the following example:

```
Field Name: Value
```

Header fields can also be entered on multiple lines by preceding the extra lines with a space of a tab. The following two examples would be interpreted identically:

```
Sentence: The cow jumped over the moon.
Sentence: The cow
  jumped over
  the moon.
```

Because the second example precedes the second and third lines with two spaces, they will be processed as the continuation of the value for the first line.

The order of the header fields is not strict in that the header fields can be entered in any desired order. However, the standard recommends that fields needed by proxy servers be entered toward the top of the list for faster retrieval and processing.

The SIP RFC specifies several header fields as required to be a valid SIP request. These fields include:

- **TO**   The TO header field specifies the logical recipient of the request. For example, 19376449090@marysville.oh.us or Tom.Carpenter@SysEdCo.com. The format of the field is as follows:

    To: Tom <sip:Tom.Carpenter@SysEdCo.com>

- **FROM**   The FROM header field indicates the sender of the request. It uses a similar format to the TO header field. The format of the field is as follows:

    FROM: Dale <sip:Dale.Thomas@SysEdCo.com>;tag=a48s

- **CSEQ**   The CSEQ header field is used to identify and order the transactions in the communication. It includes a sequence number and the method being processed. For example, for an INVITE method, the format is as follows:

    CSEQ: 5623 INVITE

- **CALL-ID**   The CALL-ID header field is the unique identifier that groups together a series of messages. It must be identical for all requests and responses sent by the UAs involved in the dialog. The format of this header is as follows:

    CALL-ID: f81d4fae-7dec-11d0-a765-00a0c91e6bf6@SysEdCo.com

- **MAX-FORWARDS** The MAX-FORWARDS header field is used to limit the number of connections or hops a request can pass through on the way to the destination. It is integer based and will be decremented by one at each stop in the path. If the MAX-FORWARDS value reaches 0 before arriving at its destination, the message is rejected with error 483 indicating too many hops. The format of the field is as follows:

  MAX-FORWARDS: 10

- **VIA** The VIA header field specifies the transport used for the transaction as well as the location where the response should be sent. The format is as follows:

  VIA: SIP/2.0/UDP srv1.SysEdCo.com;branchz9hG4bKhjhs8ass877

Additional optional headers include contact, accept, content-length, and proprietary header field specifications.

## SIP Methods

The SIP methods are the actions taken by the UAs or the requests they make. For example, when a SIP phone initiates a call, it uses the INVITE method to invite another SIP phone into the association. The SIP protocol supports several methods. These methods are listed in Table 7-1 with descriptions.

## SIP Responses

SIP responses are used to respond to methods or to report status or error information. The responses are grouped into categories, and the categories are listed in Table 7-2. While the descriptions indicate messages in 100-point ranges, it is not necessary

| TABLE 7-1 | SIP Method | Description |
|---|---|---|
| SIP Methods and Descriptions | INVITE | Begins a SIP session between two UAs |
| | BYE | Ends a call or declines a call |
| | CANCEL | Terminates any request |
| | ACK | Acknowledges receipt of an INVITE |
| | REGISTER | Registers with the SIP registrar server |
| | OPTIONS | Gets information about a server's capabilities |
| | INFO | Performs signaling within a SIP session or call |

| | SIP Response Category | Description | Examples |
|---|---|---|---|
| **TABLE 7-2**<br><br>SIP Responses | 1xx | Contains responses 100 to 199; used for informational purposes | 100 Trying, 180 Ringing |
| | 2xx | Contains responses 200 to 299; used for successful responses | 200 OK, 202 Accepted |
| | 3xx | Contains responses 300 to 399; used for redirection | 302 Moved Temporarily |
| | 4xx | Contains responses 400 to 499; used for failure responses | 404 Not Found |
| | 5xxx | Contains responses 500 to 599; used for server failure messages | 501 Not Implemented |
| | 6xx | Contains responses 600 to 699; used for global failure issues | 603 Decline |

that all values within the range be used within the SIP communications. You will recognize common responses from web sites you've visited, such as the 404 error for Not Found. The SIP responses start with HTTP responses and add several more to the list.

## Typical SIP Call

Now that you've explored the parts and pieces that work together to make SIP a functioning VoIP signaling solution, it's time to briefly explore a typical SIP call. The following list outlines the basic process used when a proxy server is not involved:

1. The calling party sends an INVITE message to the called party.
2. The called party responds with a TRYING (100) response.
3. When the phone starts ringing, the called party responds with a RINGING (180) response.
4. The calling party phone plays a ringing tone.0
5. When the called party lifts the handset, an OK (200) message is sent to the calling party.

6. The calling party sends an ACK message to the called party.

7. The RTP/RTCP sessions begin for media streaming.

While this process may seem quite lengthy, remember that all seven steps happen in computer time and not in human time. In the time it takes you to read this sentence, the entire process may have taken place (assuming the called party answers quickly).

When a proxy server is used, the only difference is that the messages from both parties are sent to the proxy first, and it forwards the messages to the appropriate endpoint. In the end, RTP and RTCP sessions still function directly between the phones for the media streams. Be sure to remember that the media streams (RTP/RTCP) do not pass through the proxy server.

## INSIDE THE EXAM

### Why Use SIP?

SIP is a significant change over H.323 or MGCP (see Chapter 8) as VoIP protocols go. While Cisco has not emphasized SIP in its certification exams or training classes, as a company, they have started to invest more into the integration of SIP into their product lines. It's clear that SIP is the wave of the near future in the VoIP market.

At this stage, you should know the basics of SIP functionality and the features that it offers. You will not be required to understand the Cisco SIP Proxy Server, which is a Linux-based server, for the CCNA Voice or CVOICE exam.

When you think about choosing a VoIP protocol for your network in the real world, keep the following advantages of SIP in mind. First, it is an open standard. This means it can be extended and implemented by anyone. Second, it uses Internet or web-like communications. This makes it easy to use in the development process. Third and final, most VoIP vendors support it. SIP has exploded in popularity in the first decade of this century and appears to be set up for continued future growth. It's very unlikely you will find yourself in a situation in the near future where a new VoIP phone from any vendor does not support SIP.

# CERTIFICATION SUMMARY

In this chapter, you learned about the Session Initiation Protocol (SIP). You learned that it is an Internet Engineering Task Force (IETF) standard defined in RFC 3261. The SIP functions and architecture were addressed as well as the SIP methods and responses.

✓ # TWO-MINUTE DRILL

## 642-436: Describe SIP

❑ SIP is defined in RFC 3261, which was accepted as a standard in 2002.

❑ SIP borrows from HTTP, SMTP, DNS, and RTP for its implementation and extends the features of these other standards where required.

❑ A SIP call is simply a communication between two or more SIP peers.

❑ The SIP initiator places the call, and the SIP invitee receives the call.

❑ The SIP location service is used to obtain information about a called party's possible locations.

❑ The SIP method is the function that a SIP request is meant to invoke.

❑ A SIP proxy may be used between two SIP peers.

❑ A SIP registrar is a server that accepts REGISTER method requests and stores the registration information in the location service.

❑ A SIP server is a SIP device that receives requests.

❑ A SIP client is a SIP device that sends requests.

❑ The user agent (UA) is the logical entity that acts as a server (UAS) or client (UAC).

❑ The UAS and UAC may operate in the same device.

❑ SIP uses ASCII text-based messages for requests.

❑ SIP uses URIs for addressing.

❑ The Cisco SIP Proxy Server is a Linux-based server and is not integrated into ISRs.

## 640-460: Describe SIP Signaling Protocols

❑ SIP uses a four-layer architecture, and the layers are syntax and encoding, transport, transaction, and transaction user.

❑ The syntax and encoding layer defines how SIP messages are structured.

❑ The transport layer defines how messages should be sent and received.

❑ The transaction layer defines how a dialog should transpire.

❑ The transaction user layer defines how the application interacts with the lower layers.

❑ SIP headers use fields and values in ASCII text encoding.
❑ Several fields are requires in a standard SIP implementation, including TO, FROM, CSEQ, CALL-ID, MAX-FORWARDS, and VIA.
❑ SIP methods include INVITE, BYE, CANCEL, ACK, REGISTER, OPTIONS, and INFO.
❑ SIP responses are categorized as informational ($1xx$), successful ($2xx$), redirection ($3xx$), failure ($4xx$), server failure ($5xx$), and global failure ($6xx$).
❑ Once a SIP call is established, the RTP/RTCP communications occur directly between the peers regardless of whether a proxy server is used.

# SELF TEST

The following questions will help you measure your understanding of the material presented in this chapter. Read all the choices carefully because there might be more than one correct answer. Choose all correct answers for each question.

## 642-436: Describe SIP

1. From what other protocol does SIP borrow response codes?
   A. Ethernet
   B. IP
   C. RTP
   D. HTTP

2. What qualifies as a SIP call?
   A. An encrypted TLS channel between two endpoints
   B. An encrypted SSL channel between two endpoints
   C. A communication between two SIP peers
   D. An IPSec association between two SIP peers

3. What service is used to obtain information about a callee's location?
   A. Location service
   B. Registrar server
   C. Proxy server
   D. UAS

4. With SIP, what defines the function a SIP request invokes?
   A. Response
   B. Method
   C. Registrar
   D. Proxy

5. What is the formal name for the generic component that receives SIP requests?
   A. UAS
   B. UAC
   C. Registrar
   D. Redirect server

6. What is the generic component that either invokes or receives requests?
   A. Registrar
   B. User agent
   C. UAS
   D. UAC

7. What format is used for SIP headers?
   A. Binary encoding
   B. ASCII encoding
   C. HEX encoding
   D. AES encryption

## 640-460: Describe SIP Signaling Protocols

8. Which one of the following is not a layer in the SIP architecture?
   A. Session
   B. Syntax and encoding
   C. Transaction
   D. Transport

9. Which of the SIP layers is responsible for getting the SIP requests to the SIP server?
   A. Transaction
   B. Transaction user
   C. Transport
   D. Session

10. Which of the following are required SIP header fields? (Choose all that apply.)
    A. FROM
    B. TO
    C. MAX-FORWARDS
    D. CONTACT

11. What SIP method is used to start a SIP call?
    A. INVOKE
    B. INVITE
    C. REGISTER
    D. INFO

**12.** What category of SIP responses includes successful responses?

    **A.** 1*xx*

    **B.** 2*xx*

    **C.** 3*xx*

    **D.** 4*xx*

**13.** What kind of responses range from 400 to 499 in the SIP response categories?

    **A.** Failure

    **B.** Success

    **C.** Informational

    **D.** Server failure

**14.** You use a SIP proxy server. A SIP call is taking place between two Cisco SIP IP phones. How is the proxy used between the two phones for the transmission of the audio data?

    **A.** It is used in a forward-only mode.

    **B.** It is used in a cache-and-forward mode.

    **C.** It is not used.

    **D.** It is used in a cache, encrypt, and forward mode.

# LAB QUESTION

You are using secure SIP and URIs for endpoint addresses. You are using standard URIs that look much like web addresses. When a call is placed to Joe Thomas in the xyznabc.net domain, what will the URI look like and why?

# SELF TEST ANSWERS

## 642-436: Describe SIP

1. ☑   **D** is correct. HTTP codes are borrowed by the SIP protocol. For example, the 404 Not Found error response is used by SIP as well as HTTP.

   ☒   **A, B,** and **C** are incorrect. SIP will operate across RTP/IP networks running on Ethernet LANs, but the response codes used in SIP are borrowed from HTTP and not Ethernet, IP, or RTP.

2. ☑   **C** is correct. A SIP call is simply defined as a communication between two SIP peers or endpoints.

   ☒   **A, B,** and **D** are incorrect. SIP calls can use TLS, but it is not required. SIP calls use TLS and not SSL in most implementations. IPSec, of course, can be used for SIP calls, but rarely is, due to the extra overhead required.

3. ☑   **A** is correct. The location service is used to get a probable location for a SIP endpoint—the "callee" in a SIP conversation.

   ☒   **B, C,** and **D** are incorrect. The registrar server places the information into the location service. The proxy server uses the location service if a proxy server is in place. The user agent server (UAS) is the callee.

4. ☑   **B** is correct. The method defines the function invoked. INVITE, CANCEL, REGISTER, OPTIONS, BYE, INFO, and ACK are all valid methods.

   ☒   **A, C,** and **D** are incorrect. The SIP response is the message sent back when a request is made. The registrar is the server responsible for adding a SIP UA to the location server. The SIP proxy may act as a go-between for SIP UAs as they establish a call.

5. ☑   **A** is correct. The component that receives SIP requests is the user agent server (UAS). The user agent (UA) plays the roles of the UAS and the user agent client (UAC).

   ☒   **B, C,** and **D** are incorrect. The user agent client (UAC) is the sender of the request. The registrar server is responsible for receiving registration requests and adding SIP UAs to the location service database. The redirect server may be used to direct a UA to the proper network or location for a UA in a different domain.

6. ☑   **B** is correct. The user agent (UA) can play the role of the UAS (receiver) or the UAC (invoker).

   ☒   **A, C,** and **D** are incorrect. The registrar server is responsible for receiving registration requests and adding SIP UAs to the location service database. The UAS is the user agent server and only receives requests and responds to them. The UAC is the user agent client and it invokes requests.

**7.** ☑ **B** is correct. SIP headers use simple ASCII text-based encoding. The headers consist of field/value pairs.

☒ **A, C,** and **D** are incorrect. Neither binary nor HEX encoding is used for SIP headers. The ASCII encoding is used and maintains a simple header format much like SMTP. AES is an encryption algorithm, and the headers are not formatted according to an encryption algorithm.

## 640-460: Describe SIP Signaling Protocols

**8.** ☑ **A** is correct. While the OSI model does include a Session layer (Layer 6 of the OSI model), the SIP architecture includes only the four layers named syntax and encoding, transport, transaction, and transaction user layers.

☒ **B, C,** and **D** are incorrect. The syntax and encoding layer is responsible for the format of the SIP messages. The transaction layer manages the transactions that take place within SIP communications. The transport layer is responsible for getting the messages to the appropriate UA.

**9.** ☑ **C** is correct. The transport layer would be responsible for getting the SIP requests to the SIP server (UAS) because it is responsible for delivery of all SIP messages (both requests and responses).

☒ **A, B,** and **D** are incorrect. The transaction layer ensures that the transactions are managed properly in SIP communications. The transaction user is the logical entity utilizing the SIP protocol. The Session layer is an OSI model layer and not a SIP layer.

**10.** ☑ **A, B,** and **C** are correct. The FROM field is required, and it indicates the sender of the SIP message. The TO field is required, and it indicates the target of the SIP message. The MAX-FORWARDS field is required, and it indicates the maximum number of allowed hops in the route to the recipient of the SIP message.

☒ **D** is incorrect. The CONTACT header field is an optional header field in SIP messages.

**11.** ☑ **B** is correct. The INVITE method is used to initiate a SIP call.

☒ **A, C,** and **D** are incorrect. No such method as the INVOKE method exists. The REGISTER method is used to register with the SIP registrar server. The INFO method is used to perform signaling within a live SIP call session.

**12.** ☑ **B** is correct. The messages from 200 to 299 (2$xx$) are reserved for successful responses. For example, response code 200 means OK.

☒ **A, C,** and **D** are incorrect. The 1$xx$ response codes are informational. The 3$xx$ response codes are used for redirection responses. The 4$xx$ response codes are failure responses.

13. ☑ **A** is correct. 4*xx* response codes indicate general failure, such as the 404 Not Found response.

    ☒ **B, C,** and **D** are incorrect. Success codes are in the 2*xx* range. Informational codes are in the 1*xx* range. Server failure codes are in the 5*xx* range.

14. ☑ **C** is correct. The actual voice data or audio data is transferred using RTP; therefore, the SIP proxy is not used during the transfer of actual audio data.

    ☒ **A, B,** and **D** are incorrect. A SIP proxy is used in forward-only mode when it is a stateless proxy, but it is only used for signaling—the audio data is sent directly between the peers using RTP. SIP proxies do not offer a cache-and-forward mode or a cache, encrypt, and forward mode in the standard.

# LAB ANSWER

The URI is likely to look something like the following:

> SIPS://JoeThomas@xyznabc.net

The SIPS portion identifies the protocol as secure SIP rather than standard SIP, which uses no encryption or authentication. The JoeThomas portion identifies the user. The @xyznabc.net portion identifies the domain.

# 8

# SCCP and MGCP

*Seldom before has any technology promised so much to so many. If you believe what you read, so-called "client-server" computer systems will cut the cost of information technology, make computers easier to use, provide unprecedented computing power, speed systems development, and transform the shape of organizations as well as the nature of management.*

—Damon Beyer, Marvin Newell, Ian Hurst, The McKinsey Quarterly, *No. 3, 1994*

W hy open a chapter on VoIP signaling protocols with a quote about client/server computing? Simple. This chapter presents the Media Gateway Control Protocol (MGCP), which is a client/server call management protocol. SIP is inherently peer-to-peer. H.323 is completely peer-to-peer when a gatekeeper is not used. MGCP cannot operate in a peer-to-peer implementation. It only supports client/server methods. The benefit of MGCP is that all client control and management is centralized. Of course, the drawback of MGCP is the same in that the centralized management can prevent calls from being placed if this central functionality goes down.

In this chapter, you will learn about both MGCP and the Skinny Client Control Protocol (SCCP). These two protocols are either proprietary to Cisco (SCCP) or were developed with heavy Cisco involvement (MGCP). Both SIP and H.323 were developed without much or any involvement from Cisco. Therefore, you might say, this chapter focuses on the Cisco proprietary technologies and Cisco-developed technologies. You'll first read about the basic uses of MGCP and SCCP and then about the protocol operations.

Interestingly, instead of transforming "the shape of organizations," the MGCP and SCCP protocols seem to be slowly fading into the background as the popularity of SIP and H.323 supplants them. However, MGCP and SCCP can certainly coexist with the more popular SIP and H.323 protocols, as you'll see in this chapter.

# 642-436: Describe MGCP

The Media Gateway Control Protocol (MGCP) is a standards-based protocol that was very popular in early Cisco VoIP networks for the entire VoIP implementation. While SIP and H.323 are growing in popularity and are likely to continue to grow with the emergence of IP service providers, MGCP still has a few key roles to play. This section will introduce you to the MGCP protocol.

## MGCP

MGCP is a client/server call management protocol with a centralized control design. MGCP servers (referenced as *call agents* in the standard) control the gateways used to connect your VoIP networks to other networks. Several gateway types are defined in the MGCP standard, including:

- *Trunking* gateways, which interface between the telephone network and a Voice over IP network.
- *Voice over ATM* gateways, which operate much the same way as Voice over IP trunking gateways, except that they interface to an ATM network.
- *Residential* gateways, which provide a traditional analog (RJ11) interface to a Voice over IP network. Examples of residential gateways include cable modem/cable set-top boxes, xDSL devices, and broadband wireless devices.
- *Access* gateways, which provide a traditional analog (RJ11) or digital PBX interface to a Voice over IP network.
- *Business* gateways, which provide a traditional digital PBX interface or an integrated "soft PBX" interface to a Voice over IP network.
- *Network access servers*, which can attach a "modem" to a telephone circuit and provide data access to the Internet.
- *Circuit switches*, or packet switches, which can offer a control interface to an external call control element.

The newest specification for MGCP is defined in RFCs 3435 and 3661. The original RFCs were 2705 and 3660, but they were superseded by the newest specification documents. The new RFCs clearly state that the gateway types may not be exclusive, but vendors may choose to implement a PBX gateway and a VoIP gateway all in one unit. Cisco ISRs are an example of gateways that may be implemented in this way.

With MGCP, dial plans are completely controlled from within the Cisco Unified Communications Manager (UCM) because the UCM is aware of all voice ports in MGCP gateways. The dial plan includes the definitions for call routing and connectivity. This centralization of intelligence makes the configuration of the MGCP gateways much simpler; however, the configurations must still be managed in the UCM.

The UDP protocol is used to send ASCII text messages between the UCM and an MGCP gateway on UDP port 2427. Because of the ASCII message format, the monitoring and debugging of MGCP messages is simple in the same way as SIP.

Several Cisco devices support MGCP, including the Cisco 2600XM series ISRs, the Cisco 2800 series ISRs, the 3700/3800 series ISRs, and the Cisco VG224 Analog Phone Gateway. It's also important to know that the Cisco Unified Communications Manager Express (CME) and the Cisco Small Business Communications System (SBCS) do not support MGCP.

e x a m

ⓦ a t c h   **Remember that CME and SBCS do not support MGCP. Because these solutions are intended for use in smaller networks, it's assumed that H.323 or SIP will be sufficient and that no enhanced gateway management will be required.**

**CERTIFICATION OBJECTIVE 8.02**

# 642-436: Describe SCCP

The Skinny Client Control Protocol (SCCP) is a Cisco protocol used for communications between Cisco IP phones (hardware and software phones) and the Cisco Unified Communications Manager (UCM) server. This section will introduce you to the SCCP protocol.

# SCCP

The Skinny Client Control Protocol (SCCP) is a Cisco proprietary protocol. This proprietary nature means that the protocol is primarily implemented in Cisco equipment and is not supported by other vendors. If you use all Cisco equipment in your environment, this is not a problem. In fact, even if you use H.323 or SIP phones from other vendors, the SCCP phones can still communicate with them on the same VoIP network. A gateway will simply have to negotiate the call in such scenarios.

on the **job**

*Using a proprietary protocol such as SCCP may be an advantage from one point of view. This perspective has to do with update times. Vendors can update their own protocols very quickly because no formal multi-party review process is required like that used for standard protocols.*

SCCP is used between the Cisco UCM and Cisco IP phone endpoints. When a Cisco SCCP phone is taken off hook, a signal is sent to the UCM to indicate the action. The UCM directs the phone to play a dial tone. For every action taken, a communication is exchanged with the UCM. This makes SCCP difficult to maintain in large-scale networks. Because the entire intelligence is in the UCM and not in the phone, intensive network communications transpire.

SCCP phones can operate in an H.323 environment. SCCP phones, when connected to Cisco UCM, can place calls to H.323 phones. This means you can implement the SCCP protocol with phones that support it (for simple and centralized management), and you can implement the H.323 protocol for the phones that do not support SCCP. In fact, mixed environments are common.

**exam**

**watch** *SCCP phones can communicate with H.323 phones. The Cisco UCM allows for the connections between the two different endpoint types.*

**CERTIFICATION OBJECTIVE 8.03**

# 640-460: Describe MGCP and SCCP Signaling Protocols

In the preceding sections, you learned about the basic use and description of the MGCP and SCCP signaling protocols. In this section, you will learn about the signaling or call exchanges that actually occur when these protocols are used.

## MGCP Signaling

Like SIP, MGCP sends its messages in plain text or ASCII text. The messages include the commands listed in Table 8-1. From this list of commands, you can see that all the basic operations of a phone call are accounted for.

Figure 8-1 illustrates an example call connection using a residential gateway. This example is also provided in RFC 3435, which defined MGCP.

Based on Figure 8-1, the following steps outline the call process:

1. The phone is taken off hook, and a NTFY message is sent to the CA. The CA responds with an ACK message.

2. The CA sends an RQNT message to the gateway. The calling phone plays a dial tone, and the residential gateway sends an ACK message to the CA.

3. The calling phone sends the digits to the gateway, and the gateway sends a NTFY message to the CA, which responds with an ACK message.

| TABLE 8-1 | Message | Description |
|-----------|---------|-------------|
| The MGCP Messages | AUEP | Audit Endpoint |
| | AUCX | Audit Connection |
| | CRCX | Create Connection |
| | DLCX | Delete Connection |
| | MDCX | Modify Connection |
| | RQNT | Request for Notification |
| | NTFY | Notify |
| | RSIP | Restart in Progress |

**FIGURE 8-1**

An MGCP call
process example

```
-----------------------------------------------------------------------
| # |     usr1     |    rgw1    |     ca     |    rgw2    |    usr2    |
|===|==============|============|============|============|============|
| 1 | offhook ->   | ntfy ->    |            |            |            |
|   |              |            | <- ack     |            |            |
|---|--------------|------------|------------|------------|------------|
| 2 | <- dialtone  |            | <- rqnt    |            |            |
|   |              | ack ->     |            |            |            |
|---|--------------|------------|------------|------------|------------|
| 3 |   digits ->  | ntfy ->    |            |            |            |
|   |              |            | <- ack     |            |            |
|---|--------------|------------|------------|------------|------------|
| 4 |              |            | <- rqnt    |            |            |
|   |              | ack ->     |            |            |            |
|---|--------------|------------|------------|------------|------------|
| 5 | <- recvonly  |            | <- crcx    |            |            |
|   |              | ack ->     |            |            |            |
|---|--------------|------------|------------|------------|------------|
| 6 |              |            | crcx ->    |            | sendrcv -> |
|   |              |            |            | <- ack     |            |
|---|--------------|------------|------------|------------|------------|
| 7 | <- recvonly  |            | <- mdcx    |            |            |
|   |              | ack ->     |            |            |            |
|---|--------------|------------|------------|------------|------------|
| 8 | <- ringback  |            | <- rqnt    |            |            |
|   |              | ack ->     |            |            |            |
|---|--------------|------------|------------|------------|------------|
| 9 |              |            | rqnt ->    |            | ringing -> |
|   |              |            |            | <- ack     |            |
|---|--------------|------------|------------|------------|------------|
|10 |              |            |            | <- ntfy    | <- offhook |
|   |              |            | ack ->     |            |            |
|---|--------------|------------|------------|------------|------------|
|11 |              |            | rqnt ->    |            |            |
|   |              |            |            | <- ack     |            |
|---|--------------|------------|------------|------------|------------|
|12 |              |            | <- rqnt    |            |            |
|   |              | ack ->     |            |            |            |
|---|--------------|------------|------------|------------|------------|
|13 | <- sendrcv   |            | <- mdcx    |            |            |
|   |              | ack ->     |            |            |            |
-----------------------------------------------------------------------
```

4. The CA sends an RQNT message to the gateway, which responds with an ACK message.

5. The CA sends a CRCX message to the gateway, which responds with an ACK message. The calling phone goes into receive only mode.

6. A CRCX message is sent to the gateway of the dialed phone, and an ACK message is sent back to the CA. The dialed phone goes into send/receive mode.

7. The CA sends an MDCX message to the gateway of the calling phone, which sends back an ACK, and the calling phone stays in receive only mode.

8. The CA sends an RQNT message to the gateway of the calling phone, which responds with an ACK, and the calling phone plays a ringback sound.

9. The CA sends an RQNT message to the gateway of the dialed phone, which responds with an ACK, and the dialed phone rings.

10. When the called user answers, the dialed phone sends an OffHook message to the gateway, which sends a NTFY message to the CA. The CA response with an ACK message.

11. The CA sends an RQNT message to the dialed gateway, and it responds with an ACK.

12. The CA sends an RQNT message to the calling gateway, and it responds with an ACK.

13. The CA sends an MDCX message to the calling gateway, and it responds with an ACK, and the calling phone is placed in send/receive mode.

14. The audio of the call can now be sent over RTP.

With H.323, the gateway is aware of the dial plan and how to reach the various destination endpoints on the VoIP network. MGCP has no such awareness of the dial plan in the gateway. MGCP depends on the call agent for all call management. In the Cisco world, this call agent is the UCM.

---

**e x a m**

**ⓦ a t c h**   *MGCP is widely used between Cisco VoIP phones and the full version of Cisco Unified Communications Manager; however, it is not used with CME (Communications Manager Express). For*   *this reason, the 640-460 exam is unlikely to demand extensive knowledge of MGCP. The 642-436 exam will require more understanding of MGCP.*

---

## SCCP Signaling

When an SCCP phone first comes online, it will register with the Communications Manager (CM), which may be either UCM or CME. The phone first announces itself to the CM and indicates its station IP port (the UDP port used for RTP communications). The CM acknowledges the registration and requests the capabilities from the phone. The phone responds with its capabilities and requests the software version from the CM. The CM responds with the software version, and then the phone requests a Phone Button Template for phone operations. The CM responds with the button template. Finally, the phone requests the date and time, and the CM responds with the requested information. At this point the phone is registered with the CM and can send and receive calls.

It's also useful to understand the messages used when establishing a phone call. The call processing signals are described in the following list:

1. The calling phone is taken off hook.
2. An OffHook message is sent to the CM.
3. The CM sends a Display Text message to the phone so that the phone's screen changes to reflect the off-hook status.
4. The CM sends a Set Lamp message to the phone to set the lamp (light) settings.
5. The CM sends a Start Tone message to inform the phone to play a dial tone.
6. The user presses a key on the keypad to dial another extension.
7. The phone sends a Keypad Button message to the CM and stops the dial tone on the phone.
8. As each keypad button is pressed, another Keypad Button message is sent to the CM.
9. The CM sends a Call Info message to the phone so the screen can be updated.
10. The phone sends a Start Tone message to the CM to indicate it is ringing for the calling party to hear.
11. The CM sends a Stop Tone message to the phone when the called party answers to indicate it should stop ringing.
12. The RTP stream ensues.

As you can see from the preceding step-by-step outline of an SCCP call, the procedure is quite simple.

---

**exam**
**Watch**

The Skinny Client Control Protocol (SCCP) is a proprietary protocol developed and implemented by Cisco. It is used between Cisco IP phones and Cisco Unified Communications Manager.

# CERTIFICATION SUMMARY

In this chapter, you learned about the basics of MGCP and SCCP. MGCP is used as a gateway to several different network types, including digital connections (such as DS0s on T1 or E1 lines), other VoIP networks, and the PSTN (public switched telephone network), POTS (plain old telephone system), or analog lines. MGCP can be used to set up calls through residential gateways and through business connections. SCCP is used between phones and the call manager (UCM or CME) to establish calls. SCCP is a client/server protocol like MGCP. SCCP sends messages back and forth for nearly every action taken because all intelligence is in the call manager and not in the phone.

# ✓ TWO-MINUTE DRILL

### 642-436: Describe MGCP

- ❏ MGCP is a client/server call management protocol with a centralized control design.
- ❏ The newest standard for MGCP is defined in RFCs 3435 and 3661. The original RFCs were 2705 and 3660, but they were superseded by the newest standards documents.
- ❏ With MGCP, dial plans are completely controlled from within the Cisco Unified Communications Manager (UCM) because the UCM is aware of all voice ports in MGCP gateways.
- ❏ The UDP protocol is used to send ASCII text messages between the UCM and an MGCP gateway on UDP port 2427.

### 642-436: Describe SCCP

- ❏ The Skinny Client Control Protocol (SCCP) is a Cisco proprietary protocol.
- ❏ SCCP is used between the Cisco UCM and Cisco IP phone endpoints.
- ❏ SCCP phones can operate in an H.323 environment. SCCP phones, when connected to Cisco UCM, can place calls to H.323 phones.

### 640-460: Describe MGCP and SCCP Signaling Protocols

- ❏ The MGCP protocol is used between the gateway and the UCM or UCM cluster.
- ❏ MGCP uses ASCII text messages such as AUEP, AUCX, CRCX, DLCX, MDCX, RQNT, NTFY, and RSIP.
- ❏ When an MGCP phone is taken off hook, the NTFY message is used to announce the event to the UCM.
- ❏ Just like SIP and H.323, RTP is used once the MGCP call is set up.
- ❏ SCCP is a client/server protocol like MGCP.
- ❏ Every button press or action taken on an SCCP endpoint causes communications to occur between the endpoint and the UCM.
- ❏ When an SCCP phone is taken off hook, the OffHook message is sent to the CM to indicate the event.
- ❏ Like MGCP, SIP, and H.323, RTP is used once the SCCP call is set up.

# SELF TEST

The following questions will help you measure your understanding of the material presented in this chapter. Read all the choices carefully because there might be more than one correct answer. Choose all correct answers for each question.

## 642-436: Describe MGCP

1. What RFC contains the most recent description of the MGCP protocol?
   A. 3435
   B. 2705
   C. 3453
   D. 2507

2. What UDP port is used for communications between the Unified Communications Manager and the MGCP gateway?
   A. 23
   B. 2705
   C. 2427
   D. 3435

3. What controls the dial plans in a Cisco MGCP VoIP implementation?
   A. UCM
   B. CME
   C. Gateway
   D. Gatekeeper

## 642-436: Describe SCCP

4. On what standard is the SCCP protocol based?
   A. H.323
   B. SIP
   C. MGCP
   D. It is a proprietary protocol.

5. To what must SCCP-based phones be connected in order to place calls to H.323 phones?
   A. Gateway
   B. UCM

C. PSTN

D. DS0

6. What protocol is used to carry the audio stream when SCCP is used to set up the call?

A. SCCP

B. RTP

C. MGCP

D. SIP

## 640-460: Describe MGCP and SCCP Signaling Protocols

7. What kind of messages are sent using the MGCP protocol?

A. Binary

B. Hex

C. ASCII

D. Encrypted

8. When is RTP used in MGCP call setups?

A. After the call is set up

B. Before the call is set up

C. During stage 1 of call setup

D. During stage 2 of call setup

9. Which of the following protocols are client/server VoIP protocols? (Choose all that apply.)

A. SIP

B. MGCP

C. SCCP

D. H.323

10. What MGCP message or verb is used to modify an existing connection?

A. CRCX

B. DLCX

C. MDCX

D. AUCX

11. What MGCP message or verb is used to request a notification?

A. NTFY

B. AUEP

C. RSIP

D. RQNT

12. When an SCCP endpoint phone is taken offline, what message is sent to the call manager?
    A. OffHook
    B. Keypad Button
    C. Start Tone
    D. Stop Tone

# LAB QUESTION

You are planning a Cisco VoIP network. The network will be implemented in a small business. Approximately 30 phones will be connected to the network, and Cisco 2801 ISRs will be used as gateways and CME servers. You must choose between MGCP and H.323 as the VoIP signaling protocol. You will connect to an IP service provider. Which of the two protocols will you use and why?

# SELF TEST ANSWERS

## 642-436: Describe MGCP

1. ☑ **A** is correct. RFC 3435 defines the MGCP standard. RFC 2705 was the original 1999 standard, but it was superseded by the 2003 standard in RFC 3435.

   ☒ **B, C**, and **D** are incorrect. RFC 2705 was the original 1999 MGCP standard and is not the most recent. RFC 3453 defines Forward Error Correction (FEC) for use in multicast networks, which is not directly related to MGCP. RFC 2507 defines IP header compression.

2. ☑ **C** is correct. MGCP uses the User Datagram Protocol on port 2427.

   ☒ **A, B**, and **D** are incorrect. These ports, 23, 2705, and 3435, are invalid port designations for MGCP.

3. ☑ **A** is correct. The UCM controls the dial plans and acts as the server in the client/server relationship with the MGCP gateways.

   ☒ **B, C**, and **D** are incorrect. CME is not used with MGCP because it does not support the protocol. The gateway depends on the UCM to manage the dial plans. Gatekeepers are used in the H.323 world.

## 642-436: Describe SCCP

4. ☑ **D** is correct. The Skinny Client Control Protocol (SCCP) is a proprietary protocol developed by Cisco.

   ☒ **A, B**, and **D** are incorrect. H.323, SIP, and MGCP are separate standards from SCCP and SCCP is proprietary. While MGCP is an Internet standard, the most recent version (RFC 3435) was submitted by Cisco Systems engineers.

5. ☑ **B** is correct. The SCCP phone must be connected to the UCM in order to connect with H.323 phones.

   ☒ **A, C**, and **D** are incorrect. SCCP phones can work with a gateway that does not support connections with H.323. The UCM must specifically be available for this interoperability. There is no requirement for a connection to the PSTN or across a DS0 trunk.

6. ☑ **B** is correct. The Real-time Transport Protocol (RTP) is used to transport the audio stream of the phone conversation for H.323, SIP, MGCP, and SCCP.

   ☒ **A, C**, and **D** are incorrect. SCCP, MGCP, and SIP are all signaling protocols. They are used to establish the connection, but RTP is used to transport the audio streams.

## 640-460: Describe MGCP and SCCP Signaling Protocols

**7.** ☑ **C** is correct. Plain text ASCII messages are sent for MGCP verbs or commands.

☒ **A**, **B**, and **D** are incorrect. Binary is used for Ethernet headers, and Hex may be used in some formats, but not with MGCP. MGCP does not use encrypted headers or commands.

**8.** ☑ **A** is correct. RTP is used after the call is set up to transfer the RTP audio stream.

☒ **B**, **C**, and **D** are incorrect. Because RTP is used to transfer the audio stream, it is used after the call is set up and not before or during any stages.

**9.** ☑ **B** and **C** are correct. MGCP and SCCP are both client/server protocols. With MGCP, the phone or the gateway is the client and the CM (the UCM) is the server. With SCCP, the phone is the client and the CM is the server.

☒ **A** and **D** are incorrect. SIP and H.323 are primarily peer-to-peer protocols. The one exception is when an H.323 gatekeeper is used for RAS.

**10.** ☑ **C** is correct. The MDCX verb is used to modify a connection. For example, it may be used to change a connection from receive only to send and receive.

☒ **A**, **B**, and **D** are incorrect. The CRCX verb is used to create a connection. The DLCX verb is used to delete a connection. The AUCX verb is used to audit a connection.

**11.** ☑ **D** is correct. The RQNT verb is used to request a notification.

☒ **A**, **B**, and **C** are incorrect. The NTFY verb is used to send a notification. The AUEP verb is used to audit an endpoint. The RSIP verb is used to indicate that a restart is in progress.

**12.** ☑ **A** is correct. The OffHook message indicates that the receiver has been taken off hook and that the phone is ready to place a call.

☒ **B**, **C**, and **D** are incorrect. The Keypad Button messages are used to send the phone button signals. The Start Tone message is used to indicate a dial tone should be played. The Stop Tone message is used to indicate that the ringing sound should no longer be played—usually because the called phone has been answered.

# LAB ANSWER

Answers may vary, but in most scenarios like this, you will use H.323 (or possibly SIP, but it wasn't mentioned in the question). MGCP requires the Cisco Unified Communications Manager (UCM), which is the full Cisco gateway and VoIP management solution. The Call Manager Express is being used in this network, which does not support MGCP. For this reason, you will need to use H.323 for the VoIP signaling protocol.

# 9
# Understanding Cisco Unified Communications

> *Communications have to be effective, simple to use and provide the flexibility to accommodate a variety of methods for businesses to enable their employees to be more effective.*
>
> —*Zig Serafin*

The modern business professional communicates with dozens of people every week, or for some, every day. To make these communications simpler and more efficient, it's essential to bring the different communication channels as close together as we can. This bringing together of the communication channels is what we call *unified communications*. Unified communications or unified messaging lets us check our e-mail, voice mail, faxes, and blog comments all in one location. This one location may be our desktop e-mail application, our wireless cellular phone, or our desktop Cisco IP phone. Whatever the device or software, unified communications will be a big part of the future responsibilities for IT professionals.

Cisco has a vision for unified communications known as the *Cisco Unified Communications Architecture*. This vision is built around Cisco VoIP technologies. In this chapter, you will learn about the Cisco Unified Communications Architecture and several of the technologies used within this architecture. In the next chapter, you'll learn more details about the specific hardware used to make all of this happen.

As you'll see while reading this chapter, the technologies required to make communications effective, simple, and flexible are themselves quite complex. The goal is to make communications simple for the users even if complexity still exists for the implementer. This reality is not necessarily bad news. After all, if it was so simple to implement unified communications that anyone could do it, we wouldn't need trained IT professionals, and that would mean that many passionate technology enthusiasts would be unable to find employment doing what they love. Thankfully, it seems there will always be a new trend in technology, and right now that trend is heavily focused on unified communications.

# 640-460: Describe the Components of the Cisco Unified Communications Architecture

The Cisco Unified Communications Architecture is a collection of infrastructure and endpoint devices and software that allows for simplified call processing and messaging services in a Cisco environment. In this section, you will learn about the infrastructure, the endpoints, the call processing agents, the Unified Communications (UC) features, and the applications in and of a UC environment.

## UC Infrastructure

For any network technology, the infrastructure includes the devices that form the highway across which the network communications occur. You can think of your network interface card as the entrance ramp onto the highway and of the switchport as the merge lane that allows your packets onto the actual highway. Once your packet is on the highway (in the memory of the access layer switch), the infrastructure ensures that the packet reaches the appropriate destination. While you learned about the network infrastructure in detail in Chapter 2, it's important here that we summarize the key features a UC infrastructure must provide. These features are:

- Reliable delivery
- Acceptable uptime

### Reliable Delivery

Reliable delivery is achieved through QoS mechanisms. Priority lanes should be created for the VoIP traffic much like the high-occupancy vehicle (HOV) lanes common throughout the United States. In a network infrastructure, these priority lanes are created using QoS tags so that the routers can identify the traffic as VoIP traffic and route it with priority over standard data traffic. Reliable delivery should also be considered from a performance perspective. We not only want the data to reach its destination, but we also want it to reach the destination in an acceptable amount of time. QoS can also help achieve this desired performance.

## Acceptable Uptime

The requirement of acceptable uptime could also be stated as tolerable downtime. The real question is, how much downtime can you tolerate from your phone system? Traditional PBX systems offer uptimes from 99.99 to 99.999% per year. This rating equals around 125 minutes of downtime per year in a 9:00 to 5:00 environment. Is this what you require out of your VoIP network? If it is, redundancy and quality equipment will be keys to your success. From a redundancy perspective, you must consider both network hardware redundancy and power redundancy. By "quality equipment," I simply mean that you need hardware that is able to run for months without requiring a reset. This usually means going with trusted vendors such as Cisco who offer stable hardware.

To achieve redundancy of network hardware, you will need to implement more routers than required to get the network up and running. For example, Figure 9-1 shows a non-redundant network that would work just fine. However, we have one device that presents a single point of failure. If Router1 fails, Network A cannot communicate with Network B, and vice versa. In the case of Figure 9-1, the single router and the switches are the network infrastructure.

Now, consider Figure 9-2. The same network has been made redundant through the use of extra routers. If Router1 fails, the devices on the networks can use Router2 to communicate. They would simply need to be configured with multiple gateways. The network infrastructure now has two routers and the switches to provide the infrastructure. The switches are still a single point of failure; however, you can reduce the potential number of impacted users when a switch fails by using multiple switches with fewer switchports. For example, you could accommodate 150 users on a subnet using eight 20-port switches rather than three 50-port switches. If a switch failed, 20 users would be impacted instead of 50 users.

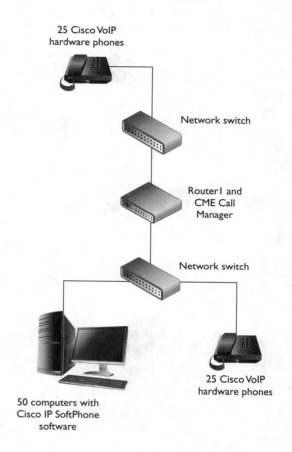

**FIGURE 9-1**

A non-redundant network infrastructure

25 Cisco VoIP hardware phones

Network switch

Router1 and CME Call Manager

Network switch

50 computers with Cisco IP SoftPhone software

25 Cisco VoIP hardware phones

on the
**Job**

*Many would suggest that switches are not a part of the infrastructure. In the Cisco world, a switch is usually considered part of the infrastructure if endpoints do not connect with it directly. The switches that connect endpoints are at the access layer or at the edge of the network, much like a merge lane on a highway.*

FIGURE 9-2

A redundant
network
infrastructure

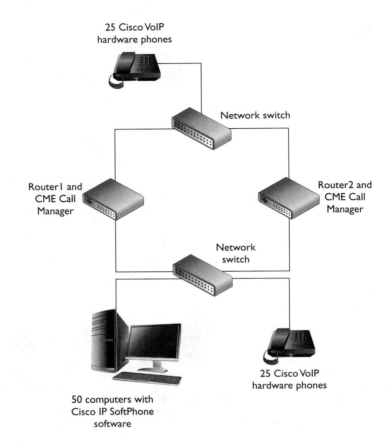

25 Cisco VoIP
hardware phones

Network switch

Router1 and
CME Call
Manager

Router2 and
CME Call
Manager

Network
switch

50 computers with
Cisco IP SoftPhone
software

25 Cisco VoIP
hardware phones

To implement redundant power supply, you will typically use an uninterruptable power supply (UPS) unit. The routers and switches can be powered by the power company through the UPS. Should the power company supply break for a few seconds, the UPS can keep the routers and switches up and running. Depending on the power method used for the phones (for example, you may be using PoE [Power over Ethernet] to power the phones), the users may still be able to place calls during a power outage.

## UC Endpoints

At the remote end of the network is the total opposite of the network infrastructure. Here we have the UC endpoints. The UC endpoints typically fall into one of two categories: hardware or software IP phones. A hardware-based IP phone is a specialized device that looks just like a traditional analog PBX phone. A software-based IP phone runs on a computing device such as a handheld computer, a laptop, or a desktop PC or MAC. The Cisco IP SoftPhone is a computer-based software package that acts as a VoIP endpoint on the network.

The UC endpoints act as the entry point and endpoint for audio streams on the VoIP network. From a transmission perspective, the IP phone creates the digital audio stream from incoming analog signals received through the IP phone's handset microphone or a connected microphone, such as the microphone included in a headset. From a reception perspective, the IP phone creates the analog audio stream from the incoming VoIP data and sends the analog data to the speaker in the IP phone.

In addition to the audio processing, IP phones send and receive management information. For example, many IP phones include LCD screens for the display of information such as the currently connected phone, the date and time, and status information for the VoIP network. Most newer Cisco phones now support XML data so that applications can be developed to display just about anything you can imagine on the LCD screens.

Cisco IP phones provide several features that allow them to function well in a UC implementation. These features include:

- Support for multiple codecs, such as G.711 and G.729
- Power over Ethernet (PoE) support for inline power supply from the switch
- LCD interface for the display of messaging information
- User customization for speed-dial and other keys

Chapter 10 provides more information on the hardware used to implement IP phones in a Cisco network.

## Call Processing Agents

The call processing agent is responsible for processing calls. This definition may sound simple, but it is exactly what the call processing agent must do. Call processing includes the following tasks:

- Receive a request for a call.
- Locate the appropriate dial-peer to place the call.
- Establish the connection for the call, or provide the needed information for that connection, depending on the protocol used (H.323, SIP, MGCP, or SCCP).

- Monitor the call and report on the performance and quality of the communications.
- Terminate the call.

In addition to these basic tasks, the call processing agent may provide on-call messaging so that the user can be notified of new voice mails, incoming calls, and other alerts that may be sent to the phone. The call processing agent should also be aware of any connected messaging systems including voice mail, faxing, and e-mail. Cisco provides several call processing agent solutions, including:

- **Cisco Unified Communications Manager Express (CME or CUCME)** The CME solution runs on an ISR such as the Cisco 2800 series or the 3800 series. It will also work on the 1800 series. Older versions of the CME will run on the 1700, 2600, and 3600 series ISRs as well. The CME solution is intended for small to medium organizations that connect with PSTN- and IP-based service providers. The CME can be managed from the IOS command line or from a web-based GUI interface. The CME supports up to 250 IP phones.

- **Cisco Unified Communications Manager (CUCM)** The CUCM solution is able to scale for very large networks and supports the full feature set of a Cisco call processing agent. CUCM runs on the Cisco 7800 series Media Convergence Servers, which are servers authorized for and dedicated to running Cisco UC solutions. CUCM provides greater availability than CME or CUCM Business Edition. CUCM can be installed in clusters, and each cluster can support up to 30,000 phones with interconnections allowed between the clusters.

- **Cisco Unified Communications Manager Business Edition** The Business Edition of CUCM is a step above the CME and functions on a dedicated server. The CUCM Business Edition is a Linux-based appliance server that supports up to 500 IP phones.

- **Cisco Smart Business Communications System (SBCS)** The SBCS solution is implemented through UC500 series appliances. These devices are specialized routers that have the call processing agent and network routing and switching functionality built in. Support for 8 to 48 phones may be included depending on the license and model purchased.

Table 9-1 provides a comparison reference for these Cisco call processing agents.

| TABLE 9-1 | Cisco Call Processing Agents Comparison |

| Call Processing Agent | Phones Supported | Platform |
|---|---|---|
| Cisco Unified Call Manager Express (CME) | Up to 250 | Integrated Services Routers (ISRs) |
| Cisco Unified Communications Manager (CUCM) | Up to 30,000 phones per cluster, with multiple clusters supported | Media Convergence Servers |
| Cisco Unified Communications Manager Business Edition | Up to 500 phones | Media Convergence Servers |
| Cisco Smart Business Communications System (SBCS) – UC500 series | Up to 48 phones | Specialized router in the UC500 series |

## Messaging

To provide voice mail, e-mail, calendaring, and faxing for your VoIP users, Cisco provides the Unity series of solutions. Three levels are available within the Unity products. The levels are Cisco Unity Express, Cisco Unity Connection, and Cisco Unity.

### Cisco Unity Express

Cisco Unity Express provides support for up to 275 mailboxes and integrates voice mail, faxing, and interactive voice response solutions. Unity Express is an add-on for select Cisco ISRs. It comes with either flash memory or a hard drive for storage of messaging data. The flash version comes in the Advanced Integration Module (AIM) form factor. The Network Module (NM) form factor is used for the hard drive models.

The Unity Express module (both AIM and NM) is configured through a Linux-based interface that runs on the router. When you enter the Unity Express configuration mode, you will no longer be working with a traditional IOS command line, but with the Linux-based command line used for configuration of the Unity Express.

**watch**     *Remember that the Unity Express modules use a Linux-based command line that runs on the IOS router,*    *not the built-in IOS operating system command line.*

The following features are provided by Cisco Unity Express:

- Voice messaging and greeting services for better customer service and employee communications
- Time-card data management with TimeCardView
- Telephone prompts and a web-based interface for fast, convenient voice mail, auto attendant, and interactive voice response (IVR) administration
- Ability to view, sort, search, and play back voice messages using a Cisco Unified IP Phone display or your e-mail client
- Scalability of up to 24 concurrent voice mail or auto attendant calls and 275 mailboxes

Cisco Unity Express is aimed at the distributed enterprise, branch office, or SMB (small- and medium-size business) market. The AIM version of Unity Express supports only 50 mailboxes due to the limited memory available on flash.

## Cisco Unity Connection

The next level is the Cisco Unity Connection. Unity Connection supports up to 20,000 mailboxes per server. Unity Connection can be used as an add-on to a CUCM Business Edition installation for up to 500 users. Larger organizations can interconnect multiple Unity Connection, Unity Express, or Unity messaging products to support thousands of users.

Cisco Unity Connection provides the following features:

- Voice messaging with advanced capabilities
- Speech-enabled messaging for interface navigation and message management
- Message access from the computer desktop through web interfaces, IMAP e-mail clients, or visual voice mail on the Cisco IP Phones that support the visual voice mail feature
- Interconnectivity with Cisco Unity so that the two systems can work together for seamless communications

Cisco Unity Connection is aimed at the enterprise, commercial, and SMB markets.

## Cisco Unity

Cisco Unity, interestingly aimed at only the enterprise and commercial markets according to Cisco literature, supports up to 15,000 mailboxes per server compared with Cisco Unity Connection's 20,000. However, Cisco Unity can scale to 250,000 total network users with multiple servers, while Cisco Unity Connection can only scale to 100,000 total network users.

Cisco Unity comes in different versions for integration with different e-mail server products. For example, Cisco Unity for Microsoft Exchange works with Microsoft's e-mail server, and Cisco Unity for Lotus Domino works with IBM's e-mail server. Cisco Unity and Cisco Unity Connection both operate on dedicated servers or server appliances, while Cisco Unity runs on ISRs.

on the Job

*Always check the Cisco web site for the latest information. Many early books indicate that lower numbers of mailboxes are supported than, for example, the 15,000 referenced here. However, the information here is based on Cisco's documentation for version 8 of the Unity products at the time this book was written.*

## Auto Attendants

The interactive voice response (IVR) feature of Cisco's VoIP products allows the device or server to communicate with the calling user by playing recorded messages. For example, when you call customer service for any company, you often receive recorded messages telling you to press 1 for a specific service, press 2 for another, and so forth. These recorded messages are driven by an IVR.

An auto attendant usually uses the features of the IVR to communicate with the user and to allow for self-direction on the voice network. In other words, the user can connect with an individual within your organization without requiring the aid of an operator. You may support Auto Attendant functions for direct dialing to extensions or for access to departments. For example, the caller may press 3 for the Accounting department, which could route him to a group of potential endpoints where the first available phone rings, and an accountant would answer to assist the caller.

## Contact Center

Larger companies often have a call center or contact center that acts as the incoming hub for all calls. One or more operators or receptionists may answer these incoming calls and direct them to the appropriate departments or endpoints. To operate such a contact center, software must be implemented that supports call distribution, queue management, and call reporting.

Cisco's Unified Contact Center (UCC) provides the features required of a contact center. These features include:

■ **Automatic call distribution (ACD)**   The ACD feature allows calls to be distributed to the appropriate user or group of users. The ACD will often integrate with an IVR solution as well.

■ **Computer telephony integration (CTI)**   CTI can also be used to provide information about the caller on the computer screen of the answering user. This information may include the phone number and name of the caller if Caller ID data is provided.

■ **Collaboration features**   The Cisco UCC also provides collaboration features such as chat, e-mail, and web collaboration.

Cisco UCC comes in both Express and Enterprise editions. The UCC Express Edition supports up to 300 agents. Larger call centers will need the UCC Enterprise Edition.

# Applications in the UC Environment

CUCM and CME can provide several features that enhance the user's experience when using the VoIP network. The most important of these features are mobility, presence, and TelePresence.

## Mobility

Cisco Unified Mobility, or simply "mobility," allows users to redirect calls from CUCM to as many as four different client devices like cellular phones or wired and wireless IP phones. This feature is also known as Single Number Reach or Single Business Number Reach. Solutions available with Cisco Unified Mobility include:

■ **Device Mobility**   The Cisco Mobile Connect services, which are part of Cisco Unified Mobility, allow mobile workers to continue a call on the IP desk phone that began on another phone (such as a cellular phone) or vice versa.

■ **Mobile Voice Access**   Calls can be placed from anywhere as if the user were connected directly to the enterprise home office. The user dials into the Cisco Mobile Voice Access line from a cellular or land-line phone and then places calls across the VoIP network.

■ **Web-based Administration**   Users and the Cisco Unified Mobility system itself may be managed from a web-based interface. Users can access their profiles through the web-based interface. Administrators can manage the user profiles and the system from the web-based interface.

## Presence

Cisco Unified Presence is used to provide availability information about VoIP network users. Administrators can determine if a user is using a phone or if video conferencing is available to a user based on the phone currently in use. The Cisco Unified Personal Communicator features, such as instant messaging, presence information, and buddy lists, depend on Cisco Unified Presence. CUCM integrates with Cisco Unified Presence for sharing of status information related to registered IP phones. Cisco Unified Presence is installed on the Media Convergence Servers such as the MCS7816, 7825, 7835, or 7845 appliances.

## TelePresence

Cisco TelePresence provides the video conferencing features that allow users to attend virtual conferences as if they were sitting across from users in a conference room. It is a combination of hardware and software designed to give an experience as close to face-to-face communications as current technology allows. The TelePresence hardware and software connects with the CUCM for conference call processing and management. Figure 9-3 shows the Cisco TelePresence system components in use.

**FIGURE 9-3**

Cisco
TelePresence

# The Cisco Unified Communications Architecture

From what you've learned in this chapter so far, you know that the Cisco UC Architecture comprises several components existing at the endpoint and infrastructure layers. Infrastructure services include:

- **Voice mail**   Cisco Unity
- **Presence**   Cisco Unified Presence and TelePresence
- **Mobility**   Cisco Unified Mobility
- **Contact center management**   Cisco Unified Contact Center
- **Call processing**   CME and CUCM

The endpoints that consume these infrastructure services include:

- **Hardware phones**   Cisco IP phones
- **Software phones**   Cisco IP SoftPhone

In addition to these services and endpoints, you must consider the VoIP topology you will use for implementation of the Cisco UC architecture. You can choose from four basic topologies:

- **Single-site/Centralized processing**   In this model, you have a single location, so you use one or more CME or CUCM call agents to handle the VoIP calls. When you use more than one call agent, you are typically using a *call agent cluster*. In a cluster, one CUCM server is the publisher and the others are subscribers. Together they act as one managed system.

- **Multi-site/Centralized processing**   In this model, you have more than one location connected by WAN links. Phones at remote sites communicate over the WAN to reach the call agent and to set up calls. With this model, it's very important that the WAN links be highly reliable because even local calls within a site must process communications across the WAN to set up the call.

- **Multi-site/Distributed processing**   In this model, the WAN dependency is removed for local calls because each site has a local call processing agent (CME or CUCM server). Gateways will be used to connect the separate VoIP networks that exist within each site.

- **WAN cluster**   In this model, a cluster of CUCM servers is used, but the cluster spans WAN connections. Just as you can implement a cluster within a site, you can implement a cluster that spans sites. A highly reliable WAN connection will be required. The publisher will be at a central site where most management operations are performed. Each site will have a subscriber server.

The topology you choose will depend on the WAN links, budget, and available administration staff.

**exam**

**Ⓦatch** *Remember that both the multi-site/centralized processing model and the WAN cluster model depend on highly reliable WAN links.*

## CERTIFICATION SUMMARY

In this chapter, you learned about the Cisco Unified Communications Architecture and its various components. You began by reviewing the importance of the network infrastructure in a UC implementation. Next, you explored the functions provided by UC endpoints, including hardware and software IP phones. The call processing agents were covered next, and you learned about the differences between CME, CUCM, and the SBCS agents. Finally, you learned about voice mail and other UV features provided in a Cisco environment and the available topologies for VoIP network implementation.

# ✓ TWO-MINUTE DRILL

## 640-460: Describe the Components of the Cisco Unified Communications Architecture

❑ The UC network infrastructure includes the hardware and software used to transport the IP packets through the network to the destination.

❑ A VoIP network infrastructure must provide reliable delivery of voice packets and network redundancy for availability.

❑ Network redundancy can be achieved through the implementation of redundant routers.

❑ Power supply redundancy can be achieved through the use of a UPS system.

❑ UC endpoints are responsible for the creation of transmitted audio streams and the rendering of received audio streams.

❑ UC endpoints may be hardware devices, such as Cisco IP phones, or software solutions, such as the Cisco IP SoftPhone.

❑ Call Manager Express (CME) runs on ISRs and is intended for smaller networks with up to 250 VoIP phones.

❑ Cisco Unified Communications Manager (CUCM) Business Edition is intended for medium organizations with up to 500 phones.

❑ CUCM is intended for large organizations with up to 30,000 phones per CUCM cluster.

❑ The UC500 series is intended for small businesses with from 8 to 48 IP phones.

❑ Cisco's Unity products provide messaging services for VoIP networks.

❑ Cisco Unity Express is intended for smaller organizations or branch offices.

❑ Cisco Unity Connection is intended for larger enterprises and SMBs.

❑ Cisco Unity is intended only for larger enterprises.

❑ Integrated voice response (IVR) systems play recorded messages to the caller and allow him or her to respond with keypad presses.

❑ Auto Attendant features allow callers to direct themselves to departments or extensions through direct-dial features.

❑ Contact centers include components to provide ACD, CTI, and collaboration features.

❑ Several topologies are available for VoIP network implementations with Cisco products, including single-site/centralized processing, multi-site/ centralized processing, multi-site/distributed processing, and WAN clustering.

❑ The multi-site/centralized processing and WAN cluster topologies require highly reliable WAN links.

# SELF TEST

The following questions will help you measure your understanding of the material presented in this chapter. Read all the choices carefully because there might be more than one correct answer. Choose all correct answers for each question.

## 640-460: Describe the Components of the Cisco Unified Communications Architecture

1. You must implement a call processing agent that supports up to 125 phones. Which one of the following agents, implemented as a single device or server, will meet your needs without excessive costs?

   A. CME

   B. CUCM Business Edition

   C. UC500

   D. CUCM

2. You must implement a call processing agent that supports up to 4,300 phones. Which one of the following agents will meet your needs without excessive costs?

   A. CME 4.2

   B. UC500

   C. CUCM

   D. CME 4.3

3. What is the maximum number of phones supported by a UC500 series router running Cisco UC?

   A. 8

   B. 16

   C. 32

   D. 48

4. Which of the following are general categories of IP phones available from Cisco? (Choose two.)

   A. Analog

   B. Hardware

   C. Software

   D. Token Ring

5. What device can be used to provide power supply redundancy for the infrastructure devices in a UC architecture?

    **A.** UPS

    **B.** CME

    **C.** CUCM

    **D.** Cisco Presence

**6.** What Cisco product provides the ability to have conference calls that simulate face-to-face meetings?

    **A.** Cisco Unified Presence

    **B.** Cisco Unity Express

    **C.** Cisco TelePresence

    **D.** CME

**7.** In what form factor does the Cisco Unity Express with flash come?

    **A.** NM

    **B.** AIM

    **C.** MCS

    **D.** PVDM

**8.** What Cisco Unity product is intended only for use within large organizations?

    **A.** Cisco Unity

    **B.** Cisco Unity Express

    **C.** Cisco Unity Connection

    **D.** Cisco Unity Enterprise

**9.** Which UC architecture topology demands highly reliable WAN links and always uses a CUCM publisher and subscribers?

    **A.** Multi-site/distributed processing

    **B.** Multi-site/centralized processing

    **C.** WAN cluster

    **D.** Single-site/centralized processing

**10.** Which UC architecture topology implements call processing agents at each site in a WAN environment, but does not depend on highly available WAN links?

    **A.** Multi-site/distributed processing

    **B.** Multi-site/centralized processing

    **C.** WAN cluster

    **D.** Single-site/centralized processing

11. What feature, within a Cisco UC environment, allows callers to direct themselves to an extension or a department?

    A. Auto Attendant

    B. Voice mail

    C. TelePresence

    D. Presence

12. What feature uses recorded messages to prompt the caller for keypad presses?

    A. IVR

    B. Auto Attendant

    C. Presence

    D. Mobility

13. What feature of a Cisco UC environment allows a user to indicate up to four different phones that may receive an incoming call targeted at a single extension or phone number?

    A. IVR

    B. Auto Attendant

    C. Presence

    D. Mobility

14. Which of the following are features typically provided by contact center management software? (Choose all that apply.)

    A. ACD

    B. IP routing

    C. CTI

    D. Presence

15. On what platform does the Cisco CME solution run?

    A. Media Convergence Servers

    B. Integrated Services Routers

    C. Network Modules

    D. Advanced Interface Modules

# LAB QUESTION

You are configuring a VoIP network and must provide redundancy in the routing infrastructure. Three network segments are to be connected. One segment is using the 10.1.0.0 network block. Another is using the 10.2.0.0 block. The final segment is using the 10.3.0.0 block. Each segment will have approximately 120 IP phones. To ensure redundancy between these networks (meaning that all networks have at least two routers through which they can connect to other networks), how many routers will you require? Explain why you have selected the number of routers specified in your answer.

# SELF TEST ANSWERS

## 640-460: Describe the Components of the Cisco Unified Communications Architecture

1. ☑  **A** is correct. The Cisco Communications Manager Express (CME) can support up to 250 phones, so it will incur the least cost to your organization while providing the needed support for the 125 phones required.

   ☒  **B, C**, and **D** are incorrect. CUCM Business Edition supports many more phones than required by the scenario and would incur unnecessary costs. The same is true for CUCM. The UC500 series device could support a maximum of 48 phones and would require three devices to meet the needs in the scenario. A single ISR running CME would be less expensive than three UC500 devices running separate VoIP networks.

2. ☑  **C** is correct. CUCM must be used in this scenario in order to accommodate the large number of phones (4,300) required.

   ☒  **A, B**, and **D** are incorrect. Regardless of costs, the CME in any version and the UC500 series devices cannot handle 4,300 phones.

3. ☑  **D** is correct. While the UC500 series devices can support from 8 to 48 phones, the maximum is 48 phones.

   ☒  **A, B**, and **C** are incorrect. A UC500 series device can support 8, 16, or 32 phones; however, the maximum number supported is 48.

4. ☑  **B** and **C** are correct. Cisco offers both hardware- and software-based phones. The hardware-based phones look like traditional analog PBX phones, but work using VoIP protocols. The software-based phone is the Cisco IP SoftPhone, and it runs on a PC and requires a microphone and speakers for functionality.

   ☒  **A** and **D** are incorrect. Analog phones are not sold by Cisco; however, Cisco does offer gateways that can connect analog phones to VoIP networks. Token Ring phones are not offered by Cisco. Cisco's IP phones are Ethernet based.

5. ☑  **A** is correct. An uninterruptable power supply (UPS) may be used to provide power redundancy for infrastructure equipment.

   ☒  **B, C**, and **D** are incorrect. The CME and CUCM software solutions require a powered machine to run. The Cisco Unified Presence (not simply Cisco Presence) feature is not a power-provisioning feature.

6. ☑ **C** is correct. The Cisco TelePresence software and hardware solution allows for video conferencing that simulates face-to-face conference meetings.

   ☒ **A, B** and **D** are incorrect. The Cisco Unified Presence feature allows for user location information and other enhancements to the Cisco UC environment. The Cisco Unity Express feature provides messaging services such as voice mail. The CME is the call processing agent.

7. ☑ **B** is correct. The Advanced Interface Module (AIM) is used for the flash-based Cisco Unity Express modules.

   ☒ **A, C,** and **D** are incorrect. The Network Module (NM) format is used for the Cisco Unity Express module that includes a hard drive. The Media Convergence Server (MCS) is not used for Cisco Unity Express implementation. The PVDM (packet voice/data module) provides DSP resources in ISR gateways.

8. ☑ **A** is correct. Cisco Unity is the most powerful version of the Unity series. It is intended for use in large enterprises and not in small businesses or branch offices.

   ☒ **B, C,** and **D** are incorrect. Cisco Unity Express is intended for branch offices or small businesses. Cisco Unity Connection is intended for large enterprises and SMBs. Cisco Unity Enterprise is not a Cisco product in the Unity series.

9. ☑ **C** is correct. CUCM clusters use publishers and subscribers; therefore, the WAN cluster topology would demand highly reliable WAN links and always use publishers and subscribers.

   ☒ **A, B,** and **D** are incorrect. Multi-site/distributed processing topologies do not require highly available WAN links. Multi-site/centralized processing topologies do require highly available WAN links; however, they do not always use CUCM clusters. Single-site/centralized processing topologies may use a cluster, but they do not use WAN links.

10. ☑ **A** is correct. The multi-site/distributed processing topology implements call managers at each site location, but does not demand the same highly reliable WAN links as other topologies may because local calls are fully handled within the site, and no WAN-based CUCM cluster exists.

   ☒ **B, C,** and **D** are incorrect. The multi-site/centralized processing topology demands highly reliable WAN links because the call manager is at the central location. Because of the WAN-based cluster, the WAN cluster topology demands highly reliable WAN links. The single-site/centralized processing topology does not require WAN links and does not distribute call agents to remote sites because no remote sites exist.

**11.** ☑  **A** is correct. The Auto Attendant feature allows callers to directly dial an extension or department when calling into the VoIP network.

☒  **B, C,** and **D** are incorrect. Voice mail simply allows callers to leave audio messages in users' mailboxes. TelePresence is a video conferencing solution. Presence is used to discover a user's location and the features at that location.

**12.** ☑  **A** is correct. The IVR feature provides recorded messages to callers and processes incoming keypad presses.

☒  **B, C,** and **D** are incorrect. The Auto Attendant feature allows callers to directly dial an extension or department when calling into the VoIP network. Presence is used to discover a user's location and the features at that location. Mobility allows users to roam and to indicate a new device to which callers should be connected when they dial the user's extension.

**13.** ☑  **D** is correct. Mobility allows users to roam and to indicate a new device to which callers should be connected when they dial the users' extension.

☒  **A, B,** and **C** are incorrect. The IVR feature provides recorded messages to callers and processes incoming keypad presses. The Auto Attendant feature allows callers to directly dial an extension or department when calling into the VoIP network. Presence is used to discover a user's location and the features at that location.

**14.** ☑  **A** and **C** are correct. Automatic call distribution (ACD) is used to manage and process queues for incoming calls. Computer telephony integration (CTI) allows the phone system to send information to the answering user on his or her computer screen.

☒  **B** and **D** are incorrect. IP routing is provided by routers and not by contact center software. Presence is provided, in a Cisco UC environment, by the Cisco Unified Presence solution.

**15.** ☑  **B** is correct. The Cisco Unified Communications Manager Express (CME) runs on Integrated Services Routers (ISRs) such as the 2600, 3600, 1700, 1800, 2800, and 3800 series routers.

☒  **A, C,** and **D** are incorrect. The Media Convergence Servers (MCSs) are used to run CUCM and not CME. Network Modules (NMs) and Advanced Interface Modules (AIMs) are used for Cisco Unity Express add-ons to ISRs.

## LAB ANSWER

Answers may vary, but if your goal is to use the fewest number of routers while providing redundancy, you can use two routers each having three interfaces. The 10.1.0.0 network will connect to one of the interfaces on each router as will the 10.2.0.0 and 10.3.0.0 networks. The result will be two routes to any potential destination. If you plan to use CME, based on the number of phones (360), you will have to implement it on more than one router and then configure the appropriate gateways and dial-peers to allow for communications between the separate networks.

# 10

# Cisco VoIP Hardware and Software

> *Hardware: where the people in your company's*
> *software section will tell you the problem is.*
> *Software: where the people in your company's*
> *hardware section will tell you the problem is.*
>
> —Dave Barry, Claw Your Way to the Top

If you plan to implement a VoIP network, it's very important to select and implement the right hardware. Because Cisco hardware varies so much, specific routers, switches, and gateways are not mentioned in the CVOICE exam objectives. However, the CCNA Voice exam (640-460) does mention very specific hardware aimed at the small office, home office (SOHO) markets. For this reason, this chapter covers the UC500 series of devices and the configuration options available on them. It also covers Cisco Unity Express, which is the small business or branch office version of Cisco's voice mail and messaging solution. Before we get into these specific hardware components, we'll look at the traditional Cisco hardware that plays a role in both small and large organizations.

# Traditional Cisco Hardware

While neither exam covers the traditional Cisco hardware at the level of the CCNA exams, it is assumed that you have the knowledge of this hardware fresh in mind. In this section, you will review the basics of the Cisco infrastructure devices (routers and switches) that enable a VoIP network to function. Next, you will review the Cisco IP phone options—both hardware and software phones.

## Cisco Infrastructure Devices for VoIP

The devices used in the network infrastructure can be divided into two basic groups: routers and switches. Even the voice gateways are really nothing more than routers with special software running to perform VoIP gateway operations. For this reason, we'll explore the Cisco infrastructure devices in two sections: one section for the routers and another for the switches. The focus of our discussion will be on VoIP utilization of these devices. For more information on the routers and switches from a general-use perspective, see the book *CCNA Cisco Certified Network Associate Study Guide (Exam 640-802)*, by Richard Deal.

## Switches

The primary functions of Cisco switches in a VoIP implementation are fourfold. First, they provide access to the network, which is of course essential. Second, they configure the VLAN settings for the VoIP phones using the Cisco Discovery Protocol (CDP). Third, the Cisco switches may provide power to the IP phones using Power over Ethernet (PoE). Finally, the fourth function is QoS implementation. While the phones may be trusted to specify QoS settings, specifying the settings can also be performed at the switch as the frames enter the network.

Several switches are available for use in VoIP networks; however, you will likely want to select a switch that offers at least three features:

- Power over Ethernet (PoE) for the powering of the Cisco IP phones
- At least 100-Mbps data rates
- Sufficient ports for your needs

The vast majority of Cisco switches offer configurable QoS support as well. However, if you purchase the newer Cisco switches being sold at retail stores, keep in mind that many of them are not configurable. The phrase "unmanaged switch" is often used to indicate the positive element of this inability to configure the switch. The point of the marketing is that you don't have to manage it—you simply install it and it works. Yes, it does work. It works in the way it's configured to work from the factory, and you have no way of telling it to work any differently. In most business networks, you'll want to avoid these unmanaged switches.

Figure 10-1 shows the Cisco 3550 switch series, which offers all of the features mentioned previously and more. The Cisco 3550 was a common switch used to provide both network access and VoIP operations. The switch has been discontinued and can no longer be purchased new from Cisco. The Cisco 3750 series of switches is the recommended replacement; however, the feature set is close enough so that you can use a 3550 switch for learning in the lab and still be able to properly configure a 3750 in production environments. You are likely to continue encountering 3550 switches in production environments through 2012 or 2013, though official support for them ends in 2011.

The 2950 switch, shown in Figure 10-2, is another example of a useful switch for VoIP networks. The 2950 is considered a fixed configuration switch because it does not support add-on modules. The phrase "fixed configuration" used in Cisco's literature should not be taken to mean the same thing as "unmanaged." Cisco 2950 switches run the IOS and are fully manageable from the CLI or through various GUI tools such as the Cisco Network Assistant (CNA) application.

**FIGURE 10-1**

Cisco 3550 switch (Courtesy of Cisco Systems, Inc. Unauthorized use not permitted.)

Common tasks required to configure switches for use in VoIP networks include:

- Configuring VLANs for voice and data
- Configuring the switchports for voice access
- Enabling the CDP protocol on the appropriate switchports
- Configuring QoS settings

**FIGURE 10-2**

Cisco 2950 switch (Courtesy of Cisco Systems, Inc. Unauthorized use not permitted.)

The following commands represent typical operations on a Cisco 2950 switch:

```
Switch>enable
Switch#configure terminal
Enter configuration commands, one per line.  End with CNTL/Z.
Switch(config)#interface fastethernet0/4
Switch(config-if)#switchport mode access
Switch(config-if)#?
  cdp               Global CDP configuration subcommands
  channel-group     Etherchannel/port bundling configuration
  channel-protocol  Select the channel protocol (LACP, PAgP)
  description       Interface specific description
  duplex            Configure duplex operation.
  exit              Exit from interface configuration mode
  mac-address       Manually set interface MAC address
  mls               mls interface commands
  no                Negate a command or set its defaults
  shutdown          Shutdown the selected interface
  spanning-tree     Spanning Tree Subsystem
  speed             Configure speed operation.
  storm-control     storm configuration
  switchport        Set switching mode characteristics
  tx-ring-limit     Configure PA level transmit ring limit
Switch(config-if)#cdp enable
Switch(config-if)#mls ?
  qos  qos command keyword
Switch(config-if)#mls qos trust ?
  cos     cos keyword
  device  trusted device class
  dscp    dscp keyword
  <cr>
Switch(config-if)#mls qos trust device cisco-phone
Switch(config-if)#exit
```

## Routers

The Cisco routers used for VoIP services are also called integrated services routers (ISRs). Cisco has offered several router series over the years. Older Cisco equipment, including 1700 series, 2600 series, and 3600 series routers, can still be used to implement and test VoIP labs. The newer 800, 1800, 2800, and 3800 series of routers

Cisco 2851
router with
IP phone and
AIM-CUE Unity
Express card
(Courtesy of
Cisco Systems,
Inc. Unauthorized
use not
permitted.)

can also be used for voice services. The 800 series is really useful only in routing voice packets on a network because no voice services can be managed on the router itself. The 1800 through 3800 series routers can perform VoIP operations. Figure 10-3 shows the Cisco 2851 router with an IP phone and AIM-CUE card for Cisco Unity Express implementation.

on the
**job**

*One of my favorite Cisco routers is the 2801 ISR. This router can be used for just about any learning you need to do with modern Cisco exams. You can implement security features, voice features, the Security Device Manager, Call Manager Express, and much more with this entry-level 2800 series device. It has four expansion slots, support for onboard PVDM modules, Compact Flash–based memory (for IOS storage), and two built-in Fast Ethernet ports.*

The common tasks performed by Cisco routers in a VoIP network include:

- Acting as a VoIP gateway
- Acting as an H.323 gatekeeper
- Performing IP routing
- Implementing analog and digital ports

Common configuration tasks on Cisco routers include:

- Installing the Call Manager Express (CME) software
- Configuring CME through the CLI or web interface
- Configuring foreign exchange station (FXS) and foreign exchange office (FXO) ports
- Configuring T1 and E1 ports
- Configuring basic IP interfaces

## Cisco IP Phones

Once the routers and switches are in place, you can begin connecting the Cisco IP phones. Cisco IP phones come in two basic versions: hardware and software. Hardware-based IP phones look like traditional PBX phones we've used in our organizations for decades. Software-based IP phones run on a PC and emulate the functions of a hardware-based IP phone.

The software-based phone offered by Cisco is now called the Cisco IP Communicator to indicate that it is more than just a phone. Figure 10-4 shows the interface of the Cisco IP Communicator software running on a Windows machine. You can see that it looks much like a traditional phone.

**FIGURE 10-4**

Cisco IP Communicator interface (Courtesy of Cisco Systems, Inc. Unauthorized use not permitted.)

According to the Cisco datasheet for the Cisco IP Communicator version 2.1, the following design features are provided:

- **Eight line keys** These keys provide telephone lines and direct access to telephony features.
- **Five softkeys** These keys dynamically give you call-feature options.
- **Messages** This key provides direct access to your voice mail messages.
- **Directories** Cisco IP Communicator identifies incoming messages and categorizes them on the screen, allowing you to return calls quickly and effectively using direct dial-back capability. The corporate directory integrates with the Lightweight Directory Access Protocol Version 3 (LDAP3) standard directory.
- **Settings** This key allows you to select from a large number of ringer sounds and background images.
- **Services** Cisco IP Communicator allows you to quickly access diverse information such as weather, stocks, quote of the day, or any other web-based information. The phone uses XML to provide a portal to an ever-growing world of features and information.
- **Help** The online Help feature gives you information about the phone keys, buttons, and features.

In addition to the design features, the following calling features are supported:

- Multiple lines or directory numbers
- Configurable speed dials
- Calling name and number display
- Call Waiting
- Call Forward
- Call Transfer
- Three Way Calling (conference)
- Park
- Call Pickup

- Redial
- Call Hold
- Barge
- Call Back
- Extension Mobility

Because the Cisco IP Communicator runs on a Windows PC, it is important to consider the hardware requirements. For Windows 2000 and Windows XP, Cisco specifies the following requirements:

- Microsoft Windows 2000 Professional (Service Pack 4) or Windows XP Professional (Service Pack 2)
- Pentium P4 1.0 GHz or equivalent (Pentium P4 1.5 GHz or higher recommended)
- 1 GB RAM
- 100 MB free disk space
- Non-ISA full-duplex sound card (integrated or PCI-based) or USB sound device
- 800×600×16-bit screen resolution (1024×768×16-bit or better recommended)
- 128-kbps network connection

For Windows Vista or Windows 7, the following requirements must be met:

- Performance scores of 3 or higher
- 200 MB free disk space
- 1 GB RAM
- A non-ISA full-duplex sound card (integrated or PCI-based) or USB sound device
- A 10/100-Mbps Ethernet network interface card
- SVGA video card
- 800×600×16-bit screen resolution (1024×768×16-bit or better recommended)

**FIGURE 10-5**

Cisco hardware-
based IP phones
(Courtesy of
Cisco Systems,
Inc. Unauthorized
use not
permitted.)

The hardware-based IP phones offer several advantages over the PC-based IP phones. First, they do not run on the PC and therefore do not take away resources from other computing operations. Second, the hardware-based IP phones have a traditional handset that can be used in the same way as a home PSTN phone. Third, the interface for the hardware-based IP phones is very familiar to the users because it works exactly like the traditional phones they are used to from a dialing, answering, and basic operational perspective. Figure 10-5 shows several Cisco hardware-based IP phones. Also notice the UC500 series all-in-one router/switch/voice gateway and the Cisco Configuration Assistant (CCA) application running on the displayed monitor.

## CERTIFICATION OBJECTIVE 10.01

# 640-460: Implement UC500 Using Cisco Configuration Assistant

The UC500 series devices are aimed at the SOHO market. They come with most of the ports, software, and other components you need to implement wired networks, wireless networks, and VoIP networks. In this section, you will learn about the UC500 series features and models and then explore the configuration options available.

## Introducing UC500

The Unified Communications (UC) 500 series is part of the Smart Business Communications System (SBCS) solution. The UC500 series is aimed at small businesses, branch offices, and home offices and comes in many different editions. Details about the SBCS solution can be found at http://www.cisco.com/go/sbcs.

The Cisco SBCS solutions offer the following features:

- Telephone call-processing software with Auto Attendant, voice mail, and basic call distribution capabilities
- A full line of business phones for all types of business workers, complete with traditional and advanced features such as support for video
- Paging, conferencing, and video calls
- Integrated wireless access (select models)
- Integrated business productivity applications
- Optional ability to see availability of colleagues whether they're using a phone or PC
- Optional integration with popular customer relationship management (CRM) applications from Microsoft or Salesforce.com
- Optional integration with specialized third-party applications for increased employee productivity
- Built-in setup and management tools

The SBCS solutions include more than the UC500 series devices. Table 10-1 provides a breakdown of the components in the SBCS solution line.

**TABLE 10-1**    SBCS Components

| Component | Description |
|-----------|-------------|
| UC500 Series | Implements voice, data, and wireless communications in a single unit. Managed through embedded web-based software, a limited CLI, or through Cisco Configuration Assistant (CCA). |
| ESW500 Switches | Inexpensive switch services for small businesses and branch offices. Managed through embedded web-based software or through CCA. |
| 500 Series Routers | Devices in the 500 series that provide VPN connectivity, Internet access, enhanced security, and optional wireless networking, but no voice services. Managed through the embedded web-based software, a limited CLI, or through CCA. |
| 500 Series APs | Wireless Access Points (APs) in the 500 series. Support clustering technologies for larger networks. |
| SPA500 Series IP Phones | Small business IP phones with wideband audio, XML applications, and customizable menus. These phones are compatible with UC500 series voice gateways, SIP voice gateways, and hosted service providers. |
| 7900 Series IP Phones | The same phones used in larger VoIP networks can operate in VoIP networks using the UC500 series devices. |

Figure 10-6 shows the SBCS components including a UC500 series router/gateway, an ESW540 switch, and the SPA524 model Cisco SPA series IP phone alongside the SPA525G and a 7925 and a wireless IP phone.

Within the UC500 series of router/gateway devices, three primary lines are offered. Table 10-2 provides a breakdown of these three lines and the features they offer.

**TABLE 10-2**    UC500 Series Line and Features

| | **UC520** | **UC540** | **UC560** |
|---|---|---|---|
| Features | • 8 to 64 IP phone station support | • 8 to 32 phone station support | • 16 to 104 phone station support |
| | • 4 to 8 analog trunks or 2 to 4 BRI digital trunks | • 4 to 8 analog trunks or 2 to 4 BRI digital trunks | • 4 to 12 analog trunks or 2 to 6 BRI digital trunks |
| | • Optional single T1/E1 voice interface (PRI and CAS) | • Optional single T1/E1 voice interface (PRI and CAS) | • Optional one or two T1/E1 voice interface (PRI and CAS) |
| | • Integrated voice mail | • Integrated voice mail | • Integrated voice mail |
| | • 16 hours voice mail storage | • 32 hours voice mail storage | • 32 or 64 hours voice mail storage |
| | • Automated attendant | • Automated attendant | • Automated attendant |
| | • Integrated business productivity applications | • Integrated business productivity applications | • Integrated business productivity applications |
| | • Integrated security | • Integrated security | • Integrated security |
| | • Music on Hold | • Music on Hold | • Music on Hold |
| | • Optional on-board wireless access | • On-board wireless included | • Wireless support with the Cisco AP 500 Series Wireless Access Point |
| | • Simple system configuration and management | • Simple system configuration and management | • Simple system configuration and management |

## Introducing the Cisco Configuration Assistant

While the UC500 series routers and gateways support a minimal CLI, the primary configuration options are the web-based interface or the Cisco Configuration Assistant (CCA). The CCA is a Windows-based, Java-dependent application that can be used to configure the devices included in the SBCS series. The CCA is a free download available at http://www.cisco.com/en/US/products/ps7287/index.html. The CCA provides the following features:

- Configuration, deployment, and ongoing network management support for the Cisco Smart Business Communications System
- Setup wizards
- Multiple network views
- Simplified network reporting
- Drag-and-drop software updates
- Troubleshooting

Because the CCA is a local application (installed on your Windows desktop), the installation process is very simple. You need only specify the directory to which you wish to install, and all other defaults can be accepted. Once CCA is installed, you will launch the CCA application and configure a site to begin using the administration tools. The system requirements for CCA are listed in Table 10-3.

The first step to using the CCA is the configuration of customer sites. Don't let the phrase "customer sites" scare you. The CCA is used in organizations, and a customer site is a reference to a location that you serve as the IT support group. Of course, the CCA could also be used to manage external customer sites by a consulting agency, but this is not the intention of Cisco's naming. Figure 10-7 shows the Connect dialog box, which is used to configure and manage customer sites or to simply connect directly to a device without specifying a customer site.

| TABLE 10-3 | Component | Requirement |
|---|---|---|
| System Requirements for CCA | Operating systems | Windows: Windows XP Professional (Service Pack 1 or later) or Windows Vista Ultimate (32 bit or 64 bit); Microsoft Internet Explorer 6.0 or later, with Adobe Flash Player 10 or later; Mac OS support (requires virtualization software) |
| | Disk space | 200 MB minimum, 400 MB recommended |
| | Hardware | PC with Fast Ethernet or higher LAN port |
| | Memory | 512 MB minimum, 1024 MB recommended |
| | Processor | 1-GHz Pentium IV or higher |
| | Screen resolution | 1024×768 minimum, 1280×1024 recommended |

CCA Connect
dialog box used
to create sites

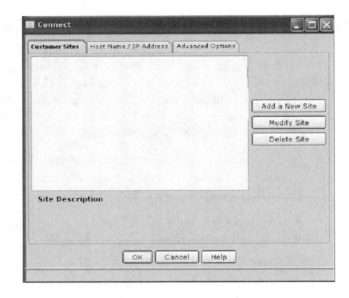

When you connect to a device or site, you will see the dashboard. Figure 10-8 provides a zoomed-out view of this dashboard. From here you can access monitoring statistics for the device or site, and you can view events and alerts as well.

*For more detailed information on using the CCA, download the Cisco Configuration Assistant SBCS Administrator Guide at http://www.cisco.com/en/ US/docs/net_mgmt/cisco_configuration_assistant/version2_1/administration_ guide/cca21_sbcs_admin_guide.pdf.*

## Configuring UC500 Devices

When you first install a UC500 device, you will need to configure several parameters and features. Most of these configuration actions can be taken within the CCA GUI interface, making the process simple. This section provides recommendations for the configuration of these various parameters. To gain access to the voice device configuration interface, simply connect to a UC500 series device with voice interfaces and select Configure | Telephony | Voice. Figure 10-9 shows the tabs available in

**FIGURE 10-8**    CCA dashboard

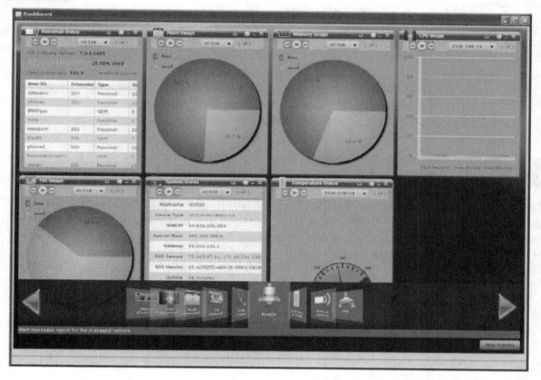

the Devices dialog box. Depending on the device to which you connect, you will see different enabled tabs in the Devices dialog box, but the optional tabs include:

- Device
- System
- Network
- AA & Voicemail
- SIP Trunk
- Voice Features
- Dial Plan
- Users

**FIGURE 10-9**

The tabs in
the Devices
dialog box

If you look closely at the CCNA Voice (Exam 640-460) objectives, you'll notice that the configuration requirements mirror these tabs almost exactly. The following sections discuss the options in each tab.

**e x a m**
**ⓦatch**

*If you are planning to take the 640-460 exam, be sure to get some hands-on experience configuring these settings with the CCA and a UC500 device.*

*If you plan to take the CVOICE exam instead, the information in this section will be a helpful review, but you will not need to understand the CCA interface.*

## Device Parameters

The device parameters include the Hardware Configuration and the Voice System Type section. In the Hardware Configuration section, you can view the router platform, which indicates the number of licensed users you can support. You can also view the following parameters:

- **Built-in Components**  These components include Unity Express modules, FXO ports, FXS ports, and switchports.
- **VIC**  This section shows the inserted VIC card if one is in use.
- **Wireless**  This section shows the wireless AP in the UC500 system if one is in use.

In the Voice System Type section, you can choose between two options:

- **Configure as a PBX**  This is the default option. Incoming calls are routed to an auto attendant or human operator and then connected to the called party.
- **Configure as a Key System**  This is not the default option. Incoming calls can be answered on any phone.

## System Parameters

On the System tab, you can configure the regional settings, which impact call tones, phone languages, date and time format, and the voice mail language. You may also configure system-wide speed-dial settings here.

## Network Parameters

The configurable network parameters include the IP information for the UC500 device and the VLAN information. Much like SOHO routers (such as Linksys and D-Link devices), the UC500 series offers simple configuration of DHCP servers and the IP address of the call manager (the CME in the Cisco world). The following parameters can be configured on the Network tab of the Devices dialog box:

- **VLAN Number**  This can be a number from 1 to 1001. This is the VLAN that will be configured as the voice VLAN.
- **DHCP IP Address Pool**  This defines the range of addresses to be configured automatically for the clients. Supporting fields include the Subnet Mask, Exclude Address From, and To fields. The DHCP IP Address Pool field will contain the subnet identifier, for example, 192.168.1.0. The Subnet Mask field will contain the appropriate mask for the subnet identifier, for example, 255.255.255.0. The Exclude Address From and To fields will include the beginning and ending addresses that define the range that should not be given out by the DHCP server, such as 192.168.1.50 to 192.168.1.59.
- **CME IP Address**  This is the IP address of the Communications Manager Express (CME) call manager server. The supporting field is the Subnet Mask field used to identify the network on which the CME server resides.

## Auto Attendant and Voice Mail

Several fields can be configured on the AA & Voicemail tab. The sections to be configured include Auto Attendant, Script Parameters, and Voicemail. In the Auto Attendant section, you can configure the phone extension of the Auto Attendant service. This is usually the main extension phone number for the organization. You can also configure the outside number (the PSTN number) used to reach the Auto Attendant. Finally, you can use the default AA script, or select a custom script you've developed.

The Script Parameters section is not used if the default AA script is selected. When a custom script is selected, you can specify the audio file to play when the different keypad numbers are pressed. The numbers 0 through 9 can be configured.

The Voice mail section lets you configure the extension and PSTN number dialed to reach the voice mail system.

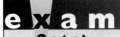

*Remember that you can configure the audio file to play for the keypad presses of 0 through 9 in the AA &* *Voicemail tab of the Devices dialog box and that these options only apply when a custom or non-default AA script is used.*

### SIP Trunks

If you are using analog connections to the PSTN through FXO ports or digital lines, you will not configure a SIP trunk. If you are using an Internet Telephony Service Provider (ITSP), you will need to configure a SIP trunk to the ITSP. To configure a SIP trunk on the SIP Trunk tab in the Devices dialog box, configure the parameters provided by your ITSP. The most current UC500 series software and CCA at the time this book was written offered support for the following service providers:

- AT&T
- Broadview
- British Telecom (BT)
- Cbeyond
- Covad
- Fibernet
- Nuvox
- One Communications
- PAETEC
- XO Communications

*Because service providers come and go, you will not be required to memorize this list of service providers for the 640-460 exam.*

## Voice System Features

The Voice Features tab includes the ability to configure the following parameters:

- **Music on Hold**   Simply select the audio file you want to play for MoH.

- **Intercom**   Phones can be enabled for intercom use if the Enable Intercom check box is checked.

- **Paging**   Paging groups can be enabled with three directory numbers (DNs) in each of a maximum of four paging group extensions.

- **Hunt Group**   Hunt groups can be enabled with a timeout value, which indicates the number of rings to try for each number in the hunt group. The hunt type can also be specified. The hunt types include sequential, longest idle, and peer. A sequential hunt type sends the call to the first DN in the hunt group and only moves on to the next DN if the first does not answer in the timeout window. A longest-idle hunt type sends the call to the DN that has been idle for the longest time (not on a call for the longest time). A peer hunt type sends the call to the next DN in the hunt group after the DN that most recently answered a call (round robin).

- **Group Pickup**   Group Pickup can simply be enabled here. Once enabled, a user can enter a code on his phone in order to answer someone else's phone in the same pickup group. Once Group Pickup is enabled, up to eight pickup groups can be specified.

- **Caller ID Block Code**   This setting specifies the number a user must dial before dialing another number to block her caller ID. The caller ID block number will be preceded by a * when dialed by the user.

- **Outgoing Call Block Number List**   This list includes numbers you do not allow internal users to dial.

- **Call Park**   Call parking allows the user to place a call on hold and resume the call from another phone. Call park slots are configured to work on special extensions.

- **Multi-party (Ad hoc) Conference**   Up to eight conference calls with up to three participants each are supported by default. Additionally, all callers must use G.711 or G.729 to reduce processing costs. However, you can enable mixed mode here if the DSP resources are available. Mixed mode allows a mixture of G.711 and G.729 users in the conference at the same time.

*Remember the three hunt types configurable in the CCA: sequential, longest idle, and peer. Also be sure to remember how they work. Sequential hunt types simply ring the first number in the list and try the next until a number answers.*

*Longest idle always rings the number that has not been on a call for the longest time. Peer always rings the number in the hunt group that immediately follows the number most recently answering a call.*

## Dial Plans

The Dial Plan tab allows you to set up the dial plan to use on your VoIP network. You can set up several dial plan parameters, including:

- Extension digit length
- Outgoing call numbering plan
- Length of area codes
- Length of local external numbers
- Digit or digits required to place long-distance calls
- Requirements for placing international calls
- Access code number for outbound call placement
- Emergency number configurations
- Processing for inbound FXO calls
- Direct Inward Dial (DID) configuration

## User Parameters

The Users tab is used to create both users and phones. Simply clicking the New button gets you started in the process. You can specify the MAC Address, phone type, primary DN (extension), user first name and last name, user ID, password, and phone-specific settings.

on the **j**ob

*The CCA interface is subject to change. When this book was written, the tabs and options were available as defined here. However, you should check the Cisco web site for documentation on the most recent version of the CCA to ensure you understand where and how to configure these options in the version you are using.*

# 640-460: Implement Voice Mail Features Using Cisco Unity Express

The Cisco Unity platform is the voice mail and messaging solution Cisco offers. It comes in many different editions, but for the 640-460 exam, you'll need to understand the basics of the Cisco Unity Express Edition. In this section, you will learn about the Cisco Unity Express hardware options and the basic configuration settings available within the system.

## Introducing Unity Express

Cisco Unity Express (CUE) is the small business edition of Cisco's voice mail and messaging solution. CUE provides voice mail services for up to 250 users in most implementations. You can use the command-line interface (CLI) or the GUI for management of the CUE modules and services. To fully understand CUE, you'll need to learn the following:

■ Unity Express hardware implementations
■ Features of Unity Express

### Unity Express Hardware

The CUE hardware comes in three basic versions:

■ **AIM-CUE**   This form factor uses the daughter card format and a flash memory module for the Linux file system and the message storage. The AIM-CUE version supports up to 50 mailboxes, six voice sessions, and a total of 14 hours of mailbox storage.

■ **NM-CUE**   This form factor uses the network module format and is shown in Figure 10-10. A hard drive is used for the Linux file system and the message storage. Up to 100 mailboxes can be created with eight voice sessions and 100 hours of mailbox storage.

■ **NM-CUE-EC**   The extended capacity of the NM-CUE version adds support for up to 250 mailboxes, 16 voice sessions, and 300 hours of mailbox storage.

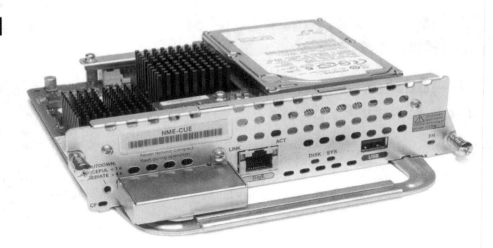

All three versions are installed in the CME router, and the NM versions provide a network interface for connecting to the CUE server. Interestingly, even though the NM versions are installed in the CME router, the internal network interfaces are not used to communicate with it. The NM version effectively acts as a Linux appliance that happens to be installed in the CME gateway router.

## Unity Express Features

CUE systems support standard voice mail features. The following features are supported by Cisco's CUE-based voice mail system:

- Command-line interface (CLI) or GUI management tools.
- CUE can integrate with multiple CME sites (up to ten are supported on NM-CUE versions only).
- CUE modules have their own embedded Linux-based operating system and processors.
- Scheduled backups of voice mail messages can be made to secure FTP servers.
- CUE modules support incremental upgrades rather than having to update the entire operating system.
- The TimeCardView add-on can be purchased to allow for time card management in an organization.
- General-delivery mailboxes (GDM) for group voice mail boxes.

- Common voice mail features, including replying, forwarding, saving, message tagging for privacy or urgency, alternative greetings, pause, fast forward, and rewind.

- Live reply allows the voice mail user either to send back a voice mail message or to call the extension at which the message was left based on the information in the message envelope (caller ID information).

- Distribution lists allow for sending voice mails to groups instead of individuals.

- CUE desktop messaging allows users to retrieve their voice mail messages as audio files in Outlook, Outlook Express, and Lotus Notes.

# Configuring Unity Express

The configuration of CUE is broken into three basic parts in the CCNA Voice objectives. First, you need to prepare the environment by configuring the required settings in the CME server to support CUE. Second, you'll configure the Auto Attendant feature. Finally, you'll perform voice mail configuration tasks. All three are addressed in the following sections.

## Preparing the Environment

Before the CUE installation and configuration can be successfully performed, you will need to prepare the CME router. First, you'll need to identify the service engine slot that contains the CUE module. The **show interfaces** command will show the interfaces, which will list the service engine slot in which the CUE module is located. Now, you can configure the service engine and the internal loopback that must be configured for everything to work properly. The following commands will work on most CME routers with a CUE module inserted:

```
interface loopback 0
 ip address 10.10.3.1 255.255.255.0
interface service-engine1/0
 ip unnumbered loopback 0
 service-module ip address 10.10.3.2 255.255.255.0
 service-module ip default gateway 10.10.3.1
ip route 10.10.3.2 255.255.255.255 service-engine1/0
```

You will need only to change the IP address configuration settings to match your environment. With these commands in the running configuration, you'll be ready to work with the service module or the CUE interface.

In addition to the IP configuration for the CUE module, you may want to enable the HTTP server so that you can use the GUI web-server interface to work with the module. To accomplish this, execute the following commands in configuration mode:

```
ip http server
ip http path flash:
```

Finally, you'll need to configure the proper ephone-dn IDs and a dial-peer for communications between the CME router and the CUE server. The following commands provide an example configuration:

```
dial-peer voice 2900 voip
 destination-pattern 29..
 session protocol sipv2
 session target ipv4:10.10.3.2
 dtmf-relay sip-notify
 codec g711ulaw
 no vad
 exit
ephone-dn 19
 number 2999
 mwi on
exit
 ephone-dn 20
 number 2998
 mwi off
 exit
```

The dial-peer ID and ephone-dn IDs can be changed as well as the numbers and IP addresses. However, it's important to know that the **codec g711ulaw** and **no vad** commands are required for proper CME and CUE communications.

Now that the CEM is set up for the CUE module to function, you can complete the standard initial configuration at the CLI. These settings include a host name, DNS server address, NTP server address, time zone configuration, and the administrator username and password. The same basic parameters you would configure for a full Cisco router should be configured for the CUE module.

## Voice Mail Configuration

The initial configuration of the CUE module is performed through an initialization wizard. The initialization wizard is accessed through the web-based interface. The following steps outline the process involved:

1. Connect to the CUE module's web server. You will use the IP address assigned to the CUE module, and connect to it using the HTTP protocol.

2. Enter the username and password for access to the module. This will be the administrator username and password configured during initial CLI setup.

3. Once the web page is displayed, select the Run Initialization Wizard option.

4. Verify the host name, username, and password and click Next.

5. Import any usernames and passwords from the CME router that you desire and click Next.

6. Configure mailbox defaults, such as the language, mailbox size (in seconds), maximum message size (in seconds), and message expiry time (in days), and then click Next.

7. Configure the call handling procedures such as the voice mail number, the operator extension, the AA access number, and operator, and then click Next.

8. Review the settings you've chosen and then click Finish.

Once the wizard is completed, you'll be shown an Initialization Wizard Status report listing the tasks taken and whether they succeeded or failed. Assuming everything was successful, at this point, the voice mail server is active and can be used by your users.

### Auto Attendant Configuration

The CUE web-based administration interface provides a GUI for Auto Attendant (AA) configuration. When you access the web-based admin, select Voice Mail | Auto Attendant to work with the AA feature. From here you can enable and disable the default AA script. You cannot modify the default, but you can create your own script if desired by clicking the Add Link button. Basic parameters that can be configured for the AA include:

- AA configuration name
- Script to be used
- Call-in number
- Maximum active sessions
- Whether the AA is enabled or disabled

*Remember that you can modify only custom AA scripts. You can enable or disable the default script, but you cannot delete, modify, or download it.*

# CERTIFICATION SUMMARY

In this chapter, you learned about the basic Cisco hardware used in a VoIP network. You first reviewed the traditional hardware such as switches and routers. Then you explored the UC500 series of devices and the Cisco Configuration Assistant used for configuration tasks. Finally, you learned about the Cisco Unity Express solution for voice mail and messaging features.

# ✔ TWO-MINUTE DRILL

### 640-460: Implement UC500 Using Cisco Configuration Assistant

❑ The Cisco Configuration Assistant (CCA) is used to configure and manage the UC500 series of devices.

❑ The CCA is a free download from Cisco.com and can be installed on a Windows 2000 or later computer.

❑ Customer sites are used to group managed devices together for monitoring and management.

❑ The Auto Attendant feature can be configured with a custom script and audio files mapped to the keypad buttons for 0 through 9.

❑ When Group Pickup is enabled, up to eight pickup groups can be defined.

❑ Three hunt group types are supported, including sequential, longest idle, and peer.

❑ The Call Park feature allows a user to place a call on hold and resume the call at another phone.

❑ By default, eight conferences with three callers in each are supported on the UC500 series devices.

❑ More conferences and mixed-mode conferencing can be used if DSP resources are available.

❑ The network parameters include the VLAN for voice connections, the DHCP pool configuration, and the location of the CME server.

### 640-460: Implement Voice Mail Features Using Cisco Unity Express

❑ The NM-CUE versions of CUE can support integration with up to ten CME sites.

❑ Before you can configure the CUE module, you must prepare the CME router by configuring the IP settings for the module and enabling the HTTP server.

❑ A dial-peer and set of ephone-dn IDs must be created for proper communications between the CME and the CUE server.

❑ The **service-module** command instead of the **interface** command is used to work with service modules.

❑ The default AA script cannot be deleted; it can only be enabled or disabled.

❑ The Initialization Wizard is used to initially configure the voice mail settings for the CUE module.

❑ Mailbox defaults include the language, mailbox size, message size, and message expiry time.

# SELF TEST

The following questions will help you measure your understanding of the material presented in this chapter. Read all the choices carefully because there might be more than one correct answer. Choose all correct answers for each question.

## 640-460: Implement UC500 Using Cisco Configuration Assistant

1. What application is primarily used to configure SBCS devices, including the UC500 series?
   A. PuTTY
   B. CCA
   C. SDM
   D. IPSec

2. What operating systems can run the Cisco Configuration Assistant natively? (Choose all that apply.)
   A. MAC OS X
   B. Windows XP
   C. Windows Vista
   D. Linux

3. When a custom script is configured for the AA from within the CCA, how many keypad digits can be associated with audio files?
   A. 9
   B. 10
   C. 0
   D. 16

4. What feature allows a user to place a call on hold and resume the call at another phone?
   A. Call parking
   B. Call forwarding
   C. Call toll
   D. Voice mail

5. What is the default number of conferences allowed on a UC500 series device?
   A. 3
   B. 5
   C. 4
   D. 8

**6.** How many callers are allowed in a conference by default on a UC500 series device?

    A. 3

    B. 5

    C. 4

    D. 8

**7.** To increase the number of allowed conferences or to implement mixed-mode conferences that use both the G.711 and G.729 codecs, what will be required?

    A. CCA 7.0 or higher

    B. UC560 series

    C. DSP resources

    D. Gigabit Ethernet interfaces

**8.** Which hunt group type routes a call using a round robin method?

    A. Sequential

    B. Looped

    C. Peer

    D. Longest idle

**9.** Which hunt group type simply routes a call to the next number in the list after the last number to which a call was routed?

    A. Sequential

    B. Looped

    C. Peer

    D. Longest idle

## 640-460: Implement Voice Mail Features Using Cisco Unity Express

**10.** How many CME sites can be integrated with a single CUE module?

    A. 1

    B. 2

    C. 5

    D. 10

**11.** Which one of the following is not a CUE mailbox default parameter?

    A. Mailbox size in seconds

    B. Message length in seconds

    C. Message expiry in seconds

    D. Language

**12.** What IP address is used to access the CUE service-module?

    **A.** The CME router's FastEthernet0/1 interface address

    **B.** The CME router's virtual interface address

    **C.** The CUE service module's IP address

    **D.** The IP address of the DNS server

**13.** You cannot delete the default AA script, but you can perform which two actions on it? (Choose two.)

    **A.** Download

    **B.** Modify

    **C.** Enable

    **D.** Disable

**14.** What two commands are required in the dial-peer for communications with the CUE service module from the CME router? (Choose two.)

    **A.** no vad

    **B.** codec g711ulaw

    **C.** codec g728

    **D.** vad

**15.** What command is used to work with a service module instead of the Cisco IOS interface command?

    **A.** service-module

    **B.** service-engine

    **C.** module-interface

    **D.** engine-interface

# LAB QUESTION

You must enable the HTTP server in a Cisco ISR so that you can work with the Unity Express module. What two commands should you use and what does each command do?

# SELF TEST ANSWERS

## 640-460: Implement UC500 Using Cisco Configuration Assistant

1. ☑ **B** is correct. The Cisco Configuration Assistant is used with the entire line of SBCS products including the UC500 series.

   ☒ **A, C,** and **D** are incorrect. PuTTY is a telnet client that may be used to gain CLI access. The Security Device Manager (SDM) is used with traditional ISR routers. IPSec is an IP security protocol solution.

2. ☑ **B** and **C** are correct. The CCA can run on any Windows operating system from Windows 2000 through to Windows 7.

   ☒ **A** and **D** are incorrect. You must use a virtual Windows operating system to run the CCA in either the MAC OS or Linux.

3. ☑ **B** is correct. Because the digits 0–9 can be assigned audio files, you can associate up to 10.

   ☒ **A, C,** and **D** are incorrect. These answers are simply incorrect.

4. ☑ **A** is correct. The call parking feature allows a user to place a call on hold and then pick it up again at another extension.

   ☒ **B, C,** and **D** are incorrect. Call forwarding allows the user to send a call to another user. Call toll references the cost of calls and is not a specific feature. Voice mail allows callers to leave messages for users.

5. ☑ **D** is correct. By default, up to 8 conferences may be run concurrently.

   ☒ **A, B,** and **C** are incorrect. These answers are simply incorrect.

6. ☑ **A** is correct. By default, up to 3 callers may participate in a single conference.

   ☒ **B, C,** and **D** are incorrect. These answers are simply incorrect.

7. ☑ **C** is correct. Digital Signal Processor (DSP) resources are required to increase the number of conferences or to allow for mixed-mode conferencing.

   ☒ **A, B,** and **D** are incorrect. The conferencing limit is configured in the CCA but imposed by the hardware and software in the UC500 series devices. The UC560 series is not a specific requirement, but the available DSP resources are. Gigabit interfaces are not required for more conference calls.

8. ☑ **C** is correct. The peer hunt group type uses a round robin method.

☒ **A**, **B**, and **D** are incorrect. The sequential hunt group type uses the next number after the first number fails to answer. The looped hunt type does not exist. The longest idle hunt type directs the call to the extension that has not answered a call in the longest time.

9. ☑ **A** is correct. The sequential hunt group type uses the next number after the first number fails to answer.

☒ **B**, **C**, and **D** are incorrect. The looped hunt type does not exist. The peer hunt group type uses a round robin method. The longest idle hunt type directs the call to the extension that has not answered a call in the longest time.

## 640-460: Implement Voice Mail Features Using Cisco Unity Express

10. ☑ **D** is correct. Up to 10 CME sites may be integrated into a single CUE module

☒ **A**, **B**, and **C** are incorrect. These answers are simply incorrect.

11. ☑ **C** is correct. The message expiry is set in days and not seconds.

☒ **A**, **B**, and **D** are incorrect. The mailbox size and message length are both specified in seconds, and the language is also a mailbox default setting.

12. ☑ **C** is correct. The service module has its own IP address, and this address is used to access the CUE module.

☒ **A**, **B**, and **D** are incorrect. These answers are simply incorrect.

13. ☑ **C** and **D** are correct. You can only enable or disable the default AA script.

☒ **A** and **B** are incorrect. You cannot download, modify, or delete the default AA script.

14. ☑ **A** and **B** are correct. You must include the **no vad** and the **codec g711ulaw** commands.

☒ **C** and **D** are incorrect. The **codec g728** command is not required, and neither is the **vad** command.

15. ☑ **A** is correct. The **service-module** command is used to work with the CUE module.

☒ **B**, **C**, and **D** are incorrect. These answers are simply invalid.

# LAB ANSWER

You must used the **ip http server** and **ip http path flash:** commands. The first command enables the HTTP web server. The second command configures the location used to access the web server files.

# 11

# Digital Signal Processors

> *One machine can do the work of fifty ordinary men.*
> *No machine can do the work of one extraordinary man.*
>
> —Elbert Hubbard

I f you've been around computers long, you know that many different types of specialized processors are used in computers today. In the 1990s, math coprocessors were introduced to offload much of the mathematical processing from the primary CPU in the machine. In the late 1990s and to this day, graphics processing units (GPUs) are used to offload the graphics processing and to enhance the graphics display capabilities of a computer. In the same way, special processors can be used to offload much of the voice processing required in VoIP networks from the Cisco ISRs main processors. As I've said in other chapters, a Cisco ISR (integrated services router) is basically a computer with special hardware and software for routing and voice call management functions. This chapter introduces a component of these gateways known as a digital signal processor (DSP), which can reduce the burden on the CPU of the router and is actually required in order to implement some VoIP features.

"Work" can be defined as performing mental or physical actions with the objective of accomplishing some goal. CPUs are generic and they are not optimized for specific tasks. An optimized processor is like Elbert Hubbard's "extraordinary man" in that it can do more of its specialized work for the cost than a generic CPU can. This optimization is the role of the DSP in voice processing and is the topic of this chapter.

## CERTIFICATION OBJECTIVE 11.01

# 642-436: Describe DSP Functionality

To plan a VoIP implementation using Cisco ISRs as gateways, you'll need to understand the digital signal processor (DSP). The DSP is a special kind of processor or microprocessor that is designed for processing digital signals. In this section, you'll gain an understanding for what DSPs are, how to choose the right DSP for your ISR, how to install that DSP once you've purchased it, and how to verify and configure the DSP resources with Cisco IOS commands.

## Introducing Digital Signal Processors

DSPs are processors dedicated to processing digital signals. Not only are they dedicated to processing digital signals, but they are also optimized for it. To understand the benefit of this optimization, consider the difference between me (a computer-and-network engineer) and a carpenter (and I don't mean in name only, like myself). My brain is not necessarily superior to the carpenter's, but I can set up a computer network many times faster than the carpenter. The carpenter's brain is not necessarily superior to mine, but he could certainly build a house many times faster than I. Through years of experience and learning, our brains have become specialized, and while they may work at the same speed, they do not allow us both to do the same thing equally well.

DSPs look much like a memory chip that you would install in a desktop computer. However, instead of having simple memory chips on board, they contain processors. Figure 11-1 shows a typical PVDM2 (packet voice/data module version 2) module that contains four DSPs.

In Cisco gateways, DSP resources are used in four primary ways (all four categorized as media processing):

- **Transcoding** In some networks, the gateway connects two different VoIP networks or even devices that use different codecs on the same network. For example, if G.729 needs to be converted to G.711, or vice versa, a DSP resource is required.

- **Conferencing** A voice conference occurs when more than two endpoints are participating in a call. Something is required to combine or mix multiple incoming audio streams into a single outgoing stream that is sent to conference participants. DSPs provide this conferencing capability.

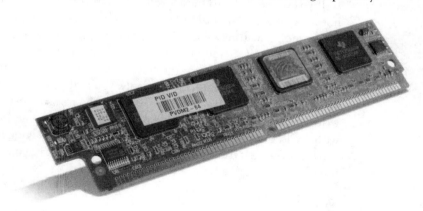

**FIGURE 11-1**

Cisco Systems PVDM2-64 containing four DSPs (Courtesy of Cisco Systems, Inc. Unauthorized use not permitted.)

■ **Voice Termination**  This function is performed when the gateway connects to the PSTN or another TDM-based voice network. The TDM communications must be terminated at the gateway and coded as VoIP packets for the internal voice network. The DSPs perform the termination and provide features such as echo cancelation, jitter management, and voice activity detection (VAD).

■ **Media Termination Point (MTP)**  The MTP is used if you place your phone on hold. There is no reason for communications to stream between your phone and the other phone while on hold. During this time the DSP can be used so the gateway can "hold" the call for you. Additionally, MTPs may bridge to connections that use different packetization periods. Finally, an MTP can transcode from G.711 a-law to G.711 μ-law, and vice versa. These last two capabilities are known as *repacketization*.

Cisco DSPs come in two forms. The first is C549. The second is the C5510, the newer DSP. The newer DSPs can handle more calls per DSP. In fact, the C5510 DSPs have about twice the processing power of the C549 DSPs.

## Selecting DSPs

The number of DSPs required for your VoIP network will depend on the technologies used on the network. Technologies that will impact your DSP selection include

■ Conferencing
■ Codec selection (codec complexity)
■ Gateway implementations

If you do not plan to support conferencing on the local VoIP network, you will not have to worry about DSP resources for conferencing. However, if you need conferencing features, you must consider the needed DSP resources. Because the determination of the number of DSPs required for a given scenario can become complex very quickly, Cisco provides a DSP calculator at http://www.cisco.com/cgi-bin/Support/DSP/dsp-calc.pl. Sadly, you will need a Cisco support account to access the page, and it was not a feature of the free support account at the time of writing. This will not be a problem if you're currently employed in an organization with a Cisco support contract; however, if you are studying for the CCNA Voice certification with the aim of acquiring such a position, you may be unable to access the calculator at this time.

Determining the DSP resources needed for a conference call is based on two primary factors. The first is the hardware module or chassis in use. For example, the NM-HDV2 module can handle from one to four PVDM2 modules. Each module can be one of the following types:

- PVDM2-8 (1/2 DSP)
- PVDM2-16 (1 DSP)
- PVDM2-32 (2 DSPs)
- PVDM2-48 (3 DSPs)
- PVDM2-64 (4 DSPs)

The second factor is the codecs used in the conference. For example, if all users use the G.711 codec, more conference calls can be handled concurrently than if users use G.729. In fact, if just one user uses the G.729 codec in a conference call, the number of concurrent calls including such a user drops by 75 percent. With a single PVDM2-8 module, an ISR running pure G.711 conferences can handle up to four concurrent conferences. If one or more participants use G.729, only one conference can be handled at a time with the same module.

The preceding information was based on the NM-HDV2 module. However, when other modules are used, or routers that have built-in support for DSP modules are used, the calculations change. If you do not have access to the DSP calculator referenced previously, you should consider accessing the following web page: http://www.cisco.com/en/US/prod/collateral/routers/ps5854/product_data_sheet0900aecd8016e845_ps3115_Products_Data_Sheet.html, which includes tables of channel densities for the different PVDM modules.

Codec complexity can also impact the number of DSPs, and therefore, PVDM modules you'll need to acquire. For example, the medium complexity codecs such as G.711 and G.726 allow for four calls per DSP. The high complexity codecs such as G.728 and G.723 allow for only two calls per DSP. Generally speaking, you will use lower complexity codecs to get more out of your DSP resources; however, you must use higher complexity codecs to consume less bandwidth on your network.

The final factor that will impact your selection of DSP resources is the ISR gateway you're using. For example, if you're using the 1700 series routers (1751 or 1760), they have built-in support for up to two PVDM modules out-of-the-box. The 2800 series routers also include this support. For the routers that do not support on-board PVDM modules, you'll need to acquire network modules such as the NM- that allow for PVDM modules to be installed.

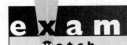

## Installing DSPs

The good news is that if you've ever installed a memory chip in a computer, you'll feel right at home installing PVDM modules that contain DSPs. The basic process for installing the DSP resources in an ISR supporting on-board PVDMs is as follows:

1. Power down and disconnect the router from the network and the power source.
2. Ensure electrostatic discharge (ESD) best practices are followed by grounding yourself.
3. Remove the router's cover.
4. Insert the PVDM module into the appropriate slot.
5. Replace the cover.
6. Connect the router to power and the network.
7. Power on the router.

If you are installing DSPs using a network module such as the NM-HDV2, you will not have to remove the cover. You should power down the router and disconnect it from the network as the preceding steps indicate. You will then remove the network module expansion cover, slide the NM-HDV2 (containing the already installed PVDM modules) into the slot, and tighten the holding screws. Reconnect the router and power it on.

## Verifying and Configuring DSPs

Once you've physically installed the DSPs, you can verify their presence with the **show voice dsp** command while in enable mode. Figure 11-2 shows the output of the **show voice dsp** command. This command will show you the DSP resources and the codec complexity configured for these resources. The **show version** command will also provide output similar to the following:

```
Cisco 2801 (revision 7.0) with 239616K/22528K bytes of memory.
Processor board ID FTX1141W0ZK
2 FastEthernet interfaces
1 Virtual Private Network (VPN) Module
2 Voice FXS interfaces
1 DSP, 8 Voice resources
DRAM configuration is 64 bits wide with parity disabled.
191K bytes of NVRAM.
500472K bytes of ATA CompactFlash (Read/Write)
```

Notice the line that reads 1 DSP, 8 Voice resources. This line shows that the PVDM module has been detected.

To begin using the DSP resources, you must assign them to a DSP farm. This is accomplished with the **dsp services dspfarm** command from within voicecard configuration mode, as shown in Figure 11-3.

With the DSP resources associated with a DSP farm, you can create DSP farm profiles. These profiles are created in dspfarm-profile configuration mode, and they assign the allowed codecs, the maximum sessions, and the association with a VoIP protocol (such as SCCP). Then the farm profile is brought online with the **no shutdown** command. This configuration is shown for a transcoding setup in Figure 11-4.

| FIGURE 11-2 |
| --- |
| The output of the **show voice dsp** command |

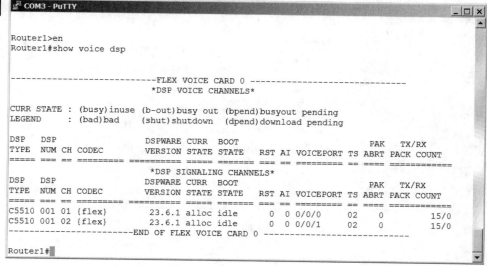

```
COM3 - PuTTY                                                              _ □ ×

Press RETURN to get started.




Router1>en
Router1#conf t
Enter configuration commands, one per line.  End with CNTL/Z.
Router1(config)#voice-card 0
Router1(config-voicecard)#?
Voice-card configuration commands:
  codec         Manage codec configuration parameters for voice card
  default       Set a command to its defaults
  dsp           Manage DSP configuration for the voice card
  exit          Exit from voice card configuration mode
  local-bypass  Enable TDM hairpinning
  no            Negate a command or set its defaults

Router1(config-voicecard)#dsp services dspfarm
Router1(config-voicecard)#exit
Router1(config)#
```

```
COM3 - PuTTY                                                              _ □ ×




Router1>enable
Router1#configure terminal
Enter configuration commands, one per line.  End with CNTL/Z.
Router1(config)#dspfarm profile 1 transcode
Router1(config-dspfarm-profile)#codec g711ulaw
Router1(config-dspfarm-profile)#codec g711alaw
Router1(config-dspfarm-profile)#codec g729ar8
Router1(config-dspfarm-profile)#codec g729abr8
Router1(config-dspfarm-profile)#codec g729br8
Router1(config-dspfarm-profile)#maximum sessions ?
  <1-3>  Number of sessions assigned to this profile

Router1(config-dspfarm-profile)#maximum sessions 3
Router1(config-dspfarm-profile)#associate application sccp
Router1(config-dspfarm-profile)#no shutdown
Router1(config-dspfarm-profile)#exit
Router1(config)#exit
Router1#
```

## CERTIFICATION SUMMARY

In this chapter, you learned about digital signal processors (DSPs) and the resources they provide to Cisco VoIP gateways. You learned about the functionality of DSPs and how to select DSPs for your needs. Next, you learned to install the DSPs and verify and configure them on a Cisco ISR router/gateway.

✓ # TWO-MINUTE DRILL

### 642-436: Describe DSP Functionality

❏ A DSP is a microprocessor dedicated to processing digital signals.

❏ DSP resources are used for transcoding, MTPs, conferencing, and voice termination.

❏ Needed DSP resources are determined based on the hardware used and the intended use of that hardware.

❏ The three basic steps for configuring DSP resources are to set the codec complexity, assign the DSPs to a DSP farm, and to configure a DSP farm profile.

❏ Verify codec complexity settings with the **show voice dsp** command.

❏ Configure codec complexity in the voicecard configuration mode with the **codec complexity** command.

❏ Use the **dsp services dspfarm** command to assign DSP resources to a DSP farm after adding a PVDM module.

❏ Use the **dspfarm profile** command to create a DSP farm profile for transcoding or conferencing.

# SELF TEST

The following questions will help you measure your understanding of the material presented in this chapter. Read all the choices carefully because there might be more than one correct answer. Choose all correct answers for each question.

## 642-436: Describe DSP Functionality

1. Which one of the following definitions best describes a DSP?
   A. A software application that optimizes the CPU for digital signal processing
   B. An add-on with dedicated processing resources for digital signal processing
   C. A data synchronization processor on a chip
   D. A SIP descrambling signal purveyor

2. Which one of the following is not a task for which DSP resources are used?
   A. Transcoding
   B. Voice termination
   C. IP routing
   D. MTP

3. What is the first step taken to configure DSP resources after a PVDM module has been added to an ISR?
   A. Configure a DSP farm profile.
   B. Configure codec complexity.
   C. Configure the FastEthernet interface 0.
   D. Assign DSP resources to a DSP farm.

4. In the following list, which actions require DSP resources? (Choose all that apply.)
   A. Transcoding
   B. RTP streaming
   C. ACL processing
   D. Conferencing

5. What command is used to view the DSP resources on an IOS-based ISR?
   A. show running-config
   B. show startup-config
   C. show voice dsp
   D. show dsp

6. What command is used to create a DSP farm profile for transcoding with an ID of 5?

   A. dspfarm profile 5 transcode

   B. dspfarm profile transcode 5

   C. create dspfarm profile 5 transcode

   D. create dspfarm profile transcode 5

7. What command, when executed in dspfarm profile configuration mode, sets the highest number of allowed concurrent sessions to five?

   A. maximum sessions 5

   B. session 5

   C. max-sessions 5

   D. maximum dsp actions 5

8. What command is used to set the codec complexity to allow for both medium and high complexity codecs?

   A. codec complexity medium high

   B. codec complexity high medium

   C. codec complexity medium and high

   D. codec complexity flex

9. What command is used to assign DSP resources to a DSP farm?

   A. dsp services dspfarm

   B. dspfarm consume all

   C. dspfarm services assign

   D. dsp assign dspfarm

10. What command is used to access a voice card for DSP farm configuration assuming the card in question is card 1?

    A. voice-card 1

    B. voicecard 1

    C. voice card 1

    D. voice 1

# LAB QUESTION

You have just installed a new DSP module of the type PVDM2-64 in a Cisco 2800 series router. What three steps should you take to configure the DSP, and what commands will you use? Additionally, what commands could you use to verify the DSP is installed and configured correctly?

# SELF TEST ANSWERS

## 642-436: Describe DSP Functionality

**1.** ☑ **B** is correct. In the Cisco world, DSP resources usually require an add-on module known as a PVDM module. The DSP resources are used for digital signal processing.

☒ **A, C,** and **D** are incorrect. These answers are not relevant to the functioning of DSP resources in a Cisco VoIP implementation.

**2.** ☑ **C** is correct. Cisco routers perform IP routing using the built-in processor and do not require DSP resources for this operation.

☒ **A, B,** and **D** are incorrect. Transcoding does require DSP resources. Transcoding is the conversion from one codec to another. Voice termination also requires DSP resources. Voice termination takes place at the point where the incoming PSTN calls must be converted to VoIP codec-based calls. MTPs (Media Termination Points) do require DSP resources.

**3.** ☑ **B** is correct. In most cases, the first configuration step should be setting the codec complexity on the voice card. The codec complexity determines how the DSP resources will be used by the router.

☒ **A, C,** and **D** are incorrect. You should configure a DSP farm profile, but this is actually the third step and not the first. The configuration for FastEthernet 0, assuming such an interface is in the router, is outside the scope of DSP resource configuration. Assigning DSP resources to a DSP farm is the second step in the process.

**4.** ☑ **A** and **D** are correct. Transcoding and conferencing both require DSP resources. DSP resources are used to convert from one codec to another with transcoding. DSP resources are used to combine multiple audio streams into one with conferencing.

☒ **B** and **C** are incorrect. RTP streaming does not require DSP resources. The DSP resources may be used for encoding before the data is streamed, but the DSP resource is not consumed to stream the data. ACL processing does not require DSP resources in any way.

**5.** ☑ **C** is correct. The **show voice dsp** command can be used to view DSP resources on a router. You can see the resource available and the codec complexity configured. You can also use the **show voice dsp detailed** command to get even more information.

☒ **A, B,** and **D** are incorrect. The **show running-config** and **show startup-config** commands are used to view the configuration in memory and the boot time configuration. In the running-config, you can see the configured DSP farms, but you cannot see the actual information about the DSP resources from a hardware level. The **show dsp** command is an invalid command.

6. ☑ **A** is correct. The **dspfarm profile 5 transcode** command is correct. The correct sequence in the command is **dspfarm profile** followed by the profile ID and then the profile type, which can be conference, mtp, or transcode.

   ☒ **B, C,** and **D** are incorrect. The command **dspfarm profile transcode 5** has the profile ID and the profile type in the wrong order. The **create dspfarm** command does not exist in the Cisco IOS.

7. ☑ **A** is correct. The **maximum sessions 5** command is correct. This command should be entered in dspfarm-profile configuration mode.

   ☒ **B, C,** and **D** are incorrect. The commands **session 5**, **max-sessions** 5, and **maximum dsp actions 5** are not valid IOS commands.

8. ☑ **D** is correct. The flex mode allows for both medium and high complexity codecs, so the command **codec complexity flex** is correct.

   ☒ **A, B,** and **D** are incorrect. These three commands are simply invalid. The **codec complexity flex** command should be used instead.

9. ☑ **A** is correct. The **dsp services dspfarm** command assigns or allocates the DSP resources to a DSP farm. The command should be entered in voicecard configuration mode.

   ☒ **B, C,** and **D** are incorrect. These three commands are invalid.

10. ☑ **A** is correct. If the voice card is voice card 1, the proper command is **voice-card 1**. The command is always **voice-card** followed by the card number. This brief command places the router into voicecard configuration mode for the specified voice card.

    ☒ **B, C,** and **D** are incorrect. These three commands are invalid.

# LAB ANSWER

The three basic steps for configuring DSP resources are to configure the codec complexity, assign the DSP resources to a DSP farm, and configure a DSP farm profile. For example, to use DSP resources for transcoding, the commands in Figure 11-5 should be used.

Now that the DSP resources are configured, you can use the **show voice dsp** command to view information about the DSP resources, as shown in Figure 11-6 with the detail option used.

You can also use the **show running-config** command to view the DSP profile in the configuration as shown in Figure 11-7.

**FIGURE 11-5**

Performing
the three
steps for basic
configuration

```
COM3 - PuTTY                                                              _□×
Press RETURN to get started.



Router1>enable
Router1#configure terminal
Enter configuration commands, one per line.  End with CNTL/Z.
Router1(config)#voice-card 0
Router1(config-voicecard)#codec complexity medium
Router1(config-voicecard)#dsp services dspfarm
Router1(config-voicecard)#exit
Router1(config)#dspfarm profile 1 transcode
Router1(config-dspfarm-profile)#codec g711ulaw
Router1(config-dspfarm-profile)#codec g711alaw
Router1(config-dspfarm-profile)#codec g729ar8
Router1(config-dspfarm-profile)#codec g729abr8
Router1(config-dspfarm-profile)#maximum sessions 4
Router1(config-dspfarm-profile)#associate application sccp
Router1(config-dspfarm-profile)#no shutdown
Router1(config-dspfarm-profile)#exit
Router1(config)#exit
Router1#
```

**FIGURE 11-6**

Viewing DSP
resources

```
COM3 - PuTTY                                                              _□×
---------------------------FLEX VOICE CARD 0 ---------------------------
                         *DSP VOICE CHANNELS*

CURR STATE : (busy)inuse (b-out)busy out (bpend)busyout pending
LEGEND     : (bad)bad   (shut)shutdown  (dpend)download pending

DSP   DSP             DSPWARE CURR BOOT                        PAK   TX/RX
TYPE  NUM CH CODEC    VERSION STATE STATE   RST AI VOICEPORT TS ABRT PACK COUNT
===== === == ======== ======== ===== ======= === == ========= == ==== ============
C5510 001 01 None      23.6.1 idle  idle     0   0             0         0/0
C5510 001 02 None      23.6.1 idle  idle     0   0             0         0/0
C5510 001 03 None      23.6.1 idle  idle     0   0             0         0/0
C5510 001 04 None      23.6.1 idle  idle     0   0             0         0/0
                         *DSP SIGNALING CHANNELS*
DSP   DSP             DSPWARE CURR BOOT                        PAK   TX/RX
TYPE  NUM CH CODEC    VERSION STATE STATE   RST AI VOICEPORT TS ABRT PACK COUNT
===== === == ======== ======== ===== ======= === == ========= == ==== ============
C5510 001 01 {medium}  23.6.1 alloc idle     0   0 0/0/0     02    0       15/0
C5510 001 02 {medium}  23.6.1 alloc idle     0   0 0/0/1     02    0       15/0
-----------------------END OF FLEX VOICE CARD 0 ---------------------------
Router1#
```

```
COM3 - PuTTY                                                          _ □ x
!
!
voice-port 0/0/0
!
voice-port 0/0/1
!
!
!
!
dspfarm profile 1 transcode
 codec g711ulaw
 codec g711alaw
 codec g729ar8
 codec g729abr8
 maximum sessions 4
 associate application SCCP
!
!
!
!
!
gatekeeper
 shutdown
!
```

# 12

# Communications
# Manager Express

12.01   640-460: Implement Cisco Unified
Communications Manager Express
to Support Endpoints Using CLI

✓    Two-Minute Drill

Q&A   Self Test

> *Well-informed people know it is impossible to transmit the voice over wires.*
> *Even if it were, it would be of no practical value.*
>
> —Boston Post, *1865*

In the early days of telephony, a living, breathing operator would sit in a room and wait for the customer to pick up her telephone handset in her home or building so that the operator could plug the wires into the right socket location to complete a call. This operator was a manual call manager, and he was there to manage the establishment of a call. Once the call was established, the calling party and the called party could communicate with each other directly, but the operator was required to establish the call. The Cisco Unified Communications Manager Express (formerly known as Call Manager Express) plays the role of this traditional operator. In this chapter, you will learn about the Communications Manager Express functionality and features and how to implement the software on Cisco integrated services routers (ISRs).

## CERTIFICATION OBJECTIVE 12.01

# 640-460: Implement Cisco Unified Communications Manager Express to Support Endpoints Using CLI

In small networks the full Unified Communications Manager is not likely to be needed. Cisco provides an alternative solution called the Cisco Unified Communications Manager Express, or CME for short, which meets the needs of small VoIP networks and branch offices. In this section, you will learn about the features of CME, the implementation process, and the configuration commands used to configure various voice features using the CME CLI.

## Introducing Communications Manager Express (CME)

Cisco CME runs on integrated services routers (ISRs) like the 2600, 3600, 2800, and 3800 series devices. No special server is needed because the CME software runs in the memory and processor of the router. The number of phones supported depends on the ISR used. Table 12-1 provides a listing of various ISR models and the number

| TABLE 12-1 | ISR Model | Maximum Supported Phones |
|---|---|---|
| | UC500 Series | 48 |
| ISRs and | 1861 | 8 |
| Maximum | 2801 | 25 |
| Phone Support | 2811 | 35 |
| | 2821 | 50 |
| | 3825 | 175 |
| | 3845 | 250 |

of phones supported on those models when running CME version 4.3 (a very popular version in modern VoIP networks).

e x a m
ⓦatch

**Remember that the CME software runs on ISRs and not on special dedicated servers. Also remember that different ISR models support different numbers of telephones.**

In addition to the number of phones supported, it's important to know which phones are supported. CME version 4.3 supports any of the following phones:

- SIP 3911
- 7906G
- 7911G
- 7920/7921G
- 7931G
- 7940G/7941G/7941G-GE/7942G/7945G
- 7960G/7961G/7961G-GE/7962G/7965G
- 7970G/7971G-GE/7975G
- 7985G videophone
- 7936/7937 conference stations

**w a t c h**   *The new CME version 8*   *likely to be tested on this version on the*
*supports up to 450 phones running on*   *current CCNA Voice and CVOICE exams.*
*Cisco 3945E ISRs; however, you are not*

The CME can act as a phone/call manager, a trunk manager, and as a connector to voice mail solutions such as Cisco Unity and Cisco Unity Express. According to Cisco's CME 4.3 datasheet, the following phone features are supported in CME 4.3:

- Maximum 250 phones per system
- Up to 34 line appearances per phone
- Attendant console functions using Cisco Unified IP Phone Expansion Module 7914
- Fast transfer: blind or consult
- Busy lamp
- Silent ringing options
- Automatic line selection for outbound calls
- Call forward on busy, no answer, and all (internal or external)
- Call-forward-all restriction control
- Do not disturb (DND)
- Feature ring with DND set
- IP phone display of DND state
- Dial-plan pattern load on SIP phones
- Diversion of calls directly to voice mail
- Customization of softkeys
- Enable and disable call-waiting notification per line
- Call waiting with overlay directory number
- Call-waiting ring
- Dual or 8 call line appearances per button
- After-hours toll-bar override
- Auto-answer with headset
- European date formats

- Hook flash pass-through across analog PSTN trunks
- Idle URL: periodically push messages or graphics on IP phones
- Last-number redial
- Live record to Cisco Unity Express mailbox
- Local name directory lookup
- On-hook dialing
- Station speed dial with configuration changes from IP phone
- System speed dial for 10,000 numbers
- Silent and feature ring options
- SIP-based line-side subscribe, providing basic presence of phone status
- Transfer to voice mail softkey
- Call barge with privacy on shared lines
- Access features using softkeys or feature access codes
- Remote teleworker IP phone support
- Dynamic hunt-group join or leave
- Support for analog phones using Cisco ATA 186 Analog Telephone Adapter or Cisco VG224 Analog Phone Gateway in SCCP mode
- Support for fax machines on foreign exchange station (FXS) ports or ATA using H.323, SCCP, or SIP
- XML application services on Cisco Unified IP display phones
- Station-to-station video with voice using Cisco Unified Video Advantage or Cisco Unified IP Phone 7985G endpoints
- Extension mobility within the single site
- Wideband audio (G.722) and iLBC (Internet Low Bitrate Codec)

Because CME runs on the ISR routers used as gateways to other networks, the following trunking features are also supported:

- Analog foreign exchange office (FXO) loop and ground start
- Ear and mouth (E&M)
- Basic Rate Interface (BRI) and Primary Rate Interface (PRI) support (NI2, 4ESS, 5ESS, EuroISDN, DMS100, and DMS250) and several other switch types are currently supported in Cisco IOS software
- Caller ID name and number

- Automatic number identification (ANI)
- Digital trunk support (T1/E1)
- Direct inward dialing (DID)
- Direct outward dialing
- E1 R2 support
- Dedicated trunk mapping to phone button
- H.323 trunks with H.450 support
- H450.12 automatic detection of H.450 support for remote H.323 endpoints
- H.323-to-H.323 hairpin call routing for non-H.450-compliant H.323 endpoints
- SIP trunks and RFC 2833 support
- Transcoding with G.711, G.729a, and iLBC
- ECMA/ISO ISDN Q.SIG supplementary services of basic calls, including:
  - Call forwarding busy, no answer, all
  - Calling name and line identification
  - Connected line and name identification
  - Message waiting indicator (MWI) and message center support
  - MWI pass-through QSIG-to-time-division multiplexing (TDM) voice mail

The CME software also supports several system features including call hold, call waiting, call transfer, intercom, hunt groups, paging, Music on Hold (MoH), and basic automatic call distribution (ACD). The software can be configured to act as a key system or as a PBX system depending on the needs of the implementing organization.

In the end, the CME software becomes the center of your small business or branch office VoIP network and plays the same roles as a traditional key system or PBX. Calls are connected through the CME, and phones are registered with and managed by the CME. It is the intelligence for your VoIP solution.

## CME Software Components

While many traders on the Internet seem to think Cisco Unified CME is a free product or that it should be, the reality is that it is licensed software running on Cisco routers. If you choose to implement CME in your organization, you'll need to acquire three different types of licenses. The first is the proper IOS (Internetwork Operating System) license. You need an IOS license that includes the voice feature

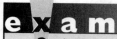

**w a t c h**
*Ensure you know the three licenses required to run CME. The three licenses are the IOS license with a voice feature set, the CME feature license, and the phone user licenses.*

set. The second license is the CME feature license. The CME feature license determines the number of phones that can be supported by the licensed router. The final license is the user license associated with each phone or at least with each user of the telephony network.

The IOS license will differ depending on the ISR on which CME is to be installed. However, you can use the Cisco Feature Navigator available at http://tools.cisco.com/ITDIT/CFN. Exercise 12-1 steps you through using the Cisco Feature Navigator to select a voice-capable IOS feature set for a Cisco 2801 router.

---

**EXERCISE 12-1**

---

### Using the Cisco Feature Navigator to Locate CME-compatible IOS Feature Sets

In this exercise, you will use Cisco Feature Navigator to select an IOS feature set for a Cisco 2801 router that will run the CME software.

#### Launching the Cisco Feature Navigator

1. Open your favorite web browser.
2. Navigate to http://tools.cisco.com/ITDIT/CFN.
3. Click the link that reads "Search by Feature."

When you select Search by Feature, a new browser window is displayed, and you can then search based on desired features.

#### Selecting the Appropriate Feature and Model

1. In the new window, click the C index in the horizontal row to jump to the features beginning with the letter C.
2. In the Available Features list, choose the CallManager Express 4.0(3) feature, and click the Add button, as seen in Figure 12-1. Communications Manager Express 4.3 will run on the same IOS versions as 4.03 as long as you are running the IOS feature set in release 12.4(15) or higher.

FIGURE 12-1 FIGURE 12-1 Selecting the desired feature

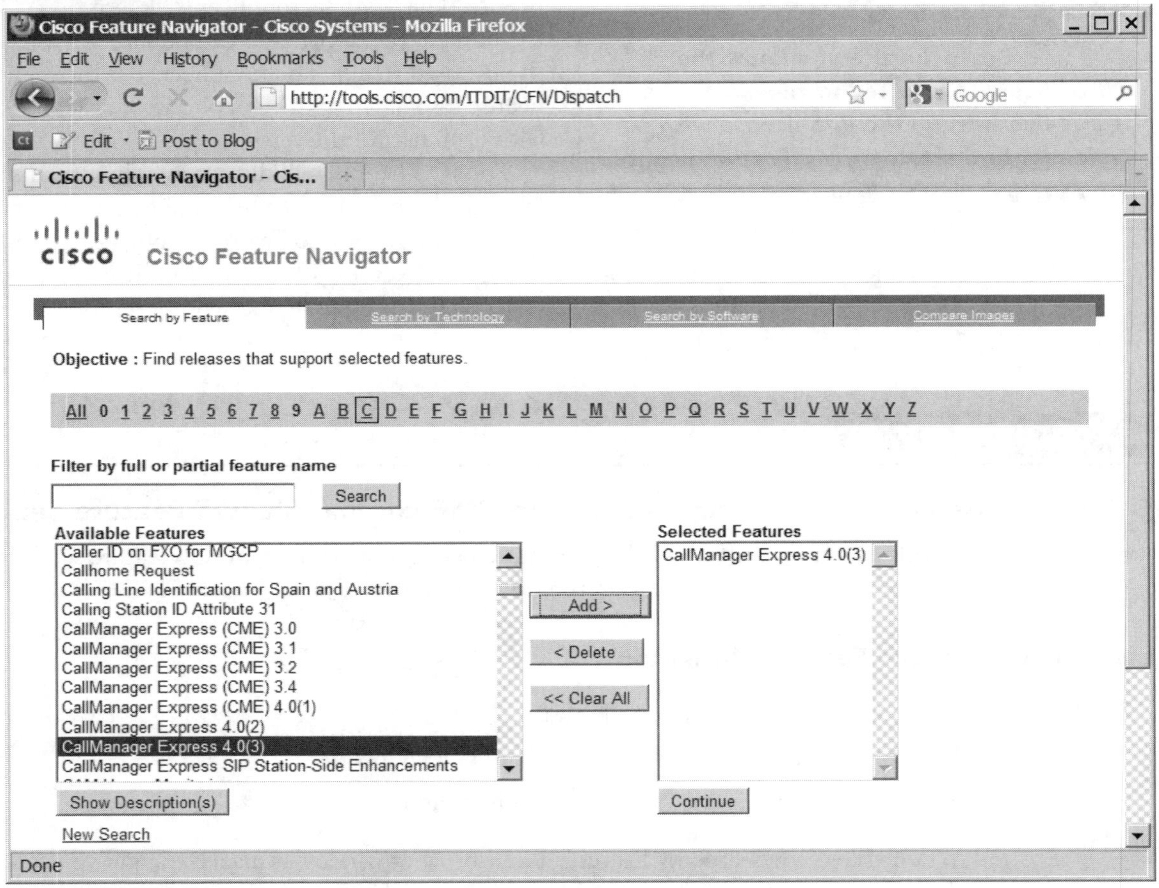

3. Click Continue to filter the results for the 2801 router.

4. On the resulting page, choose the 2801 router in the Platform drop-down list.

5. From the Major Release drop-down list, choose 12.4T, as shown in Figure 12-2.

**FIGURE 12-2**   Filtering for the router and IOS versions

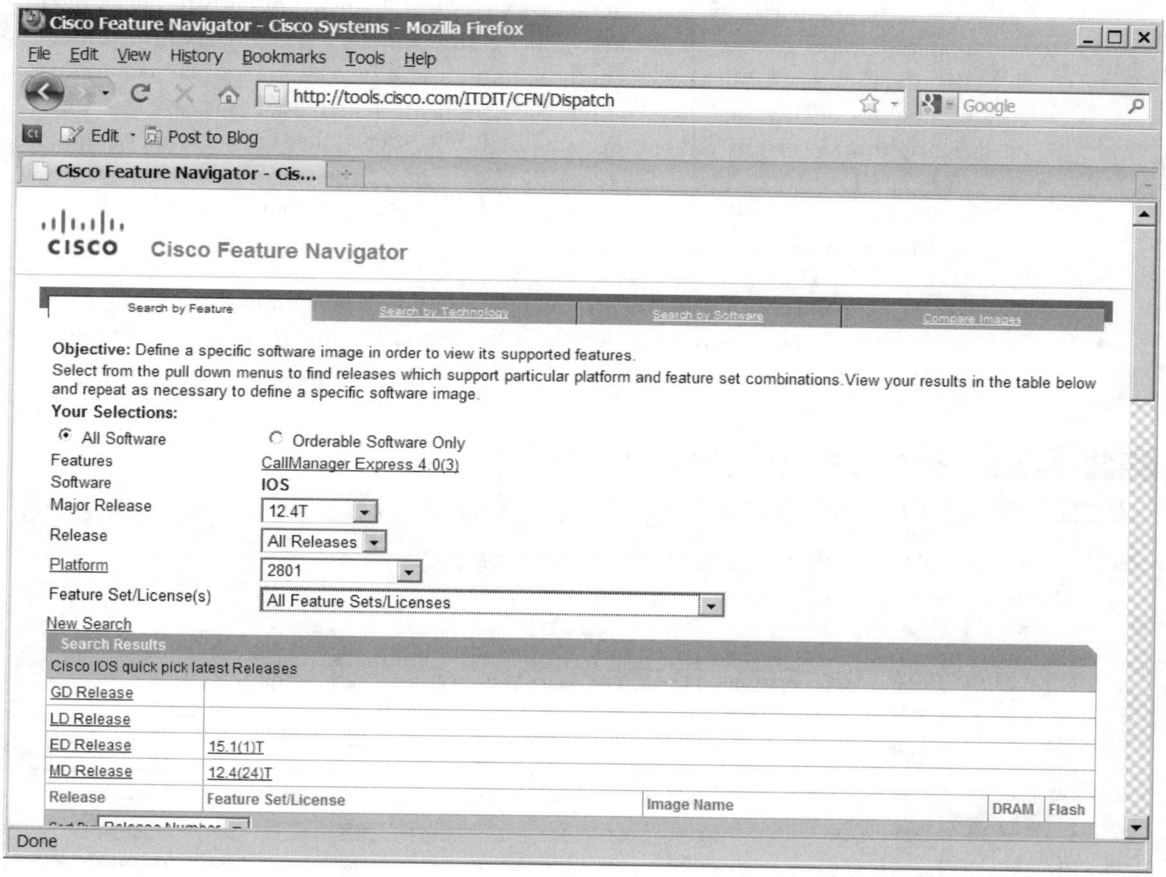

After performing steps 1–5 you should see a list of IOS feature sets that can run the Cisco Unified CME.

In addition to using the Cisco Feature Navigator, you can also use the IOS compatibility matrix available at Cisco's web site. The matrix is at http://www.cisco.com/en/US/docs/voice_ip_comm/cucme/requirements/guide/33matrix.htm, and it lists the different CME versions and the minimum IOS version required to run it. In combination with the Cisco Feature Navigator, this matrix makes it easy to select the right IOS version and feature set. The IOS compatibility matrix is shown in part in Figure 12-3.

Three file sets are required to get CME up and running on a Cisco ISR. The following list explains these three file sets:

- **IOS image** You will need an appropriate IOS image installed on the router. This book does not include the IOS installation instructions because that would have been part of your CCNA training.

| **FIGURE 12-3** | IOS compatibility matrix for Cisco Unified CME |
| --- | --- |

- **CME software** The CME software can be acquired in two modes. The basic mode includes only the CME software and the most common IP phone load files (*load files* are used to configure and enable the phones on the voice network). The full mode includes the CME software and all the currently supported phone load files.

- **IP phone load files** The IP phone load files or firmware must be placed on the TFTP (Trivial File Transfer Protocol) server so that the Cisco phones can load the software and operate on the network. In most cases, the ISR is used as both the CME router and the TFTP server. When you use the CME-full package, you will not need the separate phone load files.

on the job

*The file that contains the CME software and all IP load files and includes version 4.3 of the CME software is named cme-full-4.3.0.0.tar and can be downloaded from the Cisco software download web site if you have a customer account and have purchased the CME software license.*

The basic steps for installing CME are as follows:

1. Load the appropriate IOS image onto the router.
2. Configure basic router settings such as the IP addresses for the interfaces and the host name.
3. Extract the CME archive to the router's flash using the **archive tar** command.

These steps will install CME on the router, but much more is required to actually get the router working as a call manager. You will need to configure the following parameters:

- Set up the router to act as a TFTP server. This configuration step is performed with the **tftp-server** command in configuration mode.
- Configure the source IP address for the CME. This step is performed in telephony-service configuration mode using the **ip source-address *xxx.xxx.xxx.xxx*** command.
- Configure the maximum number of ephones and DNs. This step is performed with the **max-ephone #** and **max-dn #** commands, where # is the maximum number desired.

■ Set the firmware load files for CME to use. This step is accomplished in telephony-service configuration mode using the **load phone file** command, where **phone** is the phone model number and **file** is the filename for the specified phone. For example, a 7945 phone command would be **load 7945 SCCP45.8-3-35.loads**.

■ Create the CNF files for the phones. The CNF files are the phone configuration files, and the ISR with the CME loaded can create a default set of CNF files with the **create cnf-files** command in telephony-service configuration mode.

## Configuring DHCP and NTP for CME Operations

The Cisco IP phones must receive their IP configurations from a DHCP server. You can certainly use an existing DHCP server within your infrastructure, but it is more common to allow the CME router to lease IP addresses for the voice VLAN phones. You will also need to ensure that a network time server is available. This time server uses the Network Time Protocol (NTP).

When implementing DHCP server functions on the Cisco router, you will perform the following actions:

1. Configure DHCP exclusion addresses. These addresses will not be given out to IP phones on the network.

2. Create the DHCP pool with parameters such as the network, DNS server, default router, and additional options for the TFTP server (option 150).

3. Set up IP helper addresses if required.

exam

ⓦatch

*Remember, in the Cisco world, you create DHCP exclusions before creating the DHCP pool. This is different* *from Microsoft DHCP servers with which many network administrators have worked.*

To configure the CME router to give out IP address configurations for the phones, use the following example commands:

```
Router1> enable
Router1# configure terminal
Router1(config)# ip dhcp excluded-address 10.1.1.50 10.1.1.100
Router1(config)# ip dhcp pool Voice_Pool
Router1(dhcp-config)# network 10.1.1.0 255.255.255.0
```

```
Router1(dhcp-config)# default-router 10.1.1.1
Router1(dhcp-config)# dns-server 4.2.2.2
Router1(dhcp-config)# option 150 ip 10.1.1.1
Router1(dhcp-config)# exit
Router1(config)# exit
Router1# show running-config | section dhcp
```

In the preceding command list, the **ip dhcp excluded-address** command is used to indicate to the router that the addresses from 10.1.1.50 to 10.1.1.100 should not be given out to clients. The **ip dhcp pool** command is used to either create a pool or enter configuration mode for an existing DHCP pool depending on whether the named pool already exists. We then set the network for the DHCP pool with the **network** command and specify the gateway with the **default-router** command. The DNS server address is specified with the **dns-server** command. Finally, the **option 150** command is used to specify the IP address of the TFTP server that will host the phone load files.

The final **show running-config | section dhcp** command will list the DHCP configuration, which should look similar to the following:

```
ip dhcp excluded-address 10.1.1.50 10.1.1.100
!
ip dhcp pool Voice_Pool
 network 10.1.1.0 255.255.255.0
 default-router 10.1.1.1
 option 150 ip 10.1.1.1
 dns-server 4.2.2.2
```

on the **job**

*Only newer IOS images allow the section filter to be used with the show running-config command. For older IOS images, simply use the standard show running-config command, and scroll to the DHCP configuration section.*

If you implement DHCP on a separate router from the CME router, you may need to configure an IP helper address. The IP helper address is used when the CME router receives an IP request that it cannot service (for example, a broadcast DHCP lease request). The IP helper address is configured using the **ip helper-address** command.

Once you've configured the DHCP server pool, you can ensure that the NTP service is appropriately configured. NTP can be set up to use an Internet time server, or you can simply assign one internal server as the NTP master. To locate NTP servers on the Internet, simply visit the ntp.org web site. The NTP server is specified in configuration mode with the **ntp server server.address** command. In this case, **server.address** can be a DNS name, or it can be an IP address. To make a Cisco router the NTP master, simply execute the **ntp master** command in configuration mode.

## Understanding Key System and PBX Models

CME can run in three models. The first is the PBX model. The second is the keyswitch or key system model. The third is the hybrid model, which is a mixture of both the PBX and key system models in a single environment.

The three models operate in the traditional way that analog voice systems do. The PBX model acts like a PBX. This means that calls are routed to specific extensions or ACD queues rather than having dedicated lines. The key system model uses dedicated lines, and each phone can pick up any of the lines. The hybrid model allows some phones to operate on the key system concepts and others to operate on the PBX concepts.

## Understanding ephones and ephone-dns

Cisco CME uses ephones and ephone-dns to implement the phones within the brain of the CME router. The *ephone* is the logical representation of a physical phone. For example, you will create an ephone entry for each physical phone on your voice network. Many Cisco IP phones support multiple virtual lines. The ephone-dn (ephone directory number) is the configuration for these different lines. Therefore, a single ephone may have multiple ephone-dns.

By default, ephone-dns are single line. If you want to configure a dual-line phone, you must use the **ephone-dn # dual-line** syntax, where # is the ephone-dn identification number. To change a dual-line configuration to a single-line configuration, you must delete the existing ephone-dn and replace it with a new one.

Interestingly, you create the ephone-dns before you create the ephones. The ephone-dns define the lines, and the ephones embrace the lines (or capture them) into a specific phone's configuration. The following example code would create an ephone-dn with identification number 1 and extension 5001:

```
Router1# configure terminal
Router1(config)# ephone-dn 1
Router1(config-ephone-dn)# number 5001
```

```
Router1(config-ephone-dn)# exit
Router1(config)# exit
```

Now that we've created an ephone-dn, we can capture it into an ephone configuration by using the **ephone** command. This is accomplished with the following commands:

```
Router1# configure terminal
Router1(config)# ephone 1
Router1(config-ephone-dn)# mac-address 00cc:00cc:00cc
Router1(config-ephone-dn)# button 1:1
Router1(config-ephone-dn)# exit
Router1(config)# exit
```

From the preceding command listing, you can see that the MAC address of the phone must be known. If you are using autoregistration, you can use the **show ephone** command to see the MAC addresses of the registered phones. Once you map an ephone to a MAC address, the settings will be saved in the router's configuration.

The **button** command is used to identify the phone button that should light up when a line rings. In the preceding command example, the **button 1:1** command indicates that button 1 should light up when extension 5001 (ephone 1) is called. You will also be calling from extension 5001 (ephone 1) when you press button 1 to pick up the line. The **button** command has more options. The first number is always the phone button, and the second number is always the ephone-dn associated with that phone button; however, the colon can be replaced with different characters. For example, the command **button 1s1** would indicate a silent ring instead of a normal ring. Table 12-2 lists the options for the second space or separator character when using the **button** command.

| TABLE 12-2 | Separator Character | Meaning |
| --- | --- | --- |
| Separator Character Options for the **button** Command | : | Normal ring |
| | b | Call waiting beep, no ring |
| | c | Overlay line (with call waiting) |
| | f | Feature ring |
| | m | Monitor mode |
| | o | Overlay line (no call waiting) |
| | s | Silent ring |
| | w | Watch mode |
| | x | Overlay expansion/rollover |

## Verifying CME Endpoints

Once you've configured the ephones and ephone-dns, the endpoints should reflect this configuration. If they do not show the proper line configurations, you may need to reset or restart the phones.

The **reset** command is the sure bet, but it will take longer. When you reset the phone, it's like powering off the phone and powering it back on. The reboot will reload the firmware, user location, network location, and all parameters.

The **restart** command is the less intensive option, but may not always catch all configuration changes. A restart should process changes to the phone buttons, phone lines, or speed dial numbers. It does not require a reload of the firmware from the TFTP server, and it does not require new DHCP lease acquisitions.

**e x a m**

**ⓦatch**    *Remember that the* reset *command fully reloads the phone, and the* restart *command is less intensive. If you've simply changed the phone buttons, a* restart *will typically be sufficient.*

You can execute the **reset** and **restart** commands from within ephone configuration mode or from the telephony-service configuration mode. When used from the ephone configuration mode, only the phone currently being configured is rebooted. When used from telephony-service configuration mode, all ephones are rebooted.

## Configuring Call-Transfer

While you could categorize call transfer as one of the voice productivity features covered in the following section, it is configured so often that it warrants its own section with detailed coverage. Of course, call transfer is the feature that allows you to move an active call from one phone to another. For example, I may be on a call with a customer and need to transfer the customer to another internal employee to further assist him. The call transfer option must be appropriately configured for each ephone in order for this to work.

The call transfer option is actually configured within the ephone-dn settings for the ephone. The command used to set up call transfer is **transfer-mode**, and three transfer modes are available:

■ **Full-blind**  Full-blind is available on single-line ephone-dns, and it transfers the call without speaking with the receiving party (the phone to which the call is being transferred).

■ **Full-consult**  Full-consult is available only on dual-line ephone-dns. The sending party may speak with the receiving party before transferring the call.

■ **Local-consult**  Local-consult is a Cisco proprietary method and should only be used when older Cisco phones remain in use.

To configure call transfer, use commands similar to the following:

```
Router1# configure terminal
Router1(config)# ephone-dn 1
Router1(config-ephone-dn)# transfer-mode blind
Router1(config-ephone-dn)#exit
Router1(config)# exit
```

# Configuring Voice Productivity Features

Several voice productivity features are provided by Cisco routers running CME. These features enhance the users' experiences through added capabilities. In this section, you will learn about hunt groups, call parking, call pickup, paging, and Music on Hold.

## Hunt Groups

A *hunt group* is an ephone type that represents multiple extensions. When the hunt group extension is dialed, the extension in the hunt group take turns ringing until someone answers one of the phones. The hunt group algorithm determines the extension that rings first on the next call. Three algorithms are supported, and they were introduced in Chapter 10. The algorithms are longest-idle, peer, and sequential.

To configure a hunt group, you must have the following information:

■ **Pilot number**  This is the extension used to dial the hunt group.

■ **Algorithm type**  One of three algorithms types including longest-idle, peer, and sequential.

■ **Member list**  The ephone-dns that should be included in the hunt group.

■ **Hops**  The number of extensions the hunt group will attempt to ring.

■ **Timeout**  The length of time an extension will ring before moving to the next extension.

■ **Final number**  The number tried after the hops limit is reached.

To configure a hunt group, use commands similar to the following based on the information retrieved to define the hunt group:

```
Router1# configure terminal
Router1(config)# ephone-hunt 13 peer
Router1(config-ephone-hunt)# pilot 5050
Router1(config-ephone-hunt)# list 5001 5002 5003
Router1(config-ephone-hunt)# hops 2
Router1(config-ephone-hunt)# timeout 15
Router1(config-ephone-hunt)# final 5004
Router1(config-ephone-hunt)# exit
Router1(config)# exit
```

In the preceding command example, the extensions 5001 through 5004 may all be dialed when the hunt group extension of 5050 receives a call. Each phone will ring for 15 seconds before moving on to the next phone. Two phones will be tried, and then the phone at extension 5004 will ring until answered. In the initial **ephone-hunt** command, you can also see that this is hunt group 13, and it uses the peer algorithm.

## Call Parking

The call park or call parking feature of Cisco CME allows you to place a call on hold, but to move the call to a different extension. For example, you may be on a call at extension 5001 and want to move to 5002 to retrieve the call. To do this, you need to create park slots in an ephone-dn configuration. This way the phone at extension 5002 can pick up the call in the designated slot. The following commands illustrate this concept:

```
Router1(config)# ephone-dn 35
Router1(config-ephone-dn)# number 4001
Router1(config-ephone-dn)# park-slot
Router1(config-ephone-dn)# exit
```

Once this configuration is made, the park button on the Cisco IP phones will work. However, the call will always be parked in slot 4001. Once a call is parked in that slot, no other calls can be parked. You can alleviate this problem by simply creating multiple park slots. The parking feature will automatically use the next available park slot and report back to the phone from which the call was parked the actual park slot used.

You can also set a park timeout so that the call will ring back at the parking extension if the parked call is not picked up. For example, a customer service representative may park a call for an individual and then page the individual. If that individual does not pick up the parked call after the timeout, it will ring back to the customer service representative so that the representative may redirect the call or page the individual again.

## Call Pickup

Call pickup should not be confused with call parking. While you must pick up a parked call, that action is different from the call pickup feature. The call pickup feature allows you to pick up or answer another phone that is ringing. For example, if you are working in your office and hear the phone ringing in the office next to yours, you may need to answer that call. For this to work, a call pickup group must be created.

Call pickups can work in one of three ways:

- **Directed pickup**   The user presses the pickup button and enters the extension to answer.
- **Local group pickup**   The user presses the group pickup button, and it automatically picks up a currently ringing call.
- **Other group pickup**   When the group pickup button is pressed, the user enters the other pickup group number to automatically answer the ringing phone in that group.

Call pickup is configured within the ephone-dns. By using the **pickup-group** command, you can assign an ephone-dn to a pickup group. The following commands illustrate the simple method used to configure pickup groups:

```
Router1# configure terminal
Router1(config)# ephone-dn 5
Router1(config-ephone-dn)# pickup-group 1001
Router1(config-ephone-dn)# ephone-dn 6
Router1(config-ephone-dn)# pickup-group 1001
Router1(config-ephone-dn)# ephone-dn 7
Router1(config-ephone-dn)# pickup-group 1002
Router1(config-ephone-dn)# ephone-dn 8
Router1(config-ephone-dn)# pickup-group 1002
```

In the preceding example, ephone-dns 5 and 6 are in pickup group 1001, and ephone-dns 7 and 8 are in pickup group 1002.

## Intercoms, Paging, and Paging Groups

The intercom feature is mostly used in key system CME implementations. The best way to think of the intercom feature is like speed dialing with automatic answering. The recipient of the intercom call does not have to answer the call. The speakerphone is automatically enabled, and the caller can begin speaking. Intercoms work with two phones configured for communications. The following commands provide an example of intercom configuration:

```
Router1# configure terminal
Router1(config)# ephone-dn 25
Router1(config-ephone-dn)# number A200
Router1(config-ephone-dn)# intercom A201
Router1(config-ephone-dn)# ephone-dn 26
Router1(config-ephone-dn)# number A201
Router1(config-ephone-dn)# intercom A200
Router1(config-ephone-dn)# exit
Router1(config)# ephone 1
Router1(config-ephone)# button 2:25
Router1(config-ephone)# ephone 2
Router1(config-ephone)# button 2:26
Router1(config-ephone)# exit
```

In the preceding command examples, two ephone-dns are created (25 and 26). Notice the use of the letter A in the extension number. This prevents accidental dialing of the intercom. You can use the letters A, B, C, or D for this purpose. Also notice that ephone-dn 25 dials extension A201 for the intercom, and ephone-dn 26 dials extension A200. They are configured in reverse. Finally, we assign button 2 to ephone-dn 25 on ephone 1, and button 2 to ephone-dn 26 on ephone 2.

Now that you understand intercoms, understanding paging will be easy. This is because paging is a one-way intercom. You implement paging by creating a paging number and then assigning IP phones to the paging number. These phones will actively play the paging audio through the speakerphone whenever the paging number is used.

Paging is configured for either unicast or multicast paging. With unicast paging, a maximum of ten receiving devices can be configured. Multicast paging allows for more than ten receiving devices. The reason is simple: when sending unicast streams to each phone, the data must be transmitted multiple times on the network, and this is too inefficient to handle more than ten receiving devices at a time.

Paging groups are configured by first creating a paging ephone-dn. Once the paging ephone-dn is created, ephones can be added to the ephone-dn that is defined as paging and is called a paging-dn at this point. To configure the ephone-dn that will be the paging-dn, use commands like the following:

```
Router1# configure terminal
Router1(config)# ephone-dn 17
Router1(config-ephone-dn)# number 5151
Router1(config-ephone-dn)# paging
Router1(config-ephone-dn)# exit
```

With the preceding commands entered, the paging-dn 17 now exists. Now, to configure the ephones to use the paging-dn, execute the following commands for the appropriate ephones:

```
Router1# configure terminal
Router1(config)# ephone 1
Router1(config-ephone)# paging-dn 17
Router1(config-ephone)# exit
Router1(config)# ephone 2
Router1(config-ephone)# paging-dn 17
Router1(config-ephone)# exit
```

With the preceding commands entered, you have assigned, in this case, ephones 1 and 2 to the paging group 5151 or the paging-dn of 17. Additionally, if a user dials the number 5151, the phone extensions assigned to ephones 1 and 2 will make their speakerphones active and will play the audio spoken into the calling user's microphone.

## e x a m

**ⓦ a t c h**

*If you want to use the multicast version of paging, you will use addresses like 239.1.1.100 for the paging-dn command. However, your network infrastructure must support and allow multicasting, which is beyond the scope of the CCNA Voice and CVOICE exams.*

### Music on Hold (MoH)

MoH is used to play an audio file for the caller placed on hold when a user places that caller on hold. MoH can use a WAV or AU audio file that contains music or even spoken announcements. For example, you may have called an organization in the past that played product announcements or other helpful information as the MoH. The steps to implementing MoH are twofold:

1. Copy the audio file to the router's flash.

2. Configure the router to use the audio file.

The audio file can be copied to the router's flash using TFTP, a USB thumb drive, or by placing the flash in another device for routers that use the compact flash (CF) format such as the 2801 router.

With the audio file copied into flash, you must use the **moh** command in telephony-service configuration mode to enable the audio file. The following commands will enable an audio file named announce.wav:

```
Router1# configure terminal
Router1(config)# telephone-service
Router1(config-telephony)# moh announce.wav
Router1(config-telephony)# exit
```

As with paging, MoH can use either unicast or multicast transmission for the MoH audio file.

### Calling Privileges

In many situations, you will want to limit the privileges of users to place particular calls after operational hours. You can accomplish this by blocking calls through class of restriction (CoR), but you can also do this simply by defining after hours and then

determining the pattern for restrictions. The following commands illustrate this
method:

```
Router1(config-telephone)# after-hours day mon 17:00 8:00
Router1(config-telephone)# after-hours day tue 17:00 8:00
Router1(config-telephone)# after-hours day wed 17:00 8:00
Router1(config-telephone)# after-hours day thu 17:00 8:00
Router1(config-telephone)# after-hours day fri 17:00 8:00
Router1(config-telephone)# after-hours date dec 25 00:00 00:00
Router1(config-telephone)# after-hours block pattern 1 91..........
```

Notice that you can configure after hours by
the day or by date. Once the hours are specified,
you must decide what numbers to block after
hours. In the preceding command example, we
are blocking 9 (used to get an outside line) and
then 1 and any number to indicate that long-
distance calls should be blocked after hours.

**watch** *You can specify that a
specific phone is exempted after hours by
using the after-hours exempt command from
within ephone configuration.*

## CERTIFICATION SUMMARY

In this chapter, you learned how to plan and perform a Communications Manager
Express (CME) implementation. You learned the initial configuration steps required
and the methods used to configure various CME features, including productivity
features.

# ✓ TWO-MINUTE DRILL

## 640-460: Implement Cisco Unified Communications Manager Express to Support Endpoints Using CLI

❑ Fax machines can be connected to FXS ports on routers running CME and fax relay, or pass-through can be implemented.

❑ CME 4.3 supports a maximum of 250 phones per system.

❑ To run CME, three software components are required: the IOS image with an appropriate feature set, the CME software, and IP phone load files.

❑ The router acts as a TFTP server so the phones can download firmware images and configurations.

❑ The **tftp-server** command is used to determine the files offered by the TFTP server.

❑ The **max-ephone** and **max-dn** commands must be entered into the running configuration to determine the maximum number of ephones and directory numbers to be maintained.

❑ The **create cnf-files** command is used to create the default phone configuration files.

❑ When creating the DHCP pool, first create the DHCP exclusions with the **ip dhcp excluded-address** command.

❑ The **ip dhcp pool** command is used to create a DHCP pool.

❑ The NTP server is specified with the **ntp server** command, and the **ntp master** command can be used to make an ISR an NTP master server.

❑ Ephones represent the physical IP phones and are created with the **ephone** command.

❑ Ephone-dns represent the phone lines or extensions and are created with the **ephone-dn** command.

❑ The **button** command is used to associate a particular ephone-dn with a button on a multiline Cisco IP phone.

❑ When you want to completely reboot and reload a Cisco IP phone, execute the **reset** command.

❑ If you want to apply new button configurations, execute the **restart** command.

❏ The **reset** and **restart** commands can be executed in ephone configuration mode or telephony-service configuration mode.

❏ Call transfer can be configured as full-blind (the call is transferred without speaking to the receiving party) or full-consult (the call is transferred after speaking to the receiving party).

❏ The **transfer-mode** command is used to configure the call transfer mode for an ephone-dn.

❏ Hunt groups are used to allow an incoming call to ring multiple phones in sequence.

❏ Call parking allows a call to be placed on hold and picked up at a different phone using park slots.

❏ Call pickup allows a user to pick up a ringing phone that is in a different location.

# SELF TEST

The following questions will help you measure your understanding of the material presented in this chapter. Read all the choices carefully because there might be more than one correct answer. Choose all correct answers for each question.

## 640-460: Implement Cisco Unified Communications Manager Express to Support Endpoints Using CLI

1. You want to configure a productivity feature that will allow two phones to connect to each other and immediately activate the speakerphone for audio transmission. What feature should you configure?
   A. Call park
   B. Call pickup
   C. Paging
   D. Intercom

2. What feature is like a one-way intercom?
   A. Unicom
   B. Paging
   C. Call park
   D. Call pickup

3. When a call is parked in a park slot, how can it be picked up again?
   A. Press the pickup button and enter the slot number.
   B. Pick up the handset on the phone that represents the park slot.
   C. Plug a headset into the ISR that runs CME.
   D. Press the hold button on the phone where you wish to pick up the parked call.

4. To how many paging ephone-dns can a phone be assigned?
   A. 10
   B. 1
   C. 5
   D. 250

5. What audio formats are supported by MoH? (Choose all that apply.)
   A. MP3
   B. WAV
   C. MOV
   D. AU

6. What command is used to configure MoH?
   A. moh
   B. music-on-hold
   C. hold-music
   D. audio-playback

7. What command is used in ephone configuration mode to specify that a particular phone should be exempted from after-hours call blocking?
   A. ephone exempt
   B. after-hours exempt
   C. cb-exempt
   D. after-hours-exempt

8. What command is used to create the default phone configuration files?
   A. create cnf-files
   B. create phone-config
   C. create default
   D. create phone-config

9. What voice feature allows for an incoming call to ring a group of phones in sequence until one is answered?
   A. Conference calling
   B. Call forwarding
   C. Full-blind
   D. Hunt groups

10. What transfer mode allows a call to be transferred but does not allow the individual transferring the call to speak with the recipient of the transfer first?
    A. Full-blind
    B. Full-consult
    C. Full-auto
    D. Full-delay

11. What DHCP configuration mode command would be used to specify the TFTP server for the DHCP pool as IP 10.1.1.4?
    A. TFTP ip 10.1.1.4
    B. option 150 ip 10.1.1.4
    C. dhcp option 150 ip 10.1.1.4
    D. option 150 10.1.1.4

12. What command in DHCP configuration mode is used to specify the default router as 10.1.1.1 for the DHCP pool?

    A. gateway 10.1.1.1

    B. default-gateway 10.1.1.1

    C. router 10.1.1.1

    D. default-router 10.1.1.1

13. What ephone-dn configuration mode command is used to indicate that an ephone-dn is actually a park extension for call park?

    A. park-slot

    B. call-park

    C. call-hold

    D. park-point

# LAB QUESTION

You want to configure an ephone with an ID of 12 and a MAC address of 0c0c:0c0c:0c0c. Button 1 should be mapped to ephone-dn 12, and button 2 should be mapped to ephone-dn13 with normal rings for both. The ephone-dn 12 should be configured with extension 5001, and ephone-dn 13 should be configured with extension 5002. What commands will you type in what order?

# SELF TEST ANSWERS

## 640-460: Implement Cisco Unified Communications Manager Express to Support Endpoints Using CLI

1. ☑ **D** is correct. The intercom feature is two-way and will meet the needs of this scenario.

   ☒ **A, B,** and **C** are incorrect. Call park is used to place a call on hold in a park slot so that it can be picked up at a different phone. Call pickup is used to answer a ringing extension other than your own. Paging is used to implement a one-way intercom call to multiple receiving phones.

2. ☑ **B** is correct. Paging is used to implement a one-way intercom call to multiple receiving phones.

   ☒ **A, C,** and **D** are incorrect. Unicom is not a Cisco CME feature. Call park is used to place a call on hold in a park slot so that it can be picked up at a different phone. Call pickup is used to answer a ringing extension other than your own.

3. ☑ **A** is correct. You can press the pickup button on another phone and enter the park slot ephone-dn number.

   ☒ **B, C,** and **D** are incorrect. No phone is specifically configured as the park slot answering phone. You cannot plug a headset directly into the ISR that runs CME. The hold button is not used to pick up a parked call.

4. ☑ **B** is correct. A phone can only be assigned to one paging ephone-dn; however, the paging-dn can belong to another paging-dn, making it possible for phones to be in multiple paging groups through the hierarchy.

   ☒ **A, C,** and **D** are incorrect. These answers are simply incorrect.

5. ☑ **B** and **D** is correct. Music on Hold can use the WAV or AU format for audio.

   ☒ **A** and **C** are incorrect. Neither the MP3 nor the QuickTime MOV format is supported.

6. ☑ **A** is correct. The **moh** command is used in telephony-service configuration mode to configure the MoH audio file.

   ☒ **B, C,** and **D** are incorrect. These three commands are not valid IOS commands with or without CME installed on the router.

7. ☑ **B** is correct. The **after-hours exempt** command can be used to indicate that a specific ephone should not be constrained by after-hours rules.

   ☒ **A, C,** and **D** are incorrect. These are not valid IOS commands.

8. ☑ **A** is correct. The phone configuration files are called CNF files. The **create cnf-files** command will create the default configuration files.

   ☒ **B, C,** and **D** are incorrect. These are not valid IOS commands.

9. ☑ **D** is correct. Hunt groups are used to allow a group of phones to operate in a sequential fashion so that a first phone rings and, if after a timeout period that phone is not answered, another phone rings, and so on.

   ☒ **A, B,** and **C** are incorrect. Conference calling would be used to implement a conference call. Call forwarding allows a call to be forwarded to a different extension if you will not be at your extension for some period. Full-blind is a call transfer mode that does not allow the transferor to communicate with the transferee before the call is transferred.

10. ☑ **A** is correct. Full-blind is a call transfer mode that does not allow the transferor to communicate with the transferee before the call is transferred.

    ☒ **B, C,** and **D** are incorrect. Full-consult allows the transferor to communicate with the transferee before the call is transferred. Full-auto and full-delay are not valid call transfer modes.

11. ☑ **B** is correct. Option 150 defines the TFTP server, so the proper commands is **option 150 ip 10.1.1.4**.

    ☒ **A, C,** and **D** are incorrect. These three commands are not valid commands for configuring the TFTP server in a DHCP pool.

12. ☑ **D** is correct. The **default-router 10.1.1.1** command configures the default router for the DHCP pool.

    ☒ **A, B,** and **C** are incorrect. These are not valid IOS commands.

13. ☑ **A** is correct. The **park-slot** command is used to indicate that an ephone-dn is a call park extension.

    ☒ **B, C,** and **D** are incorrect. These are not valid IOS commands for ephon-dn configuration mode.

# LAB ANSWER

Answers may vary, but the following Cisco IOS commands executed on an ISR router running CME should provide the needed configuration:

```
Router1# configure terminal
Router1(config)# ephone-dn 12
Router1(config-ephone-dn)# number 5001
Router1(config)# ephone-dn 13
Router1(config-ephone-dn)# number 5002
Router1(config-ephone-dn)# exit
Router1(config)# ephone 12
Router1(config-ephone-dn)# mac-address 0c0c:0c0c:0c0c
Router1(config-ephone-dn)# button 1:12 2:13
Router1(config-ephone-dn)# exit
Router1(config)# exit
```

# 13

# Unified
# Communications
# Manager

> *If The Phone Doesn't Ring, It's Me.*
>
> —*Jimmy Buffett song title*

The preceding chapter covered the CME version of Cisco's call management solution. In this chapter, you'll learn about the features of the full Unified Communications Manager server. You'll learn the basic implementation process and administration tools used to work with the server-based Unified Communications Manager. In addition, a concept that applies to both the Unified Communications Manager and CME is a *dial plan*, and this topic will also be addressed in this chapter.

If, like with Mr. Buffett, the phone doesn't ring in your VoIP network, it's you—unlike him, you'll have to determine why it's not ringing. This chapter gives you the information required to plan a dialing infrastructure—known as a dial plan—so that your phones will ring.

# Unified Communications Manager

The Cisco Unified Communications Manager (CUCM or UCM) is the full enterprise version of the Cisco call management solution. UCM can be used in small businesses and branch offices, but its scalability makes it an appropriate solution for large enterprises. In this section, you will learn about UCM implementation and administration. As you learn about implementation, you will learn about the features and requirements of the UCM solution.

## UCM Implementation

Implementing UCM involves selecting the right edition and ensuring the requirements are met for the selected edition. To accomplish this, you need to understand the features provided by the different UCM editions. Additionally, you must understand the requirements for deployment, which include licensing requirements and hardware requirements.

## UCM Editions

The Cisco UCM call management solution comes in three basic editions or distributions. The first is a server-based deployment of the full UCM server software. The second is an appliance-based deployment. The third is UCM Business Edition, which is a special edition of the UCM software.

The server-based edition requires specific server hardware. You cannot simply install it on any server that meets some minimum requirements in your organization. Instead, the server must be a Cisco 7800 series Media Convergence Server (MCS) or a selected third-party server. While the supported servers are limited and you must run UCM on a supported server, the servers are effectively just servers. They have simply been approved by Cisco to provide the required uptime of a VoIP call management server.

The appliance-based edition was first released in 2006. With this deployment model, no installation is necessary. The appliance comes preconfigured with the UCM solution. The UCM database, device drivers, and general software are all bundled into the appliance for simpler deployment and support.

The appliance version of UCM supports a maintenance partition. The appliance includes two partitions: active and inactive. The active partition is the partition serving the VoIP network. The inactive partition is an exact up-to-the-minute copy of the active partition. When you want to apply an update, you can apply it to the inactive partition and then perform a switch partition reboot. The reboot will take 10–15 minutes, which is much less time than the downtime required for a traditional update to a single instance of UCM.

The UCM Business Edition (BE) is aimed at medium-sized organizations. Cisco says that BE is best for organizations with up to 20 sites and 100–350 employees. Technically, UCM BE can support up to 500 phone users. The key to UCM BE is that it includes call management, voice mail, and even WebEx. UCM BE runs on an MCS appliance and consumes 1 RU (rack unit) of rack space in your server rack.

## UCM Features

According to the Cisco datasheet for UCM 8.0, the following user features are supported by the system:

- Abbreviated dial
- Answer and answer release
- Auto-answer and intercom

- Callback busy and no reply to station
- Call connection
- Call coverage
- Call forward: All (OffNet and OnNet), busy, no answer, no bandwidth, and not registered
- Call hold and retrieve
- Call join
- Call park and pickup
- Call pickup group: Universal
- Call pickup notification (audible or visual)
- Call status per line (state, duration, and number)
- Call waiting and retrieve (with configurable audible alerting)
- Calling line identification (CLID) and calling party name identification (CNID)
- Calling line identification restriction (CLIR) call by call
- Conference barge
- Conference chaining
- Conference list and drop any party (impromptu conference)
- Dialed-number display
- Direct inward dialing (DID) and direct outward dialing (DOD)
- Directed call park with busy lamp field (BLF)
- Directory dial from phone: Corporate and personal
- Directories: Missed, placed, and received calls list stored on selected IP phones
- Distinctive ring for OnNet and OffNet status, per-line appearance, and per phone
- Do not disturb (do not ring and call reject)
- Drop last conference party (impromptu conferences)
- Extension Mobility
- Extension Mobility Cross Cluster
- Extension Mobility PIN change from phone
- Hands-free, full-duplex speakerphone

- HTML help access from phone
- HTTPS for phone services; for example, Extension Mobility
- Hold reversion
- Immediate divert to voice mail
- Intercom with whisper
- Join across lines
- Last-number redial (OnNet and OffNet)
- Login and logout of hunt groups
- Malicious-call ID and trace
- Manager-assistant service (Cisco Unified Communications Manager Assistant application) proxy-line support:
  - Manager features: Immediate divert or transfer, do not disturb, divert all calls, call intercept, call filtering on CLID, intercom, and speed dials
  - Assistant features: Intercom, immediate divert or transfer, divert all calls, and manager call handling through assistant console application
- Manager-assistant service (Cisco Unified Communications Manager Assistant application) shared-line support:
  - Manager features: Immediate divert or transfer, do not disturb, intercom, speed dials, barge, direct transfer, and join
  - Assistant features: Handle calls for managers; view manager status and calls; create speed dials for frequently used numbers; search for people in directory; handle calls on their own lines; immediate divert or transfer, intercom, barge, privacy, multiple calls per line, direct transfer, and join; send DTMF digits from console; and determine MWI status of manager phone
- Manager-assistant service (Cisco Unified Communications Manager Assistant application) system capabilities: Multiple managers per assistant (up to 33 lines) and redundant service
- Manager-assistant service now available on a Cisco Unified IP Phone with Cisco Unified Communications Manager 6.0
- MWI (visual and audio)
- Multiparty conference: Impromptu with add-on meet-me features
- Multiple calls per line appearance

- Multiple line appearances per phone
- MoH (Music on Hold)
- Mute capability from speakerphone and handset
- On-hook dialing
- Original calling party information on transfer from voice mail
- Privacy
- Real-time QoS statistics through HTTP browser to phone
- Recent dial list: Calls to phone, calls from phone, autodial, and edit dial
- Service URL: Single-button access to IP phone service
- Single-button barge
- Single-directory number and multiple phones: Bridged line appearances
- Speed dial: Multiple speed dials per phone
- Station volume controls (audio and ringer)
- Transfer: Blind, consultative, and direct transfer of two parties on a line
- User-configured speed dial and call forward through web access
- Video (SCCP, H.323, and SIP)
- VPN client on IP phone
- Web services access from phone
- Web dialer: Click to dial
- Wideband audio codec support: Proprietary 16-bit resolution; 16-KHz sampling rate codec

In addition to these shared features, you should understand the feature differences between the versions of Cisco UCM. Table 13-1 lists key ability differences between the editions of UCM.

**TABLE 13-1**    UCM Editions Capabilities Comparison

| UCM Edition | Number of Users | Deployment Model |
|---|---|---|
| Cisco UCM | 30,000 per cluster | Centralized deployment with up to 100 UCM servers in a single system |
| Cisco UCM BE | 500 | Centralized deployment |
| Cisco UCM Appliance | 30,000 per cluster | Centralized deployment with up to 100 appliances in a single system |

### UCM Requirements

The earlier versions of Cisco UCM worked on Windows or Linux. Newer versions work only on Linux. Version 4.x and earlier worked on Windows servers and are still heavily used in production environments. When you use the Cisco UCM Appliance version, requirements become a non-issue because the hardware comes with the software.

To ensure you have the proper hardware for the UCM edition you plan to run, check the Cisco web site for requirements. To learn about third-party servers that work with UCM, visit this web page: http://www.cisco.com/go/swonly.

## UCM Administration

Once you have UCM installed in your environment as an appliance or server, you can administer the server using a web-based management interface. A command-line interface (CLI) is also available for Telnet or SSH administration. Figure 13-1 shows the administration interface home page in the web-based administrator.

**FIGURE 13-1**     Cisco UCM Administration home page

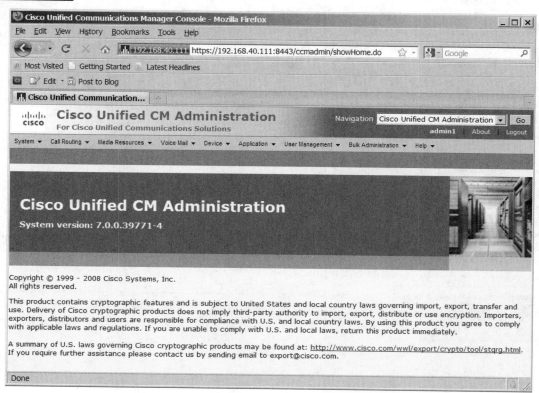

Figure 13-2 shows the interface for general configuration of the UCM server. Notice that auto-registration is disabled in the screenshot. Auto-registration is disabled by default. If you want to enable auto-registration, you would have to deselect the check box shown and add an ending directory number (DN).

Figure 13-3 shows the interface for user creation. You can specify a user ID and password as well as a PIN for voice mail access. The phone can be added and associated with the user at the same time, and you can specify the extension and extension mask.

---

**FIGURE 13-2**    The general UCM configuration page

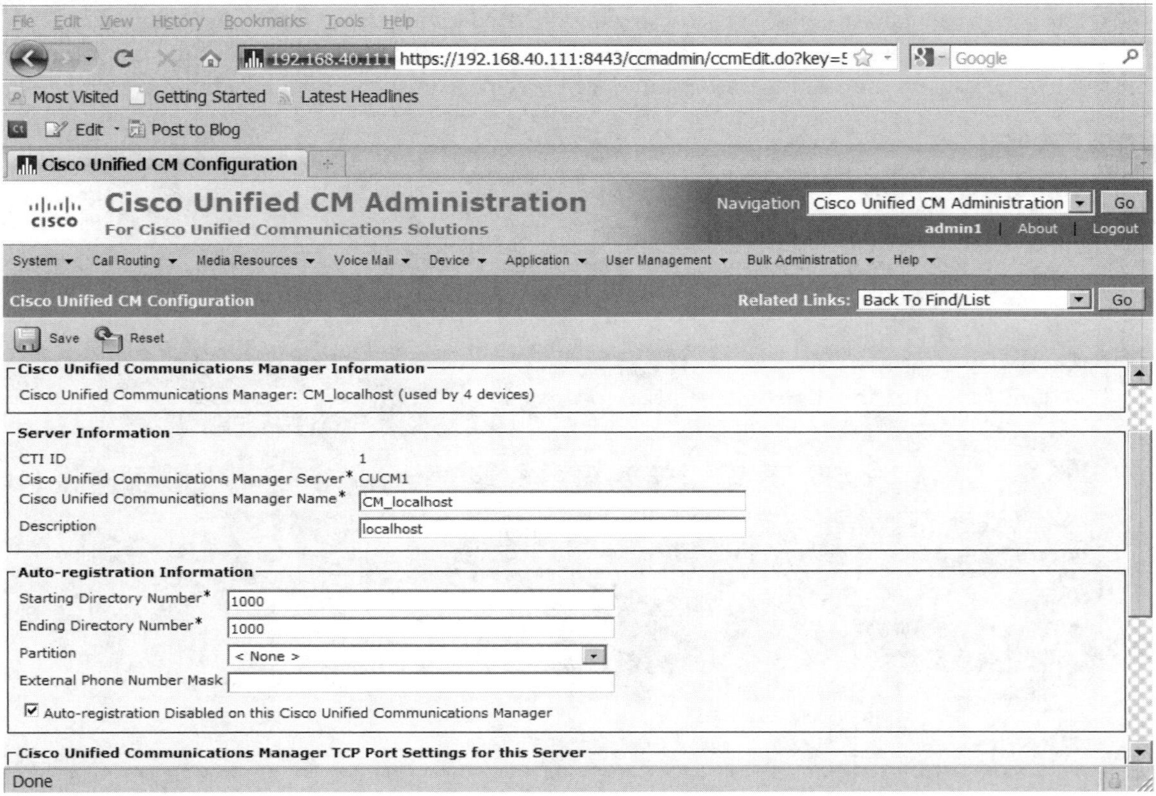

The point in showing these screens is so that you can see the simplicity of administration using the web-based interface. You will not be required to master UCM configuration for either the CCNA Voice or CVOICE exam.

The user and phone addition page

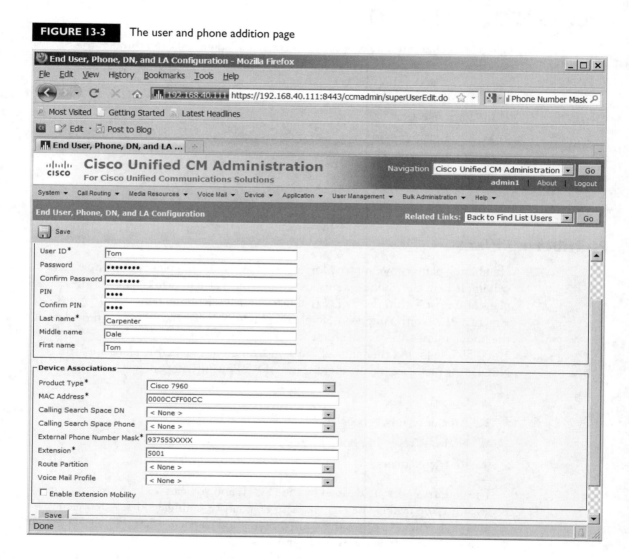

**CERTIFICATION OBJECTIVE 13.01**

# 642-436: Describe a Dial Plan

Dial plans define the way calls are connected and communicated through the network. Multiple pieces come together to form the dial plan, including:

- Numbering plans
- Path selection
- Digit manipulation
- Calling privileges
- Call coverage

This section addresses all dial plan components.

## Numbering Plans

Numbering plans come in many forms. Internal numbering plans define how you will implement the phone extensions within your voice network. Numbering plans also exist within the PSTN (public switched telephone network). In North America, the North American Numbering Plan (NANP) is used, and it provides the phone numbers we use within the United States such as 1-937-555-4567 or 1-800-555-4545. In other parts of the world, different numbering plans are used. Numbering plans are usually divided into the following components:

- Country codes
- Area or regional codes
- Node addresses or phone numbers
- Restricted digits

The country codes are defined by the ITU-T, and you can find a listing of country codes at http://en.wikipedia.org/wiki/List_of_country_calling_codes. A few example country codes include +1 for the United States and Canada, +30 for Greece, +44 for the United Kingdom, and +81 for Japan.

The area or regional codes are defined by the numbering plan used within that region. For example, North America uses the NANP plan, and the United Kingdom uses the National Telephone Numbering Plan (NTNP).

Restricted digits include listings of digits that cannot be used in specified positions within the number. Each numbering plan will limit the use of digits in order to preserve the digits for specific purposes. For example, in the NANP numbering plan, you cannot use the numbers that start with 37 or 96 in the area codes because they are reserved for future use. You also cannot assign an area code that starts with any number and ends in 11, such as 911 or 411, as these are reserved for special purposes.

The node addresses or local phone numbers are managed by the local telephone operators, which may be managed by government entities or private sector organizations.

You must be aware of the numbering plans used within the telephone network to which you connect so that you can properly manage calls coming in from the network and going out to the network. This management is accomplished through digit manipulation, which is covered in the next section.

When planning your internal numbering plan, the biggest concern is endpoint addressing. Endpoint addressing is all about the structure of your phone extensions. Sure, you could just jump in and start at extension 1 for the first phone and increase the extension numbers sequentially as you add phones, but this plan would usually result in a mess at best and in a nonfunctioning VoIP network at worst. The best practice is to following a procedure similar to the following:

1. Determine the VoIP network locations.
2. Estimate the number of extensions required at each location.
3. Create a numbering plan that will allow for routing among these locations and for future growth.

The first step is to identify network locations. For example, if you work in an organization with three sites today, it is possible that a few more sites will be added in the future. You need to consider this future growth. You also have to consider the number of extensions needed today and in the future. For this reason, today you wouldn't want a plan like the following for a network that needed 50 extensions at each of three sites:

- Site 1: Extensions 1–50
- Site 2: Extensions 51–100
- Site 3: Extensions 101–150

This plan may work fine for now, assuming you have fewer than 50 extensions at each site. However, what happens when extension 51 is needed at site 1? Now instead you have to assign extension 151 to that phone. The result is confusing to the users. You should always leave room for growth at each site. A better plan might look like the following:

- Site 1: Extensions 1000–1999
- Site 2: Extensions 4000–4999
- Site 3: Extensions 7000–7999

Do you see how this plan allows for growth? First, if you have fewer than 50 extensions at each site, you will already be able to grow the sites by 20-fold. Second, you have room for additional sites at the 2000, 3000, 5000, and 6000 extension blocks. The key principle is to leave room for growth.

## Path Selection

Path selection, or call routing, is about determining the best communications path to use for call processing and connections. Path selection can also be called "voice call flow determination." The called number will determine the path followed for the call connection. In fault-tolerant implementations, multiple paths may exist. For example, the call could be routed over a purely IP-based network or over a PSTN call leg. Call legs work together to form the complete call path.

Figure 13-4 shows an example of a VoIP call path. Notice that the call is entering on an FXS port in a gateway from an analog phone. The call passes through the IP network to another gateway to which a VoIP phone is connected. Three call legs are represented in this basic example. The link from the phone to the gateway on the FXS port is the first call leg. The router or gateway considers this an inbound call leg when a call originates from the analog phone. The router analyzes this incoming call and determines the interface through which the call should be routed and determines the outbound call leg. The outbound call leg on the first router becomes the inbound call leg on the second router. The second router looks at the inbound call leg and determines the interface through which the call should be routed and determines the outbound call leg, which ultimately reaches the VoIP phone in this scenario.

| FIGURE 13-4 | |
|---|---|
| Call legs | |

Extension: 4001     Router1 running Cisco CME     Router2 running Cisco CME     Extension: 5001

The call legs will be defined in dial peers. For example, router 1 (the leftmost router) in Figure 13-4 will have a dial peer configured that allows for the call to be routed through to router 2 when a call comes in for the VoIP phone managed by router 2. Two basic dial peer types exist. The first is a POTS dial peer, which is used for connecting to the PSTN, a PBX, or an analog device. The second is a VoIP dial peer, which is used to connect to H.323, SIP, or SCCP phones. The process used to create dial peers will be covered in Chapter 14.

## Digit Manipulation

Digit manipulation is used to alter dialed digits to match the appropriate destination. For example, on inbound calls, the number may need to be stripped of certain digits or completely changed to reflect the internal numbering plan. On outbound calls, area codes and country codes may need to be added. These basic actions are the concepts involved in digit manipulation.

Several digit manipulation techniques can be used in a Cisco environment, including:

- **Digit stripping**   Digit stripping involves the removal of unneeded digits for the target network or node and is performed when an outbound dial peer is selected and before the digits are sent out through that dial peer.
- **Forward digits**   The forward digits technique simply sends the digits through to the target network or node. Forward digits applies only to POTS dial peers.
- **Prefix digits**   The prefix digits method adds digits to the beginning of the dialed number. For example, an outside number may require a 9 prefix.
- **Number expansion**   Cisco gateways use regular expressions to perform number expansion. Number expansion is used to effectively replace a dialed number with a different number.

## Calling Privileges

Calling privileges determine which destinations a user is allowed to call. After hours privileges fall into this category, and they were covered in Chapter 12.

## Call Coverage

Call coverage is inclusive of two capabilities:

- Forwarding
- Hunting

Forwarding provides different configurations depending on whether the call origination is internal or external. Call forwarding determines what happens when a call is not answered at a target extension. The call can be redirected to a different number.

Hunting allows for a call to be routed to a group of numbers. Hunt groups define these numbers and were explained in Chapter 12.

# CERTIFICATION SUMMARY

In this chapter, you learned about the Cisco Unified Communications Manager (UCM) and dial plans. You learned that UCM comes in several editions including Business Edition, the Appliance model, and server-based implementations. You also learned about the features and requirements of the editions. Next, you explored dial plans and the components of a dial plan. Here you reviewed numbering plans, digit manipulation, call path selection, calling privileges, call coverage, and the overall VoIP call flow.

# ✔ TWO-MINUTE DRILL

## 642-436: Describe a Dial Plan

❑ A numbering plan defines how nodes will be addressed on the voice network.

❑ The North American Numbering Plan (NANP) is used on the PSTN in North America.

❑ Internal numbering plans should be carefully planned to accommodate current needs and future growth.

❑ Path selection or call routing is about determining call legs and the appropriate dialing parameters for each call leg.

❑ Digit manipulation is used to convert dialed numbers into acceptable numbers for different networks or endpoints.

❑ Digit stripping is used to remove digits from a dialed number.

❑ Prefix digits are added to the beginning of a dialed number, such as adding 9 for an outside line.

❑ Forward digits rules can be enforced to simply forward dialed digits to the next call leg.

❑ Number expansion can be used to replace dialed digits with appropriate digits for the dialed number.

❑ Any router along the VoIP call flow may perform digit manipulation.

❑ Calling privileges address the users' ability to place certain calls potentially at certain times.

❑ Call coverage includes call forwarding and call hunting or hunt groups.

# SELF TEST

The following questions will help you measure your understanding of the material presented in this chapter. Read all the choices carefully because there might be more than one correct answer. Choose all correct answers for each question.

## 642-436: Describe a Dial Plan

1. Which of the following are components of a dial plan in a Cisco VoIP telephony environment? (Choose all that apply.)
   A. Numbering plan
   B. Digit manipulation
   C. Path selection
   D. DHCP

2. What two factors must be considered when developing a numbering plan for your Cisco VoIP network?
   A. The IP addresses of the gateways
   B. The current demands
   C. The future demands
   D. The time zone in which it is to be implemented

3. What numbering plan is used in North America?
   A. NTNP
   B. NNP
   C. NANP
   D. Dial Peer

4. When a VoIP call is placed to another VoIP endpoint connected to the same router or gateway, how many call legs exist?
   A. 1
   B. 2
   C. 3
   D. 0

5. When a call is placed from an FXS port on one gateway to a VoIP phone connected to another gateway, how many call legs exist if there is a direct connection between the two gateways that can be used?

A.  1

B.  2

C.  3

D.  0

**6.** Which digit manipulation technique results in a potential complete number change when compared to the originally dialed number?

A.  Prefix digits

B.  Forward digits

C.  Digit stripping

D.  Number expansion

**7.** Which digit manipulation technique results in one or more digits being added to the beginning of the originally dialed number?

A.  Prefix digits

B.  Forward digits

C.  Digit stripping

D.  Number expansion

**8.** Which digit manipulation technique results in the digits being sent to the remote network without modification?

A.  Prefix digits

B.  Forward digits

C.  Digit stripping

D.  Number expansion

**9.** What determines the destinations to which users may place calls?

A.  Call coverage

B.  Calling privileges

C.  Digit manipulation

D.  Numbering plans

**10.** What feature provides forwarding or hunting or both?

A.  Call coverage

B.  Calling privileges

C.  Digit manipulation

D.  Numbering plans

**11.** If a call path includes three gateways running Cisco CME, which gateway(s) may modify the dialed number through digit manipulation?

A. The gateway closest to the call origination

B. The gateway farthest from the call origination

C. The central gateway

D. Any gateway in the path

**12.** You need to add a 9 to the beginning of every call placed to an outside line. What should you configure for digit manipulation?

A. A prefix

B. Digit stripping

C. Forward digits

D. Intercom

**13.** Which of the following are part of the NANP numbering plan? (Choose all that apply.)

A. Node codes

B. Country codes

C. Area codes

D. Restricted digits

# LAB QUESTION

You are creating a dial plan for an organization with four locations. Each location will require 120 extensions with the exception of one location, which will require 245 extensions. You want to ensure that you can easily grow the network in the future to include more extensions at each location, and potentially, more locations. The organization expects 10–15 percent growth each year in the number of employees, and you must implement a network that can function for at least the next ten years without upgrades (assuming no failures of hardware occur) or expansion in the future. What basic numbering plan would you recommend and why? Include in your answer the extension ranges for each location and the reason for choosing these extension ranges.

# SELF TEST ANSWERS

## 642-436: Describe a Dial Plan

1.  ☑ **A, B,** and **C** are correct. The numbering plan will determine how extensions are defined on your network. Digit manipulation will provide the plan for interacting with other VoIP or POTS networks through dial peers and dialed number changes. Path selection will determine the best route through which the call may be placed.

    ☒ **D** is incorrect. DHCP is used in a Cisco VoIP environment, but it is not part of the dial plan.

2.  ☑ **B** and **C** are correct. You must account for both the current demands and the future demands. The current demands must be accounted for to ensure that users can use the VoIP network today. The future demands must be accounted for to ensure that the network can either handle the future growth, or be extended to handle the growth.

    ☒ **A** and **D** are incorrect. The IP addresses of the gateways are important, but they are not something to consider when creating the dial plan. The time zone will be configured when setting up NTP, but it is not part of the dial plan.

3.  ☑ **C** is correct. The North American Numbering Plan (NANP) is used in North America, which includes Canada, the United States, and several other countries and islands.

    ☒ **A, B,** and **D** are incorrect. The National Telephone Numbering Plan (NTNP) is used in the United Kingdom. NNP is not a defined numbering plan. Dial peers are used to provide call paths, but they are not directly part of the numbering plan—instead, they are used to implement the network on which the numbering plan will operate.

4.  ☑ **B** is correct. Two call legs will exist. The first is between the dialing phone and the gateway. The second is between the gateway and the dialed phone.

    ☒ **A, C,** and **D** are incorrect. These answers are simply incorrect because two call legs exist in such a scenario.

5.  ☑ **C** is correct. Three call legs exist. The first call leg is between the dialing phone and the gateway. The second is between the two gateways. The third is between the dialed phone's gateway and the dialed phone.

    ☒ **A, B,** and **D** are incorrect. These answers are simply incorrect because three call legs exist.

6. ☑ **D** is correct. Number expansion is used to add to the number or to completely change it. Regular expressions are used with number expansion, and you will not be required to understand their use for the CCNA Voice or CVOICE exam.

   ☒ **A, B,** and **C** are incorrect. Prefix digits is used when you need to add a number to the beginning of a dialed number. Forward digits is used to send the entire dialed number without changes to the remote network or gateway. Digit stripping is used to remove digits before forwarding.

7. ☑ **A** is correct. Prefix digits is used when you need to add a number to the beginning of a dialed number. For example, you can use prefix digits to add a 9 when needed for an outside line.

   ☒ **B, C,** and **D** are incorrect. Forward digits is used to send the entire dialed number without changes to the remote network or gateway. Digit stripping is used to remove digits before forwarding. Number expansion is used to add to the number or to completely change it.

8. ☑ **B** is correct. Forward digits is used to send the entire dialed number without changes to the remote network or gateway.

   ☒ **A, C,** and **D** are incorrect. Prefix digits is used when you need to add a number to the beginning of a dialed number. Digit stripping is used to remove digits before forwarding. Number expansion is used to add to the number or to completely change it.

9. ☑ **B** is correct. Calling privileges can be used to limit the destinations to which calls may be placed. Calling privileges can limit certain numbers (based on wildcards) during all hours or during specific hours.

   ☒ **A, C,** and **D** are incorrect. Call coverage is used to provide forwarding or hunting. Digit manipulation is used to modify dialed numbers in order to properly complete calls. Numbering plans define the numbering for your internal extensions and how you interconnect with external voice networks.

10. ☑ **A** is correct. Call coverage is used to provide forwarding or hunting.

    ☒ **B, C,** and **D** are incorrect. Calling privileges can be used to limit the destinations to which calls may be placed. Digit manipulation is used to modify dialed numbers in order to properly complete calls. Numbering plans define the numbering for your internal extensions and how you interconnect with external voice networks.

11. ☑ **D** is correct. Any gateway can receive a call on an interface and then perform digit manipulation, if needed, before forwarding the call onto the next outbound call leg. Gateways do not have to perform digit manipulation, but they can when required.

    ☒ **A, B,** and **C** are incorrect. Because any gateway in the path can perform the digit manipulation, these answers are incorrect.

12. ☑ **A** is correct. A prefix digits configuration can be used to add a prefix to the beginning of a dialed number before sending the digits onto the next hop or the final destination.

☒ **B, C,** and **D** are incorrect. The digit stripping would be used to remove digits and not add a digit. Forward digits will send the dialed digits without change. Intercom is not a digit manipulation technique, but is used to send audio to the speakerphone of another IP phone.

13. ☑ **B, C,** and **D** are correct. The country code defines a specific country, such as the United States or Canada. The area code defines a region within that country. The restricted digits limit the numbers or digits that may be used in specific positions of the resulting telephone numbers.

☒ **A** is incorrect. Node codes are not defined in the NANP numbering plan.

# LAB ANSWER

Answers will vary, but the following plan and explanation should be similar to the plan you've developed:

> Location A: Extensions 1000–1999
>
> Location B: Extensions 2000–2999
>
> Location C: Extensions 3000–3999
>
> Location D (the larger site): Extensions 4000–4999

These extension ranges were chosen because the starting value of 120 extensions for the three smaller locations will result in 485 extensions in ten years if the growth rate holds true at the maximum of 15 percent. While this is a high growth rate, it is the rate specified in the lab. Even after ten years, the available 1,000 extensions at each site will more than accommodate the growth.

The larger location that begins at 245 extensions will grow to 991 extensions in ten years at 15 percent growth. This number is less than the 1,000 available; however, even if it is higher, the growth can be accommodated by moving up to the 5000–5999 extension range. For this reason, the range 4000–4999 was chosen for the larger location.

Finally, if new sites are added over the years, we can always use the ranges 6000–6999, 7000–7999, and so forth. The solution meets current demands and future demands as well.

# 14

# Gateways and Gatekeepers

> *Smeagol knew hobbits could not go this way. O yes, Smeagol knew.*
>
> —*Smeagol speaking of the Black Gate to Mordor in* The Lord of the Rings

Gateways and gatekeepers provide gates of different types to your VoIP network. A gate is defined as a point of entry to a space or resource, such as the Black Gate into Mordor in *The Lord of the Rings*. A gateway is a path through which the space or resource may be accessed. A gatekeeper is one who ensures that only appropriate individuals pass through the gateway and that they carry only what is allowed within the protected space or resource. The gateway into Mordor would have been the path leading up to the Black Gate. The gatekeepers would have been the sentries posted at the gate.

In a Cisco router, the gateway is the router software and hardware that allow two voice networks to communicate with each other. The gate, within the gateway, would be the interface that connects to the remote network, such as the PSTN. The gatekeeper is also software running on the Cisco router. This chapter explains both gateways and gatekeepers in greater detail than in any preceding chapters. You'll first read about gateways and then about gatekeepers.

## CERTIFICATION OBJECTIVE 14.01

# 642-436: Describe the Components of a Gateway

Voice gateways connect different voice networks. For example, they may connect your VoIP network to the PSTN, or they may connect two PBX-based voice networks together over an IP-based WAN. These connections are formed using voice ports and dial peers. In this section, you will learn about basic gateway functionality and the voice ports and dial peers used to implement these gateways.

# Gateway Functionality

Cisco voice gateways can be either digital gateways or analog gateways. Digital gateways connect to telephone service providers through ISDN, T1, or E1 lines. Analog gateways connect to either telephone service providers or analog telephony devices. Voice ports are commonly used within gateways to provide the following connection types:

- Telephone to WAN
- Telephone to PSTN
- PBX-to-PBX over WAN

When implementing telephone to WAN connections, you are either supporting internal analog or VoIP phones connecting over the WAN to remote locations in your organization or another organization to which you connect. Figure 14-1 shows the concept of the telephone to WAN implementation. The VoIP phone will connect to the gateway through standard Ethernet ports, and a digital line will usually be utilized for the WAN connection. If internal analog phones are supported, they may connect to the gateway directly using FXS (foreign exchange station) ports or through an analog to VoIP conversion device of some type.

The telephone to PSTN model uses either analog or VoIP phones within the organization and connects to the PSTN instead of to a WAN link. Figure 14-2 illustrates the telephone to PSTN implementation. With the telephone to PSTN model, the internal phones communicate with the gateway using either Ethernet communications (VoIP phones) or FXS ports (analog phones). The gateway communicates with the PSTN using analog or digital interfaces. If only a few

| FIGURE 14-1 |
| --- |

Telephone to WAN implementation

VoIP phone     Cisco gateway     WAN

**FIGURE 14-2**

Telephone
to PSTN
implementation

VoIP phone        Cisco gateway       PSTN

lines are needed, multiple FXO (foreign exchange office) ports could be used to connect to the PSTN. If several lines or channels are needed, T1 or E1 lines may be required.

With the PBX-to-PBX over WAN model, the Cisco gateways are used to form the WAN connection, and the PBX systems communicate with each other across this connection, as shown in Figure 14-3.

## Voice Ports and Usage

The preceding section mentioned several voice ports. FXS and FXO ports were mentioned as analog ports, and T1 and E1 lines were mentioned as digital ports. ISDN connections also fall into the digital port category. As you read through the rest of this chapter, you will gain the knowledge needed to choose the right voice port type for your situation. Table 14-1 provides a listing of voice ports and their uses.

## Dial Peers and Dial Peer Types

Before you can connect your Cisco router (acting as a voice gateway) to the service provider, you must install the voice port interfaces. Be sure to check the Cisco web site to ensure compatibility between the interface you plan to purchase and the router in which you plan to install it. For example, the Cisco 2801 router has WIC interface ports, but not all WIC cards will work in the router. Be sure to select adapters that work with your device.

**FIGURE 14-3**

PBX-to-PBX
over WAN
implementation

PBX     Cisco gateway     WAN     Cisco gateway     PBX

TABLE 14-1    Voice Ports and Uses

| Voice Port | Type | Uses |
|---|---|---|
| Foreign Exchange Station (FXS) | Analog | Connects analog phones and fax machines |
| Foreign Exchange Office (FXO) | Analog | Connects to the PSTN or to a PBX system |
| T1 | Digital | Connects to service providers with multiple channels |
| E1 | Digital | Connects to service providers with multiple channels |
| ISDN | Digital | Connects to service providers with multiple channels but fewer channels than T1 or E1 lines |

After installing the T1/E1, ISDN, or analog voice port, you'll need to configure the voice port with the **voice-port** command. But even after you've configured the voice port, the gateway is still not fully configured. You must configure the dial peers.

Dial peers tell the gateway when to use the voice ports and when to establish calls on the local network. A dial peer matches the dialed digits to an appropriate destination. Dial peers come in two types for telephony communications:

- **VoIP**  The VoIP dial peer is used to connect to other devices across packet-based networks. These networks include IP-based WAN links, internal LANs, and even VPN tunnels. VoIP dial peers define the IP address at which or through which a number can be reached.

- **POTS**  The POTS dial peer is used for connecting to traditional telephone networks or devices. These networks and devices include the PSTN and PBX systems. POTS dial peers are also used when a phone on one FXS port communicates with another phone on another FXS port on the same or a different router/gateway.

## CERTIFICATION OBJECTIVE 14.02

# 642-436: Implement a Gateway

In the preceding section, you learned about the components of a gateway. In this section you'll learn more specifics about gateway call routing and the analog and digital ports used within Cisco routers acting as voice gateways. You will also learn about POTS dial peer configuration commands.

## Gateway Call Routing

Gateways combine two factors to determine how to route calls. The first factor is the incoming dialed digits. The second is the dial peers and destination information on the gateway or available through a gatekeeper. The dialed digits are sent from the internal phone to the gateway and may be manipulated before being transmitted to the remote voice network. The dial peers are configured as either voice or POTS dial peers depending on the destination. With this information, the gateway can determine the best route for the call and can pass along the proper digits to eventually establish the call between two endpoints.

Calls may be routed out through analog or digital ports, which are covered in the following sections. Analog ports manage individual channels, such as FXO ports. Digital ports manage multiple channels, such as ISDN, T1, or E1 connections. Even a multi-channel connection will connect to a single port on the Cisco router. For example, a T1 line may be a full T1 line with 24 channels, but it connects to a single port that looks much like an Ethernet port on the router. The channels are separated using time slices or frequency differences, but they run on the same wires.

## Understanding Analog Ports

Analog ports connect to analog circuit providers such as the PSTN telephone companies. The ports typically connect using FXO interfaces when connecting to the telephone company or a PBX and using FXS interfaces when connecting directly to analog telephones or fax machines. These analog ports or circuits will use signaling mechanisms designed for analog communications. The following are common analog signaling methods:

- **Loop-start**   When current is flowing, the phone switch seizes a line for signaling dialed digits. When a user picks up the handset on a traditional telephone, this closes the circuit and starts the flow of current.
- **Ground-start**   When the phone grounds the ring line in the circuit, the phone switch seizes a line for signaling dialed digits. The grounding occurs for only a moment, and when detected, causes the loop to become active for digit dialing.
- **E&M wink start**   When the polarity of an E&M circuit is reversed, a line is seized for signaling dialed digits.

on the **Job**

*To learn more about analog port configurations and options, visit the Cisco .com web site at http://www.cisco.com/en/US/docs/ios/voice/voiceport/ configuration/guide/vp_cfg_analog_vps_ps6441_TSD_Products_Configuration_ Guide_Chapter.html.*

Depending on the router model, you will use different commands in global configuration mode to gain access to the voice port. On some models, you will use the **voice-port** *port* command. On others, you may use the **voice-port** *slot/port* command. On still others, you may use the **voice-port** *slot/subunit/port* command. Once you have entered voice-port configuration mode, you can configure the signaling type, tone signaling sounds, dialing type, ring frequency, ring number, ring cadence, and description. Some configuration options are available only on FXS ports, and these include ring frequency, ring number, and ring cadence. The dialing type is only available on FXO ports.

## Understanding Digital Ports

Digital ports come in two primary forms: T1/E1 and ISDN. The T1 lines can have up to 24 channels, with 23 channels usable for voice communications. The E1 lines can have up to 32 channels, with 30 channels usable for voice communications. The total data rate for a full T1 line is 1.544 Mbps with a bandwidth of 1.536 Mbps, and it is 2.048 Mbps with 1.984 Mbps in bandwidth for a full E1 line. Each channel contains 64 Kbps of bandwidth.

On digital circuits or ports, time division multiplexing (TDM) may be used. A TDM model uses time slices for specific channels, and the communication channels take turns and communicate only during their assigned time slice. The time is divided between the needed channels in order to multiplex (combine) multiple signals on the line. On a T1 line, 24 different slices or channels are provided, assuming a full T1 is purchased.

Statistical TDM reserves timeslots on the wire only when the slot is needed for data transmission. Statistical TDM allows for oversubscribing on the circuit, while traditional TDM does not allow for this feature. Statistical TDM is also known as packet-mode multiplexing.

**exam**

**Watch**
*Remember that statistical TDM can be oversubscribed, while traditional TDM cannot. Traditional TDM uses assigned timeslots for channels, and the assignments do not change. Statistical TDM requests a timeslot only when it is needed.*

Frequency division multiplexing (FDM) may also be used on digital circuits or ports. FDM uses different frequencies to send multiple signals (channels) on the same line. In fiber-optic communications, dense wavelength division multiplexing (DWDM) may be used, which is a form of FDM using different frequencies of light waves.

Digital circuits can use one of two types of signaling. The first is common channel signaling (CCS), and the second is channel associated signaling (CAS). It is easy to remember the ways in which these signaling types work. CCS has a common channel used for signaling by all other channels. With an ISDN connection, where CCS is commonly used, the data or D channel is dedicated to signaling (yes, the signals are called data and the voice data is not). Additional bearer or B channels are used to send the actual voice information. CCS is not used on ISDN connections alone; it is also used on T1 and E1 Primary Rate Interface (PRI) connections.

Channel associated signaling (CAS) uses bits on the voice channels for signaling. Each channel has 64 Kbps of bandwidth. CAS takes 8 Kbps of that bandwidth for signaling. CAS can use one of two coding types on the line. The first is Super Frame (SF), and it is older and less efficient. The second is Extended Super Frame (ESF), and it is the newer, more efficient method. Table 14-2 provides a comparison of CCS and CAS when used on T1 PRI or T1 lines.

exam

ⓦatch  *So that you can remember the method used by each signaling type, just remember that "CCS" stands for "common channel signaling," and a single channel is shared (in common) among all other channels for signaling. With CAS, the signaling is "associated" with the channel in that it is sent in-band on the channel with the voice information.*

**TABLE 14-2**   T1 CAS and T1 PRI CCS Compared

| T1 CAS | T1 PRI CCS |
|---|---|
| All 24 channels available for voice; in-band signaling may reduce quality | Full 64 Kbps available for voice calls; only 23 channels available for voice |
| 56 Kbps voice bandwidth per channel | 64 Kbps voice bandwidth per channel |
| 24 voice channels available | 23 voice channels available |
| Framing with SF or ESF | Framing with Q.931 |

When you subscribe to a digital line service, the service provider will give you all of the information you need to configure the digital ports on your Cisco gateway.

## Configuring POTS Dial Peers

At this point it is important to understand some practical configuration steps. For this example, assume that two analog phones are connected to two voice ports (FXS ports) on a single Cisco router. To configure these ports to support the two analog phones, the following actions must be taken:

1. Configure the FXS ports.

2. Create the appropriate POTS dial peers.

The commands in this section work on a Cisco 2801 with the WIC2-2FXS module installed. This module provides two FXS ports in a single module. The first thing you should do is determine the ports used to communicate with the FXS module and ports. Figure 14-4 shows the **show voice port summary** command providing the port information.

You can see from the output in Figure 14-4 that ports 0/0/0 and 0/0/1 are available. More details about each voice port can be seen with the **show voice port** command.

| FIGURE 14-4 | |
|---|---|
| Viewing available voice ports | |

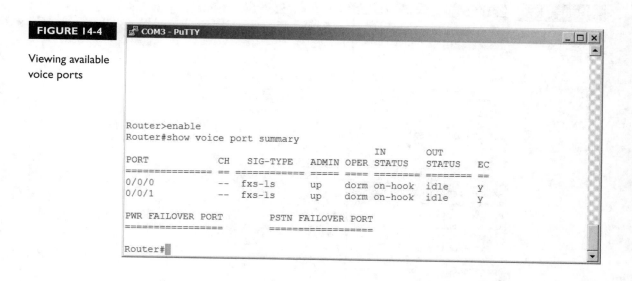

```
Router>enable
Router#show voice port summary

                                  IN       OUT
PORT            CH  SIG-TYPE   ADMIN OPER STATUS   STATUS   EC
=============== == =========== ===== ==== ======== ======== ==
0/0/0           -- fxs-ls      up    dorm on-hook  idle     y
0/0/1           -- fxs-ls      up    dorm on-hook  idle     y

PWR FAILOVER PORT            PSTN FAILOVER PORT
==================           ==================

Router#
```

To configure these voice ports, you must enter global configuration mode and then use the **voice-port** command to access the ports. Each port should be configured individually. Figure 14-5 shows the configuration of FXS port 0/0/0 on the Cisco 2801 router. For most phones the ring frequency will not be needed, and the default setting of 25 Hz will suffice.

The first configuration command in Figure 14-5 is the `description`. This property simply describes the port so you can remember its purpose. The second command is the **signal** command, which defines either `loopstart` or `groundstart` signaling. Next, we set the `cptone` or the signaling tones used, such as the dial tone. Because this phone will be used in the United States, US was chosen for the `cptone` parameter.

The `ring frequency` parameter can usually be left alone since the default is 25 Hz, and this will work with most phones. If you have an older phone connected to an FXS port and it is not working properly, try setting the ring frequency to 50 Hz. The `ring cadence` determines the length of ring time and the length of silence between rings. You can customize this or use defaults. The `pattern01` values are the default values for PSTN phones in the United States. The `station-id` name value is used for caller ID purposes so that your name can be identified when you call another party.

| FIGURE 14-5 | |
| --- | --- |
| Configuring the FXS port | |

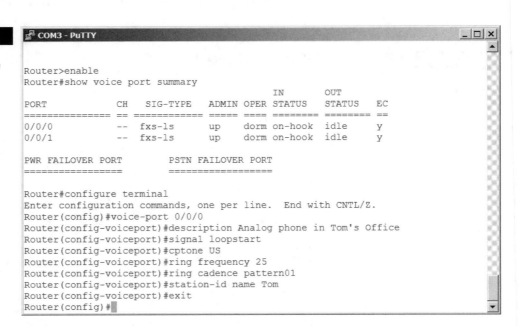

```
Router>enable
Router#show voice port summary
                                   IN       OUT
PORT            CH   SIG-TYPE   ADMIN OPER STATUS   STATUS   EC
=============== ==   ========== ===== ==== ======== ======== ==
0/0/0           --   fxs-ls     up    dorm on-hook  idle     y
0/0/1           --   fxs-ls     up    dorm on-hook  idle     y

PWR FAILOVER PORT        PSTN FAILOVER PORT
=================        ===================

Router#configure terminal
Enter configuration commands, one per line.  End with CNTL/Z.
Router(config)#voice-port 0/0/0
Router(config-voiceport)#description Analog phone in Tom's Office
Router(config-voiceport)#signal loopstart
Router(config-voiceport)#cptone US
Router(config-voiceport)#ring frequency 25
Router(config-voiceport)#ring cadence pattern01
Router(config-voiceport)#station-id name Tom
Router(config-voiceport)#exit
Router(config)#
```

These same settings should be configured for port 0/0/1, in the case of the Cisco 2801 router with two FXS ports. The `description` and `station-id` name values are likely to be the only required changes to the configuration for the other FXS port. Additionally, once the FXS ports are configured, execute the **no shutdown** command in both ports to ensure that the port is administratively up.

Now that the FXS ports are properly configured, the dial peers can be created to allow the phones connected to the FXS ports to communicate. Many first-time Cisco voice administrators are confused by the fact that they get a dial tone the moment they plug an analog phone into an FXS port. Don't let this confuse you. The supervisory signaling is active the moment you connect the phone. However, the phone numbers are assigned for FXS-port phones through dial peers, and you cannot actually call the phone until the dial peers are created.

The dial peers are created with the **dial-peer voice** command. Figure 14-6 shows the configuration of the dial peers required for the two analog phones connected to voice ports 0/0/0 and 0/0/1 to communicate with each other. Notice that two dial peers are needed. One defines the extension for the phone on voice port 0/0/0, and the other for the phone on port 0/0/1. In this example, port 0/0/0 is assigned extension 2001, and port 0/0/1 is assigned extension 2002. The **show dial-peer voice summary** command is used to verify the proper dial peers are in place and that they point to the appropriate ports.

| **FIGURE 14-6** |
| --- |
| Configuring the POTS dial peers |

```
Router>enable
Router#configure terminal
Enter configuration commands, one per line.  End with CNTL/Z.
Router(config)#dial-peer voice 10 pots
Router(config-dial-peer)#destination-pattern 2001
Router(config-dial-peer)#port 0/0/0
Router(config-dial-peer)#exit
Router(config)#dial-peer voice 11 pots
Router(config-dial-peer)#destination-pattern 2002
Router(config-dial-peer)#port 0/0/1
Router(config-dial-peer)#exit
Router(config)#exit
Router#show dial-peer voice summary
dial-peer hunt 0
                AD                              PRE PASS               OUT
TAG    TYPE  MIN  OPER PREFIX   DEST-PATTERN    FER THRU SESS-TARGET   STAT PORT
10     pots  up   up            2001            0                      up   0/0/0
11     pots  up   up            2002            0                      up   0/0/1
Router#
```

**CERTIFICATION OBJECTIVE 14.03**

# 640-460: Describe and Configure Gateways, Voice Ports, and Dial Peers to Connect to the PSTN and Service Provider Networks

In this final section on gateways, you will learn about the configuration options for VoIP dial peers and the verification commands used to ensure proper gateway configuration. First, you will review the basic dial plan components presented in Chapter 13.

## Dial Plan Components and Gateway Implementation

In the preceding chapter, you learned about dial plans and the components of a dial plan. While the dial plan includes the numbering plan you will use internally, the gateway is responsible for allowing this internal numbering plan to cooperate with the external network, such as the PSTN. For example, you may need to implement digit manipulation commands on the gateway to convert a short, internally dialed number to the full external PSTN number. Alternatively, you may need to strip an incoming call down to just the last four digits that are used as the internal extension. Either action would be performed using digit manipulation, which was also covered in Chapter 13.

Remember from Chapter 13 that the basic dial plan components include:

- Numbering plans
- Path selection
- Digit manipulation
- Calling privileges
- Call coverage

The gateway is the component that allows your numbering plan to differ from the numbering plans of the telephony networks to which you connect. It is also the gateway that, using dial peers, will determine the path selection for the calls that are placed both internally and externally. The gateways will apply digit manipulation where needed and may control the calling privileges as well. Clearly, the Cisco gateways play an important role in your VoIP network.

FIGURE 14-7

The VoIP network example for VoIP dial peers

VoIP phone (2001)          192.168.10.1                    192.168.10.2          VoIP phone (2002)

## Configuring VoIP Dial Peers

In the preceding section of this chapter, you learned to create POTS dial peers. The final dial peer type you must learn to configure is the VoIP dial peer. The same **dial-peer voice** command is used. To best understand VoIP dial peers, assume a network like the one in Figure 14-7. Notice that the VoIP phones are at extensions 2001 and 2002.

To create the dial peers for these phones to communicate with each other, a dial peer must be created on each router. The router at 192.168.10.1 will need to know that it can reach extension 2002 through 192.168.10.2. The opposite is also true in that the router at 192.168.10.2 must know that it can reach extension 2001 through 192.168.10.1. Figure 14-8 shows the configuration required on the router at 192.168.10.1.

The same basic configuration commands would be entered on the 192.168.10.2 router; however, they would be reversed. For example, the session target would change to 192.168.10.1, and the destination pattern would change to 2001.

FIGURE 14-8

Creating the dial peer on the 192.168.10.1 router

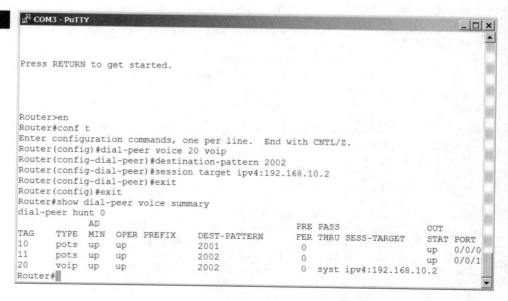

```
COM3 - PuTTY                                                              _ □ ×

Press RETURN to get started.



Router>en
Router#conf t
Enter configuration commands, one per line.  End with CNTL/Z.
Router(config)#dial-peer voice 20 voip
Router(config-dial-peer)#destination-pattern 2002
Router(config-dial-peer)#session target ipv4:192.168.10.2
Router(config-dial-peer)#exit
Router(config)#exit
Router#show dial-peer voice summary
dial-peer hunt 0
                AD                                    PRE PASS              OUT
TAG    TYPE MIN  OPER PREFIX    DEST-PATTERN          FER THRU SESS-TARGET  STAT PORT
10     pots up   up             2001                  0                     up   0/0/0
11     pots up   up             2002                  0                     up   0/0/1
20     voip up   up             2002                  0   syst ipv4:192.168.10.2
Router#
```

## Verifying Dial Plan Implementations

Cisco provides the **show voice port summary** command to view voice ports. This command can be used to view signaling types, channels, and the stats of the configured T1 or ISDN lines connected to your Cisco gateway.

Using the **show dial-peer voice summary** command, you can view a listing of all dial peers. To see the details of a dial peer, use the **show dial-peer voice *tag*** command, where *tag* is the number associated with the dial peer. Consider the following **show dial-peer voice summary** output:

```
Router1# show dial-peer voice summary
dial-peer hunt 0
                                           PASS
TAG   TYPE  ADMIN OPER PREFIX  DEST-PATTERN  PREF THRU  SESS-TARGET
110   pots  up    up                          0
111   voip  up    up           5550112        0   syst  ipv4:10.10.1.1
112   voip  up    up           5550134        0   syst  ipv4:10.10.1.1
 95   voip  up    down                         0   syst
 30   pots  up    down                         0
```

The **show gateway** command is used to view the current status of the gateway. The results of the **show gateway** command will differ depending on whether the gateway is registered with a gatekeeper. If it's registered with a gatekeeper, output similar to the following will be displayed:

```
Router1# show gateway
Gateway gateway2 is registered to Gatekeeper gk2
Gateway alias list
H323-ID gateway2
H323 resource thresholding is Enabled and Active
H323 resource threshold values:
    DSP: Low threshold 60, High threshold 70
    DS0: Low threshold 60, High threshold 70
```

When the gateway is not registered with a gatekeeper, output similar to the following will be displayed:

```
Router2# show gateway
Gateway gateway1 is not registered to any gatekeeper
Gateway alias list
H323-ID gateway1
H323 resource thresholding is Enabled but NOT Active
H323 resource threshold values:
    DSP: Low threshold 60, High threshold 70
    DS0: Low threshold 60, High threshold 70
```

# 642-436: Describe the Function and Interoperation of Gatekeepers Within an IP Communications Network

Gatekeepers are used in H.323 VoIP networks. Gatekeepers are used for several purposes, and this section will provide an overview of the terminology and functionality of a gatekeeper. You will begin by understanding the functionality of a gatekeeper or its purpose. Then you will explore the H.323 gatekeeper terminology.

## Gatekeeper Functionality

In a Cisco environment, the H.323 gatekeeper is usually a Cisco router acting as the gatekeeper. Gatekeepers are optional, but when one exists on the H.323 network, it must be used by all terminals or endpoints. The gatekeeper acts as a central database access engine for the gateways and endpoints in your network. The result is a centralized configuration location for dial plans and user accounts. The intelligence of the VoIP network is placed in the gatekeeper rather than being distributed out to all the call managers.

H.323 gatekeepers provide specific functions including four mandatory functions:

- Address resolution
- Bandwidth control
- Admission control
- Zone management

Address resolution is accomplished through the H.323 gatekeeper once a gatekeeper is added to the network. The gatekeeper knows to which call manager or router each endpoint is connected, allowing it to determine the best route to the endpoint for call setup.

Bandwidth control is used to manage the endpoints' bandwidth needs. H.225 Registration, Admission, and Status (RAS) messages are used for bandwidth control. The endpoints send a Bandwidth Request (BRQ) to the gatekeeper. The gatekeeper responds with either a Bandwidth Confirm (BCF) or Bandwidth Reject (BRJ) message.

The gatekeeper is also responsible for determining what endpoints can participate on the VoIP network through the use of admission control. The gatekeepers use H.225 RAS messages for admission control. When an endpoint wants to join the network, it sends an Admission Request (ARQ) message to the gatekeeper. The gatekeeper responds with either an Admission Confirm (ACF) or Admission Reject (ARJ) message.

Zone management is also provided by the H.323 gatekeeper. A zone is a group of H.323 nodes including gateways and endpoints that are registered with and managed by the gatekeeper. One gatekeeper is active for each zone, and a zone can span IP subnets. Zone management functions include the control of the endpoint registration process within the zone.

In addition to these four mandatory functions, several optional functions may be implemented as well:

- **Bandwidth management**   Allows the gatekeeper to reject admission to the H.323 network when insufficient bandwidth is available
- **Call authorization**   Allows for time-of-day restriction policies
- **Call control signaling**   Allows the gatekeeper to route Gatekeeper-Routed Call Signaling (GKRCS) messages between H.323 endpoints
- **Call management**   Allows for monitoring of endpoint activity for tracking busy endpoints or making call redirection decisions

## INSIDE THE EXAM

### H.323 Zones by Analogy

H.323 zones can be best understood with an analogy. I do not recall where I first heard this analogy, but know that it is not my own. To whomever the creator is, thanks for this excellent illustration of H.323 zones.

H.323 zones are a lot like departments within organizations. The department manager is responsible for workers under her authority. Twenty employees may work for this manager, and the manager is the central point of contact. The manager is aware of the status of each employee and facilitates communications with other departments. The manager is the central point of contact within the department.

The department is like the H.323 zone, and the manager is like an H.323 gatekeeper. One gatekeeper is actively in charge of each zone. Calls can be placed through the gatekeeper within the zone (intra-zone calls) and between zones (inter-zone calls). When a call is placed between zones, the gatekeeper communicates with the remote zone's gatekeeper on behalf of the endpoint placing the call.

Like the department manager, the gatekeeper is aware of all endpoints within the zone. The gatekeeper is the central server used to provide admission to the zone and control of the zone. The gatekeeper will track the status of endpoints and gateways. The gatekeeper is aware of the communication paths in the network and of the remote zone gatekeepers for inter-zone communications.

In the end, the gatekeeper manages the zone, and the zone acts as the authorization boundary for a collection of endpoints. Each zone may have one or more gateways and at least one endpoint (or terminal).

## Gatekeeper Terminology

The H.323 standard defines several terms as they apply to H.323 networks and gatekeepers. The following terms are important to properly understanding and implementing H.323 gatekeepers:

- **Call**  Point-to-point multimedia communication between two H.323 endpoints. The call begins with the call setup procedure and ends with the call termination procedure. The call consists of the collection of reliable and unreliable channels between the endpoints. A call may be directly between two endpoints or may include other H.323 entities such as a gatekeeper or MC (Multipoint Controller). In case of interworking with some endpoints via a gateway, all the channels terminate at the gateway, where they are converted to the appropriate representation for the end system. Typically, a call is between two users for the purpose of communication, but may include signaling-only calls. An endpoint may be capable of supporting multiple simultaneous calls.

- **Endpoint**   An H.323 terminal, gateway, or MCU. An endpoint can call and be called. It generates and/or terminates information streams.

- **Gatekeeper**   The gatekeeper is an H.323 entity on the network that provides address translation and that controls access to the network for H.323 terminals, gateways, and MCUs. The gatekeeper may also provide other services to the terminals, gateways, and MCUs, such as bandwidth management and locating gateways.

- **H.323 entity**   Any H.323 component, including terminals, gateways, gatekeepers, MCs, MPs (Multipoint Processors), and MCUs.

- **Multipoint Control Unit**   The Multipoint Control Unit (MCU) is an endpoint on the network that provides the capability for three or more terminals and gateways to participate in a multipoint conference. It may also connect two terminals in a point-to-point conference, which may later develop into a multipoint conference. The MCU generally operates in the fashion of an H.231 MCU; however, an audio processor is not mandatory. The MCU consists of two parts: a mandatory Multipoint Controller (MC) and optional Multipoint Processors (MPs). In the simplest case, an MCU may consist only of an MC with no MPs. An MCU may also be brought into a conference by the gatekeeper without being explicitly called by one of the endpoints.

- **Terminal**   An H.323 terminal is an endpoint on the network that provides for real-time, two-way communications with another H.323 terminal, gateway, or Multipoint Control Unit. This communication consists of control, indications, audio, moving color video pictures, and/or data between the two terminals. A terminal may provide speech only, speech and data, speech and video, or speech, data, and video.

- **Zone**   A zone is the collection of all terminals, gateways, and Multipoint Control Units (MCUs) managed by a single gatekeeper. A zone has one and only one gatekeeper. A zone may be independent of network topology and may comprise multiple network segments that are connected using routers or other devices.

A few additional terms are important in the Cisco H.323 networking world. First, a *zone prefix* is a number prefix that defines the extensions available within a zone. A zone can include multiple prefixes. A zone prefix can define a specific extension or prefixes based on wildcards such as 3.. or 4.. to indicate any extensions from 300 to 399 or 400 to 499, respectively.

Second, technology prefixes may be used. A *technology prefix* is an optional parameter that defines a prefix to indicate a specific technology is in use and that the call should be routed to the server that understands the technology. For example, the prefix 3# may be used to indicate that a fax call is being made, and the call could be routed to the server or gateway that can process the fax.

Third, when a call is unresolved by the technology prefix, the default technology prefix is used. The default technology prefix is assigned in gatekeeper configuration mode using the **gw-type-prefix** command. For example, the following command indicates that a gateway registered to process 1# calls should be used if the gatekeeper does not recognize the number or a specific technology prefix:

```
Router1(config-gk)# gw-type-prefix 1# default-technology
```

**e x a m**

**ⓦ a t c h**
        *Remember that zone prefixes define the extensions available within a zone. Technology prefixes are used to specify a particular technology such as*

*a fax or modem. The default technology prefix is used if the user does not enter a technology prefix.*

**CERTIFICATION OBJECTIVE 14.05**

# 642-436: Implement a Gatekeeper

Implementing a gatekeeper is really a three-step process. First, you will need to set up the zones and prefixes on the gatekeeper. Second, you will need to configure the gateways to use the gatekeeper. Finally, you should verify the gatekeeper's configuration is appropriate for your needs.

## Configuring Zones

Zones can be configured as local zones or remote zones. The local zone is the zone controlled by the gatekeeper on which it is created. The remote zones are zones managed by other gatekeepers. The **zone local** command is used to create the local zone. The **zone remote** command is used to specify remote zones. The following commands provide examples of zone configuration:

```
Router1(config)# gatekeeper
Router1(config-gk)# zone local gk1 sysedco.com
Router1(config-gk)# zone remote gk2 sysedco.com 10.1.4.1 123 cost 25 priority 35
Router1(config-gk)# no shutdown
Router1(config-gk)# exit
```

In the preceding example, the **zone local** command configures the `zone-name` parameter to `gk1` and the `domain-name` parameter to `sysedco.com`. The result is a local zone named `gk1.sysedco.com`. The **zone remote** command sets the remote `zone-name` parameter to `gk2` and the `domain-name` parameter to `sysedco.com`. The result is a remote zone named `gk2.sysedco.com`. Additionally, the remote zone is reachable through the IP address of `10.1.4.1` with a `cost` of `25` and a `priority` of `35`. Both the `cost` and `priority` parameters may be set to any number from 1 to 100, and the default value, when not specified, is 50. When multiple remote zones are configured, the `cost` and `priority` are used to select the first remote zone to try. A lower `cost` and higher `priority` cause the zone to be used before other zones.

With the zones enabled, you must now configure the zone prefix or prefixes. You can stay in gatekeeper configuration mode, indicated by the (`config-gk`) CLI prompt, and configure the prefixes at the same time, or you can enter gatekeeper configuration mode again, as in the following example:

```
Router1(config)# gatekeeper
Router1(config-gk)# zone prefix gk1 2...
Router1(config-gk)# exit
```

The preceding example indicates that the gk1 gatekeeper is responsible for all extensions from 2000 to 2999. If the zone includes multiple extensions, simply enter an additional **zone prefix** command for each extension or extension block by using wildcards.

Finally, you can restrict the IP subnets that should be included in the zone. This action forces IP phones on one subnet to use a particular gatekeeper, and therefore, to participate in that gatekeeper's zone. The **zone subnet** command is used to configure these restrictions, as in the following example:

```
Router1(config)# gatekeeper
Router1(config-gk)# zone subnet gk1 10.1.1.0 255.255.255.0 enable
Router1(config-gk)# exit
```

In addition to accepting specific subnets, you can configure a gatekeeper to accept all subnets with the **zone subnet gatekeeper_name default** command.

on the **Job**

*When implementing zones, know that you can manage multiple zones on a single Cisco router. Multiple zone local configurations are supported on a single router. The gatekeeper is a logical entity within the router, and it can manage multiple zones even though each zone can have only one gatekeeper.*

## Enabling Gateways for Gatekeeper Use

After the gatekeeper is enabled with zone management, prefixes, and subnets, you can enable the gatekeeper use on the gateways. Before you configure the gatekeeper settings on the gateway, you may want to shut down the gateway services. This will prevent the gateway from sending out registrations to the gatekeeper until you are completely finished with the configuration. To shut down the gateway services, execute the **no gateway** command from within global configuration mode.

With the gateway services disabled, you are ready to begin configuring gatekeeper access on the gateway router. The configuration on the gateway is performed from within interface configuration mode. The following command examples illustrate the process:

```
Gateway1(config)# interface fa0/1
Gateway1(config-if)# h323-gateway voip interface
Gateway1(config-if)# h323-gateway voip bind srcaddr 10.1.1.3
Gateway1(config-if)# h323-gateway voip id gk1 ipaddr 10.1.1.4
Gateway1(config-if)# h323-gateway voip h323-id Gateway1
Gateway1(config-if)# exit
Gateway1(config)# dial-peer voice 112 voip
Gateway1(config-dial-peer)# destination-pattern ….
Gateway1(config-dial-peer)# session target ras
Gateway1(config-dial-peer)# exit
Gateway1(config)# gateway
```

The first command changes to interface configuration mode for Fast Ethernet 0/1. The interface selected here must be the one that can communicate across the network with the gatekeeper. The **h323-gateway voip interface** command simply indicates that the current interface is the interface used for H.323 gateway functions. The next command binds the H.323 gateway to the IP address of the interface. This is the same IP address as that configured for interface Fast Ethernet 0/1 in this case. The **h323-gateway voip id** command is used to indicate the IP address of the gatekeeper and zone with which this gateway should register. Next, the H.323 ID of the gateway is specified as `Gateway1`, which would have been the default, but you can use something other than the router's host name as the registered name by using the **h323-gateway voip h323-id** command.

Now that the gateway is configured to use the gatekeeper, a single dial peer must be created to indicate that the gatekeeper should be used for all four-digit extensions. The **dial-peer** commands in the preceding example perform this operation. Notice, specifically, the **session target ras** command, which indicates that a gatekeeper (which is a RAS server) should be used for all four-digit extensions.

## Verifying Gatekeeper Configuration

After the gateways have been configured to use the gatekeeper, as explained in the preceding section, the gatekeeper operations can be verified. Several **show** commands are useful for verification, including:

- **show gatekeeper status**   This command displays the gatekeeper state, the zone name, whether accounting is enabled or disabled, security features, and the bandwidth limits and utilization.
- **show gatekeeper calls**   This command shows any calls currently in progress that were established through the gatekeeper.
- **show gatekeeper endpoints**   Interestingly, this command shows the gateways because they are considered endpoints by the H.323 standard. It's important to remember that this command is not limited to showing IP phones.
- **show gatekeeper zone**   This command displays the zone configuration information, including prefixes and subnets.

*Be sure to know which show **commands do what in relation to gatekeeper** configuration and operation verification. They are very likely to show up on the CVOICE exam.*

# CERTIFICATION SUMMARY

In this chapter, you learned about gateways and gatekeepers. These two components are very important on VoIP networks. You learned about the roles played by the gateway and how to implement a gateway by configuring voice ports and dial peers. You then learned about the functions of a gatekeeper and how to configure the gatekeeper and how to configure the gateways to use the gatekeeper.

# ✔ TWO-MINUTE DRILL

## 642-436: Describe the Components of a Gateway

❑ Cisco VoIP gateways usually run on ISRs as a component of the IOS and potentially the CME call manager.

❑ Gateways often provide telephone to WAN, telephone to PSTN, or PBX-to-PBX over WAN connectivity.

❑ FXS and FXO ports are analog voice ports.

❑ ISDN, T1, and E1 lines and ports are digital voice ports.

❑ VoIP dial peers are used to connect to other VoIP devices across packet-based networks.

❑ POTS dial peers are used to connect to the PSTN, PBX systems, or analog phone devices.

## 642-436: Implement a Gateway

❑ Gateways route calls through analog or digital ports depending on the call destination.

❑ Dial peers are used by the gateway to determine the proper call path or call route.

❑ Analog ports use loop-start, ground-start, or E&M wink start signaling.

❑ Voice ports are referenced in one of three ways within Cisco ISRs: port, slot/port, or slot/subunit/port.

❑ T1 lines use 24 channels across a single line, with each channel providing up to 64 Kbps of bandwidth.

❑ The **voice-port** command is used to enter voice port configuration mode and to configure FXS or FXO ports.

❑ The **dial-peer voice # pots** command is used to create a POTS dial peer.

## 640-460: Describe and Configure Gateways, Voice Ports, and Dial Peers to Connect to the PSTN and Service Provider Networks

❑ VoIP dial peers are created with the **dial peer voice # voip** command.

❑ VoIP dial peers use the `session target` parameter to define the IP address of the target for the dial peer.

❑ The **show dial-peer voice summary** command is used to view a basic listing of configured dial peers.

❑ The **show gateway** command is used to view the status of the gateway.

## 642-436: Describe the Function and Interoperation of Gatekeepers Within an IP Communications Network

❑ The H.323 gatekeepers are responsible for network admission control, address resolution, bandwidth control, and zone management.

❑ H.323 zones are managed by a single gatekeeper and include at least one terminal and may include multiple gateways.

❑ ARQ messages are sent to the gatekeeper to request access to the H.323 network, and the gatekeeper may respond with an ACF or ARJ message.

## 642-436: Implement a Gatekeeper

❑ The **zone local** command is used to implement local zones on a router/gatekeeper.

❑ The **zone remote** command is used to reference remote zones and gatekeepers by IP address.

❑ Zone prefixes are created with the **zone prefix** command.

❑ The **zone subnet** command is used to specify the IP subnets managed by the gatekeeper.

❑ Gateways are configured for use with a gatekeeper in interface configuration mode.

❑ The **h323-gateway** commands allow for the configuration of the gatekeeper settings on the gateways.

❑ The **show gatekeeper** commands are used to verify gatekeeper configuration.

# SELF TEST

The following questions will help you measure your understanding of the material presented in this chapter. Read all the choices carefully because there might be more than one correct answer. Choose all correct answers for each question.

## 642-436: Describe the Components of a Gateway

1. When a telephone communicates with another telephone through the gateway and the gateway is connected to another network across a WAN link, what connection type is provided by the gateway?
   A. Telephone to WAN
   B. Telephone to PSTN
   C. PSTN to Telephone
   D. PBX-to-PBX over WAN

2. Which voice port is used to connect to the PSTN or PBX systems with an analog connection?
   A. FXS
   B. FXO
   C. T1
   D. E1

3. You are implementing a VoIP dial peer. To what device may you be connecting with the dial peer?
   A. PBX
   B. Fax machine
   C. Analog phone
   D. H.323 phone

## 642-436: Implement a Gateway

4. Which of the following are valid signaling methods used on analog ports? (Choose all that apply.)
   A. Q.931
   B. Loop-start
   C. E&M wink start
   D. Ground-start

5.  When a T1 PRI CCS line is acquired as a full T1 line, how many channels are available for voice calls?

    A.  24

    B.  23

    C.  3

    D.  2

6.  You are using CAS signaling on a T1 line. How much bandwidth is available in each channel for voice calls?

    A.  64 Kbps

    B.  48 Kbps

    C.  8 Kbps

    D.  56 Kbps

7.  You want to configure a POTS dial peer for an analog phone attached to port 0/1. You want the phone to use extension 1504. Which configuration command should be entered in dial-peer configuration mode to assign the extension number desired?

    A.  port 1504

    B.  session target 1504

    C.  destination-pattern 1504

    D.  extension 1504

## 640-460: Describe and Configure Gateways, Voice Ports, and Dial Peers to Connect to the PSTN and Service Provider Networks

8.  When implementing a VoIP dial peer, which one of the following is a valid command used to create and enter dial-peer configuration mode?

    A.  dial-peer voice 15 voip

    B.  dial-peer voice 15 voice

    C.  dial-peer voice 15 pots

    D.  dial-peer voip 15 voice

9.  What command is used to show the voice ports on the machine without detailed information?

    A.  show voice port

    B.  show voice port 0

    C.  show voice port summary

    D.  show voice port brief

**10.** Which one of the following items is not shown when the **show gateway** command is executed on a gateway that is not registered with a gatekeeper?

   **A.** H.323 resource threshold values

   **B.** H.323 resource thresholding configuration

   **C.** The gateway name

   **D.** The number of dial peers on the gateway

## 642-436: Describe the Function and Interoperation of Gatekeepers Within an IP Communications Network

**11.** Which of the following are mandatory functions of a gatekeeper? (Choose all that apply.)

   **A.** Call authorization

   **B.** Address resolution

   **C.** Admission control

   **D.** Call control signaling

**12.** What message is used to request admission to the H.323 network?

   **A.** ACF

   **B.** ARQ

   **C.** HELLO

   **D.** ARJ

**13.** What is used to define the extensions included within a zone?

   **A.** Zone prefixes

   **B.** Endpoints

   **C.** MCUs

   **D.** Terminals

## 642-436: Implement a Gatekeeper

**14.** You are entering commands on Router1. What command is used in gatekeeper configuration mode to create the zone Router1 will manage?

   **A.** zone remote

   **B.** zone current

   **C.** zone local

   **D.** current zone

**15.** In what configuration mode will you configure the gateways to use a gatekeeper?
   A. Gateway configuration mode
   B. Gatekeeper configuration mode
   C. Interface configuration mode
   D. Voice port configuration mode

# LAB QUESTION

You have configured a gatekeeper and need to verify proper gatekeeper configuration. What commands will you type to verify the configuration, and why will you type these commands?

# SELF TEST ANSWERS

## 642-436: Describe the Components of a Gateway

1. ☑ **A** is correct. The telephone to WAN connection provides voice connections across WAN interfaces.

   ☒ **B, C,** and **D** are incorrect. The telephone to PSTN connection provides voice connections with the PSTN. The PSTN to telephone connection is automatically created when the telephone to PSTN connection is established. The PBX-to-PBX over WAN connection provides a connection between two PBX systems over WAN interfaces.

2. ☑ **B** is correct. The foreign exchange office (FXO) port is used to connect to PBX systems and the PSTN. FXO ports are analog interface ports and provide a single channel in normal utilization.

   ☒ **A, C,** and **D** are incorrect. Foreign exchange station (FXS) ports are used to connect to analog phones, fax machines, and potentially other analog telephony devices. T1 ports are digital. E1 ports are digital.

3. ☑ **D** is correct. An H.323 phone is a VoIP endpoint that is reached directly using VoIP dial peers.

   ☒ **A, B,** and **C** are incorrect. PBX systems, fax machines, and analog phones are all analog devices and would be reached with POTS dial peers and not directly with VoIP dial peers.

## 642-436: Implement a Gateway

4. ☑ **B, C,** and **D** are correct. Loop-start, E&M wink start, and ground-start are all valid signaling methods on analog ports.

   ☒ **A** is incorrect. Q.931 is used on ISDN ports and some other digital interfaces.

5. ☑ **B** is correct. Twenty-three channels are available on a T1 PRI CCS line, which is the most common line chosen, with 64 Kbps of bandwidth each. The 24th channel is used for signaling, hence, common channel signaling (CCS).

   ☒ **A, C,** and **D** are incorrect. Twenty-four channels are available with T1 CAS, but each channel has only 56 Kbps of bandwidth because the signaling is passed on the voice channels. Three channels come with ISDN lines, with one channel used for signaling. Two channels is simply an incorrect answer.

6. ☑ **D** is correct. Because CAS signaling uses channel associated signaling on the voice channels, only 56 Kbps of bandwidth is available.

   ☒ **A, B,** and **C** are incorrect. On T1 CCS lines, 64 Kbps of bandwidth is available. The answers 48 Kbps and 8 Kbps are simply incorrect.

7. ☑ **C** is correct. The **destination-pattern** configuration command is used to assign the extension.

   ☒ **A, B,** and **D** are incorrect. The **port** command is used to assign the voice port as a destination for a local voice port POTS dial peer. The **session target** command is used with a VoIP dial peer. The **extension** command is invalid and does not exist.

## 640-460: Describe and Configure Gateways, Voice Ports, and Dial Peers to Connect to the PSTN and Service Provider Networks

8. ☑ **A** is correct. The **dial-peer voice 15 voip** command is a valid example of both creating the dial peer and entering dial peer configuration mode.

   ☒ **B, C,** and **D** are incorrect. These commands are either invalid or used to create a POTS dial peer. The command **dial-peer voice 15 pots** is valid for creating a POTS dial peer. Answers B and D are simply invalid commands.

9. ☑ **C** is correct. The **show voice port summary** command is used to summarize the voice ports.

   ☒ **A, B,** and **D** are incorrect. The **show voice port** command shows the details of each voice port. The **show voice port 0** command would show the details of voice port 0. The **show voice port brief** command is invalid.

10. ☑ **D** is correct. The number of dial peers is not listed in the output of the **show gateway** command.

    ☒ **A, B,** and **C** are incorrect. The H.323 resource threshold values and configuration status are listed in the output. The gateway name is also displayed in the output.

## 642-436: Describe the Function and Interoperation of Gatekeepers Within an IP Communications Network

11. ☑ **B** and **C** are correct. Address resolution and admission control are mandatory functions of an H.323 gatekeeper.

    ☒ **A** and **D** are incorrect. Call authorization and call control signaling are optional functions of an H.323 gatekeeper.

12. ☑ **B** is correct. The ARQ message is sent to request admission to the H.323 network.

☒ **A, C,** and **D** are incorrect. The ACF message is a confirmation of admission sent in response to an ARQ message. The HELLO message is not part of the gatekeeper protocols. The ARJ message is a rejection of admission sent in response to an ARQ message.

13. ☑ **A** is correct. Zone prefixes are used to define the telephone extensions managed in a given zone.

☒ **B, C,** and **D** are incorrect. Endpoints, MCUs, and terminals in no way define the extensions. Endpoints and terminals may be given extensions, but the zone prefixes determine the extensions managed within the zone. MCUs are used to aggregate multiple voice streams into one and perform other voice operations on the network.

### 642-436: Implement a Gatekeeper

14. ☑ **C** is correct. The **zone local** command is used to define the local zone or zones managed by the local gatekeeper service on the router.

☒ **A, B,** and **D** are incorrect. The **zone remote** command is used to configure remote zones managed by other gatekeepers for access to those zones. **Zone current** and **current zone** are invalid commands.

15. ☑ **C** is correct. Interface configuration mode is used to configure the gatekeeper. You will also be required to create appropriate dial peers in dial-peer configuration mode, but this mode was not a listed option.

☒ **A, B,** and **D** are incorrect. Gateway configuration mode is used to configure various gateway settings, but the gatekeeper use is defined in interface configuration mode. Gatekeeper configuration mode is used to make the router a gatekeeper. Voice port configuration mode is used to configure voice ports.

## LAB ANSWER

Answers may vary; the following commands may be used:

- **show gatekeeper status**   Displays the gatekeeper state, the zone name, whether accounting is enabled or disabled, security features, and the bandwidth limits and utilization.
- **show gatekeeper calls**   Shows any calls currently in progress that were established through the gatekeeper.
- **show gatekeeper endpoints**   Shows the gateways because they are considered endpoints by the H.323 standard. It's important to remember that this command is not limited to showing IP phones.
- **show gatekeeper zone**   Displays the zone configuration information including prefixes and subnets.

# 15

# IP-to-IP Gateways

> *A lot of people had Atari video game machines. And so the idea was,*
> *well maybe you can take an Atari video game machine, where people plug in a game*
> *cartridge, and plug in a modem, and tie that into a telephone, and essentially turn that*
> *game in the machine into an interactive terminal.*
>
> —Steve Case, Cofounder of America Online

A gateway, as you've learned in preceding chapters, is a device that connects to different networks. The networks may be different in type or simply different in management. An IP-to-IP gateway connects two IP networks. One of the IP networks is your internal network. The other IP network is the service provider's network. The role of the IP-to-IP gateway is to connect the two. This functionality is not unlike connecting your Atari to an online network service. Without the connection through the cartridge, the Atari stands alone (internal communications only); however, when you add the online cartridge, you can communicate with the world. You might say that old Atari cartridge that was planned was a form of gateway to a new world of online discovery.

In this chapter, you'll learn about the IP-to-IP gateway. You'll first learn about its features and purpose. Then you'll learn about the various configuration commands and actions needed to get an IP-to-IP gateway up and running for your VoIP network. Finally, you'll learn the commands used to verify the gateway is configured correctly.

## CERTIFICATION OBJECTIVE 15.01

# 642-436: Describe the IP-to-IP Gateway Features and Functionality

An IP-to-IP gateway connects two IP networks and may convert VoIP signaling protocols between them. In this section, you will learn about the features of an IP-to-IP gateway and the basic functionality it provides.

## IP-to-IP Gateway Features

In the Cisco world, the IP-to-IP gateway is known as the Cisco Unified Border Element (UBE). As far as the hardware goes, the UBE is like other gateways in that it can be any of several Cisco ISRs. Instead of using voice cards (FXO, T1, or E1) and signaling, UBE gateways use IP connections to the service provider.

| | |
|---|---|
| *While the objectives for the CVOICE exam indicate that you should understand an IP-to-IP gateway, Cisco no longer calls their solution by* | *that name. What was once called the Cisco Multiservice IP-to-IP Gateway is now called the Cisco Unified Border Element (UBE).* |

The Cisco UBE sits between two IP networks and terminates and originates the signaling and media streams for VoIP calls. The UBE, in some ways, acts as a proxy. The calls terminate and reoriginate at the UBE. The signaling reorigination includes SIP and H.323 and the conversion between the two. The media stream reorigination includes both RTP and RTCP. The UBE is a Cisco IOS feature, which is also known as a session border controller (SBC). In the simplest of explanations, UBE connects VoIP dial peers. An inbound dial peer is connected with an outbound dial peer, and the dial peers may be associated with different ports or destination IP addresses.

It's important to know that only specific IOS images support the UBE. The feature sets that support UBE are listed in Table 15-1. Note that the special IPIPGW IOS image is even named based on this support.

| TABLE 15-1 | Cisco IOS Feature Sets Supporting UBE |
|---|---|

| IOS Feature | Set Description |
|---|---|
| INT VOICE/VIDEO, IPIPGW, TDMIP GW AES | Referenced by the code "adventerprisek9_ivs" in the IOS image filename. IP Services with AES encryption capabilities. |
| INT VOICE/VIDEO, IPIPGW, TDMIP GW | Referenced by the code "ipvoice_ivs" in the IOS image filename. Provides VoIP features in full with basic routing functions as well. |
| ADVANCED ENTERPRISE SERVICES | Referenced by the code "adventerprisek9" without the "_ivs" code appended in the IOS image filename. An all-in-one feature set version of the IOS. |
| SP SERVICES | Referenced by the code "spservicesk9" in the IOS image filename. Intended for use within service provider networks. |
| IP VOICE | Referenced by the code "ipvoice" without the "_ivs" code appended in the IOS image filename. Provides basic VoIP services and features and basic IP routing features. |

## INSIDE THE EXAM

### Cisco IOS Feature Sets?

Because the CVOICE exam requires that you understand the basics of configuring an IP-to-IP gateway or the Cisco UBE, it is important to understand feature sets. You may have a Cisco 2801 ISR, for example, but still be unable to implement it as a Cisco UBE because it runs the wrong IOS feature set. Of course, you can purchase the license for the feature set you need or download it from your Cisco account, assuming you have the appropriate support level, but it is still an important consideration when implementing Cisco UBE.

If you're relatively new to the Cisco world, but have used Windows servers and clients for many years, you may find it easier to understand IOS feature sets by relating them to Windows editions. For example, Windows Server 2008 comes in several editions including Web, Standard, Enterprise, and Datacenter. As you move up through the more advanced editions, more features and capabilities are added. For example, the Web edition cannot act as a domain controller.

While the hardware on which it runs could be a domain controller, the functionality is limited by the running edition. To make the machine a domain controller, you would have to upgrade the OS to at least the Standard edition.

The same is true for Windows clients. For example, Windows 7 comes in several editions, including Home, Home Premium, Professional, Enterprise, and Ultimate. If you have the Home edition, you cannot join the machine to a domain. You would have to upgrade to at least the Professional edition to perform this action. In summary, different editions of Windows servers and clients offer different features.

I've shared this comparison to help you see that what Cisco is doing is really nothing new or unique in the industry. If you want a certain set of features, you have to make sure you have the right version of the software. The Cisco IOS is no different. This is not only true for Cisco UBE implementations, but for many other voice features as well.

The Cisco UBE gateway device will support most VoIP functions that are needed for the gateway and general VoIP communications. Table 15-2 lists the primary features of the UBE gateway.

| TABLE 15-2 | Cisco UBE Features |

| Feature | Details |
| --- | --- |
| Protocols | H.323 and SIP |
| Media Modes | Media flow-through and media flow-around |
| Media Support | RTP and RTCP |
| Transport Mode | TCP, UDP, and TCP-to-UDP internetworking |
| Fax Support | T.38 fax relay, fax pass-through, and Cisco fax relay |
| Modem Support | Modem pass-through and Cisco modem relay |
| Dual-Tone Multifrequency (DTMF) | H.245 alphanumeric, H.245 signal, RFC 2833, SIP notify, and Key Press Markup Language (KPML) |
| Call Admission Control (CAC) | Resource Reservation Protocol (RSVP), maximum calls per trunk, CAC based on IP circuits, CAC based on total calls or CPU use or memory use threshold |
| Quality of Service (QoS) | IP Precedence and Differentiated Services Code Point (DSCP) marking |
| Network Address Translation (NAT) traversal | NAT traversal support for SIP phones as well as stateful NAT traversal |
| Codecs Supported | G.711, G.722, G.723, G.726, G.728, G.729, and iLBC |
| Security | IP Security (IPSec), Secure RTP (sRTP), and Transport Layer Security (TLS) |

## IP-to-IP Gateway Functionality

The Cisco UBE functionality can be summarized as follows: The UBE acts as a VoIP gateway in the same basic way as a PSTN-to-IP gateway. In other words, the UBE joins two IP-based VoIP call legs instead of a PSTN and IP call leg. Cisco UBE can connect any of these combinations of IP voice networks:

- H.323-to-H.323
- H.323-to-SIP
- SIP-to-SIP

If your service provider (SP) uses SIP and you use H.323, Cisco UBE can convert the signaling between the two protocols to allow for connectivity. Even if you use H.323 and your SP uses the same protocol, the UBE will terminate and reoriginate the signaling and media streams. The result is that Cisco UBE can function in one of two ways:

- Internetworking between like networks
- Internetworking between different networks

When internetworking between like networks, the same VoIP signaling protocol is used on both networks. When internetworking between different networks, the networks use different VoIP signaling protocols such as H.323 and SIP.

In addition to the considerations related to signaling, you must consider how the media (the voice RTP streams) will flow from one network to the other. The UBE, as was previously stated, is effectively a proxy. It receives the signals from one side (for example, the internal interface) and reoriginates them for output on the other side (for example, the external interface). However, the UBE has to address the media streams as well as the signaling information. For this, the UBE can either use media flow-through or media flow-around.

Figure 15-1 depicts the architecture of a media flow-through implementation. Notice that the signaling goes to the Cisco UCM and then through the UBE. The media (RTP stream) goes from the phones to the UBE. The UBE introduces delay in the communications process and may not provide acceptable performance for the VoIP calls. This is particularly true if the UBE device is used for additional data networking purposes.

Figure 15-2 depicts the architecture of a media flow-around implementation. As you can see, the media now goes directly from phone to phone. Interestingly, the

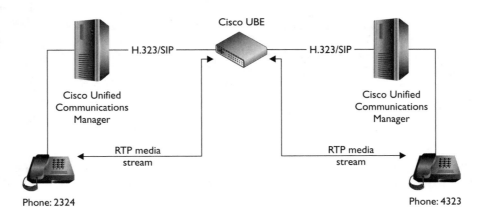

**FIGURE 15-1**

The UBE media flow-through architecture

Cisco UBE

H.323/SIP — H.323/SIP

Cisco Unified Communications Manager

Cisco Unified Communications Manager

RTP media stream

RTP media stream

Phone: 2324

Phone: 4323

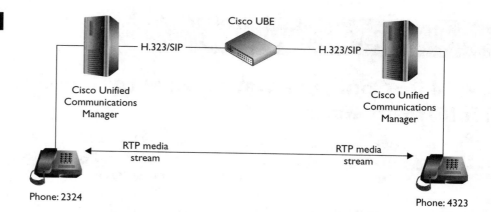

**FIGURE 15-2**

The UBE media flow-around architecture

actual data packets may still traverse through the device that is acting as the UBE; however, the UBE service will no longer terminate and reoriginate the media stream packets. The result is less delay and potentially improved quality for the VoIP call.

The Cisco UBE is a gateway and therefore supports gateway functionality including the following tasks:

- **DTMF relay**   This task allows for the dual-tone multifrequency (DTMF) dialed digit signals to pass through to the remote IP network.
- **Fax and modem relay or pass-through**   Because fax machines and modems use sound signals to transfer information, they must either be relayed or passed through with a lossless codec to function properly.
- **Media stream handling and speech path integrity**   This task ensures that the media stream is set up appropriately and has a route through which to travel without corruption or interruption.
- **Dial peers and codec filtering**   The gateway can limit the codecs allowed between configured dial peers.
- **Digit translation and call processing**   The gateway can translate dialed digits into appropriate structures for the destination VoIP network.
- **Carrier ID handling**   The UBE gateway supports carrier ID detection and processing.
- **Gateway-based billing**   Most useful for service providers, this feature provides extensive accounting for billing purposes.
- **Termination and reorigination of signaling and media**   The gateway decapsulates the arriving packets and encapsulates them for the destination network.

**CERTIFICATION OBJECTIVE 15.02**

# 642-436: Configure Gatekeeper to Support an IP-to-IP Gateway

When the Cisco UBE is deployed in an H.323 environment with a gatekeeper, the gatekeeper must be configured to support the UBE gateway. This section provides the commands required to perform this configuration.

## Cisco Gatekeeper Configuration Commands

Configuring a gatekeeper to support the Cisco UBE is a simple and straightforward process. You will perform the actions in gatekeeper configuration mode. For the Cisco H.323 gatekeeper to work with the UBE, via-zones must be configured. According to Cisco's "Configuring Cisco Unified Border Element with Gatekeeper" configuration guide:

> Via-zone gatekeepers differ from legacy gatekeepers in how LRQ and ARQ messages are used for call routing. Using via-zone gatekeepers will maintain normal clusters and functionality. Legacy gatekeepers examine incoming LRQs based on the called number, and more specifically the dialedDigits field in the destinationInfo portion of the LRQ. Via-zone gatekeepers look at the origination point of the LRQ before looking at the called number. If an LRQ comes from a gatekeeper listed in the via-zone gatekeeper's remote zone configurations, the gatekeeper checks to see that the zone remote configuration contains an invia or outvia keyword. If the configuration contains these keywords, the gatekeeper uses the new via-zone behavior; if not, it uses legacy behavior.
>
> For ARQ messages, the gatekeeper determines if an outvia keyword is configured on the destination zone. If the outvia keyword is configured, and the zone named with the outvia keyword is local to the gatekeeper, the call is directed to a Cisco Multiservice IP-to-IP Gateway in that zone by returning an ACF pointing to the Cisco Multiservice IP-to-IP Gateway. If the zone named with the outvia keyword is remote, the gatekeeper sends a location request to the outvia gatekeeper rather than the remote zone gatekeeper. The invia keyword is not used in processing the ARQ.

In other words, remote and local zones must be configured on the gatekeeper. The outvia keyword is used to determine if a local Cisco UBE is available for processing the call. To configure remote zones, use commands like the following:

```
Router1> enable
Router1# configure terminal
Router1(config-gk)# zone remote spGK spname 10.16.193.158 1719 invia myGK outvia myGK
Router1(config-gk)# exit
```

The key command is the **zone remote** command, which uses the following syntax:

**zone remote** *gatekeeper-name domain-name* [*ras-IP-address*] [**invia** *inbound-gatekeeper* | **outvia** *outbound-gatekeeper* [**enable-intrazone**]]

To configure local zones, use commands like the following:

```
Router> enable
Router# configure terminal
Router(config)# gatekeeper
Router(config-gk)# zone local myGK mydom.com 10.16.193.158 invia myGK outvia myGK enable-intrazone
Router(config-gk)# exit
```

The key command here is the **zone local** command, which uses the following syntax:

**zone local** *gatekeeper-name domain-name* [*ras-IP-address*] [**invia** *inbound-gatekeeper* | **outvia** *outbound-gatekeeper* [**enable-intrazone**]]

For more details on configuring gatekeepers for functionality with a Cisco UBE, read the "Configuring Cisco Unified Border Element with Gatekeeper" configuration guide available at www.cisco.com/en/US/docs/ios/voice/cubegk/configuration/guide/ve-gk-config.html.

*Remember that you must use a via-zone to allow a gatekeeper to work with the Cisco UBE and that the* zone local *and* zone remote *commands are used to accomplish this configuration.*

**CERTIFICATION OBJECTIVE 15.03**

# 642-436: Configure IP-to-IP Gateway to Provide Address Hiding

Cisco UBE supports IP address hiding in order to ensure that the UBE is the only point of signaling and media entry or exit in all communications scenarios. This section provides instructions for IP address hiding when using Cisco UBE.

## Hiding Addresses

Like most Cisco IOS-based activities, IP address hiding is accomplished by first entering enable mode and then entering configuration mode. Next, you will enter the VoIP voice-service configuration mode and use the **address-hiding** command. The following example illustrates this process:

```
Router1> enable
Router1# configure terminal
Router1(config)# voice service voip
Router1(conf-voi-serv)# address-hiding
Router1(conf-voi-serv)# exit
```

The key command here is the **address-hiding** command. It's very easy to remember because you type no parameters when entering the command. To disable address hiding, you will simply execute the **no address-hiding** command.

**CERTIFICATION OBJECTIVE 15.04**

# 642-436: Configure IP-to-IP Gateway to Provide Protocol and Media Interworking

The Cisco UBE needs to be configured for both signaling and media internetworking. The protocol or signal internetworking is related to the H.323 and SIP protocols. The media internetworking is about determining whether you want to implement media flow-through or media flow-around. In this section, you will learn the commands for both operations.

# Providing Protocol Internetworking

As you learned earlier in this chapter, you can implement Cisco UBE to connect networks in three possible scenarios:

- H.323-to-H.323
- H.323-to-SIP
- SIP-to-SIP

Configuring protocol internetworking is about choosing these network types and informing the UBE of their existence. The good news is that the commands are very simple. You will use the **allow-connections** command from VoIP voice-service configuration mode. The following example illustrates the available commands:

```
Router1> enable
Router1# configure terminal
Router1(config)# voice service voip
Router1(conf-voi-serv)# allow-connections h323 to h323
Router1(conf-voi-serv)# allow-connections sip to sip
Router1(conf-voi-serv)# allow-connections h323 to sip
Router1(conf-voi-serv)# allow-connections sip to h323
Router1(conf-voi-serv)# exit
```

You can probably guess which command does what based on the syntax. To be clear, you set up an H.323-to-H.323 UBE with the **allow-connections h323 to h323** command. For SIP-to-SIP you use the **allow-connections sip to sip** command. Finally, for h.323-to-sip you use the two commands **allow-connections h323 to sip** and **allow-connections sip to h323**.

# Providing Media Interworking

In addition to signaling protocol conversion and internetworking, you must configure the media flow. The media flow is not configured from within the VoIP voice-service configuration like the protocol internetworking. Instead, you will configure media flow within the dial peers. As an example, consider the following commands:

```
Router1> enable
Router1# configure terminal
Router1(config)# dial-peer voice 4300
Router1(conf-dial-peer)# description Destined for UCM at local site
Router1(conf-dial-peer)# destination-pattern 4...
```

```
Router1(conf-dial-peer)# session target ipv4:10.1.1.1
Router1(conf-dial-peer)# dtmf-relay h245-alphanumeric
Router1(conf-dial-peer)# codec transparent
Router1(conf-dial-peer)# media flow-around
Router1(conf-dial-peer)# exit
Router1(config)# dial-peer voice 5300
Router1(conf-dial-peer)# description Destined for UCM at remote site
Router1(conf-dial-peer)# destination-pattern 5...
Router1(conf-dial-peer)# session target ipv4:10.2.2.1
Router1(conf-dial-peer)# codec transparent
Router1(conf-dial-peer)# media flow-around
Router1(conf-dial-peer)# exit
```

The key command in this dial-peer listing is the **media flow-around** command. This command tells the UBE to allow the RTP media to pass through without termination and reorigination. If the **media flow-through** command had been used, the UBE would have acted as a proxy for the RTP streams as well as for the signaling protocols. If you do not specify a **media** command in the dial peer, the default is **media flow-through**.

The extra command included in the preceding listing is the **codec transparent** command. This command tells the UBE to allow codec negotiation between the endpoints and to leave the codec information untouched. Even when transparent codecs are allowed, the UBE must support the codec being used.

### CERTIFICATION OBJECTIVE 15.05

# 642-436: Configure IP-to-IP Gateway to Provide Call Admission Control

Sometimes a busy signal is good. Not for the caller, but for your network. Why is this? If too many calls come through the Cisco UBE, all the calls will suffer in quality. Call admission control (CAC) allows you to limit the number of incoming calls so that the calls that are processed have acceptable quality. This section provides the commands used to enable Cisco UBE CAC.

## Call Admission Control Configuration

CAC comes in three basic types in the Cisco world. These types include local, measurement based, and resource based. The three types can be described as follows:

- With local CAC, the gateway evaluates all connections to determine if it can handle another connection.

- With measurement-based CAC, packets are sent onto the WAN for the purpose of measuring the connection. Once the connection is measured, the CAC can be configured accordingly. Advanced Voice BusyOut (AVBO) and PSTN fallback are used to provide measurement-based CAC.

- With resource-based CAC, you utilize gatekeepers to make sure the call limit is managed so that QoS is provided overall. The Resource Reservation Protocol (RSVP) is used with a gatekeeper to provide this CAC method.

The simplest way to enable CAC on your UBE gateway is to use the maximum connection limit. This limit can be established in the VoIP dial peers. For example, assuming you want to limit VoIP dial peer number 50 to 10 connections, you would execute the following commands:

```
Router1> enable
Router1# configure terminal
Router1(config)# dial-peer voice 50
Router1(config-dial-peer)# max-conn 10
Router1(config-dial-peer)# exit
```

## CERTIFICATION OBJECTIVE 15.06

# 642-436:Verify IP-to-IP Gateway Implementations

## Configuration Verification

Because the Cisco UBE supports both H.323 and SIP protocols, you should be aware of troubleshooting and verification commands for each. Table 15-3 provides verification commands for the H.323 and SIP in UBE implementations.

| TABLE 15-3 | H.323 and SIP Cisco UBE Verification Commands |

| Command | Purpose |
| --- | --- |
| show call active voice | To display call information for voice calls that are active or in progress |
| show call active fax | To display fax transmissions currently in progress |
| show call history voice | To display the call logs of historical voice calls |
| show call history fax | To display the history of fax calls |
| show dial-peer voice | To display and verify proper dial-peer configuration |
| show running-config | To verify which connection types are allowed (H.323-to-H.323, H.323-to-SIP, or SIP-to-SIP) |
| show voip rtp connections | To view the active RTP media stream connections |

In addition to the commands in Table 15-3, you can use several debug commands to test H.323 and SIP configurations on UBE gateways. The commands include:

- **debug cch323 all**   Provides debugging output for H.323 errors, H.225 and H.245 protocols, RAS, and general H.323 events.
- **debug ccsip all**   Provides debugging output for SIP errors, events, states, messages, and calls.
- **debug h245 events**   Provides debugging output for H.245 events. Remember, H.245 is about feature negotiation in VoIP communications.
- **debug voip ipipgw**   Provides debugging output for the Cisco Multiservice IP-to-IP Gateway (IPIPGW), now known as the Cisco UBE. This debugging command reveals the inbound and outbound call leg processing.

**exam**

ⓦ**a t c h**   *Memorize this list of debug commands for exam day. You are very likely to see them crop up somewhere—not only* *in the areas of IP-to-IP gateway, but in other VoIP troubleshooting scenarios as well.*

# CERTIFICATION SUMMARY

In this chapter, you learned about the IP-to-IP gateway or the Cisco Unified Border Element (UBE). You learned that the UBE is used to connect two IP networks. The UBE supports H.323 and SIP protocols and can perform media flow-through or flow-around for the RTP media streams. You can implement call admission control (CAC) on the UBE, and you can use several commands to verify and troubleshoot the configuration.

✔ # TWO-MINUTE DRILL

### 642-436: Describe the IP-to-IP Gateway Features and Functionality

❑ The IP-to-IP gateway feature is now called the Cisco UBE gateway.

❑ The Cisco UBE gateway connects two IP networks together for VoIP servicing.

❑ Both H.323 and SIP protocols are supported by the Cisco UBE.

❑ Cisco UBE is an IOS feature, and the appropriate feature set must be used.

❑ DTMF signaling can be accomplished with H.245 signals, H.245 alphanumeric, SIP notify, and the Key Press Markup Language (KPML).

❑ Both modem and fax relay and pass-through are supported in UBEs.

❑ Cisco UBE supports both IP precedence and DSCP marking for QoS.

### 642-436: Configure Gatekeeper to Support an IP-to-IP Gateway

❑ To enable a gatekeeper to support a Cisco UBE gateway, you must configure via-zones.

❑ Via-zones are configured using the **zone remote** and **zone local** commands.

### 642-436: Configure IP-to-IP Gateway to Provide Address Hiding

❑ Address hiding ensures that the UBE is the only point of signaling and media entry or exit in all scenarios.

❑ The **address-hiding** command is executed in VoIP voice-service configuration mode to enable address hiding.

### 642-436: Configure IP-to-IP Gateway to Provide Protocol and Media Interworking

❑ The **allowed-connections** command is used to specify the protocol internetworking with Cisco UBEs.

❑ When no **media** command is entered as part of a dial peer, **media flow-through** is the default.

❑ The **codec transparent** command allows the two endpoints to negotiate the codec used; however, the Cisco UBE must support the negotiated codec as well.

## 642-436: Configure IP-to-IP Gateway to Provide Call Admission Control

❑ CAC can be implemented as local, measurement-based, or resource-based technology.

❑ With local CAC, the gateway evaluates all connections to determine if it can handle another connection.

❑ With measurement-based CAC, packets are sent onto the WAN with the purpose of measuring the connection. Once the connection is measured, the CAC can be configured accordingly.

❑ With resource-based CAC, you utilize gatekeepers to make sure the call limit is managed so that QoS is provided overall. RSVP is used for resource-based CAC.

❑ The **max-conn** command is used in dial-peer configuration mode to limit the number of allowed connections on a given WAN link.

## 642-436: Verify IP-to-IP Gateway Implementations

❑ The **show active voice** and **show call history voice** commands are used to view current and past VoIP call information.

❑ The **show dial-peer voice** command will be used to verify proper configuration of codec transparency or media flows (flow-through and flow-around).

❑ The **debug cch323 all** and **debug ccsip all** commands are used to view detailed information about H.323 and SIP processes, respectively.

❑ The **debug voip ipipgw** command is used to view information about inbound and outbound call leg processing.

# SELF TEST

The following questions will help you measure your understanding of the material presented in this chapter. Read all the choices carefully because there might be more than one correct answer. Choose all correct answers for each question.

## 642-436: Describe the IP-to-IP Gateway Features and Functionality

1. What is the primary purpose of the Cisco UBE gateway?
   A. To connect two different physical layer networks
   B. To provide a bridge between Ethernet and Token Ring networks
   C. To connect two different VoIP networks
   D. To connect two different directory service networks

2. What must be installed on a Cisco ISR in order to implement it as a UBE gateway?
   A. The right IOS version and feature set
   B. The IPIPGW software module
   C. The IPIPGW interface module
   D. The SDM

3. Which of the following DTMF signaling methods are supported on a UBE gateway? (Choose all that apply.)
   A. SS7
   B. H.245
   C. SIP Notify
   D. KPML

4. What two methods are supported for QoS on the Cisco UBE?
   A. IP precedence
   B. DSCP marking
   C. TQC marking
   D. Six Sigma

## 642-436: Configure Gatekeeper to Support an IP-to-IP Gateway

5. What must be configured and implemented in order to allow a Cisco UBE to be used by a gatekeeper?
   A. The proper sRTP parameters
   B. The proper cRTP parameters
   C. An IPX interface
   D. Via-zones

## 642-436: Configure IP-to-IP Gateway to Provide Address Hiding

**6.** What command is used to provide hiding of IP addresses on the Cisco UBE gateway?
   A. address-hiding
   B. address hiding
   C. hide ip
   D. hide-ip

**7.** What is the benefit of IP address hiding when using a Cisco UBE gateway?
   A. It's more difficult to hack into the network.
   B. It's easier to monitor network traffic.
   C. It ensures that the UBE is the only point of signaling and media entry.
   D. It ensures that the CME is the only point of signaling and media entry.

## 642-436: Configure IP-to-IP Gateway to Provide Protocol and Media Interworking

**8.** What command is used to implement SIP-to-SIP on a Cisco UBE gateway?
   A. allowed-connections sip
   B. allowed-connections sip to sip
   C. allowed-connections sip-to-sip
   D. allowed-connections sip only

**9.** You want the RTP media to go from one phone to another through the UBE without termination and reorigination. What command should you type while in dial-peer configuration mode?
   A. media flow-through
   B. media passthrough
   C. media flow-around
   D. RTP passthrough

## 642-436: Configure IP-to-IP Gateway to Provide Call Admission Control

**10.** What command is used in dial-peer configuration mode to limit the number of concurrent connections that can pass through the dial peer?
   A. limit-conn
   B. max-conn
   C. upper-conn
   D. conn-limit

11. What kind of CAC sends packets onto the WAN to determine the quality of the WAN link and implement CAC accordingly?

    A. Local CAC

    B. Measurement-based CAC

    C. Resource-based CAC

    D. Gatekeeper CAC

12. What two components must be in place and configured to use resource-based CAC?

    A. H.323 gatekeeper

    B. SIP proxy

    C. RSVP

    D. DiffServe

## 642-436: Verify IP-to-IP Gateway Implementations

13. What command is used to view the dial peers on a gateway?

    A. show dial-peer voice

    B. show running-config

    C. show active voice

    D. show call history voice

14. What command is used to view the current voice connections on a gateway?

    A. show active voice

    B. show call history voice

    C. show dial-peer voice

    D. show interfaces

15. What debugging command will reveal SIP events and errors?

    A. debug voip ipipgw

    B. debug h323 all

    C. debug ccsip all

    D. debug sip all

# LAB QUESTION

You want to verify the proper configuration of the Cisco UBE on a Cisco 2801 ISR. You specifically want to see the following information:

- The H.323-to-SIP gateway setting for allowed connections
- The current voice connections
- The error information for both SIP and H.323
- The media flow configuration for the calls

For each set of information, what command will you execute?

# SELF TEST ANSWERS

## 642-436: Describe the IP-to-IP Gateway Features and Functionality

1. ☑ **C is correct.** The primary purpose of the UBE gateway is to connect two different VoIP networks, which may use the same signaling protocols or different signaling protocols.

   ☒ **A, B,** and **D** are incorrect. While gateways can be used to connect any other three networks or services, the Cisco UBE gateway does not serve these purposes.

2. ☑ **A is correct.** The Cisco ISR must have the right feature set, which requires a specific version (or higher) of the IOS with that feature set included.

   ☒ **B, C,** and **D** are incorrect. No software or hardware module must be added and the Security Device Manager (SDM) is not required.

3. ☑ **B, C,** and **D** are correct. You can use H.245, SIP Notify, or KPML to transfer DTMF signals through the UBE gateway.

   ☒ **A** is incorrect. SS7 signaling is not directly supported on the UBE gateway as part of the border controller functionality.

4. ☑ **A** and **B** are correct. Both IP precedence and DSCP marking are supported for QoS on the Cisco UBE.

   ☒ **C** and **D** are incorrect. TQC marking is not a QoS method supported on Cisco routers. Six Sigma is a management and processing methodology and has no bearing on QoS.

## 642-436: Configure Gatekeeper to Support an IP-to-IP Gateway

5. ☑ **D is correct.** The gatekeeper uses via-zones to know when to route to the UBE and when the VoIP call can be handled internally.

   ☒ **A, B,** and **C** are incorrect. sRTP and cRTP are not required parameters for gatekeeper configuration in relation to the Cisco UBE gateway. IPX interfaces are not used for VoIP networks.

## 642-436: Configure IP-to-IP Gateway to Provide Address Hiding

6. ☑ **A is correct.** The simple **address-hiding** command is used to hide IP addresses.

   ☒ **B, C,** and **D** are incorrect. Address hiding, hide ip, and hide-ip are invalid commands. They perform no function on Cisco IOS routers or within the Cisco UBE gateway.

**7.** ☑ **C** is correct. Address hiding ensures that the UBE is the only point of signaling and media entry or exit in all scenarios.

☒ **A, B,** and **D** are incorrect. Address hiding does not make it more difficult to hack into the network, and it does not make it easier to monitor network traffic. Additionally, the UBE is the only point of signaling and media ingress and egress for the network, not the CME.

## 642-436: Configure IP-to-IP Gateway to Provide Protocol and Media Interworking

**8.** ☑ **B** is correct. The proper command for SIP-to-SIP implementation is the **allowed-connections sip to sip** command.

☒ **A, C,** and **D** are incorrect. You cannot simply indicate allowed-connections sip and implement SIP-to-SIP. You should not include hyphens between the sip to sip clause in the **allowed-connections** command. No such option as sip only exists for the **allowed-connections** command.

**9.** ☑ **C** is correct. The **media flow-around** command should be used. This command indicates that the media (RTP stream) should not be terminated and reoriginated by the UBE.

☒ **A, B,** and **D** are incorrect. The **media flow-through** command indicates that the UBE should terminate and reoriginate the RTP media streams. The media passthrough and RTP passthrough commands are not valid IOS commands.

## 642-436: Configure IP-to-IP Gateway to Provide Call Admission Control

**10.** ☑ **B** is correct. The **max-conn** command is used to limit the number of connections that can concurrently pass through a dial peer. For example, **max-conn 12** would limit the dial peer to 12 concurrent connections.

☒ **A, B,** and **C** are incorrect. limit-conn, upper-con, and conn-limit are invalid IOS commands within the dial-peer configuration mode.

**11.** ☑ **B** is correct. Measurement-based CAC sends packets onto the WAN in order to measure the performance of the WAN. The CAC is then dynamically configured based on the results.

☒ **A, C,** and **D** are incorrect. Local CAC uses simple connection limits or is bound by the literal input source (such as a single POTS line). Resource-based CAC uses gatekeepers and RSVP. Gatekeeper CAC is not a Cisco term.

**12.** ☑ **A** and **C** are correct. Resource-based CAC requires both a gatekeeper and the RSVP protocol support on the endpoints and the gateways.

☒ **B** and **D** are incorrect. A SIP proxy is not required and DiffServe is not used.

### 642-436: Verify IP-to-IP Gateway Implementations

13.   ☑   A is correct. The **show dial-peer voice** command will list all voice dial peers. You can also specify the **show dial-peer voice #** command to view a specific dial peer by number.

☒   B, C, and D are incorrect. The **show running-config** command will show the IOS configuration, but it does not include details about the dial peers. The **show active voice** and **show call history voice** commands show information about active and historical calls, but they do not show dial-peer configuration information.

14.   ☑   A is correct. To view the currently active voice connections, use the **show active voice** command.

☒   B, C, and D are incorrect. The **show call history voice** command shows the buffered information about past calls and it does not show information about active calls. The **show dial-peer voice** command will list all voice dial peers. The **show interfaces** command shows information about the physical and virtual interfaces in the router.

15.   ☑   C is correct. The **debug ccsip all** command will show errors and other events related to the SIP protocol.

☒   A, B, and D are incorrect. The **debug voip ipipgw** shows inbound and outbound call leg processing information. The **debug h323 all** command is invalid. To view H.323 errors and events, you would use the **debug cch323 all** command instead. The debug sip all command is invalid. The **debug ccsip all** command will show errors and other events related to the SIP protocol.

## LAB ANSWER

The lab requested four specific things:

    1. The H.323-to-SIP gateway setting for allowed connections

    2. The current voice connections

    3. The error information for both SIP and H.323

    4. The media flow configuration for the calls

To accomplish the viewing of this information, you must use the following commands (with numbers matched to the objectives):

    1. Use the **show running-config** command to verify that the allowed connections h323 to sip entry is in the configuration.

    2. Use the **show active voice** command to view the current voice connections.

    3. Use the **debug ccsip all** and **debug cch323 all** commands to see the error information for SIP and H.323.

    4. Use the **show dial-peer #** command to view the media flow configuration for a specific dial peer.

# 16

# Fax and Modem over IP

> *What, exactly, is the internet? Basically it is a global network exchanging digitized data in such a way that any computer, anywhere, that is equipped with a device called a "modem," can make a noise like a duck choking on a kazoo.*
>
> —Comedian Dave Barry

**M**odems were among the first devices that allowed for long-distance communications using computers. Fax machines allowed you to send pictures and text over the phone lines to anyone else having a fax machine. In their day, fax machines were amazing technological advances. Today, we are mostly stuck using these archaic solutions because so many business processes came to depend on them, and business processes are hard to change. E-mailing a scanned page or picture is a far superior solution to faxing. Wireless network connections to the Internet or to the corporate network are many times faster than modems. However, the old technology still remains, and we must support it—even if it does sound like a "duck choking on a kazoo."

This chapter helps you understand how you can support analog communication technologies in modern VoIP implementations. These analog methods (modems and fax machines) use sound to send information. Because of this technology selection, we must find a way to get the sound through the VoIP network without losing characteristics that define the information in the analog signal. This is where fax and modem pass-through and relay play a big role. In this chapter, you'll first learn about the problems involved in supporting fax and modem communications on VoIP networks, and then you'll learn about the solutions.

**CERTIFICATION OBJECTIVE 16.01**

# 642-436: Implement Fax and Modem Support on a Gateway

Many business processes still depend on fax support and some depend on modems. Modems are used less often these days, but their use still lingers on for remote area connections. The Cisco Voice (CVOICE) exam 642-436 requires that you understand how to allow for fax and modem communications through a voice gateway. This section covers the information you'll need to know for the exam as well as for real-world applications of the knowledge.

# Fax and Modem Problems on VoIP Networks

If you've ever had the pleasure of picking up a phone handset only to hear modem communications or a fax transfer, you know that fax machines and modems use sound to transfer information across the PSTN. One sound can represent a 0 bit, and another sound can represent a 1 bit, allowing for the transfer of any binary-based information (and, remember, all computer information is binary information). More complex modulation techniques can use more sounds for the transfer of more information at faster rates. For this reason, we have 300-bps modems all the way through to 56-kbps modems.

The "mod" (or "mo") in "modem" stands for "modulator," and the "dem" in "modem" stands for "demodulator." A modem modulates data onto analog sound waves for transfer across the telephony network. It also demodulates data off of the analog sound waves at the receiver. Through this process communications can occur over great distances. These modems must operate within the frequency boundaries of the PSTN and are therefore limited in bandwidth and data rates. Additionally, poor line quality can force the data rate to be lowered because the sound signals are not passing through cleanly.

In much the same way that poor line quality can cause a modem to reduce the rate or even drop the connection, VoIP networks can hinder modem communications. You've learned about codecs elsewhere in this book, and you understand that they may compress the audio data. As the data is compressed the MOS (Mean Opinion Score) is reduced. The MOS value is a measurement of the signal's perceived quality. If the perceived quality is reduced, it is because the real quality is reduced. This reduction in quality is like having a poor line from the modem's perspective, and it will either greatly reduce the data rate or make communications impossible.

Fax machines use modem technology to send scanned documents across the PSTN lines. They are susceptible to the same problems as modems. Fax machines operate at lower data rates than the fastest modems, but they can still experience communications problems when the data rate is significantly reduced. For this reason, we must have a solution to both fax and modem communications problems that occur across our VoIP networks.

## Solutions to Fax and Modem Problems

Three solutions are available for fax and modem communications on Cisco VoIP networks. The first solution is fax and modem relay, the second is fax and modem pass-through, and the final is store and forward. This section discusses the solutions for fax and modem problems together for a simple reason: fax machines use modems to transmit data. Therefore, both fax machines and modems require the same basic solutions.

### Fax and Modem Relay

Fax and modem relay sends the fax from a receiving router to a destination router using either a proprietary Cisco protocol called Cisco Fax Relay or the T.38 standard. The T.38 standard is an ITU recommendation, and the Internet Society (ISOC) has defined the MIME registration for T.38 in RFC 3362.

Figure 16-1 illustrates the concepts of fax and modem relay. Notice that the fax message comes into the voice gateway on a PSTN connection using T.30, which is the traditional PSTN faxing standard. Next, the gateway converts the incoming communications to the T.38 standard and sends it out on the VoIP network. The end voice gateway converts the T.38 communication back to T.30 standard fax data to send to the receiving fax machine, which may be connected via the PSTN or more likely to an FXS port on the voice gateway.

When using the T.38 fax relay, the two fax machines believe they are communicating directly with each other using a dedicated analog telephone connection. The T.38 translation and transmission process is transparent to the sending and receiving fax machines. Cisco voice gateways support T.38 for SIP, MGCP, and H.323 protocols.

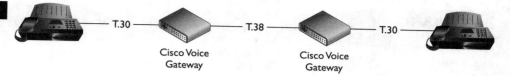

**FIGURE 16-1**

Fax and modem relay

If you do not specify the T.38 fax relay, most Cisco voice gateways default to using the Cisco Fax Relay. This proprietary fax relay solution works only between Cisco voice gateways and is not supported by voice gateways from other vendors. For this reason, more networks are using T.38 today when fax relay is needed. The standard works as well or better than the proprietary solution, so it makes sense to use this compatible standard instead of the incompatible proprietary protocol.

Like fax relay, modem relay converts the analog modem signals at the incoming voice gateway and transports them across the IP network as digital packets. Cisco voice gateways use the Simple Packet Relay Transport (SPRT) protocol to transmit the modem packets across the IP network. The UDP protocol is used to transport the SPRT packets. The entry-point voice gateway demodulates the modem's signals and converts them to SPRT packets. These packets are sent to the exit-point voice gateway. The exit-point voice gateway re-creates and re-modulates the modem signal to pass to the receiving modem.

Modem relay supports the following features:

- Modem data rates of up to 33.6 kbps can be supported. Faster modems must be trained down to the supported data rates.

- IP signaling protocols that support modem relay include SIP, H.323, and MGCP.

- Relay switchover occurs when a modem call is detected. This includes changing to the G.711 codec, disabling voice activity detection (VAD) and echo cancellation, and implementing special jitter buffers.

## Fax and Modem Pass-Through

Fax and modem pass-through should be used only if you are connecting with a non-Cisco voice gateway that does not support fax relay. Fax relay is more reliable than fax pass-through. Fax and modem pass-through require the G.711 codec with VAD and echo cancellation disabled. The incoming fax or modem communications are transported using the G.711 codec. However, the Cisco voice gateway detects the fax or modem and changes to a 10-ms packetization period. Because of the smaller packetization period, the fax and modem relay requires 96-kbps data rates for the fax or modem data sent across the IP network instead of the normal 80-kbps data rates for the 20-ms packetization period.

**FIGURE 16-2**

Fax and modem
pass-through

Figure 16-2 illustrates the topology of fax and modem pass-through. The difference between Figure 16-1 and 16-2 should be clear. Fax and modem relay uses UDP across IP and consumes little overhead above that required to send the actual fax data. Fax and modem relay is a much more efficient solution than fax and modem pass-through.

## Store and Forward

Store and forward is a fax-only solution, but it is the most interesting of the three. With store and forward, the fax comes into the router, and the router terminates the fax communications. In other words, the router is the fax machine, and it converts the fax into an e-mail message with an attached TIF image file. The e-mail is sent to the configured destination. Additionally, internal users can e-mail a TIF file to the router (voice gateway), and the router can send the TIF file as a fax message to a remote fax machine. Figure 16-3 illustrates this concept.

In the Cisco world, two types of store and forward faxing are available. On-ramp faxing occurs when a fax comes in from the PSTN or external voice network. With on-ramp faxing the voice gateway converts an incoming fax to an e-mail. Off-ramp faxing occurs when an e-mail comes into the voice gateway and is converted to a fax for transmission. With off-ramp faxing the voice gateway converts an incoming e-mail to an outgoing fax communication.

**FIGURE 16-3**

Store and
forward faxing

# Configuring Cisco Gateways to Support Fax and Modem Communications

Now that you understand the differences between the three types of fax and modem communications solutions, it's important that you understand how to configure the two most frequently used solutions: relay and pass-through. In this section, you'll learn the basic Cisco commands for configuring both solutions.

## Fax and Modem Relay Configuration

Fax and modem relay can be configured for each dial peer, or it can be configured globally. To configure the relay settings globally, you will enter the voice service configuration mode and use the **fax** command. The following commands illustrate this method:

```
Router> enable
Router# configure terminal
Router(config)# voice service voip
Router(config-voi-serv)# fax protocol t38
Router(config-voi-serv)# exit
```

Notice the **fax** command. This is the key command for globally configuring fax and modem relay. When the t38 parameter is used, the router knows to convert all incoming faxes to the T.38 standard format and to send them across the IP network.

To configure fax and modem relay within a dial-peer, use commands like the following:

```
Router> enable
Router# configure terminal
Router(config)# dial-peer voice 300 voip
Router(config-dial-peer)# fax protocol t38
Router(config-voi-serv)# exit
```

As the preceding listing shows, the only real difference between global configuration and dial-peer configuration is the use of the **dial-peer** command on configuration mode instead of the **voice service voip** command.

In addition to the configuration of the T.38 protocol for the dial-peer, you should disable VAD and echo cancellation. You disable VAD in the dial-peer configuration mode with the **no vad** command. You disable echo cancellation in voice port configuration mode with the **no echo-cancel enable** command.

## Fax and Modem Pass-Through Configuration

Fax and modem pass-through are configured in the same way as fax and modem relay. The difference is in the **fax** command used. Consider the following example:

```
Router> enable
Router# configure terminal
Router(config)# voice service voip
Router(config-voi-serv)# fax protocol pass-through g711ulaw
Router(config-voi-serv)# exit
```

Remember that you can use the g711ulaw or g711alaw parameters. G.711 a-law is typically used outside the United States, and G.711 μ-law is used within the United States.

# CERTIFICATION SUMMARY

In this chapter, you learned about the problems associated with faxing and with modem communications on VoIP networks. You then learned about the three primary solutions to these problems in a Cisco VoIP network. The three solutions are fax and modem relay, fax and modem pass-through, and store and forward faxing.

# TWO-MINUTE DRILL

## 642-436: Implement Fax and Modem Support on a Gateway

- ❑ Fax machines and modems use sound waves to transfer digital or computerized information.

- ❑ VoIP codecs compress sound waves, reducing their quality, which may prohibit or diminish communications.

- ❑ The Cisco modem relay feature uses the Simple Packet Relay Transport (SPRT) protocol to transport the modem data across the IP network.

- ❑ SPRT relies on the UDP protocol for data transmission.

- ❑ When modem relay is used, relay switchover occurs when a modem call is detected. This includes changing to the G.711 codec, disabling voice activity detection (VAD) and echo cancellation, and implementing special jitter buffers.

- ❑ Fax and modem pass-through allows for the communications to pass through the IP network in a VoIP G.711 tunnel.

- ❑ Fax and modem pass-through is less efficient than the fax and modem relay solution.

- ❑ Store and forward faxing uses e-mail to transmit the fax across the IP network.

- ❑ On-ramp store and forward faxing occurs when the voice gateway receives a fax from the PSTN and forwards it to the destination as an e-mail.

- ❑ Off-ramp store and forward faxing occurs when the voice gateway receives an e-mail from a source and forwards it to the destination fax machine as a fax message.

- ❑ The **fax protocol** command is used to specify **pass-through** or **t38** for fax calls in global configuration mode.

- ❑ You can also use the **fax protocol** command from within dial-peer configuration mode.

- ❑ The **no echo-cancel enable** command should be used on the voice port to disable echo cancellation for incoming fax lines.

- ❑ The **no vad** command should be used when configuring fax communications within dial-peers.

# SELF TEST

The following questions will help you measure your understanding of the material presented in this chapter. Read all the choices carefully because there might be more than one correct answer. Choose all correct answers for each question.

## 642-436: Implement Fax and Modem Support on a Gateway

1. Why do fax and modem communications often have problems on VoIP networks?
   A. Because VoIP networks cannot send sound information
   B. Because VoIP networks often compress sound information
   C. Because VoIP networks will not allow fax or modem communications
   D. Because modems were designed in the 1970s

2. What do fax machines and modems use to transfer data?
   A. Sound waves
   B. RF waves
   C. Ocean waves
   D. Emotional waves

3. What protocol is used by Cisco voice gateways when modem relay is enabled?
   A. SRTP
   B. ICMP
   C. TCP
   D. SPRT

4. Which transport protocol is used by the Simple Packet Relay Transport protocol?
   A. TCP
   B. UDP
   C. FTP
   D. HTTP

5. When modem relay is used and a modem call is detected, what three things occur during relay switchover? (Choose three.)
   A. The codec is changed to G.711.
   B. The call is ended.
   C. VAD is disabled.
   D. Echo cancellation is disabled.

6. What codec is used for fax and modem pass-through?
   A. G.729
   B. G.728

    **C.** G.711

    **D.** G.726

**7.** Which one of the following methods is the most efficient for handling fax calls on VoIP networks?

    **A.** Pass-through

    **B.** Walking the fax over to the recipient's office

    **C.** Relay

    **D.** Running the fax over to the recipient's office

**8.** What fax solution for VoIP networks uses e-mail in the process?

    **A.** Relay

    **B.** Pass-through

    **C.** Sneakernet

    **D.** Store and forward

**9.** The voice gateway receives a fax and converts it to an e-mail. What store and forward type is being handled?

    **A.** On-ramp

    **B.** Off-ramp

    **C.** Exit-ramp

    **D.** Entrance-ramp

**10.** What command is used from within dial-peer configuration mode to set up fax relay?

    **A.** fax protocol

    **B.** voip relay

    **C.** voip protocol

    **D.** t36 protocol

**11.** What command is used to disable echo cancellation, and in what context should it be used?

    **A.** **no echo-cancel enable** should be used in dial-peer configuration mode.

    **B.** **no echo-cancel enable** should be used in voice service configuration mode.

    **C.** **no echo-cancel enable** should be used in voice port configuration mode.

    **D.** **echo-cancel disable** should be used in dial-peer configuration mode.

# LAB QUESTION

You must select a fax and modem solution for your VoIP network. You use both Cisco voice gateways and gateways from another vendor. You want to use a fax relay solution that will work with both gateway types. The other vendor supports the ITU standard for fax relay. What fax relay protocol will you use and why?

# SELF TEST ANSWERS

## 642-436: Implement Fax and Modem Support on a Gateway

1. ☑ **B** is correct. Depending on the VoIP codec used, heavy compression may be in place. This compression can result in a degraded audio signal, which can prevent fax machines and modems from working properly.

   ☒ **A, C,** and **D** are incorrect. VoIP networks can send sound information; in fact, they're designed to do just that. VoIP networks will allow fax and modem communications. Though modems were designed in the 1970s, with ever-increasing speeds since that time, they can work on VoIP networks with proper implementation procedures.

2. ☑ **A** is correct. Both fax machines and modems use sound waves to transfer data. The data is modulated onto the sound waves and demodulated off of them.

   ☒ **B, C,** and **D** are incorrect. RF waves are used for wireless communications. Ocean waves do not transfer information because they cannot be controlled. Emotional waves sometimes just hurt.

3. ☑ **D** is correct. The Simple Packet Relay Transport (SPRT) protocol is used to transport the data across the IP network.

   ☒ **A, B,** and **C** are incorrect. SRTP is the secure RTP protocol and is not used in this scenario. ICMP is used by PING and other diagnostic protocols in the TCP/IP suite. TCP is a transport protocol and is not used by SPRT.

4. ☑ **B** is correct. UDP is used to transport SPRT packets.

   ☒ **A, C,** and **D** are incorrect. TCP is a transport protocol, but it is not used by SPRT. FTP and HTTP are not transport protocols.

5. ☑ **A, C,** and **D** are correct. When relay switchover occurs, the codec is changed to G.711, VAD is disabled, and echo cancellation is disabled. Additionally, special jitter buffers are implemented.

   ☒ **B** is incorrect. The call is not ended when a fax or modem connection is detected.

6. ☑ **C** is correct. G.711 is used for fax or modem pass-through.

   ☒ **A, B,** and **D** are incorrect. G.729, G.728, and G.726 would cause too much audio data loss to allow for reliable fax or modem communications; therefore, they are not used for fax or modem pass-through.

7. ☑ **C** is correct. Fax or modem relay is more efficient than fax or modem pass-through.

   ☒ **A, B,** and **D** are incorrect. Fax pass-through incurs more overhead than fax relay. Walking or running the fax over to the recipient's office may vary in efficiency, but they do not occur on the VoIP network.

8. ☑ **D** is correct. The store and forward method uses e-mail to transfer the fax to the destination or to convert the e-mail to a fax for sending.

   ☒ **A, B,** and **C** are incorrect. Neither relay nor pass-through uses e-mail. Sneakernet is a colloquial term for physically carrying information from one place to another.

9. ☑ **A** is correct. With on-ramp store and forward communications, the voice gateway receives a fax from the PSTN and converts it to an e-mail for the destination.

   ☒ **B, C,** and **D** are incorrect. With off-ramp store and forward communications, the voice gateway receives an e-mail and converts it to a fax. "Exit-ramp" and "entrance-ramp" are not terms used in store and forward configurations.

10. ☑ **A** is correct. The **fax protocol** command is used within both dial-peer configuration mode and voice service configuration mode.

    ☒ **B, C,** and **D** are incorrect. The **voip relay, voip protocol,** and **t36 protocol** commands are not valid IOS commands for fax relay configuration.

11. ☑ **C** is correct. The **no echo-cancel enable** command should be used on the voice port that receives incoming fax or modem calls.

    ☒ **A, B,** and **D** are incorrect. The **no echo-cancel enable** command can only be used in voice port configuration mode. The echo-cancel disable command is invalid.

# LAB ANSWER

You should use the T.38 fax relay protocol because it is the ITU standard protocol. T.38 is supported by both Cisco and other vendors. The Cisco Fax Relay protocol is proprietary and should not be used in scenarios like the one described.

# 17

# Troubleshooting VoIP Problems

> *It's not that I'm so smart, it's just that I stay with problems longer.*
>
> —*Albert Einstein*

The ability to troubleshoot network problems is an important skill set for any network engineer, but this is particularly true for the VoIP engineer. VoIP, as you've learned in the preceding chapters of this book, introduces unique challenges to networked communications. In this chapter, you'll explore the basic troubleshooting processes that can be used to locate a network problem. Then you'll look specifically at the troubleshooting methods employed with various Cisco systems. These systems include Cisco Unified Communications Manager Express, Cisco Unity Express, and the UC500 series of small business devices.

# Troubleshooting Methods

Humans have been solving problems for as long as we have existed. Troubleshooting is problem solving; however, systematic troubleshooting is a very organized problem-solving approach. As a Cisco VoIP network administrator, you should understand different troubleshooting methodologies and the benefits that come from using them.

## Troubleshooting Methodologies

A methodology can be defined as a standard way of doing something; therefore, a troubleshooting methodology is a standard way to troubleshoot. A methodology helps to ensure that you do all the things you need to do to complete a task or set of tasks. Also, it provides you with collective knowledge when developed over time. *Collective knowledge* is knowledge that you do not personally possess and yet benefit from. For example, most of us have never researched the statistics on whether wearing a seatbelt is safer than not wearing a seatbelt when we drive; however, we trust the research done by others, and therefore, we wear our seatbelts (it also helps to motivate us when the law requires it). A good troubleshooting methodology will cause you to take steps for which you may not fully understand the purpose, but for which you will still get the benefit. For example, you may not know all the benefits of documentation, but you will still reap those benefits if you perform it.

I will share four different methodologies with you in this section as well as one concept that will help you in the troubleshooting process. The four methodologies are:

- REACT
- OSI Model
- Hardware/Software Model
- Symptom, Diagnosis, and Solution

## REACT

Early in my information technology career, I worked as a helpdesk analyst and a telephone troubleshooter. I found that I would frequently forget to do an important thing in the troubleshooting process that would cost me minutes or even hours of time—not to mention the added stress. For this reason, I developed an acronym to remind me of the stages I should go through when troubleshooting a problem. This way, I can work through the acronym until I reach a solution. I always reach a solution by the end of the acronym. The reality is that sometimes the solution is a complete reload of firmware and settings for some devices, and sometimes it is a complete reload of the operating system on a client computer; however, more often than not, I find a simpler solution.

The REACT acronym stands for five stages or phases of troubleshooting:

- Research
- Engage
- Adjust
- Configure
- Take Note

I'll cover each one briefly in the following sections so that you can understand how they fit together and why I go through these stages.

**Research**    Around 1997 I was trying to resolve a problem with a Microsoft Access 95 database. Every time the user tried to open the database, she received an error that read, "A device attached to the system is not functioning." When I see an error about a device, the first thing I think of is hardware. I spent more than two hours trying to verify that all the hardware was functioning properly, and of course, it was. By the end of the day, I went home tormented by my failure to resolve the problem (hopefully, you're not like me and I'm the only one who suffers like this when I can't fix a computer problem).

The next day, I decided to do some research, so I opened the MSDN CD (that's right, it used to fit on one CD and have plenty of space left over). I searched for the error message and found that the error could be generated if VBRUN300.DLL was corrupt. If you haven't been around long, VBRUN300.DLL was used by all Visual Basic 3.0 applications. The only problem was that Microsoft Access and this database did not rely on the Visual Basic 3.0 runtime for anything; however, my mind was racing. I suddenly realized the implications: if the corruption of VBRUN300.DLL could cause the error, maybe any corrupt DLL could cause the error. I reinstalled Microsoft Access, and the error went away.

You are probably wondering what the moral of this intriguing story is. The moral is that I could have saved the first two hours of work with a few minutes of research. My new standard became: Research at least 10 to 15 minutes before moving to the Adjust stage with any new problem that requires troubleshooting. Not all problems require troubleshooting, and the confusion that usually comes into play is the result of misunderstanding what troubleshooting really is. Here is my favorite definition:

*Troubleshooting is the process of discovering the unknown cause and solution for a known problem.*

If you know the solution to a problem, you are repairing and not troubleshooting. You start with Research only when it is a real troubleshooting scenario according to this definition. In the end, by researching for just 15 minutes, you find that the cause and solution are often learned without spending any time adjusting various settings and parameters to resolve the issue. For example, if my wireless VoIP phone cannot connect to the wireless LAN and is receiving a specific error message on the screen, I will search for this error message at Google.com (or another search engine) to see what I can discover. I may also search the Cisco web site. If I don't find the cause or solution, I will usually get direction so that I can focus on the right area as I move to the Engage or Adjust stages.

**on the job**

*I have found that some of my best search results lead me to discussion forums where others have experienced similar difficulties. The forum thread may not provide a direct solution, but it can often help me focus my thinking in the right direction.*

The most important information base that you can search is the organization's internal documentation. If you work in a standardized environment (meaning that systems are configured according to a standard baseline and then customized for specific uses), it is highly probable that the same problems will creep in again and again until you locate the source of the problem. Once the problem source is located, it should be documented. You may also want to go back to your baseline and make necessary changes to prevent the problem from occurring. However, the main focus of this discussion is on research, and the act of documenting your solution will be helpful to you and any other administrator who faces the same or similar problem. Documentation is discussed more in the later section called "Take Note," but know that your organization's internal database of problem solutions will be one of the most valuable sources you build over time.

At the end of the Research phase, I may have a solution to my problem. If that is the case, I will resolve the problem and move to the final phase so that I can document the problem and solution for future reference. If my research has only given me direction or has yielded no results after a few minutes, I will move on to the next phase: Engage.

**Engage**   While you may be eager to move from the Research phase to the Adjust phase, you should engage the user if he or she is involved in the problem. Avoid the temptation of jumping right in and making changes. You may engage the user before researching the problem, or you may only gather summary information about the problem before doing the research. Either way, these first two phases are essential, and you may find yourself in a reciprocal process alternating between researching and engaging for some time.

When you engage the user, ask a question like, "Do you know if anything has changed about your system in the past few days?" Notice I didn't say, "Did you change anything?" The latter question will usually cause people to become defensive and will fail to get you any valuable information. The users do not usually have any knowledge of what caused the problem, but when they do, it can save you hours or even days of trouble. Always engage the user. Other questions that might be beneficial include:

- Have you seen any strange activity in the area lately (rogue access points [APs] in wireless VoIP implementations, hackers roaming around)?
- Did the problem begin only recently, or has it been happening for some length of time?
- Are you aware of any others experiencing similar difficulties?
- When was the last time it worked?
- Is the device turned on? (Seriously.)

This last question is probably the most commonly asked question in the history of technical support, and it is still a very important question. With modern complex systems, it is very possible that the user has powered on one component of the system and not another component. Sometimes you can save the user from embarrassment by asking him or her to power cycle everything. This way, if the user did not have the hardware powered on, he or she will not have to admit it. The big key is to always handle users tactfully because you will definitely find it easier to work with users who enjoy being around you.

If you are using the newer operating systems and a software-based IP phone, you may be able to take advantage of new features that allow you to get the needed information without relying on the user. For example, in Windows Vista and Windows 7, the Reliability Monitor is an exceptional tool for viewing the historical problems and changes on a computer. To access the Reliability Monitor, press the Windows key on the keyboard (or click the Start button), type **Reliability Monitor**, and then press ENTER (or click the View Reliability History link that is displayed). You will see a screen similar to the one in Figure 17-1. Notice that the Reliability Monitor shows the application failures as well as software and driver installations and removals.

Now that the Research and Engage phases are complete, it's time to move on to the Adjust phase if the problem is still unresolved. If the problem is solved, you can skip ahead to the Configure and Take Note phases and document the problem and solution, or simply close the trouble ticket if the problem is a common recurring issue.

**Adjust**  Interestingly, we've just now arrived where I see many techs, VoIP administrators, or network administrators in general, beginning. Don't feel bad—I've done it many times myself. Through years of experience, I've found that I can save hours of difficulty by moving through the Research and Engage phases before the Adjust phase. Keep in mind that I'm going to spend 10 to 15 minutes in most situations in these first two phases. I find that I'm more frequently finished with the first two phases in five or ten minutes. At one point, I tracked the results of using this methodology with all of my troubleshooting cases for six months. During this time I had to troubleshoot 206 unique problems (I dealt with hundreds of common problems during the same period). With 117 of the problems, I found the solution in the first two phases. This result meant that I solved more than half of the problems in less than 10 to 20 minutes.

With the remaining 89 problems, I moved on to the Adjust phase. This is the phase where you begin trying different things to see if you can track down the source of your problem. You might try updating the firmware on a wireless VoIP phone or

**FIGURE 17-1** The Windows 7 Reliability Monitor

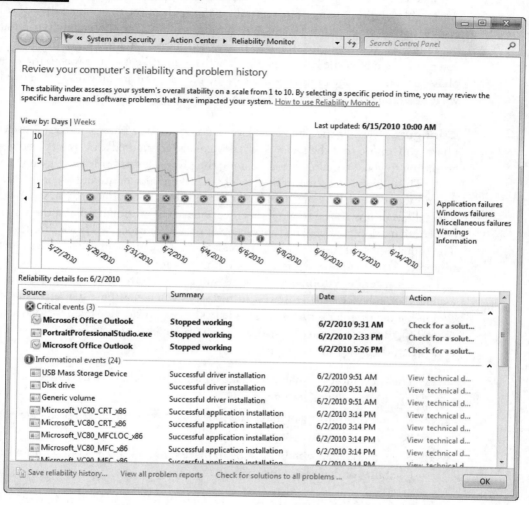

AP. You may try installing new device drivers for a client adapter in order to make them more compatible with the VoIP software you are using. You could also change settings or disable features to see if the problem goes away. The point is that this is where you begin the "technical" side of troubleshooting. While many techs begin here, you will have an advantage because you are starting this phase with a more accurate view of the problem.

Once you've completed these first three stages, you'll have come to a solution. Again, this solution is sometimes reinstalling the application, reinstalling the operating system, or reloading factory defaults and starting over with the configuration of a router, but things are working again. You may have your solution after the Research phase, or you may have it after the Engage phase. Whether you make it all the way to the Adjust phase, or you solve the problem earlier in the process, you are now ready to move to what I call the ongoing stability phases: Configure and Take Note.

**Configure**    This is the first of the two ongoing stability phases. In the Configure phase, you ensure that the systems and devices are configured and are operating according to your standards before leaving the physical area (or remote management tool). This allows you to maintain a standardized environment, and a standardized environment is usually more stable. Of course, with a reinstallation, you will need to reinstall according to the original specifications for the installation and then apply any configuration changes that have been approved or processed since that time. The primary goal of this phase is to provide consistency in your environment and to improve troubleshooting processes moving forward.

In a consistent environment, you can assume certain things. For example, you can assume that a device has the newest firmware, or you can assume that an operating system has a particular service pack loaded. The real world, however, introduces great difficulty in the area of consistency. For an environment to be and remain consistent, the following things must all be true:

- The users must be unable to make configuration changes that affect the consistency of the configurations.
- All administrators who have the power to make configuration changes must be consistent in the changes they make.
- Some automated system must be in place that adjusts the configurations of all machines or devices simultaneously.

As you can see from these three requirements, it is very difficult to have a truly consistent environment because of the human factor. However, even an environment that is mostly consistent makes troubleshooting much easier because the likelihood of an administrator implementing a bad configuration is lower than that of a user or customer. This ratio is not based on some superior intellect of the administrator; it is simply based on the training and area of specialty of the administrator. In the end, configuring your machines and devices to a standard specification generally reduces support costs by reducing support incidents.

**Take Note**   This final phase completes the process and ensures that you get the greatest benefit out of this methodology going forward—this is the second ongoing stability phase. By documenting your findings, what I call "Take Note," you provide a searchable resource for future troubleshooting. For example, the situation I shared earlier where the device error was generated should be documented, and I suggest documenting the following at a minimum:

- The problem with any error messages if they existed
- The cause concisely explained
- The solution with any necessary step-by-steps
- Any learned principles, such as a DLL being referenced as a device by the operating system

If your organization does not provide a centralized trouble ticket–tracking system or helpdesk solution, consider creating your own database. You can use any desktop database application like Microsoft Access or FileMaker. Just be sure you can document the needed information and query it easily. I tracked the 206 unique problems in an Access 2.0 database back in the late '90s. It worked fine for me, and a similar solution can still work for a small organization. However, web-based trouble ticket– or call-tracking systems seem to be the direction in which helpdesk applications are going, and I certainly find them useful as well. One benefit of a web-based system is that you may be able to access it from home or from any location where you have web access. This way you can check in for new problems at any time. If you have remote access to systems, you may even be able to resolve the problem without ever going on-site. Many open source web-based helpdesk or problem-tracking systems exist.

This first methodology, REACT, is my own methodology. It is the one that I use for every new and unique problem I face and is depicted in Figure 17-2. Through the years, I've incorporated some of the concepts of the OSI model methodology and systems thinking into my processes as well, but REACT still provides the basic framework in which I operate. Next, you will learn about the OSI model methodology.

## OSI Model

The OSI model is an excellent thinking tool for designing and understanding networks; however, it can also be used for troubleshooting purposes. When using the OSI model as a troubleshooting methodology, you will go up or down the OSI

**FIGURE 17-2**

Tom's REACT
troubleshooting
methodology

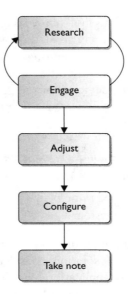

model, analyzing the system at each layer. This process allows you to break the problem into logical sections and then verify that the system is operating properly in each of these sections (OSI layers). You may choose to analyze only Layers 1 through 3, or you may choose to evaluate all seven layers (or even eight layers if you're including the user layer, which is sometimes called Layer 8).

on the job

*The ISO standard for the OSI model does not mention a Layer 8; however, many network administrators and engineers use this term to refer to the user. For example, a Layer 8 problem is a reference to a user mistake.*

**Layer 1**  Layer 1 is the Physical layer, and analyzing it would mean evaluation of the LAN client devices or infrastructure devices to ensure that they are working properly at the hardware and possibly driver level. For example, is the radio still functioning appropriately in a wireless NIC or not? With client devices, this can be tested quickly by removing the wireless LAN client device (assuming it's a USB, CardBus, or another kind of removable device) and installing it in another computer that is using the same model device and is working. If the new computer stops working too, the wireless LAN device is most likely at fault at the hardware level or the internal software level (firmware). If it is the wireless AP that is suspected and you have a spare, you could load the identical configuration on the spare, and place it in the same location to see if the problem persists. If it does not persist with the new

AP, again, the radio—or some other hardware/firmware issue—may be failing. If the problem is suspected to be in a Cisco router, you may have to simply run diagnostic show commands to locate the problem. If you have an identical spare router, you could use it, but it's not common to have such a spare sitting in storage.

An additional key is to evaluate the hardware used by Layer 1 (sometimes called Layer 0). On the wired network, you may also evaluate patch panels, connectors, and cabling. Another area where failure may occur in wireless VoIP connections in relation to Layer 1 is the Ethernet connection between the AP and the wired LAN. If your clients are authenticating and associating with the AP, but they cannot obtain an IP address from your DHCP server (assuming you're using one), the Ethernet connection may not be working. Go to a wired client, and try to connect to the AP via the Ethernet connection. Can you? If not, verify that the Ethernet cable is good, that the port on the switch is working, and that the Ethernet port in the AP is still functioning (by connecting directly to the AP and trying to connect).

These same guidelines apply whether or not you are troubleshooting a wired or wireless connection. Consider replacing cables as well as NICs to test the Physical layer. Also, keep in mind that many Physical layer problems will exist in hardware other than the end nodes, such as in switches and routers. You will also want to consider testing at higher layers first. If you can PING a device on the network, but your VoIP softphone is not working, the Physical layer is not the likely problem.

**Layer 2**   The second layer you will usually evaluate is Layer 2, the Data Link layer. This is where the bridges and switches perform their magic. Make sure the switch ports are still working properly (though this is really a Layer 1 issue), that VLANs are configured appropriately, and that port security settings are set accurately on your switches. Check the configuration in your bridge or bridges to ensure that they are configured correctly. Be sure the wireless link on all wireless bridges is still working and that the signal strength is still acceptable for operations. Since wireless bridges evaluate incoming frames and forward them based on information in the frame, be sure that the bridging rules or filters are set up appropriately. Of course, with both bridges and switches, the problem can be at the cable and connector level, which you will check at Layer 1.

The same rule applies to Layer 2 when it comes to troubleshooting this layer. If you can PING a device on the network, but your VoIP phone does not work, the Data Link layer (Layer 2) is most likely functioning just fine. When working with hardware VoIP phones, you may not have the ability to perform PING tests. In these scenarios you can simply attempt to connect with a different phone to see if the problem is resolved. If it is, it is likely a hardware failure or a configuration problem somewhere in the settings of the phone. While the OSI model of troubleshooting usually involves a logical flow up or down through the layers, it is also important to think of the layers as a systematic whole and to remember that you should sometimes jump straight to Layer 3 to rule out problems in lower layers. At the same time, you may be able to PING a device and assume that Layer 2 is fine, when the specific problem is in the VLAN assignment for the VoIP phone. Remember that you cannot always rule out VLAN problems at Layer 2 with a Layer 3 PING.

**Layer 3**    If you've evaluated the radios, NICs, cabling, and connectors at Layer 1 and you've checked the bridges and switches at Layer 2 and you've still not found a solution, you might have to move on to Layer 3, the Network layer. Here you'll need to check the routing tables to ensure proper configuration. Make sure any filters applied are accurate. Using common desktop operating system tools like ipconfig, traceroute, pathping, ping, and arp, you can ensure that you can route data from one location on the network to another.

Layer 3 is all about the network topology at a logical level. This means that you will be considering the network from a segmentation and routing perspective. You will need to ensure that the VoIP device is properly configured with default router settings, DNS server settings, and a valid IP address/subnet mask pair.

**Upper Layers**    Finally, if you've tested the first three layers and can't find a problem there, the network infrastructure is probably working fine. It's time to move to the upper layers, which are layers 4 through 7. These layers are called the Transport (4), Session (5), Presentation (6), and Application (7) layers. Look at the configuration settings in your applications and client software for VoIP utilization. Be sure that the authentication mechanisms are installed and configured correctly. Try using different tools and software that provide the same basic functionality. Do they work? If so, there may be a compatibility problem with the specific application you're using and the hardware on which it is operating.

One important lesson to take away from this section is that you cannot become narrow in your focus. If you insist on investigating only one layer of the OSI model, you will likely fail to find a solution or even the cause of your problem. This is why many techs will begin by attempting basic PING commands and traceroute commands in order to verify the functionality at Layers 1 through 3 quickly. If these commands work, the problem preventing appropriate communications is likely an upper layer issue, with the exception of VLAN misconfigurations.

As you can see, the OSI model of troubleshooting can help you both focus on and move through a sequence of testing procedures until you find the true source of the problem. I've only touched on the concept here, but you can take it further by learning more about what happens at each layer and the tools that can be used to test at each layer. For example, you can use a spectrum analyzer to test and troubleshoot the Physical layer and a protocol analyzer to inspect the Data Link layer of LANs.

## Hardware/Software Model

The hardware/software model is a troubleshooting methodology that attempts to narrow the problem to either hardware or software. Certain problems are commonly hardware problems, and others tend to be software problems. Many administrators will attempt to troubleshoot software first and then hardware. Others will do the opposite. In most cases, the situation will help you to determine which should be your first point of attack. If everything is working in a system except one application, that is often a good sign that the software is the problem. If multiple applications that use the same hardware are experiencing the same problem, that is often a good sign that the hardware is the problem. These are not absolute rules, but they are good general guidelines.

You will also want to consider the speed with which you can "swap out" the hardware. For example, a laptop PC card can be exchanged very quickly if you have a handy spare. It may be faster to swap the card and see if the problem goes away than to begin troubleshooting software settings. If the problem is resolved by swapping the hardware, you have resolved the issue. If it has not been resolved, then you can begin the more time-consuming process of software testing. Of course, some hardware cannot be swapped so easily, and in those cases you will likely perform some hardware tests through vendor utilities, or you will inspect the software configuration.

**Hardware Problems**   LANs have hardware problems that present specific symptoms. While I cannot provide you with an exact list of symptoms mapped to problems, the list in Table 17-1 is a good place to start.

| TABLE 17-1 | Hardware Problems and Symptoms |
| --- | --- |

| Problem | Symptoms |
| --- | --- |
| Client adapter failed | Device driver will not load, client cannot connect, OS reports errors loading the device |
| Firmware outdated | No support for newer security features, poor performance, reduced stability |
| Improper antenna installed or antenna disconnected with a wireless device | RF coverage in the wrong place, signal too weak at a distance |
| Bad cables | Could cause improper power for PoE devices or low SNR for antennas; could cause intermittent connection problems for wired links |

| TABLE 17-2 | Software Problems and Symptoms |
|---|---|
| **Problem** | **Symptoms** |
| Client software misconfigured | Client cannot connect, cannot receive an IP address, unable to browse the network |
| Improper passphrase entered | Client associated with the AP, but cannot log onto the wireless network; client connected to the wired LAN, but cannot place phone calls |
| DHCP server down | Client connects physically, but cannot acquire an IP address |
| RADIUS server down | Client associates with the AP, but cannot log onto the network when using a Robust Security Network (RSN) for a wireless LAN |

**Software Problems**    Table 17-2 lists common software problems and their symptoms.

## Symptom, Diagnosis, and Solution

Because certain symptoms usually surface with specific problems, many issues can be resolved in a similar way to human health issues. Look at the symptom, identify the most likely cause (diagnosis), and then treat it (solution). Repeat this process until the problem is resolved.

**Symptom**    Defining the symptoms means gathering information about the problem. What is happening? Where is it happening? What technology is involved? Which users, if any, are involved? Has it always been this way? Answering questions like these will help you determine the various details about the problem. Good questions are at the core of effective problem definition.

**Diagnosis**    Based on the information gathered from your symptoms analysis, what is the most likely cause, or what are the most likely causes? You can treat one or all, but you will most likely learn more by treating one cause at a time. Try one solution based on your diagnosis first and evaluate the results. This gives you expert knowledge over time or what some call "intuition."

**Solution**    The solution is the potential fix for the problem. You may try replacing a CardBus PC network card because you determine that, based on the symptoms, the most likely cause is a failed card. After replacing the card, you note that you are experiencing the same problem. Next, you may decide to try both cards in another machine that is currently using the same card model and is working. When you do this, both cards work in the other computer. Next, you may attempt to reload the drivers in the malfunctioning computer, but this doesn't help either. In the end, you discover that the CardBus port is experiencing intermittent failures in the malfunctioning laptop. You send it to the vendor for repairs.

This illustration demonstrates the diagnosis and solution method—what I call the Adjust phase in my REACT methodology. You make changes and try different tactics until something solves the problem. You document the solution for future reference, but you also mentally document it. This is called experience, and as you get more of it you approach the level of expertise that helps you solve problems more quickly. For this reason, I look at problems as stepping-stones to a better future because solving this network or computer problem today will only make me more able to solve similar and different problems tomorrow.

## Systems Thinking

Now that we've covered four effective troubleshooting methodologies, we'll look at an important concept that will make you a better troubleshooter. This concept is called systems thinking. Systems thinking is the process of analyzing all interdependent components that compose a system. In other words, it is the opposite of being narrow-minded in the troubleshooting process. I've seen administrators blame everything from network connectivity to application errors on an operating system or a particular brand of PC instead of looking for the actual problem. While some operating systems and some PC brands may seem more prone to problems than others, the reality is that probably thousands of individuals out there have had the opposite experience as you. In other words, if you like the computers from company A because they are very stable and you don't like the computers from company B because of your experience with them, there is likely someone (or thousands of someones) out there who feels exactly the opposite because of his or her experience. This reality doesn't mean you're wrong and they're right; it simply means that we often shape our opinions based on individual experiences that may not reflect the larger reality. Systems thinking can help us avoid these mind traps.

I remember when Packard Bell computers were very popular. IT professionals tended to dislike the machines because they were integrated. The sound card was built-in. The video was built-in. The drive controller was built-in. Do you see a pattern that is similar to almost every computer on the market today? Few systems do not have integrated sound, video, and drive controllers today; yet, this was the thing that gave Packard Bell's systems a bad name—at least in part. If memory serves me correctly, the bad name also had to do with poor support, but you can see how blinders can keep us from troubleshooting the real problem. Obviously, the integrated components were not the real culprit since most machines are designed that way today.

The point is simple: rather than focusing on a vendor that I do not like, I must focus on the actual problem and seek a solution. When I do this, I'm less likely to just reinstall every time a problem comes up. I want to ask questions like:

- What are the systems or devices between this device and the network or device with which it is attempting to communicate?
- What other devices are attempting to communicate with the same system at this time?
- What has changed in the environment within which the system operates?
- Has the system been physically moved recently?

Asking these kinds of questions causes you to evaluate factors that are more related to the actual system you have in place and less related to the vendors that have provided the components. Indeed, if a vendor has provided you with bad components over a period of time, you will likely discontinue partnering with that vendor; however, blaming the problem on a single vendor every time does not help me solve the problems I am facing right now. For that, I need systems thinking and a good methodology.

Whether you adopt one or more of these methodologies, pursue another methodology, or create one of your own, you should consider how you troubleshoot problems and then be sure it is an efficient and effective process.

# General VoIP Troubleshooting

It is important, both for the CCNA Voice exam and your efforts in troubleshooting networks, that you understand many of the common symptoms and problems that occur in VoIP networks. The CCNA Voice objectives do not list specific symptoms; however, I will cover 10 specific symptoms and 14 common problems in the following sections.

## Common Symptoms

The first piece of information you have when troubleshooting is a collection of one or more symptoms. Understanding these symptoms and the common problems that can cause them is very important. You will learn about the symptoms first, and then we will move on to the common problems.

### Poor Voice Quality

Voice or call quality is a subjective term that describes how accurately the human voice is digitized and transmitted as a voice signal. It is a subjective term because voice quality is based on the perception of the hearer and is impacted by that hearer's experience. For example, if the hearer has been exposed to very high quality audio communications, he or she will be more likely to notice poor voice quality on a VoIP conversation. By the same token, a person who has not been exposed to such quality is less likely to perceive the same voice signal as being poor. This reality is not unlike the experience we've had with high speed Internet. I have very fast Internet throughput at my home. I consider it high speed. When I go to a hotel with less than 1/10 the throughput, I don't consider that high speed even though the hotel does. A fast Internet connection to one is a slow connection to another.

Even with this subjectivity, an industry standard for judging voice quality has been developed. This standard is known as the Mean Opinion Score (MOS). The MOS is based on responses from a group of participants, and it attempts to remove some of the subjectivity through the process of averaging the participants' responses.

Factors that impact voice quality include clarity, delay, and echo. Clarity is a perceptual measurement of an original sound compared with a digitized signal. Delay causes the perception of a continuous voice signal (like the continuous sound waves in a face-to-face communication) to be lost. Echo causes the voice signal to be reflected back toward the speaker. This echo can result in overlapping sounds and can reduce quality.

## Clipping

Clipping occurs when parts of the sound waves are lost during digital communications. This can occur as a result of many different problems:

- Processing overload on the encoder due to insufficient hardware
- Dropped packets between the sender and receiver due to media errors or other problems
- Overflows or underflows on the jitter buffer
- Network latency causing too much delay and forcing dropped packets
- Using a half-duplex speakerphone

When full-duplex speakerphones are used, they usually sample the environment to build a digital image of the noise floor within the area. This image is used to distinguish between a human speaker and the background noise. Half-duplex speakerphones do not do this and may interpret the background noise as a human speaking, which may in turn result in clipping.

Whatever the cause, remember that clipping is the loss of portions of sound within the digital stream of communications.

## Echo

Echo occurs when the person speaking hears what he or she said a few milliseconds after having said it. The effect is very similar to what you experience when you speak loudly into a cave. When echo is involved in a telephone conversation, it can become very frustrating to the participants; however, echo is a normal occurrence on the PSTN and even on private voice networks. The goal is to remove or minimize as much echo as possible.

Echo can be resolved through impedance matching in the cabling systems, reducing delay as much as possible, and using echo suppression and/or cancelation. Echo cancellers are installed at a local site to prevent an echo from returning to the remote site. If you have a VoIP network that interconnects multiple locations, you may consider installing an echo canceller at each site. Echo cancellers are usually implemented on the VoIP gateway's PSTN interface.

## Delay

Delay is the time it takes for a packet to travel across a network. As a packet traverses the network, it must pass through switches, routers, and other devices. Each of these devices can introduce delay. Delay can cause loss of call clarity, clipping, and other problems on VoIP networks, so you should attempt to minimize delay as much as possible. Implement paths between calling partners that introduce as few handling delays as possible. Use the fastest technology your budget will allow (for example, use gigabit Ethernet instead of 100 Mbps whenever possible).

Audio codecs will introduce different transcoding delays as well. Table 17-3 provides a listing of common delays introduced by the different codecs.

The reality is that the codec-induced delay is directly related to the amount of compression. G.729 compresses the audio very tightly, where G.711 doesn't compress it at all. It is important, however, when looking at these delays introduced by transcoding, that you do not forget the reduction in delay provided by the smaller data size.

| TABLE 17-3 | Transcoding Delay (ms) | Codec |
|---|---|---|
| | 0.125 | G.722 |
| Codec-Introduced Delay | 0.75 | G.711 PCM audio |
| | 1 | G.726 and G.727 |
| | 3 to 5 | G.728 |
| | 10 | G.729 and G.729a |
| | 30 | G.723 and G.723.1 |

## No Dial Tone

If a user takes the phone off-hook and does not receive a dial tone, the problem could be one of many possibilities. The possibilities include:

- Configuration issues
- A digital signal processing (DSP) problem
- A software bug or malfunction
- Hardware failure

## Cross Talk

When an electrical signal in one cable causes a voltage fluctuation in another cable, cross talk occurs. With telephone signals, cross talk may be detected as a faint background conversation. When the signal from another line bleeds into your line, the conversation on the other line may come through.

Longer cables are more susceptible to cross talk, and poorly terminated cables may also increase its occurrence. Cross talk is rated as near end cross talk (NEXT). NEXT is measured by intentionally introducing a signal on one line and measuring the strength of that signal on an adjacent line. The difference between the proper signal on the main line and the cross talk signal on the adjacent line is known as signal-to-noise ratio (SNR). A higher SNR is desirable.

## Dropped Calls

A call can be dropped for a number of reasons. One of the users may have inadvertently pressed the End or Hang-up button. A switch may fail to forward packets quickly enough, and the call may be dropped due to inactivity. A call could be dropped because routers are reconfiguring routing paths or routing tables, and this process can detract from the ability to forward the voice packets. In addition, all of the typical reasons network connections fail will apply to VoIP connections.

**w a t c h** *Remember that it is possible for two VoIP phones to maintain a connection as long as they can communicate with each other over* *the network. If neither phone can reach the call manager, but both phones can communicate with each other, the call may not be dropped.*

## Blocked Calls

When a call is blocked, the dialer receives a busy signal. Grade of service (GoS) expresses the probability that a single call will be blocked. A system has a high GoS if calls go through on the first try. When some calls receive a busy signal, the GoS is lower; however, it is usually acceptable to have some calls receive a busy signal. The question is one of how many calls per hundred or thousand that you can tolerate being blocked.

GoS, then, is the probability that a given call will be blocked on the first try during the busy hour of phone operations. The formula for calculating GoS is:

$$GoS = bC/cC$$

where bC is equal to the number of blocked first attempt calls in the busy hour and cC is the number of completed first attempt calls in the same time window. If 312 calls are completed on the first try and 17 calls receive a busy signal, the calculation is as follows:

$$GoS = 17/312 \text{ or } GoS = 0.054$$

A GoS of 0.054 means that 54 calls out of every 1,000 calls, or 5.4 percent of calls, will usually be blocked on the first try during the busy hour.

## Loss of Features

Cisco IP phones stay in touch with the Cisco Communications Manager software by transmitting KeepAlive messages. Three sequential failed KeepAlive messages within an active call will cause the message "CM Down, Features Disabled" to appear on the phone. This state will prevent features such as conference calling, call parking, and call holding from functioning. The cause may be a network problem between the phone and the Call Manager, or it may be a problem within the server or phone software.

## Poor Video Quality and Video Frame Loss

If you are streaming video as well as audio, video quality may also be an issue. Like voice packets, video packets arriving out of sequence or with high levels of delay will cause poor quality in the rendered video. When using the H.323 protocol, the required bandwidth for video is about 384 kbps plus 25 to 30 percent more for signaling overhead. This is usually rounded to approximately 480 kbps of required bandwidth. To resolve video quality and frame loss problems, you might consider using multiple parallel flow paths for the data transfer. You can also implement load balancing or load splitting for the video processing.

H.323 has some very tight constraints for video transfer. The packet loss for H.323 video must be less than 1 percent. Jitter has to be less than 30 milliseconds, and latency must be between 150 and 200 milliseconds in one direction.

To assist in the reduction of negative outcomes on packet-based networks, consider classifying video with QoS tools. You can use IP precedence solutions like DiffServ and queue the video packets with Low Latency Queuing (LLQ) or Weighted Fair Queuing (WFQ) so that the packets move out of the network nodes as quickly as possible.

## Common Problems

Now that you have learned the basics of the different trouble symptoms that you are likely to encounter on a converged network, you can explore the problems that may cause these symptoms to arise. While it is important to have and master excellent troubleshooting tools, it is equally important to understand common points of failure so you can focus your efforts. Table 17-4 provides a listing of the common problems you are likely to encounter.

## Troubleshooting Tools

It's one thing to have a good methodology and to understand the common symptoms and problems that occur on a converged network. It's another thing to know how to use the right tools to analyze and discover what's really happening on your network. This section will introduce a number of IP troubleshooting tools that you may find useful when you're analyzing your next big problem. These tools are used within Windows and Linux operating systems and may be available within some Cisco routers. For example, the PING command can be used from within many Cisco devices. The tools covered include:

- PING
- TraceRt
- PathPING
- ARP
- NSLookup
- Hostname
- NetStat

| TABLE 17-4 | Problems and Definitions |

| Problem | Definition |
| --- | --- |
| Media errors | Bad optic terminations or RF connectors. Poor shielding or damaged cables. |
| Packet or data loss | A measurement of the number of packets lost compared with the total sent. |
| Protocol mismatch | Using an inefficient protocol or improperly labeling packets for Label Switch Routers (LSRs). |
| Jitter | Variableness in the rate of delay. |
| Port settings | Port settings include perimeter firewall ports and client firewall ports. H.323 requires that UDP ports 1718 and 1719 be open. It also requires that TCP ports 1720 and 1503 be open. RTP and RTCP video and audio streams use dynamic ports from 1024 to 65,535 on TCP or UDP. |
| Configuration settings | Improper configuration settings can wreak havoc on a VoIP network. |
| Packet reordering | When routers are congested or traffic is improperly prioritized, VoIP packets may arrive out of sequence more than they normally would. This disorder results in packet resequencing, which can impact voice quality. |
| MTU issues | When a small maximum transfer unit (MTU) size is configured, it can cause fragmentation. This fragmentation can result in extra processing delay. |
| Bandwidth restrictions | VoIP requires consistency in bandwidth availability in order to operate smoothly. Bursty network communications can impact this and lower voice quality. |
| Router misconfigurations | It is not uncommon to see routers running multiple routing protocols (like RIP, OSPF, or IGRP) when only one or two of the protocols are actually needed. These extra routing protocols can degrade network performance. |
| QoS tags being dropped | Not all devices support QoS tags, and as a router extracts the IP packet out of an Ethernet frame, the QoS information can be lost during re-encapsulation. Be sure to select infrastructure devices that support the QoS technology you plan to implement. |
| IP packet loss | Due to UDP's connectionless nature and the fact that many VoIP protocols rely on it, IP packets can be lost, and this could be due to slow routers and other slow devices on the infrastructure. |
| Backup over the network | Many organizations are now performing data backups across the network. This activity can generate a large amount of network traffic. The backup packets should be tagged as a lower priority transfer than voice and video. You can configure the interleaf ratio so that five or more voice packets are sent for every one of the backup packets. |
| Hardware failure | For any networking technologies to function, all intermediate hardware devices must continue to function. A common problem causing VoIP and other networking communication symptoms is simple hardware failure. |

## PING

PING stands for Packet Internet Groper and is a command used to test IP connectivity. It is very useful when you are unsure if your network connection is even operating at the Network layer. The **PING** command varies slightly from one operating system to another, but most operating systems that support TCP/IP also support the **PING** command. Even Windows for Workgroups 3.11 (many years ago) included a **PING** command when you installed the TCP/IP protocol. The following exercise will walk you through using PING on a Windows machine.

### EXERCISE 17-1

### Using the PING Command

In this exercise, you will use the **PING** command to verify that a remote system is functioning on the network. You will also use the command to perform a continuous PING to test for intermittent problems. Finally, you'll see how you can increase and decrease the size of the PING request.

#### Verify a Remote System Is Functioning

1. Open a Command Prompt window.
   a. Click Start | All Programs | Accessories and select Command Prompt.
2. Type **PING remote_system_IP**.
   a. For example, if you are testing the remote system at 10.10.10.100, you would type **PING 10.10.10.100**.

#### Perform a Continuous PING

1. Open a Command Prompt window.
2. Type **PING –t localhost** and press ENTER.

You will notice that the **PING** command requests a response from the local machine periodically and without ceasing. If you want to test for intermittent network problems, use the **PING –t** command against a remote machine. You can stop the perpetual PING by pressing CTRL-C.

### Increase or Decrease the Size of the PING Request

1. Open a Command Prompt window.

2. Type **PING —l 10240 localhost** and press ENTER.

The default PING request size is 32 bytes. The —l switch allows you to increase or decrease this size. Using the —l switch with the —t switch can be very useful when troubleshooting latency or dropped packet problems.

## TraceRt

The **TraceRt** (trace route) command provides you with a simple method for testing the intermediate devices between two endpoints. For example, if you are working at a computer with the IP address of 10.10.10.200 and you want to test the route to 10.10.50.200, you would type the following command:

```
TRACERT 10.10.50.200
```

The **TraceRt** command also provides several switches for manipulating the command. Table 17-5 outlines these switches.

Remember that operating systems implement similar tools in different ways. For example, the MAC OS has a TraceRoute command as opposed to the Windows **TraceRt** command.

**TABLE 17-5**  TraceRt Switches

| Switch | Description |
|---|---|
| —d | Does not resolve addresses to host names. This switch can speed up the TraceRt processing. |
| —h *maximum_hops* | Specifies the maximum number of hops to trace. |
| —j *host* | Forces TraceRt to route through a given host. |
| —w timeout | Specifies the timeout value, in milliseconds, for each reply. |
| —R | Traces the round-trip path for IPv6 connections. |
| —S *source_address* | Specifies the source address to use for IPv6. |
| —4 | Forces the use of IPv4. |
| —6 | Forces the use of IPv6. |

### PathPING

PathPING is a newer command-line tool for Windows systems that allows you to PING the devices along the path to a destination. Unlike TraceRt, PathPING also reveals the number of sent packets compared to the number of dropped or lost packets. For this reason, PathPING is an excellent tool for troubleshooting dropped packets in voice networks. The command uses the switches listed in Table 17-6.

### ARP

The Address Resolution Protocol (ARP) is used to resolve IP addresses to MAC addresses for LAN packet delivery. Directly linked Ethernet devices communicate with each other based on their MAC addresses; however, routers receive packets destined for IP addresses. Some mechanism must be used to resolve these IP addresses to MAC addresses, and this is where the ARP cache is utilized.

When a machine needs to resolve an IP address to a MAC address, it will first look in the ARP cache. The ARP cache contains a listing of previously resolved IP-to-MAC mappings. To see the ARP cache on Windows:

1. Open a Command Prompt window.
2. Type **ARP  −a** and press ENTER.

Figure 17-3 shows sample output from the ARP command on a Windows Vista client. You can see the MAC addresses of the local network interfaces as well as the devices to which the machine has connected. For more detailed information, type **ARP −a −v**, which will provide you with a verbose listing of the ARP cache. To clear the ARP cache, simply type **ARP −s \*** and all entries will be deleted.

| TABLE 17-6 | PathPING Switches |
| --- | --- |

| Switch | Description |
| --- | --- |
| −g *host* | Same functionality as the −j switch in TraceRt |
| −h *maximum_hops* | Specifies the maximum number of hops across which the connection should be traced |
| −i *address* | Tells PathPING to use the specified source IPv6 address |
| −n | Same functionality as −d in TraceRt |
| −q *number_of_queries_per_hop* | Specifies the number of PINGs to execute against each device in the path |
| −w *timeout* | Specifies how long to wait, in milliseconds, for each query reply |
| −4 | Forces the use of IPv4 |
| −6 | Forces the use of IPv6 |

**FIGURE 17-3**

ARP output

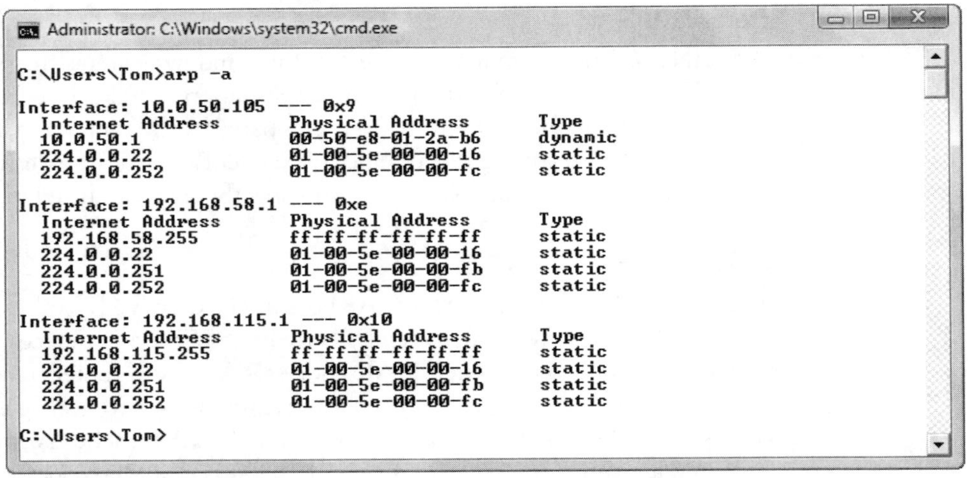

```
Administrator: C:\Windows\system32\cmd.exe

C:\Users\Tom>arp -a

Interface: 10.0.50.105 --- 0x9
  Internet Address      Physical Address      Type
  10.0.50.1             00-50-e8-01-2a-b6     dynamic
  224.0.0.22            01-00-5e-00-00-16     static
  224.0.0.252           01-00-5e-00-00-fc     static

Interface: 192.168.58.1 --- 0xe
  Internet Address      Physical Address      Type
  192.168.58.255        ff-ff-ff-ff-ff-ff     static
  224.0.0.22            01-00-5e-00-00-16     static
  224.0.0.251           01-00-5e-00-00-fb     static
  224.0.0.252           01-00-5e-00-00-fc     static

Interface: 192.168.115.1 --- 0x10
  Internet Address      Physical Address      Type
  192.168.115.255       ff-ff-ff-ff-ff-ff     static
  224.0.0.22            01-00-5e-00-00-16     static
  224.0.0.251           01-00-5e-00-00-fb     static
  224.0.0.252           01-00-5e-00-00-fc     static

C:\Users\Tom>
```

## NSLookup

If you are finding it impossible to connect to devices based on their DNS or host names, you can use the NSLookup tool to query the DNS server. This tool can perform both forward and reverse lookups as well as special operations for service records. For example, to resolve the IP address of a web site, type **NSLOOKUP website_domain_name**. The result will be the IP address of the web site and the name of the DNS server that resolved the host name to the IP address. You can also use NSLookup in interactive mode by typing **NSLOOKUP** and pressing ENTER. Figure 17-4 shows the NSLookup tool working in interactive mode.

**FIGURE 17-4**

NSLookup in interactive mode

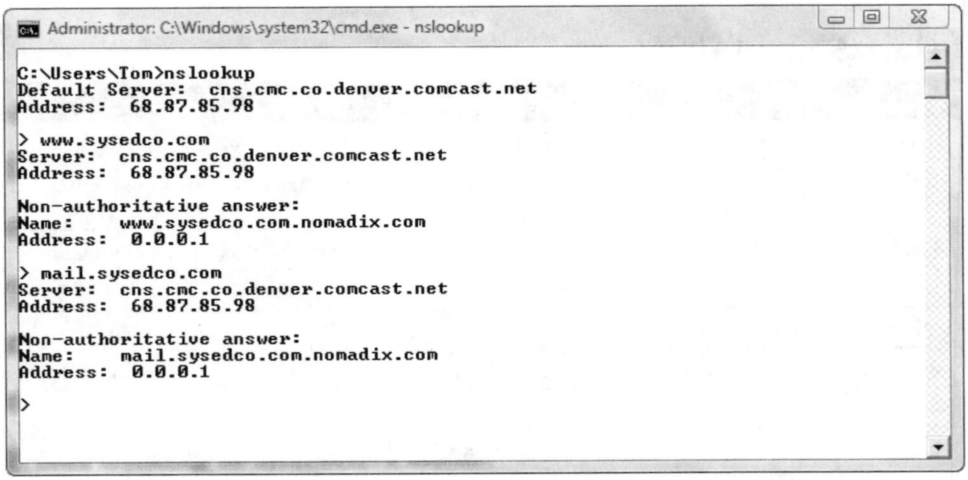

```
Administrator: C:\Windows\system32\cmd.exe - nslookup

C:\Users\Tom>nslookup
Default Server:  cns.cmc.co.denver.comcast.net
Address:  68.87.85.98

> www.sysedco.com
Server:  cns.cmc.co.denver.comcast.net
Address:  68.87.85.98

Non-authoritative answer:
Name:    www.sysedco.com.nomadix.com
Address:  0.0.0.1

> mail.sysedco.com
Server:  cns.cmc.co.denver.comcast.net
Address:  68.87.85.98

Non-authoritative answer:
Name:    mail.sysedco.com.nomadix.com
Address:  0.0.0.1

>
```

## Hostname

Hostname is a simple command-line tool that reveals the local machine name. Typing **hostname** at the command prompt will return the host name of the computer. You can get the same information by typing **ECHO %computername%**. The latter method has been available for many years in Windows systems, and the former method is more recent.

## NetStat

NetStat is a command-line tool that reveals network interface statistics. You can view both statistics related to communications and the currently open connections with this tool. Figure 17-5 shows the command-line options available for NetStat.

One of the useful features of the **NetStat** command is the ability to view statistics for a specific protocol. For example, you can view only TCP statistics, only IP statistics, and only UDP statistics. The **NetStat –s –p TCP** command, for example, will display only statistics for TCP communications. Figure 17-6 shows the output for viewing TCP, IP, and UDP statistics, respectively.

**FIGURE 17-5**

NetStat options

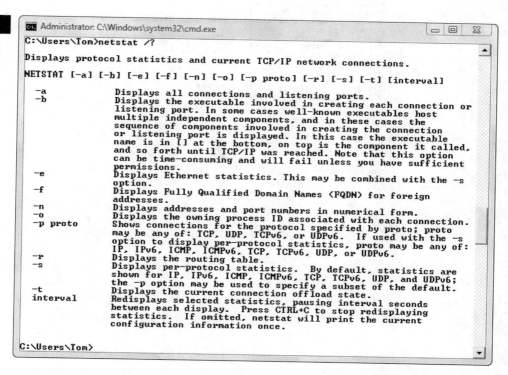

```
Administrator: C:\Windows\system32\cmd.exe                                    □ ▣ ⬜

C:\Users\Tom>netstat -s -p tcp

TCP Statistics for IPv4

    Active Opens                        = 494
    Passive Opens                       = 119
    Failed Connection Attempts          = 20
    Reset Connections                   = 176
    Current Connections                 = 8
    Segments Received                   = 15392
    Segments Sent                       = 14919
    Segments Retransmitted              = 109

Active Connections

    Proto  Local Address          Foreign Address        State
    TCP    10.0.50.105:49679      cg-in-f104:http        CLOSE_WAIT
    TCP    10.0.50.105:49680      cg-in-f104:http        CLOSE_WAIT
    TCP    10.0.50.105:49685      cg-in-f147:http        CLOSE_WAIT
    TCP    10.0.50.105:49686      cg-in-f147:http        CLOSE_WAIT
    TCP    127.0.0.1:49227        Tom-PC:49228           ESTABLISHED
    TCP    127.0.0.1:49228        Tom-PC:49227           ESTABLISHED
    TCP    127.0.0.1:49244        Tom-PC:49245           ESTABLISHED
    TCP    127.0.0.1:49245        Tom-PC:49244           ESTABLISHED

C:\Users\Tom>netstat -s -p ip

IPv4 Statistics

    Packets Received                    = 13938
    Received Header Errors              = 0
    Received Address Errors             = 827
    Datagrams Forwarded                 = 0
    Unknown Protocols Received          = 0
    Received Packets Discarded          = 7782
    Received Packets Delivered          = 28708
    Output Requests                     = 22060
    Routing Discards                    = 0
    Discarded Output Packets            = 193
    Output Packet No Route              = 9
    Reassembly Required                 = 0
    Reassembly Successful               = 0
    Reassembly Failures                 = 0
    Datagrams Successfully Fragmented   = 0
    Datagrams Failing Fragmentation     = 0
    Fragments Created                   = 0

C:\Users\Tom>netstat -s -p udp

UDP Statistics for IPv4

    Datagrams Received    = 5341
    No Ports              = 1347
    Receive Errors        = 6442
    Datagrams Sent        = 6292

Active Connections

    Proto  Local Address          Foreign Address        State

C:\Users\Tom>
```

**CERTIFICATION OBJECTIVE 17.01**

# 640-460: Explain Basic Troubleshooting Methods for Cisco Unified Communications Manager Express

As with most anything you troubleshoot, the first step that you should take with a Cisco Unified CME configuration is to verify proper settings. If the settings are incorrect, the device will not perform as needed. In this section, you will learn about several commands that can be used to verify CME configuration settings.

## Verifying CME Settings

One of the most important commands on a Cisco router that is used to run Cisco Unified CME is the **show running-config** command. In addition to this common command, several troubleshooting show commands may be helpful. Table 17-7 provides a reference for these commands.

| TABLE 17-7 | CME IOS Troubleshooting Commands |

| Command | Purpose | Example |
|---|---|---|
| debug ip | To analyze DHCP communications | debug ip dhcp server events |
| debug tftp events | To analyze TFTP events such as Cisco IP phone firmware downloads | debug tftp events |
| show telephony-service | To view the CME settings and information | show telephony-service tftp-bindings |
| debug ephone | To verify that the ephone registration process is working | debug ephone register |
| show ephone | To determine the state of an ephone (registered, unregistered, or deceased) | show ephone attempted-registrations |

In addition to these commands, you can also use the CME router to ping the Cisco IP phones to troubleshoot the communications between the router and the phone. Some phones may respond to only one out of every two ping requests, but this is normal behavior because the router pings at a higher rate than the phone allows.

CME questions are likely to be on both the CVOICE and the 640-460 exams. Make sure you understand how to view information about CME with the show telephony-service **command and that you** understand when to use the debug ephone and show ephone **commands.**

## CERTIFICATION OBJECTIVE 17.02

# 640-460: Explain Basic Troubleshooting Methods for Cisco Unity Express

Cisco Unity Express is an AIM-CUE module installed in a Cisco router. It may come preinstalled in the UC500 series devices. To troubleshoot Cisco Unity Express, you'll need to be able to verify that the service module is detected and that the configuration is appropriate. This section provides an overview of troubleshooting commands for the Cisco Unity Express module.

## Cisco Unity Express Troubleshooting Commands

If the Cisco Unity Express module, which provides voice mail and auto-attendant features, is not functioning, you should first verify that it has been detected by the Cisco IOS. This can be accomplished easily with the following command:

```
Router1# show run | inc interface Service-Engine
```

If the device has been detected, you should see output indicating that a new interface Service-Engine line has been added to the running-config. If no results are shown, it indicates that the router has not detected the module. Try reseating the module or replace it if the router functions otherwise but does not detect the module.

If the Cisco router still detects the module but it is not working, the next step is to verify the proper configuration. To do this, you must first gain access to the service module. Access the service module with the following command:

```
Router1# service-module service-engine 1/0 session
CUE>
```

This command assumes that the Unity Express module is addressed as 1/0. If not, you'll simply change the command to match the address of your service module. Remember, this address can be identified by looking at the running-config. Notice that the prompt changes once you've accessed the service module. Once you've accessed the service module, you must again enter enable mode to perform any useful functions as follows:

```
CUE> enable
Password:
CUE#
```

Now you can begin verifying proper configuration. The Unity Express module requires that appropriate license files be installed. To verify the license, use the following command:

```
CUE# show software license
```

You should see results that indicate a license file is installed and the number of mailboxes the license supports.

In worst-case scenarios, you can reset the Unity Express module to factory defaults. If you take this drastic action, all configuration and data will be lost, so this action should be taken with caution. You will be warned by the device should you choose to perform this action. To reset to factory defaults, execute the following commands:

```
CUE> offline
CUE (offline)> restore factory default
```

After executing the **offline** command, you'll be asked to verify the action. Simply type **Y** and press ENTER. You'll also be asked to verify the second command. Type **Y** and press ENTER if you're absolutely certain you must take this last-resort action.

**CERTIFICATION OBJECTIVE 17.03**

# 640-460: Explain Basic Maintenance and Troubleshooting Methods for UC500

The UC500 series does not have the power of a Cisco ISR with CME and Unity Express modules; however, while it cannot scale to the sizes of an ISR, it does have many similar troubleshooting features. This section will explore a few of the troubleshooting methods you can use with the UC500 series of equipment.

## UC500 Troubleshooting Commands

Unlike the ISR-based VoIP solutions from Cisco, the majority of the troubleshooting in the UC500 series is accomplished within the graphical user interface. However, the UC500 does have a basic command-line interface (CLI) that may be used for troubleshooting purposes. To access the CLI, connect an Ethernet cable to one of the switch ports on the UC500 device and to your computer. You can now telnet into the device by connecting to its configured IP address. From here you can use basic IOS commands such as **show version**, **show running-config**, and **show interfaces.** These commands can be useful in verifying proper configuration.

**e x a m**

**ⓦatch**

*If you can gain access to a UC500 series device to work with the CCA and web-based interface before exam day, it will greatly increase your chances of successfully answering questions related to this series. If you are taking the CVOICE exam instead, you will not need to know anything about the UC500 series management interfaces.*

# 640-460: Describe How QoS Addresses Voice Quality Issues

One of the key factors in a successful VoIP network is the impact of quality of service (QoS) on the network. When QoS is properly implemented, even a 100-Mbps network can handle many more calls than it can when no QoS is implemented or when QoS is implemented improperly.

You may remember from earlier chapters that VoIP communications require low levels of delay and jitter in order to function properly. In this section, you'll learn about the three stages of QoS functionality, QoS trust boundaries, and the Cisco Auto-QoS implementation process.

## Three Stages of QoS Functionality

QoS works by classifying, marking, and queuing the IP packets on the network. These actions represent the three stages of QoS functionality. *Traffic classification* involves identifying the packets and classifying them into different priorities. In the Cisco world, we typically create voice VLANs and data VLANs. If IP packets are in the voice VLAN, we assume they require the voice priority. This makes classification simpler. Network devices can also classify packets by looking at the IP data types and placing them into the appropriate classification.

Based on the classification of the IP packet, *traffic marking* flags the packet so the rest of the network devices can simply forward the data using queues based on these flags. Cisco IP phones will use the class of service (CoS) values for this flagging purpose. Eight priority levels are available in the CoS field of the Ethernet frame header. Voice traffic is flagged with a CoS value of 5. Standard unmarked data is given a CoS value of 0. The higher values indicate high priorities. Table 17-8 documents the eight classes and their common uses. Based on the values in this table, you can see that the actual highest priority for data packets is 5 because

| TABLE 17-8 | Class | Applications |
|---|---|---|
| CoS Classes and Applications | 0 | Best effort data |
| | 1 | Considered background data |
| | 2 | Considered excellent effort |
| | 3 | Considered for critical non-streaming applications |
| | 4 | Usually used for video data |
| | 5 | Express Forwarding (EF) traffic such as VoIP |
| | 6 | Used for IP routing protocols |
| | 7 | Used for IP routing protocols |

classes 6 and 7 are reserved for routing protocols. The CoS values are used with the Differentiated Services (DiffServ) QoS solution. IEEE 802.1p defines QoS as a standard.

Once the traffic is marked, it can be placed in the appropriate queue for matched priority processing. *Traffic queuing* is the process of prioritizing the outbound packets so that the higher priority packets are sent first. The queuing technique recommended for voice data is known as Low Latency Queuing (LLQ), and it assists in the removal of jitter, delay, and packet loss in the voice communications. The Cisco auto-QoS feature implements LLQ by default.

## QoS Trust Boundaries

The QoS trust boundary defines the point at which we trust devices to properly tag or mark the packets with QoS information. For example, you can trust at four primary levels:

- All endpoints
- Cisco IP phones
- Access layer (switches)
- Distribution layer (switches and routers)

If you trust all endpoints, then you can accept the QoS tags placed on the packets coming into any interface on your switches. This trust boundary works best on strictly managed environments. If you trust Cisco IP phones, you are indicating that only IP phone endpoints can apply the QoS markings. You can also indicate that any switch can apply the QoS markings (the access layer) or that only the distribution layer switches can.

To configure the trust boundary, use the **auto qos voip** command with any of the following parameters:

- **Cisco-phone**  This parameter indicates that only hardware-based Cisco IP phones will be trusted to apply the CoS markings. The Cisco Discovery Protocol (CDP) is used to verify that it is indeed a Cisco phone.

- **Cisco-softphone**  Like the **cisco-phone** parameter, this option uses CDP for verification; however, it will allow for the QoS markings from software-based Cisco IP phones.

- **Trust**  This option indicates that the switch should trust any CoS markings it receives. This option is used on all interfaces that connect your switches and routers within your infrastructure so that the QoS markings can pass throughout the infrastructure and be honored for priority queuing.

## Implementing Auto-QoS

To indicate that you only trust markings from a hardware-based Cisco IP phone, execute the following command:

```
SwitchA(config-if)#auto qos voip cisco-phone
```

The command should be executed while in the interface configuration mode for the switch port you wish to configure.

You should execute the following command on infrastructure interfaces to allow QoS markings to be processed and honored:

```
InfraSwitch(config-if)#auto qos voip trust
```

As you can see, Cisco auto-QoS is easy to configure. These simple commands do it in just a few moments. However, these commands enable many different, more complex commands to make QoS happen on your Cisco network. The following items are configured automatically when using the **auto qos voip** command:

- MLS trusts are configured based on the trust boundary specified. For example, the **auto qos voip cisco-phone** command would result in a **mls qos trust device cisco-phone** entry in the running configuration.

- The weighted round robin (WRR) queues are configured. You will notice several entries in the running configuration for **wrr-queue** commands. These commands configure and apply CoS maps.

*Make sure you know the* auto qos voip *commands for the exam.*
*Understand the different trust boundaries they define and the basic features they enable.*

## CERTIFICATION SUMMARY

In this chapter, you learned about troubleshooting methods and specific Cisco commands that can be used to verify configurations and to troubleshoot problems related to VoIP implementations. You first learned about the need for troubleshooting methodologies and then explored troubleshooting tips for Cisco Unified CME, Unity Express, UC500 devices, and voice quality issues.

# ✓ TWO-MINUTE DRILL

## 640-460: Explain Basic Troubleshooting Methods for Cisco Unified Communications Manager Express

❑ The **show running-config** command can be used to view the running configuration on a CME router just like any other ISR router.

❑ The CME router and telephony services can be configured from a web browser if the **ip http server** command is enabled.

❑ The **debug tftp events** command will allow you to view attempts to access the TFTP files when phones download firmware.

❑ The **debug ip dhcp server events** command is used to monitor DHCP activity. IP phones must acquire their IP configuration from DHCP, and this command helps troubleshoot the DHCP process.

❑ The **show telephony-service** command is used to view information about CME.

❑ You can ping the Cisco IP phones from a router in order to troubleshoot communications.

❑ To troubleshoot the IP phone registration process, use the **debug ephone** command.

## 640-460: Explain Basic Troubleshooting Methods for Cisco Unity Express

❑ You should see an entry in the running-config for the service module if the router has detected the Cisco Unity Express module. Use the **show running-config** command to view the running-config.

❑ Access the Unity Express module with the **service-module service-engine 1/0 session** command.

❑ Once in the service module command prompt, you must use the **enable** command to enter configuration or enable mode just like the native router.

❑ To view the current software license for the Unity Express module, execute the **show software license** command when at the service module command prompt.

❑ As a last resort, you can return the Unity Express module to the factory defaults with the **restore factory default** command. The module must be offline in order to execute the factory restore process.

❑ If the factory defaults are restored, all data and configuration settings are removed.

## 640-460: Explain Basic Maintenance and Troubleshooting Methods for UC500

❑ The UC500 series offers a command prompt interface similar to the standard IOS; however, it has limited functionality.

❑ Telnet can be used to access the CLI of a UC500 series device through the standard switch ports on the device.

❑ The most common way to access and troubleshoot the UC500 series is through the web-based interface or the Cisco Configuration Assistant (CCA). Both methods offer a GUI interface for configuration verification and status review.

## 640-460: Describe How QoS Addresses Voice Quality Issues

❑ The class of service (CoS) QoS solution allows for eight classes.

❑ Classes 0 through 5 are used for data. Classes 6 and 7 are used only by routing protocols.

❑ VoIP data typically receives class 5 markings.

❑ The three stages of QoS processing are traffic classification, traffic marking, and traffic queuing.

❑ Cisco's auto-QoS feature uses Low Latency Queuing (LLC) for VoIP traffic.

❑ The **auto qos voip** command is used to configure Cisco auto-QoS.

❑ Three options exist for the **auto qos voip** command: **cisco-phone**, **cisco-softphone**, and **trust**.

❑ The **cisco-phone** option limits the QoS markings to those applied by a Cisco IP phone.

❑ The **cisco-softphone** option allows the Cisco software-based IP phone on a PC to apply QoS markings.

❑ The **trust** option accepts all QoS marking sources and is usually used only within the infrastructure devices in the distribution and core layers.

# SELF TEST

The following questions will help you measure your understanding of the material presented in this chapter. Read all the choices carefully because there might be more than one correct answer. Choose all correct answers for each question.

## 640-460: Explain Basic Troubleshooting Methods for Cisco Unified Communications Manager Express

1. What command must be entered into the router's configuration in order to access CME from a web browser?
   A. ip http server
   B. enable http
   C. http server
   D. ip http-server

2. You want to monitor DHCP activity on the CME router. What command should you enter?
   A. ip dhcp monitor
   B. debug dhcp server events
   C. debug ip dhcp server events
   D. ip dhcp server events

3. What **show** command is used to view information about CME settings and data?
   A. show interfaces
   B. show telephony-service
   C. show ip interface
   D. show cme-service

4. What command can you enter into a Cisco router to troubleshoot ephone registration processes?
   A. debug ephone
   B. debug ip-telephony
   C. debug telephony-service
   D. debug ip rtp packets

## 640-460: Explain Basic Troubleshooting Methods for Cisco Unity Express

**5.** What command is used to access the Unity Express service module assuming it is at the 1/0 address?

A. interface service-engine 1/0

B. interface service-module 1/0

C. service-module service-engine 1/0

D. service-engine service module 1/0

**6.** What command can be used to view information about the licensing for your Unity Express module in a Cisco router?

A. show software license

B. show run | inc license

C. show run | inc certificate

D. show software license

**7.** What is lost if you reset a Unity Express module to factory defaults? (Choose all that apply.)

A. Data

B. Configuration settings

C. Memory

D. FastEthernet 0 IP settings

**8.** What command is used to reset a Unity Express module to factory defaults?

A. restore factory default

B. reset factory default

C. reload factory default

D. del running-config

**9.** What command must be executed before reloading the factory defaults?

A. unprotect

B. offline

C. exit

D. disable

## 640-460: Explain Basic Maintenance and Troubleshooting Methods for UC500

**10.** How can you access the CLI for a UC500 series device?

A. Telnet in through the switch port

B. Telnet in through the default VPN tunnel

C. Connect a keyboard and monitor to the device

D. Use a video and keyboard switchbox

**11.** What application is typically used to configure, troubleshoot, and monitor a UC500 series device?

    **A.** CCA

    **B.** SDM

    **C.** SNMP

    **D.** RTP

### 640-460: Describe How QoS Addresses Voice Quality Issues

**12.** How many classes are defined within the CoS classes?

    **A.** 4

    **B.** 8

    **C.** 12

    **D.** 7

**13.** What class is usually used for VoIP data as a CoS marking?

    **A.** 1

    **B.** 0

    **C.** 7

    **D.** 5

**14.** Which CoS classes are used for endpoint data on Ethernet networks?

    **A.** 0–5

    **B.** 1–5

    **C.** 6–7

    **D.** 0–7

**15.** What is the command to enable QoS on a Cisco switch with the trust boundary as the hardware-based IP phones?

    **A.** auto qos voip cisco-softphone

    **B.** auto qos voip phone

    **C.** auto qos voip cisco-phone

    **D.** auto qos voip trust

# LAB QUESTION

You are configuring QoS on a Cisco switch. You want to ensure that CoS markings are received from hardware-based Cisco phones and Cisco softphones. You do not want to trust any other devices. You also want to enable the web-based access to the CME. What commands can you type on the Cisco switch and the CME router to accomplish this? On which device will you type the commands?

# SELF TEST ANSWERS

## 640-460: Explain Basic Troubleshooting Methods for Cisco Unified Communications Manager Express

1. ☑ **A** is correct. The HTTP service must be started. You can use the **ip http server** command or the **ip http secure-server** command to start the service. The latter enables the HTTPS server.

   ☒ **B, C,** and **D** are incorrect. The commands enable http, http server, and ip http-server simply do not exist within the Cisco IOS with CME installed or without it installed.

2. ☑ **C** is correct. The **debug ip dhcp server events** command will enable output detailing the DHCP activity within the Cisco router.

   ☒ **A, B,** and **D** are incorrect. No such commands as the ip dhcp monitor, debug dhcp server events, or ip dhcp server events exist.

3. ☑ **B** is correct. The **show telephony-service** command can be used to view information about CME on a Cisco ISR.

   ☒ **A, C,** and **D** are incorrect. The **show interfaces** command is used to view information about Ethernet, WAN, and other interfaces. The **show ip interface** command is used to show information about IP configurations on the router. The show cme-service command is not a valid command.

4. ☑ **A** is correct. The **debug ephone** command will allow you to view detailed activity information related to IP phone registrations.

   ☒ **B, C,** and **D** are incorrect. The debug ip-telephony and debug telephony-service commands are invalid commands. The **debug ip rtp packets** command is useful for VoIP analysis in that it shows the RTP header information; however, it does not help in troubleshooting ephone registration processes.

## 640-460: Explain Basic Troubleshooting Methods for Cisco Unity Express

5. ☑ **C** is correct. The **service-module** command is used to enter the management mode for any service module, including the Unity Express module.

   ☒ **A, B,** and **D** are incorrect. All of these commands are invalid and serve no purpose within the Cisco IOS.

**6.** ☑ **D** is correct. The proper command is **show software license**, and the command should be executed from within the service-module prompt and not the native IOS prompt.

☒ **A, B,** and **C** are incorrect. All of these commands are invalid and serve no purpose within the Cisco IOS. Licensing information is not stored in the running-config of the router.

**7.** ☑ **A** and **B** are correct. You will lose both the data on the module and the configuration if you reset to factory defaults.

☒ **C** and **D** are incorrect. The memory will not be changed because it is a hardware element. The FastEthernet 0 interface, if the router has one, will not be impacted because it is a separate interface.

**8.** ☑ **A** is correct. The **restore factory default** command resets the Unity Express module to factory defaults. This command should be used with great caution because all data and configuration settings will be lost.

☒ **B, C,** and **D** are incorrect. These commands are not valid commands for resetting factory defaults on Unity Express modules.

**9.** ☑ **B** is correct. The **offline** command should be executed to take the Unity Express module offline for reconfiguration.

☒ **A, C,** and **D** are incorrect. The unprotect command is not a valid command for Unity Express modules. The **exit** command is used to return to native IOS mode from within the service-module command prompt. The disable command is not valid within the Unity Express module.

## 640-460: Explain Basic Maintenance and Troubleshooting Methods for UC500

**10.** ☑ **A** is correct. The Telnet protocol is supported on the switch ports. You can also use the serial interface with a terminal emulator program.

☒ **B, C,** and **D** are incorrect. No VPN tunnel exists by default on a UC500 series device. No ports exist to connect a keyboard or monitor. A video and keyboard switchbox will not work since no keyboard and monitor ports exist.

**11.** ☑ **A** is correct. The Cisco Configuration Assistant (CCA) is typically used for the management of UC500 series devices. You may also use the web-based interface for management of the device.

☒ **B, C,** and **D** are incorrect. The Security Device Manager (SDM) is used with Cisco ISRs. The SNMP protocol is used to manage and monitor devices, but it is not used to configure UC500 series devices. The RTP protocol is used to carry voice communications.

## 640-460: Describe How QoS Addresses Voice Quality Issues

12. ☑ **B** is correct. Eight classes are defined as class 0 through 7.

    ☒ **A, C, and D** are incorrect. Because eight classes are defined, all of these answers are incorrect.

13. ☑ **D** is correct. Class 5 is typically used for voice data on a VoIP network.

    ☒ **A, B, and C** are incorrect. Class 1 is defined as background data. Class 0 is defined as best effort data. Classes 6 and 7 are used for routing protocols.

14. ☑ **A** is correct. Classes 0 through 5 are used for endpoint data.

    ☒ **B, C, and D** are incorrect. Classes 1–5 are used for endpoint data, but class 0 is as well. Classes 6 and 7 are used for routing protocols. Because classes 6 and 7 are used for routing protocols, it is untrue that classes 0–7 are used for endpoint data.

15. ☑ **C** is correct. The **auto qos voip cisco-phone** command is used to indicate that hardware-based Cisco phones are trusted to mark IP packets with CoS information.

    ☒ **A, B, and D** are incorrect. The **auto qos voip cisco-softphone** command is used to trust computer-based softphones from Cisco. The **auto qos voip phone** command is invalid because the **phone** parameter is not used. The **auto qos voip trust** command allows for CoS marking from any device.

# LAB ANSWER

You will need to add three commands to complete this lab. The first two commands must be added on the appropriate switch ports and they are:

```
auto qos voip cisco-phone
auto qos voip cisco-softphone
```

The third command should be executed on the CME router and it is:

```
ip http server
```

You could also use the **ip http secure-server** command to use HTTPS instead of the unprotected HTTP.

# 18
# Securing VoIP Networks

> *One thing is certainly true about this field of study—it never gets boring.*
>
> —*Gregory B. White*, Security+ Certification All-In-One Exam Guide,
> *on the topic of information security.*

Some people call them hackers. I prefer to call them crackers or attackers; however, regardless of their name, they are an evolving and morphing collective. This group of technically savvy and intensely creative individuals continues to surprise us each month as they develop new techniques for penetrating our networks and systems. While we spend our days implementing, maintaining, and troubleshooting these networks and systems to enable our users to get business results, the attackers often have no such time constraints. Since such a time investment disparity exists, it is essential that we also collaborate to gather our collective protection knowledge as a unit.

Indeed, attackers are developing new methods nearly every day. As network administrators and security practitioners, we must evolve with them. We may not have the time to perform the research that leads to vulnerability discovery and protection against those vulnerabilities, but we must make the time to learn of these vulnerabilities and solutions through books, web sites, magazines, and conferences.

For this reason I have provided extended security information beyond that required by the CCNA Voice exams. In this chapter, you will learn about the threats, vulnerabilities, and exploits to which all networks—including VoIP networks—are vulnerable. You will also learn about some specific vulnerabilities that apply only to VoIP networks. In the last section of this chapter, you will learn about the secure RTP (sRTP) protocol in more detail than presented in Chapter 5.

# Information Security Concepts

Information and network security technologies exist to protect our data and systems from attackers or crackers. You can truly understand why the security technologies are needed only if you understand the attack methods and tools. This section will not be an exhaustive treatment of the cracking world, but it should give you enough information to help you understand why the technologies covered in the last half of the chapter are so important. Here, I'll cover the following major topics:

- Importance of Security
- Threats, Vulnerabilities, and Exploits Defined
- Attack Points
- Hacking Examples
- 0-Day Hacks
- VoIP-Specific Hacks

# Importance of Security

The importance of security varies by organization. The variation exists due to the differing values placed on information and networks within organizations. For example, organizations involved in banking and health care will likely place a greater priority on information security than organizations involved in selling greeting cards. However, every organization needs to classify data so that it can be protected appropriately. The greeting card company will likely place a greater value on its customer database than it will on the log files for the Internet firewall. Both of these data files have value, but one is more valuable than the other and should be classified accordingly so that it can be protected properly. This process is at the core of information security, and it can be defined as follows:

1. Determine the value of the information in question.
2. Apply an appropriate classification based on that value.
3. Implement the proper security solutions for that classification of information.

As an example, your organization may choose to classify information in three categories: internal, public, and internal sensitive. Information classified as internal information may require only appropriate authentication and authorization. Information classified as public information may require neither authentication nor authorization. The internal sensitive information may require authentication, authorization, and storage-based encryption.

You can see why different organizations have different security priorities and needs from this very brief overview of information classification and security measures. It is also true, however, that every organization is at risk to certain threats. Threats like Denial of Service (DoS), worms, and others are often promiscuous in nature. The attacker does not care what networks or systems are damaged in a promiscuous attack. The intention of such an attack is often only to demonstrate the attacker's ability or to serve some other motivation for the attacker, such as curiosity or need for recognition.

Since many attacks are promiscuous in nature, it is very important that every organization place some level of priority on security regardless of the intrinsic value of the information or networks they employ.

## Statistics

Various organizations perform surveys and gather statistics that are useful in gaining a perspective on the need for security. One such organization is *InformationWeek* magazine. Their 2008 security survey ("2008 Security Survey," June 2008) showed that complexity is the greatest difficulty in securing systems. In fact, 62 percent of respondents cited complexity as the biggest security challenge. Administrators are dealing with varied data types, and that data is often unclassified. Without classification, it's difficult to determine how to protect the data. There is good news, however, in *InformationWeek*'s survey: solutions exist that can help reduce the likelihood of a security incident. According to the survey, the following solutions were selected by the indicated percentage of respondents:

- Firewalls (63 percent)
- Antivirus (59 percent)
- Encryption (46 percent)
- VPNs (45 percent)
- Strong passwords (40 percent)
- Spam filtering (35 percent)
- E-mail security (34 percent)

Another organization that reports on the state of information and systems security is the Computer Security Institute (CSI). CSI has performed their annual security survey for more than ten years, and the statistics show that security should be a very important part of any organization's budget and plans. For the five years preceding the 2007 survey, the results showed a drop in the average organization's losses due to cybercrime; however, the 2007 survey reported a significant rise in estimated losses. The good news is that the 2007 losses are still lower than those reported in 2002. This continued lower loss rating may indicate that we are doing a better job of securing our data and assets, or it may only indicate that we are spending less on hardware and software, and therefore, losing less when these assets are stolen or compromised.

The following statistics represent just a few of the important reports from the 2007 CSI Computer Crime and Security Survey:

- 25 percent of responding organizations spend between 6 and 10 percent of the annual IT budget on security.

- 61 percent of responding organizations still outsource no security functions.

- 46 percent indicated that they had experienced a security incident in the previous 12 months, and 10 percent indicated that they were unsure.

- 26 percent of the total responding pool indicated that there had been more than 10 incidents in the previous 12 months.

- Only 36 percent indicated that they accrued no losses due to insider threats, which means that 64 percent experienced an insider attack that led to losses.

- The most common type of attack was the simple abuse of Internet access by valid users.

- Viruses were also a common attack problem, with 52 percent reporting such attacks.

- Only 5 percent reported telecom fraud, and 13 percent reported system penetration; however, it is important to know that some experts estimate as many as 85 percent of all attacks go undetected.

It is clear from these statistics that threats are real and security is important. The statistics show us what is happening, but the theory can help us gain an understanding of why these attacks occur.

## Theory

Why does a seemingly unprovoked attacker attack? This is an important question, but it is difficult to answer with certainty. We are, after all, dealing with human nature. It is easy to understand why an employee who is terminated decides to attack: that employee may want revenge. It is even easy to understand why a competitor might attack: to gain the upper hand on your organization. But why might script kiddies (those who lack deep technical understanding but have the ability to run scripts or follow instructions) choose to attack your organization?

One theory says that they don't choose your organization. Instead, the suggestion is that the attackers are promiscuous. They don't care who the target is, but will attack any target that is vulnerable to a particular exploit. Attacks from script kiddies often fall into this category. These attackers will scan hundreds or even thousands of networks, looking for any network that is vulnerable. When a vulnerable network is found, the attacker will launch other scripts or utilities against the network to penetrate it and gain access to data and resources. This method may also be used by skilled crackers who wish only to gain control of the network and resources so that an attack may be launched against a primary target using these easily penetrated resources. A distributed DoS (DDoS) attack would be an example of just such an attack. This is more than a theory, however; it is a reality. Script kiddies exist in the many thousands and are a prime threat for any organization. This theory says that one form of attack is the promiscuous attack, but another theory explores the motivations of the attackers more deeply and suggests that underlying motives may move the attacker against your organization.

Whether the thinking is correct or incorrect doesn't matter. All that matters is that the attacker perceives your organization to be a threat to something he or she values. These values may include environmental concerns, freedom of speech concerns, freedom from government, or any other value that the attacker holds in high esteem. If the attacker sees your organization as a threat to the realization of these values, this perception may be the motivation for the attack. Depending on the attacker's values, he or she may attempt only to deface your web site or to completely destroy data and systems. Either way, we must protect against these individuals as well.

What is the difference between these two attacker types and why does it matter? The big difference is the answer to the question, "Why?" Why does the attacker want to attack your network or systems? If the attack is promiscuous in nature, traditional protection mechanisms will likely suffice. If it is targeted, the attacker will most likely be willing to spend much more time attempting to penetrate your network, and stronger security mechanisms will be needed. You will need to evaluate your organization's risk of being an intentional target based on strong motivations or of being a promiscuous target based on weak motivations. Additionally, you must remember that even an attack that is promiscuous in nature may be intended to harm another organization through the utilization of your resources.

## Reality

All of these statistics and theories, which I've only covered here in part, lead us to an important reality: Every organization must deal with information, network, and systems security. Protection methods must be considered for the information. These methods will include authentication, authorization, accounting, and encryption. For the network systems, you will need to implement authentication and authorization to ensure that only the assigned personnel may administer the devices. For the systems security, you should ensure secure management of your application code-base and secure programming practices. This picture is the big picture. Throughout the rest of this chapter, you'll learn the finer details of how attackers gain access to your networks, your systems, and ultimately your information.

*One of the key tasks you should perform to secure your VoIP and data networks is a thorough security audit. The security audit will help you locate areas of vulnerability so that you can lock them down. It may also result in more thorough security procedures for ongoing secure management.*

## Threats, Vulnerabilities, and Exploits Defined

A *threat* is defined as an individual, group, circumstance, or event with potential to cause harm to a system. The only requirement for a person or event to be considered a threat is the potential for harm. Certainty is not required. Threats fall into two general categories: intentional and unintentional. Intentional threats include all threats that have intellect behind them. Stated differently, intentional threats are those threats that are planned and executed by an individual or a group of people. Unintentional threats include those events or circumstances that are often called acts of God. Lightning strikes, hurricanes, accidents of any kind, and other similar events are unintentional threats; however, these unintentional threats must be accounted for as well.

A *vulnerability* is defined as a weakness in a system or object. The object may be part of a system, or it may be an independent entity. For example, a VoIP router may be considered as an independent entity or as part of a larger networked system. As an independent entity, the router may have vulnerabilities; however, if you plan to implement the router as part of a larger system, that system must be checked for vulnerabilities as a whole. New vulnerabilities that were nonexistent in individual objects are often discovered when those objects are used together as a system because of the newly introduced network communications. For example, there may be no vulnerabilities in a given software module, but when that module communicates with another module, the communication channel may introduce a new vulnerability.

The discovery of vulnerabilities is known as *vulnerability analysis*. Vulnerability analysis may be performed by a software or hardware vendor in order to test their solutions. It may also be performed by organizations implementing the solution in order to ensure the privacy and protection of their data. In most cases, it will be performed by both the vendor and the implementing organizations. This dual testing is needed because the implementing organizations will be deploying the solution in an environment that is foreign to the vendor and may therefore introduce new vulnerabilities.

An *exploit* is a specific method used to expose and take advantage of a vulnerability. Exploits introduce threats because of vulnerabilities. An exploit may be a procedure that an attacker must perform, or it may come in the form of source code that must be executed.

When an attacker wishes to gain access to a network, he will go through the following basic steps:

1. Scan for devices on the network.
2. Scan for services on those devices.
3. Discover the versions of the running services.
4. Research vulnerabilities.
5. Launch an exploit based on one or more vulnerabilities.

This step-by-step process shows that attacking a network is a simple process. You simply have to have the right tools. For instance, on a Windows system, you could use nMap or Angry IP Scanner to find the devices, services, and versions. These Windows tools are free to download. Next, you can search the Internet for known vulnerabilities, and then you can take advantage of those vulnerabilities through exploits. In many cases, you can download free applications that are specially designed to launch the exploit. As an illustration, AirCrack is a program designed specifically for cracking WEP (Wired Equivalent Privacy) and WPA (Wi-Fi Protected Access) keys on wireless networks and may be used to hack into a weak wireless VoIP network.

When the tools are easy to get and the instructions are easy to follow, the threat increases. This increase is due to the fact that script kiddies can easily launch the exploit. For this reason, WEP cracking of wireless voice links must be considered a valid threat to all organizations since promiscuous attackers can use the exploit against them. WEP cracking is used as an example here, but any other exploit that is similar in nature (it can be acquired and executed without in-depth technical knowledge) should be considered a threat, and protection against it should be part of all security policies and procedures.

## Attack Points

When you are considering the threats to a converged voice and data network, a good starting place is to document the various attack points. An attack point is an entry point to the system or a location within the system that an attacker may attempt to penetrate. At a minimum, the following attack points should be considered:

- ■ Networks
- ■ Servers
- ■ Storage
- ■ Authentication Systems
- ■ Encryption Systems

## Networks

The earliest voice and data networks were wired only; however, with the standardization of wireless technologies in the late 1990s, wireless VoIP has become very popular. We must consider both wired and wireless networks and the potential vulnerabilities they introduce.

**Wired**   Wired networks may be exploited by gaining access to an insecure port or by penetrating the network through a secured port. If the network is connected to the Internet, the Internet connection may also be exploited. Another method of exploit is through dial-up connections. Dial-up connections are becoming increasingly rare, but they do still exist.

An insecure wired port is an Ethernet (or some other wired network standard) port that is enabled and not protected with authentication. IEEE 802.1X is a standard that defines mechanisms for securing such a port. Some organizations choose to implement 802.1X, while others choose to resolve the issue by disabling any unused ports until they are needed. The latter method leaves the network vulnerable to human error or forgetfulness. The 802.1X solution is preferred as long as a secure extensible authentication protocol (EAP) implementation is used.

If a port is insecure, an attacker may connect to the port and begin scanning and ultimately attacking the network. Prime targets include ports in conference rooms, unused offices, and remote areas of warehouses or manufacturing plants. These ports should certainly be secured or disabled anytime they are not in use.

One of the most commonly used attack points is an organization's Internet connection. Many administrators have noted more than a thousand attack attempts in a single day. If you have an Internet connection (hopefully a good firewall), and the connection attempts can be logged, you should enable this logging. After a few days you can look at the log to see how many connection attempts are being made against ports that are commonly attacked. You may be surprised by the number of attempts.

**Wireless**  Wireless networks are vulnerable to penetration through Internet facing connections just like wired networks; however, wireless networks also introduce entirely new vulnerabilities. Instead of focusing on ports, you must focus on connections. Wireless networks allow client devices to connect to the network without the use of preassigned ports. For this reason, disabling ports is not an option. MAC filtering has been used in the past in an attempt to accomplish security at the same level as port management; however, MAC filtering is very weak since an attacker may monitor the network and discover valid MAC addresses. Once the valid addresses are known, the attacker may reconfigure her device to use an allowed MAC address. For this reason, you should consider MAC filtering as a security myth and not as a security solution.

In fact, many myths are associated with wireless security. I'll cover just a few of them here:

- MAC Filtering
- SSID Hiding
- All Modern Equipment Uses "Better WEP"
- Wireless Networks Can't Be Secured

**MAC Filtering**  Vendors of wireless devices and books on wireless networking often provide a list of the "Top 5" or "Top 10" things you should do to secure your wireless LAN. This list usually includes MAC filtering and SSID hiding or cloaking. The reality is that neither of these provides a high level of security. MAC addresses can easily be spoofed, and valid MAC addresses can be identified in just a few moments. For example, an attacker can eliminate the AP in an infrastructure BSS (Basic Service Set) by looking for the MAC address that sends out beacon frames. This will always be the AP in the BSS. With this filtered out of the attacker's protocol analyzer, he has only to find other MAC addresses that are transmitting with a destination MAC address equal to that of the AP. Assuming the captured frames are data frames, the attacker now knows a valid MAC address.

MAC filtering will make it more difficult for an attacker to access your network. The attacker will have to go through the process I've just outlined (or a similar process) to obtain a valid MAC address to spoof. However, you are adding to your workload by implementing such MAC filtering, and you have to ask, "Am I getting a good return on investment for my time?" The answer is usually no. Assuming you are using TKIP (Temporal Key Integrity Protocol) or CCMP (counter mode with cipher block chaining-message authentication code) with a strong EAP type for authentication (or even pre-shared keys), this will be so much more secure than

MAC filtering could ever hope to be that it makes the extra effort of MAC filtering of minimal value. I recommend that you do not concern yourself with MAC filtering in an enterprise or SMB implementation. It may be useful in a SOHO (small office, home office) implementation, but I even question its value then.

**SSID Hiding**    Hiding or cloaking the SSID (service set identifier) of your wireless LAN falls into a similar category as MAC filtering. Both provide very little in the way of security enhancement. Changing the name of your SSID from the vendor defaults can be very helpful because it will make dictionary attacks against pre-shared key implementations more difficult. This is because the SSID is used in the process of creating the pair-wise master key. Hiding the SSID only makes it difficult for casual eavesdroppers to find your network.

Hiding the SSID also forces your valid clients to send out probe requests in order to connect to your wireless LAN, whether using the Windows Wireless Zero Configuration (WZC) utility or your vendor's client software. This activity means that, when the user turns on his or her laptop in a public place, the laptop is broadcasting your SSID out to the world. This could be considered a potential security threat since a rogue AP of any type can be configured to the SSID that is being sent out in the probe requests. Software-based APs can respond to random SSIDs generated by WZC, but hiding your SSID effectively makes every wireless LAN client in existence vulnerable to such attacks since they will all have to send probe requests with the SSID.

I always recommend changing the SSID from the default, but I never recommend hiding the SSID for security purposes. Some people will hide the SSID for usability purposes. Turning off the SSID broadcast in all APs' Beacon frames will prevent client computers from "seeing" the other networks to which they are not supposed to connect. This may reduce confusion, but SSID hiding should not be considered a security solution.

**All Modern Equipment Uses "Better WEP"**    When the initial scare hit, many vendors looked for solutions to the weak IVs (initialization vectors) used in the WEP implementations that existed at the time. Eventually, many vendors began implementing newer WEP solutions that attempted to avoid the weak IVs. As early as 2003, I noticed people posting on the Internet and saying that the newer hardware didn't have this problem. In fact, I have a network-attached storage device that was purchased in 2005 that includes a built-in AP. This device is running the most recent firmware from the vendor (D-Link, in this case), and I can connect a brand-new Intel Centrino chipset laptop to the device using WEP. While monitoring from another computer, I am able to capture weak IVs and crack the WEP key in a matter of minutes. You simply cannot trust that a vendor has actually implemented algorithms that protect you against WEP weaknesses just because the hardware is newer. Instead, you need to monitor the communications with the device in order to determine if weak IVs are being used. It's easier to implement WPA or WPA2, so I recommend that.

**Wireless Networks Can't Be Secured**    Don't allow these last few false security methods to keep you from implementing a wireless LAN. Wireless LANs can be implemented in a secure fashion using IEEE 802.11i (Clause 9 of IEEE 802.11-2007) and strong EAP types. In fact, they can be made far more secure than most wired LANs, since most wired LANs do not implement any real authentication mechanisms at the node level. If you buy into the concept that wireless LANs cannot be secured, and you decide not to implement a wireless LAN for this reason, you will likely open your network to more frequent rogue AP installations from users who desire wireless access to the network. The simplest way to avoid or at least diminish the occurrence of user-installed rogue APs is to implement a secure wireless LAN for the users. In the end, wireless LANs can be secured, but you must be aware of the security myths surrounding them.

on the
**job**

*If you would like to learn much more about wireless networks and wireless security and their impacts on VoIP, consider reading the CWNA/CWSP All-in-One Guide published by McGraw-Hill. The book also helps you prepare for the CWNA and CWSP certification examinations.*

## Servers

The second attack point that I will cover is the server or servers on your network. Servers are used to store data, provide services to users, or provide services to other systems. Many servers are running Linux or Windows operating systems, and these systems are heavily targeted by attackers because of their popularity. Attack methods include:

- Exploiting known vulnerabilities
- Exploiting configuration errors
- Exploiting running services

Attackers can locate known vulnerabilities using search engines, discussion forums, and other web sites. Common web sites used for vulnerability discovery include:

- Microsoft.com/security
- MilW0rm.com
- Zone-H.org
- HackerWatch.org
- Secunia.com/community

As a network administrator, you should visit these web sites regularly to keep your knowledge up-to-date in the hardware, operating systems, and applications you are utilizing.

Configuration error exploits can often be avoided by implementing a strong security management process. The process would usually include threat and vulnerability analysis, security policy development, and policy implementation. By implementing configurations based on solid security policies, you reduce the likelihood of configuration errors. However, it does require a team effort because each technician must abide by the policies when configuring a device. An attacker requires only one misconfigured device to gain entry to the network. Auditing and security assessments may also be used to ensure proper configuration.

Many services are insecure regardless of the implementation method used. For example, Telnet sends authentication credentials as clear text when implemented according to the standards. This insecurity is why SSH is recommended for Cisco ISRs instead of Telnet. FTP also sends the username and password in the clear. Passwords sent as clear text can be easily retrieved using protocol analyzers. This statement is particularly true of wireless networks that do not implement encryption, such as wireless hotspots and older networks, because they are more vulnerable to undetected eavesdropping than wired networks.

## Storage

Many storage attacks are really authentication attacks. The attacker performs password guessing, password sniffing, or offline password cracking in order to gain access to the storage location.

In addition to authentication attacks, an attacker may take advantage of vulnerabilities inherent in the embedded operating system of the device. For example, many Network Attached Storage (NAS) devices use embedded Linux. Since the operating system is implemented through firmware, the administrator may fail to update the operating system as often as normal computers running the same operating system. This delay can result in vulnerabilities being exposed for longer periods. The moral of the story is simple: update the firmware on your devices anytime a security vulnerability is patched and the firmware does not introduce problems into the system. If you cannot update the firmware because the vendor is no longer updating it, consider placing the device behind a router or firewall that can be used to block all traffic that may result in the exploiting of the vulnerability.

## Authentication Systems

Authentication systems are used to validate user identities and allow for authorization of the users for access to resources. Authentication systems are based on credentials. Credentials can include any of the following three types:

- Something you know
- Something you have
- Something you are

Something you know includes passwords and personal identification numbers (PINs). Something you have includes keys, smart cards, and RFID (radio frequency identification) chips. Something you are includes biometrics such as fingerprint scanners, retina scanners, and even weight measurements.

Authentication systems can be attacked by exploiting weak protocols, weak credential stores, or weak credentials. Weak protocols are protocols that are implemented poorly. The passwords may be sent across the network, or another vulnerability may be inherent in the system. Weak credential stores are exploited by cracking the encryption used on the store or by simply accessing the credential store when no encryption is implemented. Weak credentials are usually weak passwords. Today, weak passwords are passwords that are less than eight characters and those passwords that do not include multiple character types. However, a password such as "thehorsejumpedoverthemoononabroom" is very secure even though it does not contain multiple character types. The ultimate determiner of the strength of a password, with few exceptions, is the size of the password pool. The unusually long password referenced here is more than 30 characters long. A 30-character password with only lowercase letters is part of a password pool that includes 254,186,582,832,900,000,000,000,000,000,000,000,000 possible passwords. This number represents more than 254 undecillion passwords. To put it into perspective, you could guess 100 trillion passwords each second, and it would take more than 40 quadrillion years to guess the password on average.

The math in the preceding paragraph assumes a blind brute force attack, but clearly even with advanced methods including rainbow tables and intelligent algorithms, it would take far too long to make it worth the attempt. However, you must consider whether it is feasible to ask users to remember 30-character passwords. This is why we usually require shorter passwords with character complexity. The pool is still large, but the password is shorter and may be easier to remember.

My point with this example is simple: if you have strong enough passwords, you will be safe enough for most data. If you feel passwords cannot be made strong enough, due to the human element (for example, writing passwords on sticky notes), you should consider other authentication methods such as smart cards or biometrics.

## Encryption Systems

Sensitive data should be encrypted in two places: during transit and during storage. Encryption for transmitted data is processor intensive and may introduce additional processing delay in VoIP systems; however, the trade-off may be worth it if security is of utmost importance to your organization. In-transit encryption solutions are vulnerable to various sniffing attacks. For example, WEP encrypts traffic for wireless LANs, but the algorithm and keys were improperly implemented resulting in the ability to easily crack the WEP key and then gain access to the transmitted data.

Storage encryption is most frequently attacked by attacking the key store. You may have noticed that I'm not mentioning brute force methods with encryption. Brute force is seldom used to crack any encryption scheme due to the time required. Even DES (Digital Encryption Standard) at 40 bits takes too long for most attacks. For this reason, attackers will usually look for vulnerabilities in the key store or in the method used to access the key store. I give an example of this in the "Hacking Examples" section of this chapter under the title "Encryption Hacks."

# Hacking Examples

With an awareness of the common attack points, you're ready to investigate a few hacking examples. You will improve your understanding of security by learning about specific hacking methods. In the next few pages, I'll present various hacks that can be used against a selection of the attack points previously discussed.

## Network Hacks

Cracking WEP is a perfect example of a network hack. The Wired Equivalent Privacy (WEP) protocol is used to encrypt data on wireless LANs and to authenticate users to the wireless LAN based on the fact that the user knows the WEP key. There are numerous problems with the WEP protocol that result in the ability to crack it easily.

An understanding of the basic WEP process will help you to understand the weaknesses that are covered next. The WEP process starts with the inputs to the process. These inputs include the data that should be encrypted (usually called plaintext), the secret key (40 bits or 104 bits), and the IV (24 bits). These inputs are passed through the WEP algorithms to generate the output (the ciphertext or encrypted data).

Since WEP is a Layer 2 security implementation, it doesn't matter what type of data is being transmitted as long as it originates above Layer 2 in the OSI model. To encrypt the data, the RC4 algorithm is used to create a pseudorandom string of bits called a *keystream*. The WEP static key and the IV are used to seed the pseudorandom number generator used by the RC4 algorithm. The resulting keystream is XORed against the plaintext to generate the ciphertext. The ciphertext alone is transferred without the keystream; however, the IV is sent to the receiver. The receiver uses the IV that was transmitted and the stored static WEP key to feed the same pseudorandom number generator to regenerate the same keystream. The XOR is reversed at the receiver to recover the original plaintext from the ciphertext.

WEP was never intended to provide impenetrable security, but was only intended to protect against casual eavesdropping. With the rapid increase in processor speeds, cracking WEP has become a very short task, and it can no longer be considered for protection against any organized attack. The weaknesses in WEP include the following:

- Brute force attacks
- Dictionary attacks
- Weak IV attacks
- Re-injection attacks
- Storage attacks

In late 2000 and early 2001, the security weaknesses of WEP became clear. Since then many attack methods have been developed, and tools have been created that make these attack methods simple to implement for entry-level technical individuals.

The *brute force* attack method is a key-guessing method that attempts every possible key in order to crack the encryption. With 104-bit WEP, this is really not a feasible attack method; however, 40-bit WEP can usually be cracked in one or two days with brute force attacks using more than 20 distributed computers. The short timeframe is accomplished using a distributed cracking tool like jc-wepcrack.

jc-wepcrack is actually two tools: the client and the server. You would first start the tool on the server and configure it for the WEP key size you think the target wireless LAN uses and provide it with a pcap file (a capture of encrypted frames) from that network. Next, you launch the client program and configure it to connect to the server. The client program will request a portion of the keys to be guessed and will attempt to access the encrypted frames with those keys. With the modern addition of Field Programmable Gate Arrays (FPGAs), which are add-on boards for hardware acceleration, the time to crack can be reduced by more than 30 times. In fairness, the 20 computers would have to be P4 3.6-GHz machines or better. If you chose to go the FPGA route, you would be spending a lot of money to crack that WEP key. Since smart enterprises will no longer be using WEP, you would not likely gain access to any information that is as valuable as your hacking network.

The *dictionary* attack method relies on the fact that humans often use words as passwords. The key is to use a dictionary-cracking tool that understands the conversion algorithm used by a hardware vendor to convert the typed password into the WEP key. This algorithm is not part of IEEE 802.11 and is implemented differently by the different vendors. Many vendors allow the user to type a passphrase that is then converted to the WEP key using the Neesus Datacom or MD5 WEP key-generation algorithms. The Neesus Datacom algorithm is notoriously insecure and has resulted in what is sometimes called the Newsham-21-bit attack because it reduces the usable WEP key pool to 21 bits instead of 40 when using a 40-bit WEP key. This smaller pool can be exhausted in about 6–7 seconds on a P4 3.6-GHz single machine using modern cracking tools against a pcap file. Even MD5-based conversion algorithms are far too weak and should not be considered secure because they are still used to implement WEP, which is insecure due to weak IVs as well.

The *weak IV* attacks are based on the faulty implementation of RC4 in the WEP protocols. The IV is prepended to the static WEP key to form the full WEP encryption key used by the RC4 algorithm. This means than an attacker already knows the first 24 bits of the encryption key since the IV is sent in cleartext as part of the frame header. Additionally, Fluhrer, Mantin, and Shamir identified "weak" IVs in a paper released in 2001. These weak IVs result in certain values becoming more statistically probable than others and make it easier to crack the static WEP key. The 802.11 frames that use these weak IVs have come to be known as *interesting* frames. With enough interesting frames collected, you can crack the WEP key in a matter of seconds. This reduces the total attack time to less than 5–6 minutes on a busy WLAN. The weak IVs discovered by Fluhrer, Mantin, and Shamir are now among a larger pool of known weak IVs. Since 2001, another 16 classes of weak IVs have been discovered by David Hulton (h1kari) and KoreK.

What if the WEP-enabled network being attacked is not busy and you cannot capture enough interesting frames in a short window of time? The answer is a *re-injection* attack. This kind of attack usually re-injects ARP packets onto the wireless LAN. The program aireplay can detect ARP packets based on their unique size and does not need to decrypt the packets. By re-injecting the ARP packets back onto the wireless LAN, it will force the other clients to reply and cause the creation of large amounts of wireless LAN traffic very quickly. For 40-bit WEP cracking, you usually want around 300,000 total frames to get enough interesting frames and for 104-bit WEP cracking you may want about 1 million frames.

*Storage* attacks are those methods used to recover WEP or WPA keys from their storage locations. On Windows computers, for example, WEP keys have often been stored in the registry in an encrypted form. An older version of this attack method was the Lucent Registry Crack; however, it appears that the problem has not been fully removed from our modern networks. An application named *wzcook* can retrieve the stored WEP keys used by Windows' Wireless Zero Configuration. This application recovers WEP or WPA-PSK keys (since they are effectively the same, WPA just improves the way the key is managed and implemented) and comes with the Aircrack-ng tools used for cracking these keys. The application works only if you have administrator access to the local machine, but in an environment with poor physical security and poor user training, it is not difficult to find a machine that is logged on and using the wireless LAN for this attack.

WEP makes up the core of pre-RSNA security in IEEE 802.11 networks. I hope the reality that WEP can be cracked in less than 5 minutes is enough to make you realize that you shouldn't be using it on your networks. The only exception would be an installation where you are required to install a wireless LAN using older hardware and you have no other option. I've encountered this scenario in a few churches where I've assisted in their network implementation. The problem was not with the infrastructure equipment in any of the scenarios. The problem was with the client devices that the church members wanted to use to connect to the wireless LAN. These devices did not support WPA or WPA2, and we were forced to use either WEP or no security at all. While WEP can certainly be cracked quickly, at least it has to be cracked. Open System authentication with no WEP, WPA, or WPA2 security is just that: open.

In the end, businesses and organizations that have sensitive data to protect must take a stand for security and against older technologies. This means that you should not be implementing WEP anywhere in your organization. When you have the authority of a corporation, the government, or even a nonprofit oversight board, you can usually sell them on the need for better security with a short (5 minutes or less) demonstration of just how weak WEP is. If you're implementing Voice over wireless LAN, these insights will be tremendously valuable.

## Password Hacks

Most computer access controls are based on passwords. Weak passwords are one of the most serious security threats in networking, for obvious reasons. Intruders easily guess commonly used and known passwords, such as "password", "admin", and so on. Short words or strings of characters are often at risk from a brute force password attack program, and passwords made from words found in the dictionary can be guessed using dictionary attacks.

All of this information is common knowledge to security administrators, but what is not commonly considered is that passwords flow from client to server across unsecured networks all the time. In the past, there was a common misconception that wired networks were secure, but wireless LANs have opened the eyes of many administrators and attackers that networking systems using passwords passed in clear text across any medium are vulnerable to interception. For this reason, password encryption has become very popular along with security mechanisms, such as Kerberos, that implement such encryption. Two auditing tools often used by administrators and hackers alike to view clear text passwords are Win Sniffer and ettercap.

**Win Sniffer**    Win Sniffer is a password capture utility capable of capturing FTP, HTTP, ICQ, Telnet, SMTP, POP3, NNTP, and IMAP usernames and passwords in a shared medium networking environment such as wireless APs or wired hubs. Win Sniffer is installed on a Windows-based computer, usually a laptop being used to audit wireless networks. In a switched network, Win Sniffer can capture only passwords that originate from either the client that sent the password or the server that sent the client the information directly. Win Sniffer can be used to capture your own passwords (when saved in applications) when you forget them. Sample output from Win Sniffer is shown in Figure 18-1.

Consider Figure 18-2 in which the user is checking e-mail over an unencrypted wireless LAN segment. An attacker is scanning the wireless segment using a password sniffer and picks up the user's e-mail login information and the domain from which the user is checking the e-mail. The attacker now has access to the user's e-mail account and can read all of the user's e-mail.

FIGURE 18-1

Sample password
output from Win
Sniffer

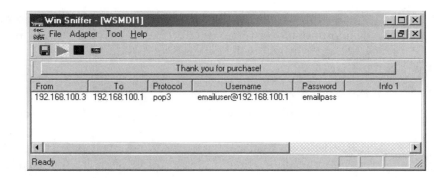

Public access wireless networks (hotspots) such as those found in airports or in metropolitan areas are some of the most vulnerable areas for user attacks. Users that are not familiar with how easy it is to obtain their login information through a peer-to-peer attack unknowingly check their e-mail or access their corporate network—even VoIP systems—and end up giving access to their accounts to a hacker. Once hackers obtain a valid login to a corporate account, they are now well equipped to try to obtain further access into the network to locate more sensitive information.

FIGURE 18-2

Obtaining
passwords from
unsuspecting
users

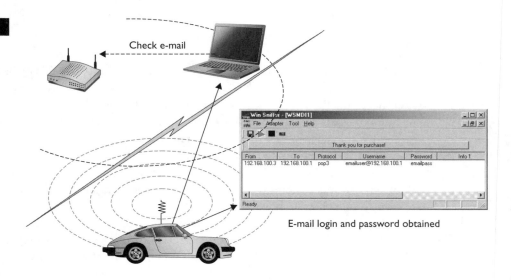

**Revelation**    On Windows systems, a tool that can be used to discover passwords is Revelation. This program will allow you to drag a curser over a password field in any login dialog box or web page and have the password revealed. Of course, to use this tool, the user would have to have left his or her computer logged on, and you would have to have the ability to run the tool. However, with users saving their passwords in web forms so frequently today, this tool can reveal passwords for many situations. To protect against it, you can disallow the tool from running through Windows Group Policies or disallow users from saving their passwords. Neither method will provide complete protection, but they can provide extra protection and make it more difficult for the attacker. For example, the attacker would have to use a hex editor to modify the binary file (revelation.exe) in order to get around the hash-based Group Policies in Windows Server 2003 and supported by Windows XP clients. Revelation can be used on wired and wireless systems in order to discover passwords.

**ettercap**    Written by Alberto Ornaghi and Marco Valleri, ettercap is one of the most powerful password capture and auditing tools available today. ettercap supports almost every operating system platform and can be found at http://ettercap. sourceforge.net. ettercap is capable of gathering data even in a switched environment, which far exceeds the abilities of most other audit tools. ettercap uses a menu-style user interface, making it user friendly. Some of the features available in ettercap are:

- Character injection into an established connection: A user can inject characters to a server (emulating commands) or to a client (emulating replies) while maintaining a live connection.
- SSH1 support: A user can analyze usernames and passwords, and even the data of the SSH1 connection. ettercap is the first software capable of analyzing an SSH connection in full-duplex mode.
- HTTPS support: A user can sniff HTTP-SSL data even if the connection is made through a proxy.
- Remote traffic through a GRE tunnel: A user can analyze remote traffic through a GRE tunnel from a remote router.
- PPTP broker: A user can perform man-in-the-middle attacks against PPTP tunnels.

- Plug-ins support: A user can create plug-ins using the ettercap's API. Many plug-ins are included in the base package.
- Password collector for: Telnet, FTP, POP, RLogin, SSH1, ICQ, SMB, MySQL, HTTP, NNTP, X11, Napster, IRC, RIP, BGP, SOCKS-5, IMAP4, VNC, LDAP, NFS, SNMP, Half-Life, Quake 3, MSN, and YMSG.
- Packet filtering/dropping: A user can configure a filter that searches for a particular string (even hex) in the TCP or UDP payload and replace it with a new string or drop the entire packet.
- OS fingerprinting: A user can fingerprint the operating system of the victim host and its network adapter.
- Kill a connection: From the connections list, a user can kill all the connections he or she chooses.
- Passive scanning of the LAN: A user can retrieve information about any of the following: hosts in the LAN, open ports, services version, host type (gateway, router, or simple host). and estimated distance (in hops).
- Check for other poisoners: ettercap has the ability to actively or passively find other poisoners on the LAN. These would be devices that have hacked the arp cache to point to improper devices and is known as arp poisoning.
- Bind sniffed data to a local port: A user can connect to a port on a client and decode protocols or inject data.

In addition to these features, the newer versions of ettercap support internal WEP decryption for wireless packets. When you provide the WEP key, which you must know or have previously cracked, the packets can be decrypted on-the-fly for storage and later viewing.

**L0phtCrack**    In many cases, operating systems implement password authentication and encryption at the application layer. Such is the case with Microsoft Windows file sharing and NetLogon processes. The challenge/response mechanism used by Microsoft over the years (and over several operating system and service pack upgrades) has changed from LM (weak), to NTLM (medium), to NTLMv2 (strong). Before NTLMv2, tools such as L0phtCrack could easily crack these hashes. It is important to properly configure your Windows operating system to use NTLMv2 and not to use the weaker versions. This process must be accomplished manually, and instructions can be found at www.technet.com.

L0phtCrack, also known by the newer name LC5 (short for L0phtCrack version 5), is a password auditing and recovery tool created by L0pht Heavy Industries, now owned by @stake. L0phtCrack is used to audit passwords on Windows operating systems. L0phtCrack can capture password hashes in many different ways, but two in particular that auditors frequently attempt are file share authentication and network logons. L0phtCrack can capture these challenge/response conversations and derive the password. The stronger the challenge/response mechanism used, the more difficult it is for L0phtCrack to crack them. The output of a password recovery session in L0phtCrack version 4 (LC4) is shown in Figure 18-3.

Once the intruder has captured the targeted password hashes (as many as deemed appropriate in a given audit), the hashes are imported into LC4's engine, and a dictionary attack automatically ensues. If the dictionary attack is unsuccessful, a brute force attack automatically begins. The processor power of the computer doing the audit will determine how fast the hash can be broken. L0phtCrack has many modes for capturing password hashes and dumping password repositories. One mode allows for "sniffing" in a shared medium (such as wireless), while another goes directly after the Windows Security Access Manager (SAM).

**FIGURE 18-3**

Sample password auditing output from L0phtCrack 4

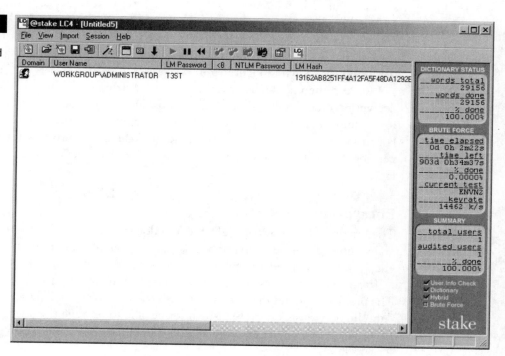

Windows 2000 Service Pack 3 introduced a new feature called "SysKey," short for "System Key." This feature, implemented by running the syskey.exe executable file, encrypts the SAM such that L0phtCrack cannot extract passwords from it as was possible before it was encrypted. L0phtCrack has the capability of letting the auditor know that he or she is auditing a SAM that has been encrypted so the auditor will not waste much time attempting to extract that password.

on the **Job**

***While L0phtCrack will still work for password auditing, Symantec acquired @stake in 2004 and discontinued support for L0phtCrack version 5 (LC5) and all other versions. They cite U.S. government regulations on export as the reason for the dismissed support.***

**LRC**    Proxim OriNOCO PC Cards store an encrypted hash of the WEP key in the Windows registry. The Lucent Registry Crack (LRC) is a simple command-line utility written to decrypt these encrypted values. The problem is getting these values from another computer—one that has the WEP key installed that the attacker wants to obtain. This task is accomplished through a remote registry connection. The attacker will make a remote registry connection to the target computer using the tools in Window's Registry Editor on his own computer. Once the hacker is connected, he must simply know where the key is located in the registry in order to copy and paste it into a text document on his computer. These encrypted strings are stored per profile, as shown in Figure 18-4.

LRC can then be run against this encrypted string to produce the WEP key. The decryption process takes about 1–2 seconds. Once the attacker has the WEP key, it is a simple matter of plugging it into his computer to gain access to the network. For this reason, wireless end users should implement peer attack safeguards such as personal firewall software or IPSec policies. The LRC operation process is shown in Figure 18-5.

## Encryption Hacks

The Encrypting File System (EFS) in Windows 2000 and later operating systems is an example of storage encryption. It is also an example of potential weaknesses in encryption systems. EFS is vulnerable to key store attacks.

In any encryption system, the most difficult thing to do is to protect the key store. The problem is found in the method used to access the keys. If a user needs to decrypt data she previously encrypted, she must be able to retrieve the encryption key. EFS encrypts the file encryption key (FEK) with the user's public key. This process

OriNOCO WEP key in encrypted form stored in the Windows registry

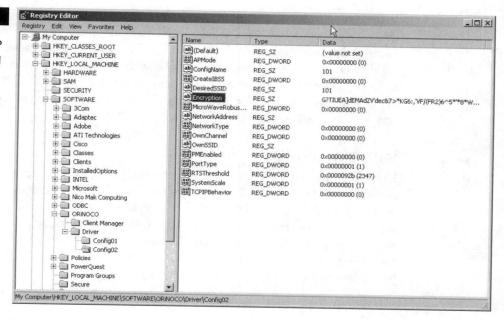

means that the user's private key will be needed to decrypt the FEK, which will be used to decrypt the file. The question is, how does the user access her private key? The answer is simple: automatically.

By default, when the user opens a file that is encrypted by EFS, the user's private key is automatically retrieved, and the FEK is then decrypted followed by the decryption of the data file. As long as the user is logged on, it all happens automatically. This process reveals the potential weakness: the user's authentication credentials.

**FIGURE 18-5**

LRC cracking the encryption used for safeguarding WEP keys

EFS uses a solid encryption algorithm with a sufficient key length; however, the user's password may be very weak, and this reality introduces an important vulnerability into the system. If the attacker can guess the user's password, all of the data encrypted by that user will now be accessible to the attacker in many, if not most, scenarios. However, this is not a unique problem with EFS. If a user implements the very popular Pretty Good Privacy (PGP) desktop encryption system and uses weak passphrases, the data may be equally vulnerable.

## VoIP Eavesdropping

Eavesdropping in VoIP is different from the traditional eavesdropping in data networks, but the basic concept remains the same. In a data network, you capture data packets and reassemble data files. In a VoIP network, you must intercept the signaling and associated media streams of a call, and then reassemble this data into an audio stream or file for listening. The signaling messages use separate network protocols (that is, UDP or TCP) and ports from the media itself. Media streams usually are carried over UDP/RTP. The process basically involves three steps:

1. Capture and decode the RTP packets.
2. Rebuild a session.
3. Save the rebuilt session as an audio file, or play the session from the application.

All three steps can be performed in WireShark, which is a free protocol analyzer. To protect against this, you must use encryption or a network topology and security mechanisms that prohibit network sniffing (such as a switched infrastructure that is properly secured); however, encryption is the best choice. Encryption is best because eavesdropping is passive and very difficult to detect.

## Social Engineering

Social engineering is defined as persuading someone to give you or tell you something that they should not give you or tell you through the manipulation of human or social interactions. Successful social engineering attacks occur because the target might be ignorant of the organization's information security policies or intimidated by an intruder's knowledge, expertise, or attitude. Social engineering is one of the most dangerous and successful methods of hacking into any IT infrastructure. If defeating WEP has stumped the hacker, the hacker might try to trick an employee who is authorized to have the WEP key into giving up this information. Once the hacker has the WEP key, the hacker will enter it into his own computer and use the available monitoring tools or protocol analyzers to capture sensitive data in real time, just as though there were no security. For this reason, social engineering has the potential of rendering even the most sophisticated security solution useless.

Hackers are not always like they are portrayed in movies: the cigarette-smoking, caffeine-loaded teenager in a dark room in a basement with multiple high-speed connections to the Internet, loud music, and plenty of spare time. Many times the most successful and damaging network intrusion is accomplished in broad daylight through clever efforts of someone who walks into a business like they own it. In the very same manner, a hired professional security auditor should openly attempt intrusion as one tactic of testing security policy adherence.

There are some well-known targets for this type of attack:

- The helpdesk
- Contractors
- Employees

**The Helpdesk**   The helpdesk is in place to assist those individuals who need help with some aspect of a computer or network. It becomes quite awkward in many situations for the helpdesk not to provide answers to questions when the person on the other end of the line seems to know what they need. It is not an easy task to train helpdesk personnel not to be helpful in certain situations; nevertheless, this type of education is crucial to corporate network security. The helpdesk should be trained to know exactly which pieces of information related to the wireless network should not be given out without the proper authorization or without following specific processes put in place by security policy. Items that might be marked for exclusion are:

- SSID of access points
- WEP key(s)
- Physical locations of infrastructure devices
- Usernames and passwords for network access and services (that is, e-mail)
- Passwords and SNMP strings for infrastructure devices
- VoIP solutions in use

The auditor should (and the hacker *will*) use two particular tactics when dealing with helpdesk personnel:

- Forceful, yet professional language
- Playing dumb

Both of these approaches have the same effect: getting the requested information. Helpdesk personnel understand that their job is to help people with their problems. They also understand that their manager will not be happy with them if their customers are not happy with the service they are receiving. By threatening to speak with the manager, the social engineer can get the helpdesk person to give over the requested information just to appease and settle down the social engineer. Some people are just naturally insecure when dealing with personal conflict, and some people are easily intimidated by anyone with an authoritative voice. Both of these situations can be used to the advantage of the social engineer. The human factor has to be overcome with training, discipline, and repetitively following documented procedures.

Playing dumb is a favorite of many social engineers. The helpdesk person is usually disarmed and stops paying attention when they figure out that the person to whom they are speaking knows very little. This situation is exacerbated when the "dumb" customer is overly polite and thankful for the help. It's important that a helpdesk person be alert to this tactic at all times. A social engineer is likely to call over and over, hoping to speak with different representatives, and taking different approaches with each.

**Contractors**   IT contractors are commonplace at many businesses today, and very few, if any, are put through organizational security training. Few are given a copy of the company security policy or required to sign privacy agreements. For this reason, and because IT contractors, like the helpdesk people, are there to help, IT contractors can be especially good targets for social engineers. Contractors are aware of the specific details about network resources because they are often on-site to design or repair the network. In wanting to be helpful to their customer, contractors often give out too much information to people who are not authorized to have such information. For this reason, strong security solutions that rely on multi-factor authentication are recommended.

**Employees**   Since people spend many hours each day with each other at their work location, they often share private information—such as network login information—with one another. It is also common to see that same login information on sticky notes under keyboards and on monitors. Another problem is that most computer users are not computer network or security savvy. For this reason, they might not recognize spyware, hack attempts, or social engineering.

VoIP technology is still very new to many organizations. Employees who are not educated about network security may not realize the dangers that unauthorized access via the network can pose to the organization and to them personally. Specifically, nontechnical employees who use the network should be aware of the fact that their computers can be attacked in a peer-to-peer fashion at work, at home, or on any public wireless network if the device uses wireless networking. Social engineers take advantage of all of these facts and even engineer elaborate stories that would fool almost anyone not specifically trained to recognize social engineering attacks.

Similar to social engineering is shoulder surfing. Shoulder surfing is a nontechnical way of capturing information. As its name implies, you simply watch over the user's shoulder to see what information you can gather. Frequently, users enter their passwords slowly enough that you can see what they are typing. At other times, you can see configuration screens with information about SSIDs for WLANs, pre-shared keys when WPA-Personal is being utilized, VoIP configuration settings, encryption passwords, and more.

## 0-Day Hacks

In the end, you must stay up-to-date on the various vulnerabilities that may pose a threat to your network. You may have noticed that most of the chapter so far has not been specific to VoIP networks. Why is this? Simple: VoIP networks are vulnerable to the same exploits as traditional wired and wireless networks. This does make your efforts somewhat easier if you're already familiar with network security; however, you must remember that the impact of security technologies can be detrimental on VoIP networks. As an example, the implementation of encryption for VoIP calls could be just enough to take your network latency to an unacceptable level. Balancing between security and performance is an important issue in VoIP networks. The phrase "0-day hacks" is a reference to the newest attack methods in use. You will need to frequent web sites mentioned in this chapter in order to keep your knowledge fresh.

## VoIP-Specific Hacks

While VoIP networks are vulnerable to the same attacks as other data networks, it is dangerous to assume that you need to protect only against traditional network attacks in VoIP implementations. The majority of attacks will indeed be typical network attacks; however, there are specific attacks to which VoIP networks and devices are vulnerable.

Theft of service is important to consider. If an attacker can gain access to your VoIP network as a valid client, she may place long-distance calls across your PSTN trunks. This can cause performance problems for your valid users and increase the cost of your telephone service.

Voice spam is another potential problem. Vishing (similar to its cousin—phishing) is used to gather information from unsuspecting VoIP users. The attacker may spoof her caller ID information so that the victim trusts the caller's credibility. In the end, the attacker is performing social engineering, but she is taking advantage of the weaknesses in many VoIP implementations.

In addition to the attack methods that are somewhat unique to VoIP implementations, there are hacking tools designed for hacking VoIP protocols and systems. Table 18-1 lists many of these tools and their capabilities.

**TABLE 18-1**    VoIP Attack Tools

| Attack Tool | Capabilities |
| --- | --- |
| SIP-scan | This tool can scan a range of IP addresses looking for SIP devices. |
| SIP-kill | A tool for small-scale DoS attacks that can kill a SIP session. |
| SIPcrack | This tool includes two programs: SIPdump and SIPcrack. SIPdump sniffs SIP logins off the network, and SIPcrack brute forces the password. |
| VoIPong | Sniffs all VoIP conversations off the wire and automatically saves each conversation to a sound file. Support is included for SIP and H.323. Only G.711 calls can be decoded. |
| SIPp | A testing tool and traffic generator for the SIP protocol. It can be used to connect with alternate CID information and to simply monitor SIP traffic statistics. |

# Security Solutions

If you look at the Computer Security Institute's annual security surveys, you will notice one startling thing: every year a large percentage of respondents indicate that no security incidents occurred within their organizations. I suppose you could indicate such, if an incident is defined as a security breach that causes known losses; however, if you remove the word "known," so that it is defined as a security breach that causes losses, it seems to me that the only responses to the survey question could be yes or unsure. If I am sure that a security incident has not occurred, I probably don't understand security.

The real issue here seems related to the definition you choose to use for the word "incident." The term *incident* commonly means a single or distinct event, and there is no indication that the event was actually observed, analyzed, or detected by anyone. Many security resources define an incident as a detected security event that adversely affects systems or data. This definition is not effective since an incident may occur without detection. For this reason, I prefer to define incident using the Sans.org security terminology glossary's definition: "an adverse network event in an information system or network or the threat of the occurrence of such an event."

This thinking comes from another quote by Bruce Schneier, one of the world's foremost experts on security, who says, "there's no such thing as absolute security." You can rephrase this quote with a different focus to say, "If your system is completely secure, your users can't use it." If you decide to implement a firewall filtering rule that disallows traffic destined for TCP port 21, you've just made it impossible for users to connect to FTP servers through that firewall. The decision has forced a trade-off: you aren't susceptible to direct FTP server attacks, but you can't use the FTP server through the firewall.

With this understanding, you will explore the different security solutions available to you. You will learn how they help to protect your converged network, but unlike in many books, you'll also be told the reality of how they can impact the network negatively. Stated differently, you'll learn about the trade-offs. These trade-offs become very important in VoIP networks because performance is paramount to success. By keeping the following concepts in mind, you will make better decisions related to network security in general and VoIP security specifically:

- A system cannot be made absolutely secure and still provide a useful function to the users.
- Incidents occur whether you detect them or not.
- Higher security requirements usually result in lowered usability or lowered performance or both.

# Concepts and Components of Security Design

We'll look at security design and implementation from four perspectives:

- Network Design and Security
- Perimeter Security Solutions
- Connectivity Solutions
- Security Monitoring

In addition to these categories, we'll also review specific VoIP tools and technologies that provide solutions to security issues in converged networks.

## Network Design and Security

Security should be designed into a system or network. It should not be an afterthought. You will have a more secure network when security is designed into the implementation from the start. Instead of thinking of specific attacks and specific countermeasures alone, you may want to consider security as a system. A system is defined as a group of independent but interrelated elements that form a whole.

A good example of the fact that security is a system is a bank vault. A bank vault is usually thought of as a single entity that helps to protect valuables, but it is actually a group of independent and interrelated elements. The vault combination lock is combined with procedures and policies as well as alarms and response mechanisms to form the whole of the bank vault. Additionally, many vaults are layered: one door opens the vault, and smaller doors may open compartments within the vault.

Security design is about building systems and implementing layers that help to protect valuable assets. When you design a security system, you are designing a unique system that is aimed at keeping certain actions—attacks—from working.

You are designing a system to protect against intelligent, intentional, and malicious attacks. This process is very different from safety management, where you are protecting against unintentional problems that occur randomly. Security attacks may be intentional and occur at specially selected times that provide the attacker with the greatest opportunity.

Two key principles assist in security design: layered security and isolation. Layered security implies that more than one protection mechanism is used between an attack point and a valued resource. Layered security is sometimes called "defense in depth." Isolation provides virtual or literal separation of one set of users or services from another set of users or services.

### Demilitarized Zones and Perimeter Networks

A demilitarized zone (DMZ) is a concept borrowed from military operations. It defines a portion of the network that is not as secure as the rest of the network. The DMZ is usually located between the private network and the Internet or another external network. DMZs are also known as perimeter networks since they exist at the edge of the private network. The DMZ acts as a location for Internet service servers and as a point of inspection and authentication for access into the internal or private network.

Most organizations will choose to place a firewall between the Internet and the DMZ. An additional firewall will usually be placed between the DMZ and the private network. This dual-firewall implementation allows for reduced restrictions at the ingress to the DMZ from the Internet and increased restrictions at the ingress from the DMZ to the private network. Figure 18-6 provides an example of a DMZ or perimeter network.

**FIGURE 18-6**

Demilitarized zone

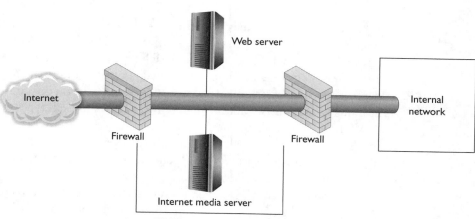

DMZ/Perimeter network

**VLANs**    Virtual LANs or VLANs are used to segment a physical network into multiple logical networks. VLANs operate within the switches and routers on your network, and client computers are usually unaware of their participation in a VLAN. To the client computers, the VLANs look and operate just like a physically segmented LAN. For this reason, VLANs can be used to provide increased security on converged networks.

The most common way to use VLANs with VoIP is to configure at least two VLANs. The first VLAN will be used for data traffic and the second for voice traffic. Since VLANs are a logical grouping of devices that may or may not be physically near each other, they can be used to group both directly connected and indirectly connected devices into logical arrangements.

If you've worked with VLANs, you know that devices in one VLAN cannot communicate with devices in another VLAN without the configuration of some sort of trunking protocol or routing solution. However, you should not assume that the segregation provided is a solid security solution by itself. VLAN protocols were not designed with security as the primary intent and can be compromised with the right knowledge.

### Perimeter Security Solutions

Should you decide to implement a perimeter network or DMZ, you will need to understand the technologies used to implement it. These technologies include firewalls, proxies, and network address translation devices. It is important that you understand the functions provided by each of these devices and the different implementation methods that they offer.

**Firewalls**    A *firewall* may be defined as a logical or physical break in the network links where network packets may be accepted, rejected, or stored for further evaluation. Firewalls come in different types, and each type provides different filtering processes. Some firewall devices can implement several types of filtering. Firewalls may be deployed as hardware appliances or as services running on operating systems such as Linux or Windows. Table 18-2 lists the common firewall types.

Without a firewall, any network connected to the Internet is more vulnerable to attacks. The firewall will prevent entry of specific types of communications or of all communications from or to specific IP addresses. Additionally, many vendors provide rule sets that will automatically configure your firewall to protect against many common attacks. However, it is up to the administrator to continue managing the firewall in order to protect against any new threats that may be introduced.

| TABLE 18-2 | Firewall Types |
| --- | --- |

| Firewall Type | Description |
| --- | --- |
| Packet filtering | A firewall that evaluates the received packets and determines the appropriate action based on rules. |
| Stateful inspection | A firewall that can eliminate packets originating outside the network that are not part of a current session or connection. |
| Application layer firewall | A firewall that can filter communications based on application types and that is aware of applications regardless of the port (TCP or UDP) used. Also known as proxy firewalls. |
| Desktop | A desktop firewall runs on the client computers connected to your network. Each computer runs a local copy of the firewall and may have different rules. |

on the **job**

*A newer approach to security is the unified threat management (UTM) method. UTM devices and applications provide traditional firewall functions while also implementing spam filtering, virus detection, and intrusion detection. Since most UTM solutions are single-box solutions, the complexity of implementing multiple security devices is removed.*

**Proxies**    Proxy servers act as intermediaries between two communicating devices or networks. Proxy servers allow caching of web pages for improved efficiency in browsing and filtering of web content. Proxy servers are often used by organizations to prohibit access to particular web sites, and many organizations disallow direct access to the Internet. In a converged network, proxy servers may introduce problems with VoIP communications if the servers do not support VoIP protocols. For this reasons, many organizations allow VoIP communications that need to traverse the Internet to bypass the proxy and use the proxy server only for web browsing.

**Network Address Translation and Port Address Translation**    Instead of providing public IP addresses to each VoIP phone or desktop computer on your network, you may decide to implement private IPv4 addressing. The following addresses are reserved for internal private use:

- 10.*x.x.x*
- 172.16.*x.x*–172.31.*x.x*
- 192.168.*x.x*

For example, you could use the IP addresses ranging from 10.10.10.1 to 10.10.10.254 to implement a 254-node network. The devices using these IP addresses will not be able to communicate on the Internet. Instead, they will need to communicate through a device that can translate private addresses to Internet addresses. *Network Address Translation (NAT)* servers perform this operation. A NAT server sits between your network and the Internet, or between your network and your DMZ in some cases. The internal users communicate with the NAT server, and the NAT server maintains sessions for those users with the Internet locations the users are requesting. NAT is one of the major reasons that IPv4 has continued as the most popular communications protocol. Without NAT, or a similar technology, we would have been forced to upgrade to IPv6 with the explosion of nodes connected to the Internet.

Do not confuse NAT with PAT. *Port Address Translation (PAT)* is very different from NAT. While NAT is about managing IP address translation, PAT can perform IP address translation as well as Layer 4 port translation. PAT servers usually have only one Internet-facing IP address, and all communications coming out of the network appear to originate from that one address. NAT servers may have multiple Internet-facing IP addresses. With *NAT*, the Internet-facing addresses may be assigned to an internal IP address for the duration of a session, or they may be used in a round-robin fashion. With *PAT*, the single IP address is used for outbound communications, and the inbound communications are automatically redirected to the appropriate internal IP address based on the PAT routing table.

Because VoIP protocols use two communication channels for the calls, NAT and PAT servers may introduce problems. The NAT server can usually initiate the call, but the audio may work only in one direction, or the audio may not work at all. This failure is caused by communicating through the NAT device. The NAT device does not know that the two streams (signaling and audio) are for the same communication. You can resolve this issue in several ways:

- Don't use NAT or PAT.
- Implement IP tunneling through the NAT device to the remote network, and run the VoIP connection through the tunnel. This will introduce extra latency.
- Use VoIP-aware NAT or PAT devices.

## Connectivity Solutions

One of the key security solutions that should be implemented on a converged network is secure connectivity. Secure connectivity includes authentication to the network, confidentiality of network communications, and accounting.

**Authentication**   One of the important components of a security strategy is an identity management system. The system provides a storage location for identity objects usually called user accounts. An identity management system also provides one or more methods for connecting to the storage location and proving identity ownership—a process known as authentication. User accounts are objects that identify and are owned by users. These objects provide properties for use by authentication systems and network operating systems. In addition to user accounts, certificates, biometrics, tokens, and other credentials may also be used for authentication and identity management.

Without a clear understanding of authentication and identity management, you will have difficulty installing a secure converged network. There are both basic and advanced authentication systems, and many systems include the ability to support both system types. For example, Windows Server systems allow for advanced authentication mechanisms through the Internet Authentication Service (Microsoft's RADIUS implementation) and for basic authentication using simple passwords against the Active Directory database. Both methods serve a valid purpose and are best for certain scenarios. Determining which method is right for your scenario is the first step to secure authentication.

In addition to selecting advanced or basic authentication methods, you must determine whom to authenticate. Do you wish to authenticate the clients only? Do you need to validate the authentication server as well? When both the client and the authentication server or authentication device are authenticated, this is known as *mutual authentication*. Mutual authentication helps prevent the introduction of rogue authentication devices to your network. Client-only authentication allows the network to "feel" secure, while mutual authentication allows both the clients and the network to have confidence and trust in the connections.

Authentication should not be confused with authorization. *Authentication* can be defined as proving a person or object is who or what he, she, or it claims to be. *Authorization* is defined as granting access to a resource by a person or object. Authorization assumes the identity has been authenticated. If authentication can be spoofed or impersonated, authorization schemes fail. From this, you can see why authentication is such an integral and important part of network and information security.

Advanced authentication systems generally utilize stronger credentials and better protection of those credentials than basic authentication systems. The strength and protection of the credential is determined by the effort it takes to exploit it. A password-protected credential is usually considered weak when compared with biometric-protected credentials. This, in some cases, is a misconception, because strength of authentication really depends on how the authentication information (the credential and proof of ownership) is sent across the network. If you were to implement a biometric system, such as a thumb scanner, and the client sent the credentials and proof of ownership (a unique number built from the identity points on the user's thumb) to the server in clear text, it is no more secure than a standard password-based system; however, I am not aware of any biometric authentication system that sends the authentication data as clear text.

The key element, which will provide a truly strong authentication pathway, is the encryption or hashing of the user credentials, or at least the proof of identity information. This can be accomplished with Virtual Private Networking (VPN) technology or with well-designed authentication systems. One example of a well-designed authentication system is 802.1X with a strong EAP type. 802.1X and EAP types are used to secure both wired and wireless connections.

You use authentication every day of your life. For example, when you are at a seminar and the speaker says he is an expert on the topic of his speech, you use authentication mechanisms to verify this information. In other words, you listen to the information he delivers and use it to determine if he is truly an expert. In addition, suppose someone walks up to you and says, "Hi, my name is Bill and I am tall." You would look at him and compare his height with a height you consider to be tall and authenticate whether he is truly tall or not. If he is not tall, by your standards, he will lose *credibility* with you.

Remember the word "credentials"? Consider other important "cred" words: credit, credibility, and credentials. Do you see how they are all related? They all have to do with having proof of something. When you have good credit, you have proof of your trustworthiness to pay debts. When you have credibility, you have proof that you are authentic, persuasive, and dynamic. When you have credentials, you have an object or the experience that proves your skill or identity. Authentication results in the verification of credentials.

Advanced authentication is more secure than basic authentication because advanced mechanisms are used to protect the user's credentials. This usually means protecting a username and password pair, but it can also include protecting a user/ certificate combination, a user/machine combination, or any other user/object combination used to identify a specific user. In addition to the extra protection offered by advanced authentication systems, when 802.1X-based systems are used, you have the benefit of standards-based technology. This means that hardware from many different vendors is likely to support the authentication process. Sometimes driver or firmware upgrades are required, but often a path can be taken to implement the authentication mechanism.

To increase security, you should avoid basic authentication mechanisms such as the password authentication protocol (PAP), which sends the password as clear text across the network. Another example of a basic authentication protocol would be Basic Authentication to web servers. This authentication mechanism is part of the HTTP standard, but the passwords are sent across the network using a reversible encryption algorithm. Use an authentication system that provides for better protection of credentials, and you will go a long way toward a more secure network.

Many different credential solutions are available for securing your networks. It's important to select the right system for your needs. In this process you will consider the primary features of a credential solution and whether you need a multi-factor authentication system. In addition, you should be aware of the various credential types available to you.

A credential solution should provide a means of user or computer identification that is proportional to your security needs. You do not want to select a credential solution that places unnecessary burdens on the users and results in greater costs (of both time and money) than the value of the information assets you are protecting. You should evaluate whether the selected authentication solution provides for redundancy and integration with other systems such as Active Directory or Lotus Notes. The system should also support the needed credential types such as smart cards and/or biometrics. In addition, consider the following factors when selecting a credential solution:

- The method used to protect the credentials
- The storage location of the credentials
- The access method of the credential store

If an authentication system sends the credentials as clear text, a protection method is effectively nonexistent. Advanced authentication systems will protect the user credentials by encrypting them or avoiding the transmission of the actual credentials in the first place. Instead of transmitting the actual credentials, many systems use a hashing process to encode at least the password. *Hashing* the passwords means that the password is passed through a one-way algorithm resulting in a fixed-length number. This number is known as the hash of the password, or the message digest. The hash is stored in the authentication database and can be used as an encryption key for challenge text in a challenge/response authentication system.

The credentials, both username and password (or hash) or certificates, must be stored in some location. This storage location should be both secure and responsive.

It must be secure to protect against brute force attacks, and it must be responsive to service authentication requests in a timely fashion. Certificates are usually stored in a centralized certificate store (known as a certificate server or certificate authority) as well as on the client using the certificate for authentication. Both locations must be secure, or the benefit of using certificates is diminished. In addition to the standard certificate store, users may choose to back up their certificates to disk. These backups are usually password protected, but brute force attacks against the media store may reveal the certificate given enough time. For this reason, users should be well-educated in this area and understand the vulnerability presented by the existence of such backups.

Access methods vary by authentication system and storage method, but there are standards that define credential access methods. One example is LDAP (Lightweight Directory Access Protocol). LDAP is a standard method for accessing directory service information. This information can include many objects, but is usually inclusive of authentication credentials. LDAP is, or can be, used by Lotus Notes, Novell's Directory Services, and Microsoft's Active Directory among others.

Sometimes, one type of authentication is not sufficient. In these cases, multi-factor authentication can be used. Multi-factor authentication is a form of authentication that uses more than one set of credentials. An example of a *multi-factor authentication* process would be the use of both passwords and thumb scanners. Usually, the user would place her thumb on the thumb scanner and then be prompted for a password or PIN (personal identification number) code. The password may be used for network authentication, or it may only be used for localized authentication before the thumb data is used for network authentication. However, in most cases the password and thumb data are used to authenticate to the local machine and then to the network or just to the network alone. A common example of multi-factor authentication would be your ATM card. You have the card and you know the PIN (something you have and something you know).

There are many common credential types. They include:

- Username and password
- Certificates
- PACs (Privilege Attribute Certificates)
- Biometrics
- Tokens

Username and password pairs are the most popular type of credential. They are used by most network operating systems including Novell NetWare, Linux, Unix, and Windows. Due to the human factor involved in the selection of the password, they often introduce a false feeling of security. This is because the chosen password is usually too weak to withstand dictionary attacks, and depending on the length of the password, certainly brute force attacks. In addition, the passwords are often written down or stored in plain text files on the system and then changed infrequently, resulting in a longer attack opportunity window.

An alternative to username and password pairs is certificates. To use certificates throughout an organization, a certificate authority must exist. This certificate authority can be operated by the organization or an independent third party. In either case the costs are often prohibitive to widespread use due to the need for an extra server or even a hierarchy of servers. Small- and medium-sized organizations usually opt for server-only certificates or no certificates at all because of the cost of implementation. A full PKI (Public Key Infrastructure) would usually consist of more than one certificate authority. Each certificate authority would be a single server or cluster of servers. The PKI is the mechanism used for generation, renewal, distribution, verification, and destruction of user and machine certificates.

The Privilege Attribute Certificate (PAC) is used by the Kerberos authentication protocol in Windows 2000 and higher (Windows XP and Windows Server 2003 as well as newer versions). The PAC contains the authorization data for the user and includes group memberships and user rights. This feature means that the user's group assignments and right assignments are transferred as a portion of the ticket granting ticket (TGT)—a feature of the Kerberos authentication protocol.

Yet another authentication credential is you. Biometrics-based authentication takes advantage of the uniqueness of every human and uses this for authentication purposes. For example, your thumb can be used as a unique identifier as can your retina. The balancing of cost and security is important with biometric credentials. While hair analysis could be used to authenticate a user, the cost and time involved is still too high for practical use. Today, both thumb scanners and retina scanners are becoming more popular.

Two common types of authentication tokens are software based and hardware based. Software-based authentication token systems often run on PDAs or cell phones, so users can launch the application on their mobile device and retrieve an authentication code. This code is usually used in conjunction with a password or PIN, essentially creating a two-factor authentication system. The hardware-based token systems usually provide a keychain-sized device that, with the press of a button, will show the current authentication code. This code, again, is used with a password or PIN. Most token systems work off of a time-synchronized (or some other synchronization point) algorithm that generates proper codes in the software system or hardware device. This means that a valid code today will not work tomorrow and provides greater security.

**Virtual Private Networks**   A Virtual Private Network (VPN) is implemented by creating an encrypted tunnel between two endpoints over a public network. The same technologies originally introduced for public network use are also used on private networks today. Since VPNs are used on both public and private networks, the qualification of running on a public network is no longer necessary. Today a connection is considered a VPN connection if it uses VPN technologies such as authentication and encryption, which are the two requirements of a secure VPN solution. Figure 18-7 shows an example implementation of a VPN connection across the Internet. In this case, it is a site-to-site VPN. All traffic between the sites is routed through the VPN connection.

In addition to the site-to-site VPN connection, you may choose to implement any of the following VPN solutions:

- **Device-to-device**   These VPN connections are made directly between two devices on a network in order to provide additional security.

- **Remote client connections**   Remote users can use a VPN client program to connect to the organization's network across the Internet.

- **Wireless security VPNs**   VPNs are used for wireless security when the wireless client connects to an insecure public hotspot.

The last bullet point warrants some further explanation. The user may connect his laptop to a coffee shop hotspot that uses no encryption. Next, the user can launch a VPN client connection across the Internet to his organization's home office. Now all Internet traffic will be routed through the VPN connection to the home office and then back out from the home office to the Internet. This solution prevents wireless eavesdropping when no actual wireless security is available. Once the VPN is established, the user may also launch a software VoIP application and initiate calls without fear of someone listening in on the calls.

Many VPN technologies are available, but the two most common solutions are the Point-to-Point Tunneling Protocol (PPTP) and the Layer 2 Tunneling Protocol

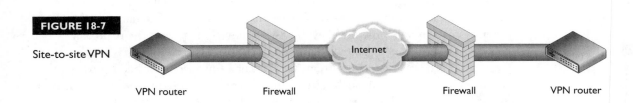

**FIGURE 18-7**

Site-to-site VPN

VPN router          Firewall                    Internet                    Firewall          VPN router

(L2TP) with IPSec. The latter is considered the most secure. The key decision factors include the authentication method and encryption used by the VPN solution. Weak authentication equals a weak VPN regardless of the encryption strength. Weak encryption equals a weak VPN regardless of the authentication strength. Both factors must be strong for the VPN solution to be considered secure. For this reason, early PPTP implementations are not recommended, and even the recent implementations are not considered as secure as a solid implementation of L2TP with IPSec. The variance is partly because L2TP and IPSec provide you with many options for authentication and encryption. You can choose the level of security you need with more granularity than with PPTP.

**Encryption**    The foundation of a VPN is encryption. Once the user is authenticated, if no encryption is used, you still do not have a VPN. For example, you could create an L2TP tunnel between two endpoints without using encryption. This would result in tunneled communications, but it would not be a VPN. In most cases, IPSec is used to establish the encryption for the L2TP tunnel in an L2TP/IPSec VPN solution.

Encryption is the process of encoding information so that it can be unencoded given the appropriate algorithm and inputs. Most encryption systems use an algorithm with a key and some data as the inputs. When encrypting, the system will use the key and the data to generate the cipher text. When decrypting, the system will use the cipher text and the key to regenerate the original data. Consider the following algorithm:

$$3 \times k + D \times k = cipher\ text$$

where $k$ is the encryption key and $D$ is the original data. This algorithm could be used to encrypt any base 10 number. For example, assume you want to encrypt the number 12 with a key of 7. The algorithm would look like this:

$$3 \times 7 + 12 \times 7 = 105$$

The resulting cipher text, 105, can be decrypted to retrieve the original data as long as the proper algorithm is applied and the correct key is known. Here's the decryption algorithm:

$$(cipher\ text - 3 \times k)\ /\ k = original\ data$$

The resulting algorithm would look like this for our example:

$$(105 - 3 \times 7)\ /\ 7 = 12$$

While this is not an implemented encryption algorithm (the actual algorithms are binary and much more complex), it shows how you can use the same algorithm with different encryption keys to encrypt data. Having the algorithm does not automatically allow you to decrypt the data with certainty. You must know the key that was used for encryption.

Many encryption standards exist. Table 18-3 lists the most common encryption algorithms.

**VoIP Encryption Solutions**    The encryption solutions will vary depending on the VoIP technology you implement. SIP uses standards from the IETF, and H.323 uses standards from the ITU. Table 18-4 lists the ITU specifications known as the H.235 hierarchy. These standards are used in H.323 VoIP networks when security is required. One of the major enhancement to H.323 version 6 and the H.235 standards at that level is the inclusion of sRTP. sRTP is the Secure Real-time Transport Protocol, and it provides the same functionality as RTP while adding secure communications.

SIP uses the standards created by the IETF. These standards implement existing security standards for VoIP. The standards include Transport Layer Security (TLS), Secure/Multipurpose Internet Mail Extensions (S/MIME), and Secure Real-Time Protocol (sRTP). SIP essentially relies on an existing security layer beneath the VoIP communications in the OSI model rather than implementing security within the VoIP protocols themselves. TLS is used to protect the signaling, and sRTP is used to protect the voice payload. Additionally, S/MIME may be used to secure both the signaling and the payload.

**TABLE 18-3**    Encryption Standards

| Encryption Algorithm | Type | Applications |
|---|---|---|
| Digital Encryption Standard (DES) | Block | Data encryption; communications encryption. |
| Advanced Encryption Standard (AES) | Block | Data encryption; communications encryption. |
| Triple DES (3DES) | Block | Data encryption; communications encryption. Used to increase the strength of DES on system that cannot implement AES. |
| RC4 | Stream | Data encryption; communications encryption. |
| Message Digest 5 (MD5) | Hashing | Digital signatures; password storage; data integrity. |
| Secure Hashing Algorithm 1 (SHA-1) | Hashing | Digital signatures; password storage; data integrity. |

**TABLE 18-4**  H.323 Security Solutions Using H.235

| Standard | Definition |
|---|---|
| 235.1 | Basic or baseline security profile. Includes only authentication and integrity of signaling streams. |
| 235.2 | Signature security profile. Specifies methods for distribution of digital signatures used to secure the signaling stream. |
| 235.3 | Hybrid profile. Used to combine 235.1 and 235.2. |
| 235.4 | Direct and selective routed call security. Implements symmetric key management. |
| 235.5 | Secure authentication in RAS using weak shared secrets. |
| 235.6 | Voice encryption profile. This profile must be supported if the VoIP system requires encryption of the actual voice data. |
| 235.7 | Usage of the MIKEY key management protocol for sRTP. |
| 235.8 | Key exchange for sRTP using secure signaling channels. May include end-to-end security or only security in sensitive areas of the network. |
| 235.9 | Support for security gateways. |

**Accounting**  The term *accounting* is used to reference any method or system that provides recordkeeping and activity tracking. In network security, an accounting system at its most basic level is a logging system that logs the activity occurring on the network. Authentication gets you onto the network. Authorization gets you into things on the network. Accounting keeps a record. Accounting is important for incident response, and it is also important as a tool for baseline analysis and anomaly detection. Advanced accounting systems are called intrusion detection systems or intrusion prevention systems.

## Security Monitoring

The security technologies presented in this chapter can help protect your network from an attack; however, new attack methods are continually being developed, and you must have a solution that allows you to monitor for both the older and newer attacks. The technologies that assist you with this effort include:

- Intrusion Detection and Intrusion Prevention Systems
- Antivirus and Antispyware Solutions

**Intrusion Detection and Intrusion Prevention Systems**  An *intrusion detection system* (IDS) detects many security-related incidents and logs the information. An IDS may notify an administrator of suspect activity. Incidents that may be detected by an IDS include unwanted connections, high bandwidth consumption, attacks based on signatures, and anomalies in network activity. Signature-based detection relies on patterns that exist within attack scenarios. Anomaly-based detection relies on comparisons with the baseline (normal operations) of network activity.

An *intrusion prevention* system (IPS) goes one step further than the IDS solution. Intrusion prevention systems may prevent an attack by disallowing connections from suspect devices or even by shutting down services that are under attack.

**Antivirus and Antispyware Solutions**  A computer program with the ability to regenerate itself is called a *virus*. A virus may or may not harm the infected computer. Viruses may lay dormant for some time before they attack the infected host machine. A *worm* is a self-replicating application that requires no user action for reproduction. Viruses usually require human interaction in some way, whereas worms do not.

Malware is software designed to cause harm to a computer. A type of malware is the Trojan horse. Named after the ancient fabled gift, the Trojan horse enters the computer under the guise of a useful program or utility. Once in the machine, it may infect the machine with a virus or worm, or it may download other Trojans.

Similar to the Trojan horse is the spyware or adware villain. Spyware is installed on your computer and reports back to the source. Adware is installed on your computer and causes unwanted ads to display on your screen. Additionally, spyware and adware combinations are common.

To protect your network from these malware applications, you will need to run antivirus and antispyware applications. The two basic types of antimalware applications are ingress and host-based. Ingress applications reside at the entry point of the data, and host-based antimalware applications run on the host devices. An example of an ingress antimalware application would be an e-mail server scanner. This software would scan e-mail messages as they enter (and possibly exit) the e-mail server. If malware is detected, the message can be rejected, flagged as malware infected, or passed on without attachments.

Antivirus software must be maintained. You will need to download and apply new definition files frequently. Many antivirus applications include automatic update features so that the definitions can be maintained without the need for user interaction. The definition file includes the signatures that are used to identify known malware.

## CERTIFICATION OBJECTIVE 18.01

# 642-436: Describe sRTP

Chapter 5 briefly introduces the secure RTP (sRTP) protocol. In this chapter on security, you will learn about this protocol in greater depth. Specifically, you will learn about the features offered by sRTP, the structure of the sRTP header, and the method used to implement sRTP in a Cisco environment.

## sRTP Features

sRTP is defined in RFC 3711. sRTP is designed to provide authentication, confidentiality, and integrity for RTP data streams and RTCP communications. According to the RFC, multiple goals were set during the development of the sRTP standard.

The security goals of the sRTP standard are to provide for the following:

- The confidentiality of the RTP and RTCP payloads
- The integrity of the entire RTP and RTCP packets, together with protection against replayed packets

According to the standard, these security services are optional and independent of each other, except that sRTCP integrity protection is mandatory. This requirement is because malicious or unintentional alteration of RTCP messages could prevent appropriate processing of the RTP data stream.

In addition to the security goals, functional goals are also specified as:

- A framework that permits upgrading with new cryptographic transforms
- Low bandwidth cost, that is, a framework preserving RTP header compression efficiency
- A low computational cost
- A small footprint (that is, small code size and data memory for keying information and replay lists)
- Limited packet expansion to support the bandwidth economy goal
- Independence from the underlying transport, network, and physical layers used by RTP, in particular, high tolerance to packet loss and reordering

The standard further states: "These properties ensure that SRTP is a suitable protection scheme for RTP/RTCP in both wired and wireless scenarios."

In addition to these goals, the sRTP standard implements some features to reduce the resources required for key management and to improve security. These features include:

- A single master key used to provide encryption keys for both sRTP and sRTCP. Each session uses a key derived from the master key so that only the master key must be maintained.

- The session keys may be refreshed at some interval in order to prevent cracking of the key. Since the key changes periodically, it will be more difficult for an attacker to gain the key and then gain access to the RTP stream data.

- sRTP allows for salting keys so that pre-computed dictionaries cannot be used to easily crack the encryption keys. The salt is typically a random or predetermined number that is appended to the keying material during encryption key generation.

**watch** *Be sure to remember the basic features provided by sRTP. You are sure to be asked about some of them on the 642-436 (CVOICE) exam.*

## sRTP Header

In Chapter 5, you learned about the RTP header and the fields that are included. The sRTP header, as shown in Figure 18-8, is the same as the RTP header with extra information for the security profile offered. As you can see in Figure 18-8, all of the standard RTP header fields are still in the sRTP header. In fact, only the sRTP MKI and Authentication Tag fields are new in the sRTP header.

The Master Key Identifier (MKI) field is optional and is defined, signaled (encoded and transferred), and used by key management. The MKI provides the identity of the master key that was used to generate the session keys for the sRTP session. These session keys are used to authenticate and encrypt the data (sRTP) or control (sRTCP) packets.

The Authentication Tag field is recommended and is used to provide the message authentication data. In an sRTP packet, the authenticated portion includes the

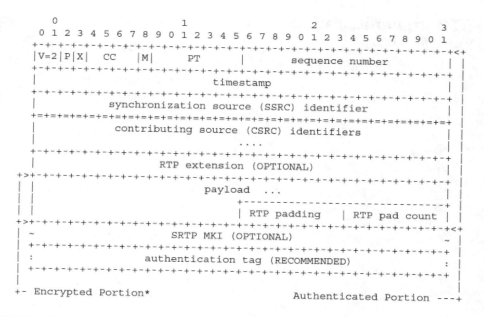

**FIGURE 18-8**

sRTP header
as depicted in
RFC 3711

RTP header and the encrypted payload. When both encryption and authentication are used, on the sending side, encryption takes place first, and then authentication information is generated against the header and encrypted data. On the receiving side, authentication is performed first and then decryption takes place. Because the sequence number is part of the RTP header, integrity is also provided by the authentication process. The end result is that sRTP provides confidentiality, integrity, and authentication.

The final elements that are new in the sRTP header are the RTP Padding and RTP Pad Count fields. The internally specified encryption solutions do not require RTP padding. The payload may vary in size with these encryption solutions. When an externally specified solution (one not referenced in RFC 3711) is used, padding may be required. This padding is required when the encryption solution requires that the payload be a certain size rather than variable in length.

**e⋋am**

**ⓦatch**

*You should know that, when the RFC 3711–specified encryption solutions are used, the payload is no larger than the unencrypted payload would be.*

*The RTP Padding and RTP Pad Count fields are used only with externally specified encryption solutions that require the payload to equate to a certain size.*

## sRTP Implementation

Thankfully, the configuration of sRTP is quite simple on Cisco ISRs. If you want to enable sRTP for a specific dial peer, you will use the **srtp** command from within dial-peer configuration mode. This command was first introduced in IOS 12.4(6)T1. The following commands will enable sRTP for the dial peer with an ID of 750:

```
Router1# conf t
Router1(config)# dial-peer voice 740 voip
Router1(config-dial-peer)# srtp
Router1(config-dial-peer)# exit
```

If you want to allow fallback to non-secure voice communications when the remote end requires it, you can use the **srtp fallback** command. By default, all dial peers inherit the sRTP setting from the global voice service. To configure sRTP for the global voice service, use commands like the following:

```
Router1# conf t
Router1(config)# voice service voip
Router1(config-voi-serv)# srtp
Router1(config-voi-serv)# exit
```

In global voice service configuration mode, you may also use the **srtp fallback** command. To disable sRTP at either the global voice service level or for an individual dial peer, simply use the **no srtp** command.

**e x a m**

**W a t c h**  *If you want to guarantee that sRTP is used or that the call cannot be placed, use the* no srtp fallback *command for the desired dial peer. This command does* *not disable sRTP, but it forces the call to use sRTP or nothing. RTP cannot be used once the* no srtp fallback *command is entered.*

# CERTIFICATION SUMMARY

In this chapter, you learned about security technologies used to ensure security on your voice and data networks. While you will not be heavily tested on the contents of the first portion of this chapter, you should know the information about sRTP covered in the last section. sRTP is used to authenticate and encrypt VoIP packets on the network. sRTP is a profile of RTP and uses AES encryption by default.

# TWO-MINUTE DRILL

## 642-436: Describe sRTP

- ❏ RFC 3711 defines both sRTP and sRTCP for security in RTP communications.
- ❏ sRTP provides both confidentiality and authentication or integrity.
- ❏ sRTP is implemented as a profile of RTP.
- ❏ A single master key may be used for derivation of encryption keys.
- ❏ Key salting may be used to assist in the prevention of pre-computational encryption attack methods (such as dictionary attacks).
- ❏ When using a master key, session keys are used to perform the encryption.
- ❏ The session keys may be periodically refreshed to further hinder encryption-cracking attempts.
- ❏ sRTP can be used in combination with cRTP.
- ❏ The Authentication Tag is used to provide authentication information in sRTP headers.
- ❏ The Master Key Identifier (MKI) field is used to identify the master key used for session key derivation.
- ❏ When encryption and authentication are used together, encryption is performed first, and then authentication information is generated against the RTP header and encrypted payload on the sending side.
- ❏ The RTP Padding and RTP Pad Count fields are required only when using an externally specified encryption solution that requires a fixed-length payload.
- ❏ The **srtp** command is used within dial peers and the voice service global configuration mode to enable sRTP or disable sRTP.
- ❏ By default, dial peers inherit the sRTP configuration from the global voice service settings.
- ❏ You can disallow fallback to RTP for a dial peer by executing the **no srtp fallback** command from within dial-peer configuration mode.

# SELF TEST

The following questions will help you measure your understanding of the material presented in this chapter. Read all the choices carefully because there might be more than one correct answer. Choose all correct answers for each question.

## 642-436: Describe sRTP

1. In what RFC is sRTCP defined?
   A. 3551
   B. 3750
   C. 3711
   D. 3550

2. What security functions are provided for RTP by sRTP? (Choose all that apply.)
   A. Confidentiality
   B. Authentication
   C. Integrity
   D. Permissions

3. To allow for the derivation of session keys, what kind of key is used with sRTP?
   A. Primary key
   B. Master key
   C. Subordinate key
   D. Peer key

4. You have implemented sRTP with a master key. Session keys are generated from the master key. The communications use an MKI and authentication tag. What key is used to perform encryption?
   A. Master key
   B. Session key
   C. MKI
   D. Authentication tag

5. What feature may be implemented in sRTP in order to prevent pre-computational encryption cracking?
   A. Master keys
   B. Session keys

    C.  Key salting

    D.  Key peppering

**6.** What can be used, in combination with sRTP, to reduce the size of RTP packets?

    A.  PKZip

    B.  RTCP

    C.  Zmodem

    D.  cRTP

**7.** In sRTP, what is used to identify the master key used for session key derivation?

    A.  MKI

    B.  Authentication tag

    C.  RTP padding

    D.  RTP pad count

**8.** When encryption and authentication are both used with sRTP, in what order are they processed?

    A.  On the sending side, encryption and then authentication; on the receiving side, decryption and then authentication

    B.  On the sending side, encryption and then authentication; on the receiving side, authentication and then decryption

    C.  On the receiving side, encryption and then authentication; on the sending side, decryption and then authentication

    D.  On the receiving side, authentication and then encryption; on the sending side, decryption and then authentication

**9.** When would the RTP Padding and RTP Pad Count fields be required with sRTP?

    A.  When the internal encryption algorithms are used and the payload is very small

    B.  Anytime the internal encryption algorithms are used

    C.  When external encryption algorithms are used that require a fixed-length payload

    D.  Anytime external encryption algorithms are used

**10.** You want to enable sRTP for a specific dial peer. In what configuration mode will you use the **srtp** command?

    A.  Global voice service configuration mode

    B.  Switch port interface configuration mode

    C.  Router port interface configuration mode

    D.  Dial-peer configuration mode

# LAB QUESTION

You are configuring your VoIP network for the use of sRTP. You use Cisco ISRs with CME and Cisco 2950 switches. The VoIP phones are powered with a power block. You want to enable sRTP by default, and you want to disable sRTP for dial-peer 650. What commands will you use on the CME router, and in what configuration mode will you execute the commands? Additionally, will any commands be required on the 2950 switches in order to enable sRTP?

# SELF TEST ANSWERS

## 642-436: Describe sRTP

**1.** ☑ **C is correct.** RFC 3711 defines both sRTP and sRTCP. The RFC specifies encryption solutions and the authentication process. It details the header format for sRTP and sRTCP packets. RFC 3711 is a profile for RTP.

☒ **A, B,** and **D** are incorrect. RFC 3551 defines the audio/video profiles for RTP. RFC 3750 defines transition scenarios for moving to IPv6. RFC 3550 defines RTP and RTCP, but not the security profile, which is defined in RFC 3711.

**2.** ☑ **A, B,** and **C** are correct. sRTP provides confidentiality (encryption) and authentication of the RTP headers and encrypted payload. Integrity is also provided because the sequence numbers in the RTP header are authenticated.

☒ **D is incorrect.** Permissions are not part of sRTP. In fact, sRTP does not provide authorization functions. Authorization should still be managed at the point of network ingress.

**3.** ☑ **B is correct.** The master key allows for a single key to be used in the generation of unique session keys within an RTP stream.

☒ **A, C,** and **D** are incorrect. No such keys as the primary key, subordinate key, or peer key are used in sRTP communications.

**4.** ☑ **B is correct.** Session keys are used to perform the actual encryption of the RTP payload. The master key is used to derive the session keys.

☒ **A, C,** and **D** are incorrect. The master key is utilized in the session key derivation process, but it is not used for the encryption of the RTP payload. The master key identifier (MKI) is a field in the sRTP header used to identify which master key was used to derive the session key. The authentication tag includes authentication information to authenticate the RTP header and encrypted payload.

**5.** ☑ **C is correct.** Key salting is a technique used to prevent pre-computational cracking. Pre-computational cracking attempts use previously generated dictionaries for cracking. The salting modifies the key enough so that it will not match the pre-computed tables.

☒ **A, B,** and **D** are incorrect. Master keys provide for simple generation of session keys, but they do not help prevent pre-computational attacks. Session keys are used to encrypt data, but in order for them to be secured against pre-computational attacks, they are often used with key salting. Key peppering is not a term used in encryption processing.

6. ☑ **D is correct.** cRTP or compressed RTP is used to reduce the size of the RTP, UDP, and IP headers. Because sRTP is implemented as a profile of RTP, cRTP can still be used in conjunction with it so that you can achieve security and reduced bandwidth at the same time. However, both sRTP and cRTP add overhead in processing and should be used only when necessary for optimal router performance.

   ☒ **A, B, and C are incorrect.** PKZip is used to compress stored data and not RTP data streams. RTCP is the Real-time Transport Control Protocol and is used for communications of RTP performance information. The old ZModem terminal protocol did offer compression, but it is not used with RTP data streams.

7. ☑ **A is correct.** The Master Key Identifier (MKI) is used to indicate the master key that was used in the session key derivation process.

   ☒ **B, C, and D are incorrect.** The Authentication Tag is a field in the sRTP header that identifies authentication information for the authentication of the RTP header and RTP payload. The RTP Padding and the RTP Pad Count fields are used only when encryption algorithms that require fixed-length payloads are used.

8. ☑ **B is correct.** Because the encrypted payload is authenticated in its encrypted state, when both encryption and authentication are used, the encryption must happen first and then the authentication on the sending side. The converse process occurs on the receiving side. The encrypted data must first be authenticated while in its encrypted state, and then the data (payload) may be decrypted.

   ☒ **A, C, and D are incorrect.** Remember that the data is encrypted and then authenticated as encrypted data. This sequence forces the only possible processing order on the sender and receiver. On the sender, we encrypt and then authenticate. On the receiver, we authenticate and then decrypt.

9. ☑ **C is correct.** The RTP Padding and RTP Pad Count fields are used when an externally specified (not identified in RFC 3711) encryption algorithm that requires a fixed-length or equally divisible length payload size is used. For example, the algorithm may require that the payload be divisible by 256 bits. This algorithm may require padding. The internally specified algorithms have no such requirements.

   ☒ **A, B, and D are incorrect.** When the internal encryption algorithms are used, no length requirements are in place for the payload. For this reason, the RTP Padding and RTP Pad Count fields are not required when the internally specified algorithms are used. Only externally specified algorithms that require a fixed-length or divisible-length payload will require the padding fields in the sRTP header.

**10.** ☑ D is correct. You should execute the **srtp** command in the dial-peer configuration mode.

☒ A, B, and C are incorrect. If the **srtp** command is used in the global voice service configuration mode, it will apply to all dial peers by default. You do not use the **srtp** command with either switch port interfaces or router port interfaces. The **srtp** command is only supported on dial peers and on the global voice service configuration mode.

# LAB ANSWER

You will not have to execute any commands on the switches. The switches will use Layer 2 forwarding and RTP as well as RTCP run on top of UDP, which is a Layer 4 protocol. The switches will simply forward on the RTP packets whether they use sRTP or standard unencrypted and unauthenticated RTP.

Because you want to enable sRTP by default, you should execute the **srtp** command while in global voice service configuration mode. This will enable sRTP for all dial peers by default. For dial-peer 650, you should execute the **no srtp** command while in the dial-peer configuration mode. This action will override the default settings coming from the voice service configuration.

# A

## About the CD

T he CD-ROM included with this book comes complete with MasterExam, CertCam videos from the author, and an electronic version of the book. The software is easy to install on any Windows 2000/XP/Vista/7 computer and must be installed to access the MasterExam feature. You may, however, browse the electronic book and the CertCam video training directly from the CD without installation. To register for the bonus MasterExam, simply click the Bonus MasterExam link on the main launch page, and follow the directions to the free online registration.

## System Requirements

The software requires Windows 2000 or higher and Internet Explorer 6.0 or above and 20 MB of hard disk space for full installation. The electronic book requires Adobe Acrobat Reader.

# Installing and Running MasterExam

If your computer CD-ROM drive is configured to auto-run, the CD-ROM will automatically start up upon your inserting the disc. From the opening screen you may install MasterExam by clicking the MasterExam link. This will begin the installation process and create a program group named LearnKey. To run MasterExam, use Start | All Programs | LearnKey | MasterExam. If the auto-run feature did not launch your CD, browse to the CD and click the LaunchTraining.exe icon.

## MasterExam

MasterExam provides you with a simulation of the actual exam. The number of questions, the type of questions, and the time allowed are intended to be an accurate representation of the exam environment. You have the option to take an open book exam, including hints, references, and answers, a closed book exam, or the timed MasterExam simulation.

When you launch MasterExam, a digital clock display will appear in the bottom right corner of your screen. The clock will continue to count down to zero unless you choose to end the exam before the time expires.

# CertCam Video Training

CertCam .avi clips provide detailed examples of key certification objectives in audio video format direct from the author of this book. These clips walk you step-by-step through various system configurations. You can access the clips directly from the CertCam table of contents by clicking the CertCam link on the main launch page. The CertCam .avi clips are recorded and produced using TechSmith's Camtasia Producer. Since .avi clips can be very large, ExamSim uses TechSmith's special .avi codec to compress the clips. The file named tsccvid.dll is copied to your Windows\ System folder during the first auto-run. If the .avi clip runs with audio but no video, you may need to reinstall the file from the CD-ROM. Browse to the Programs\ CertCams folder, and double-click the tscc.exe file.

# Electronic Book

The entire contents of the Study Guide are provided in PDF. Adobe's Acrobat Reader has been included on the CD.

# Help

A help file is provided through the help button on the main page in the lower-left corner. An individual help feature is also available through MasterExam.

# Removing Installation(s)

MasterExam is installed to your hard drive. For best results removing programs, use the Start | All Programs | LearnKey | Uninstall option to remove MasterExam.

# Technical Support

For questions regarding the content of the electronic book, MasterExam, or CertCams please visit www.mhprofessional.com or e-mail customer.service@mcgraw-hill.com. For customers outside the 50 United States, e-mail international_cs@mcgraw-hill.com.

## LearnKey Technical Support

For technical problems with the software (installation, operation, removing installations), please visit www.learnkey.com, e-mail techsupport@learnkey.com, or call toll free at (800) 482-8244.

# Glossary

**access control**   The prevention of access to resources by unauthorized users and systems.

**access device**   A common term for a networking device through which client devices connect to a network; for example, a typical access point device.

**ad hoc network**   An alternate term often used to reference an independent basic service set (IBSS) or a peer-to-peer network in a wireless LAN (local area network).

**address signaling**   The method used to transmit dialed digits on telephony networks. Dual-tone multifrequency (DTMF) is a common address-signaling system.

**Advanced Encryption Standard (AES)**   The encryption standard that replaced the Digital Encryption Standard (DES) in order to improve encryption strength. It is based on the Rijndael algorithm.

**a-Law**   A compressing and expanding (companding) algorithm used outside the United States and Japan.

**Application layer**   The layer of the OSI model (see *OSI model*) that provides access to the lower OSI layers for applications and provides information to applications from the lower OSI model layers. Also known as Layer 7.

**area code**   A three-digit prefix identifying the geographic region to which calls should be routed.

**authentication**   A process that results in the validation or invalidation of user or system credentials.

**authentication server**   A device that provides 802.1X authentication services to an authenticator in an 802.1X/EAP implementation.

**authenticator**   A device at one end of a point-to-point LAN (local area network) segment that facilitates the 802.1X authentication of the device at the other end in an 802.1X/EAP implementation.

**bandwidth**    Either the difference between the upper and lower frequencies used by a wireless channel, or the sheer amount of data that may be communicated through the channel including all frame protocol overhead, or sometimes the number of payload bits that can be communicated through the channel in a second—more properly called *throughput*.

**B-channel**    An ISDN bearer (B) channel that carries voice, video, or data.

**binary**    Data represented as 1's or 0's.

**bit**    An individual information element that can be equal to 1 or 0. A single bit can represent any two values to an application.

**byte**    A collection of bits. Usually 8 bits in computer systems.

**call admission control (CAC)**    A system that allows you to manage VoIP call volumes when quality of service controls are insufficient.

**call agent**    The component containing the call-forwarding logic in an MGCP network implementation.

**call detail record (CDR)**    A record of the details of a call including time, duration, and source.

**capacity**    The amount that can be contained or managed. System capacity is usually a measurement of storage space or data space. In communications systems, capacity is a reference to the amount of data that can be transferred through the system in a given window of time.

**central office (CO)**    A location including one or more PSTN switches. The CO may be connected with other telephone systems.

**channel**    An instance of communications medium (radio frequency bandwidth) used to pass information between two communicating stations (STAs).

**circuit switching**   A switching method used to reserve a route or path between the two endpoints that need to communicate.

**cluster**   In a Cisco VoIP network, a logical collection of call managers (Cisco Unified Communications Manager or Cisco Unified Communications Manager Express).

**coaxial cable**   Networking cable that is implemented with a center conductor made of copper surrounded by a shielding made of some type of plastic. Also known as coax.

**codec**   An abbreviation for coder/decoder. A method used to convert analog signals to digital signals and vice versa. Examples include G.711, G.729, and G.728.

**contact center**   A location or call center that processes PSTN, VoIP, e-mail, instant messaging, and other forms of customer contact.

**convergence**   The process of bringing voice, multimedia, and data communications together on a shared network.

**core device**   A common term for a networking device that neither connects to client devices nor provides services to the network other than packet forwarding.

**coverage**   A term used to refer to the physical space covered by an access point. An administrator might say that she needs to provide coverage in the Accounting department, meaning that she needs to be sure the RF signal from the access point is of acceptable quality in that physical area that contains the Accounting department.

**Data Link layer**   The layer of the OSI model (see *OSI model*) that is responsible for physical network management such as the detection of errors in the physical media and for locating and transferring data on the physical medium such as Ethernet. This is where MAC frames and data reside. Also known as Layer 2.

**data rate**   The rate at which bits are communicated in a WLAN during a single frame transmission. In a wired LAN, it is the rate at which bits are communicated. This rate may vary in a WLAN.

**D-channel**   An ISDN channel used for signaling information with the Q.931 signaling protocol. The D-channel is the data (D) channel, and the B-channel is the bearer (B) channel.

**demilitarized zone (DMZ)**   A network, usually at the perimeter, that resides between a private network and a public network such as the Internet.

**Denial of Service (DoS)**   An attack that is used to prevent valid users from accessing a network or system.

**dial peer**   A configuration set with the needed information for reaching phone extensions. Created with the **dial-peer** command in Cisco routers.

**dial plan**   A collection of components with instructions for reaching phone extensions including a numbering plan.

**distribution device**   A common term for a networking device that does not connect to client devices but that provides services to the network such as packet filtering and forwarding; sometimes used to describe access point–to–access point bridging.

**encapsulation**   The process of enveloping information within headers so that the information can be passed across varied networks.

**encryption**   The process of obfuscating data so that it cannot be viewed by non-intended systems or individuals.

**extensible authentication protocol (EAP)**   A standards-based model used to implement various authentication types such as certificates and pre-shared keys or passphrases.

**FCC**   The Federal Communications Commission (FCC) is responsible for defining limitations and allowances for radio frequency communications—among other things—in the United States and its territories. They define the regulations that are then implemented in IEEE and other standards.

**fiber optic cable**  A high-speed cabling technology that transmits light across glass fibers instead of electricity across copper wires.

**foreign exchange office (FXO)**  Analog port in a Cisco gateway used to connect to a PBX or the PSTN.

**foreign exchange station (FXS)**  Analog port in a Cisco gateway used to connect to analog terminals such as analog phones or fax machines.

**fragmentation**  The process of converting a single frame into multiple smaller frames in order to reduce retransmission overhead when occasional interference corrupts one part of the overall transmission in a wireless LAN (local area network). Also, the process of converting large TCP packets into multiple IP (Internet Protocol) payloads for transmission in wired or wireless LANs.

**frequency**  The rate at which an RF (radio frequency) wave, or any wave, repeats itself, commonly measured in hertz, MHz, or GHz.

**gatekeeper**  A device used on converged networks. Provides switching for VoIP communications. Provides registration, admission control, and monitoring.

**gateway**  A Cisco router that converts between two different telephone networks, such as VoIP and the PSTN.

**H.323**  A suite of protocols designed to support voice and multimedia communications across unreliable networks like TCP/IP (Transmission Control Protocol/Internet Protocol).

**IEEE**  The Institute of Electrical and Electronics Engineers specifies standards based on regulations defined by regulatory bodies.

**IEEE 802.3**  The standard that defines wired Ethernet networking.

**IEEE 802.11**  The standard that defines the use of radio frequency signals to implement wireless LANs.

**IEEE 802.1X**   A standard, independent of the IEEE 802.11 standard, that defines port-based authentication. This standard is reference by IEEE 802.11 (after the 802.11i amendment) as being used to implement a Robust Security Network (RSN).

**interference**   That which occurs when RF energy in the same frequency corrupts RF communications.

**jitter**   The uneven arrival of packets with variations in delay.

**key system**   A phone system where any phone can be used to answer any incoming line call.

**local exchange**   Everything from the customer location to the central office.

**Low Latency Queuing (LLQ)**   A queuing solution that gives priority to specific traffic types.

**Media Gateway Control Protocol (MGCP)**   A gateway and VoIP control protocol that provides call routing intelligence to the call manager, such as Cisco Unified Communications Manager.

**μ-Law**   A compressing and expanding (companding) algorithm used in the United States and Japan.

**MOS**   The Mean Opinion Score (MOS) is a subjective rating of the quality of a given multimedia or VoIP codec. Scores range from 1 (very bad) to 5 (excellent). A score of 4.0 or higher is usually considered very good.

**network**   A group of connected or interconnected people or things. In computer networks, it is a group of connected or interconnected computer systems.

**Network layer**   The layer of the OSI model (see *OSI model*) that is responsible for actual data transfer between logical devices. The Internet Protocol lives here. Also known as Layer 3.

**network protocol**   A collection of rules, recommendations, and options used to facilitate communications between computing devices.

**Nyquist theorem**   A guideline that indicates a waveform should be sampled at twice the highest frequency to provide acceptable audio quality.

**octet**   A term that describes 8 bits of data. A byte is generally thought to be 8 bits, but a byte can be fewer than 8 bits, and it can be more than 8 bits. An octet is specifically an 8-bit byte.

**OSI model**   The Open Systems Interconnection (OSI) model provides a common basis for the purpose of system interconnection and includes a seven-layer approach. (See *Application layer, Presentation layer, Session layer, Transport layer, Network layer, Data Link layer,* and *Physical layer.*)

**packet switching**   A switching method used to segment a message into small parts and then send those parts across a shared network. Unlike circuit switching, a dedicated connection is not required. Also known as "datagram switching."

**Physical layer**   The layer of the OSI model (see *OSI model*) that provides the actual transfer of bits on the network medium. Also known as Layer 1.

**Power over Ethernet**   A standard method for providing power to network devices over Ethernet cables. Also called PoE.

**Presentation layer**   The layer of the OSI model (see *OSI model*) that provides presentation services such as encryption and syntax management. Also known as Layer 6.

**Private Branch Exchange (PBX)**   A phone switch located within and owned by a private organization. A PBX will usually connect to the PSTN, or it may connect through the Internet to other PBX systems.

**protocol**   See *network protocol.*

**protocol analyzer**   A tool used to decode packets on a network.

**Public switched telephone network (PSTN)**   The PSTN is the public telephone network. Also known as plain old telephone system (POTS).

**quality of service (QoS)**   A term applied to a required level of quality. QoS is implemented through different technologies such as DiffServ, ToS, MPLS, and RSVP. A collection of technologies providing the capability of processing different traffic types with different priorities.

**Real-time Transport Protocol (RTP)**   A protocol used to carry voice packets on an IP network.

**Real-time Transport Control Protocol (RTCP)**   A protocol used to monitor RTP communications and provide feedback for service improvement and processing.

**routing**   The process of moving data packets from one network to another.

**segmentation**   The process of segmenting or separating the data into manageable or allowable sizes for transfer. Also known as fragmentation in the lower levels of the OSI model.

**Session layer**   The layer of the OSI model (see *OSI model*) that provides for session initiation and management. This layer provides for connections between applications on a network. The functions of the Session layer are handled by TCP in the TCP/IP (Transmission Control Protocol/Internet Protocol) suite, or they may be handled by upper layer protocols. Also known as Layer 5.

**SIP**   The session initiation protocol (SIP) is a call control protocol and is an alternative to H.323 for voice and multimedia communications.

**throughput**   The rate at which payload data can be transferred through a system.

**traffic shaper**   A device that allows network managers to control the data on their network more granularly. The manager may be able to block or slow particular types of traffic.

**Transport layer** The layer of the OSI model (see *OSI model*) that provides for data transport. This is the layer that most resembles the Transport layer of the TCP/IP model. Also known as Layer 4.

**trunk** A connection used to tie voice networks (such as PBX implementations) together.

**twisted pair cables** Networking cables that are implemented using multiple conductor cables. These cables are twisted in pairs. Both unshielded and shielded twisted-pair cables exist.

**virtual private network (VPN)** A session between two endpoints that encrypts all data transmitted across that session. Data is routed through the session as if it were a physical connection.

**VLAN** A virtual local area network (VLAN) is a virtual network segment enabled through a Layer 2 switch that supports VLAN protocols. Nodes from many physical network segments are made to appear as if they were on the same segment by the VLAN switch.

**VoIP** Voice over IP uses the traditional IP network to send voice data for communications.

**VoWLAN** IP telephony over the WLAN (wireless local area network) is the use of a WLAN to transport IP voice communications.

**Wi-Fi Alliance** An organization that certifies equipment to be interoperable with other equipment in the WLAN industry based on their certification standards.

# INDEX

## E

## O

## P